The Social Animal

Books by Elliot Aronson

Handbook of Social Psychology (with G. Lindzey), 2nd ed., 1968–1969

Theories of Cognitive Consistency (with R. Abelson et al.), 1968

Voices of Modern Psychology, 1969

The Social Animal, 1972, 1976, 1980, 1984, 1988, 1992, 1995, 1999, 2003, 2008, 2011, 2018

Readings About The Social Animal, 2019, 1972, 1976, 1980, 1984, 1988, 1992, 1995, 1999, 2003, 2008, 2011

Social Psychology (with R. Helmreich), 1973

Research Methods in Social Psychology (with M. Carlsmith & Ellsworth), 1976

The Jigsaw Classroom, 1978

Burnout: From Tedium to Personal Growth (with A. Pines & D. Kafry), 1981

Energy Use: The Human Dimension (with P. C. Stern), 1984

The Handbook of Social Psychology (with G. Lindzey), 3rd ed., 1985

Career Burnout (with A. Pines), 1988

Methods of Research in Social Psychology (with Ellsworth, M. Carlsmith, & Gonzales), 1990

Age of Propaganda (with A. R. Pratkanis), 1992, 2000

Social Psychology: Volumes 1, 2, & 3 (with A. R. Pratkanis), 1992

Social Psychology: The Heart and the Mind (with T. Wilson & R. Akert), 1994

Nobody Left to Hate: Teaching Compassion After Columbine, 2000

Social Psychology: An Introduction (with T. Wilson, R. Akert, & S. Sommers), 2002, 2005, 2007, 2010, 2013, 2016

The Adventures of Ruthie and a Little Boy Named Grandpa (with Ruth Aronson), 2006

Mistakes Were Made (But Not By Me) (with Carol Tavris), 2007, Rev. ed., 2015

Not By Chance Alone: My Life as a Social Psychologist, 2010

Books by Joshua Aronson

Improving Academic Achievement, 2002

The Scientist and The Humanist (with M. H. Gonzales and C. Tavris) 2010

Twelfth Edition

The Social Animal

Elliot Aronson
University of California, Santa Cruz

with Joshua Aronson
New York University

 worth publishers
Macmillan Learning
New York

Vice President, Social Sciences and High School: Charles Linsmeier
Director of Content and Assessment, Social Sciences: Shani Fisher
Executive Program Manager: Christine Cardone
Assistant Editor: Melissa Rostek
Executive Marketing Manager: Katherine Nurre
Marketing Assistant: Chelsea Simens
Director of Media Editorial, Social Sciences: Noel Hohnstine
Assistant Media Editor: Nik Toner
Director, Content Management Enhancement: Tracey Kuehn
Managing Editor: Lisa Kinne
Senior Content Project Manager: Vivien Weiss
Project Manager: Priyanka Sharma, Lumina Datamatics, Inc.
Media Producer: Eve Conte
Senior Workflow Supervisor: Susan Wein
Senior Workflow Project Manager: Lisa McDowell
Photo Editor: Sheena Goldstein
Director of Design, Content Management: Diana Blume
Cover and Text Design: Victoria Tomaselli
Composition: Lumina Datamatics, Inc.
Printing and Binding: LSC Communications
Cover Drawing: Tom Durfee

Library of Congress Control Number: 2017962739

ISBN-13: 978-1-4641-4418-9
ISBN-10: 1-4641-4418-4

Printed in the United States of America
Second printing

Worth Publishers
One New York Plaza
Suite 4500
New York, NY 10004-1562
www.macmillanlearning.com

To Vera, of course

Contents

Saul Steinberg, *Untitled drawing*, ink on paper.
Originally published in *The New Yorker*, May 29, 1965.
© The Saul Steinberg Foundation / Artists Rights Society (ARS), New York.

The Story of This Book

In 1970, when I was a relatively young professor at the University of Texas, I received an offer I couldn't refuse. I was invited to spend the year in a beautiful location, while being awarded my full academic salary and doing absolutely nothing—not a bad deal!

The location was a rustic hilltop on the edge of the Stanford University campus, a short drive from San Francisco, my favorite city in the world. The institution on the gorgeous hill is a think tank called the Center for Advanced Study in the Behavioral Sciences. In addition to a year's salary, the good folks at the Center for Advanced Study provided me with an office, all the secretarial help I might need, access to a very good library, free lunch, and the opportunity to schmooze with a couple of dozen distinguished scholars, if I chose to or not—in case I preferred to hang out in the theater district of San Francisco or go skiing in the High Sierras. There were no strings attached.

So there I was, with a whole year in which to do anything my heart desired, and what did I do? I chose to barricade myself in my office on the hill and write this book. How come? If there's a single reason, it's that, a few months earlier, I heard myself tell 600 students in my introductory social psychology class that social psychology is a young science—and, in retrospect, that semi-apology made me feel like a coward.

Let me explain: We social psychologists are fond of saying that social psychology is a young science—and, relative to most scientific disciplines (e.g., biology, astronomy), that is an accurate statement. Of course, astute observers have been making interesting pronouncements and proposing exciting hypotheses about social phenomena at least since the time of Aristotle, but these pronouncements and hypotheses were not seriously tested until well into the twentieth century. The first systematic social psychological experiment was conducted by Norman Triplett in 1898 (he measured the effect of competition on performance), but it was not until the middle of the twentieth century that experimental social psychology really took off, primarily under the inspiration of Kurt Lewin and his talented students.

In a deeper sense, however, for me to have stated that social psychology is a young science was something of a cop-out—a way of pleading with my students not to expect too much from us. Specifically, it was my way of dodging the responsibility for, and avoiding the risks inherent in, applying our findings to the problems of the world we live in. In this sense, stating that social psychology is a young science was akin to confessing that we might not be ready to say anything important, useful, or relevant to the lives of my students.

But after reflecting on that statement for a while, I came to realize that it was not only cowardly, but it was also misleading; in fact, I didn't really believe that social psychology was irrelevant to our lives. I didn't believe it in 1970, and I certainly don't believe it now. So, when I was handed that wonderful opportunity to take time off, I was determined to set the record straight. The purpose of this book was and still is to spell out the relevance that social psychological research might have for helping us understand and perhaps begin to solve some of the most important problems besetting contemporary society.

Most of the data discussed in this volume are based on experiments; most of the illustrations and examples, however, are derived from current social problems—including prejudice, propaganda, war, alienation, aggression, unrest, and political upheaval. This duality reflects two of my own biases—biases that I cherish. The first is that the experimental method is the best way to understand a complex phenomenon. It is a truism of science that the only way to really know the world is to reconstruct it. That is, to truly understand what causes what, we must do more than simply observe; rather, we must be responsible for producing the first "what" so that we can be sure that it really caused the second "what." My second bias is that the only way to be certain that the causal relations uncovered in experiments are valid is to bring them out of the laboratory and into the real world. Thus, as a scientist, I like to work in a laboratory; as a citizen, however, I like to have windows through which I can look out upon the world. Windows, of course, work in both directions; we often derive hypotheses from everyday life. We can best test these hypotheses under the sterile conditions of the laboratory. At the same time, in order to keep our ideas from becoming sterile, we must take our laboratory findings back out through the window to see if they hold up in the real world.

So, that is how I spent the year doing anything I wanted to do: I wrote this book. From the outset, it has been a personal book, in the sense that it contains a lot of my own ideas about what is most important in our field. This decision made it imperative for me to write in the first person singular, describing, in an intimate way, what I have discovered and what I believe to be the state of our science. (Unlike any textbook at the time, in *The Social Animal* the little word "I" appears over and over again.) Much to my delight, it soon became apparent that students enjoyed reading it. They particularly liked the personal touch, as well as its application to their lives. *The Social Animal* became one of the most popular and enduring texts in the field. As a consequence, my work was not finished—not by a long shot. In order to keep up with research in the field and dramatic changes in the world, I found it necessary to revise and update the book about every four years.

When I first set pen to paper (literally!) in 1970, I was a promising young man, some 38 years old. As I tell you this story, in the summer of 2017, I have magically evolved into a grizzled old geezer (you can do the math). I now must admit that I am too old to revise the book by myself. Fortunately, I found the perfect co-author for this, the twelfth edition. His name is Joshua Aronson, a brilliant, experienced social psychologist who has done impressive research both in the laboratory and in the helter-skelter of the real world. He also happens to be my son. Needless to say, Joshua has his own ideas about social psychology—and that is how it should be. His contributions are many and varied. They have added a special luster to this edition; as has the work of my long-time collaborator Carol Tavris, who served as developmental editor for this edition and, with her usual delicate touch, seamlessly melded my work and Joshua's. She also not-so-delicately pressed and prodded us to make our deadlines.

And so, what is different in this edition? Joshua and I have reexamined every chapter afresh, removing some of the research and theories that were "hot" years ago but have not stood the test of time and replication; we have reorganized and streamlined every chapter to keep the narrative clear as we integrated new material. Recent studies that inform our understanding of contemporary events have replaced dated ones—for example, how decision-making has been influenced for better and worse by the internet, how the rise of information bubbles and self-confirming media sources shape our nation's polarized beliefs and behavior, the emotional downside of the constant social comparisons generated on Facebook, and the rise of terrorist groups such as ISIS. However, I feel strongly that bringing a book "up to date" does not mean removing the iconic stories of our government's mistakes in Vietnam and Iraq, and of the tragedies at Jonestown, Columbine, and Heaven's Gate. The dates of these events are old, but the social-psychological lessons to be learned from them are not dated. I want students to understand that what happened *then* applies just as powerfully to what is happening *now*.

Elliot Aronson
October 2017

Acknowledgments

This book is now in its twelfth edition. In the first edition, I was moved to acknowledge my indebtedness to my friend and mentor, Leon Festinger. It goes without saying that I still feel gratitude and affection for that good and great man. If anything, these feelings have intensified over the years. I loved being his student—and I guess I will never stop being his student. In 1989, Leon died, marking the end of an important era in social psychology. He is sorely missed, not only by those of us who knew and loved him, but also by anyone who has been influenced by his research and theories; this would include just about anyone who has ever been a student of social psychology.

As this book and I have grown older, I have become increasingly aware of my indebtedness to my own students. Every four years, as I begin revising the book, I am struck by the realization that these are not simply my own ideas—rather, they are ideas I have developed in collaboration with my students. Over the past five decades, I have been blessed with a great many outstanding students, from my very first research assistants in 1960 (Merrill Carlsmith, Tony Greenwald, and John M. Darley) to my students at the University of California, Santa Cruz. They have all taught me a great deal, and it is a pleasure to acknowledge my debt to all of them. I have also enjoyed talking with and stealing ideas from some remarkably gifted colleagues. Two of them in particular, Anthony Pratkanis and Carol Tavris, have contributed a great deal to the continued improvement and updating of this book. It is a pleasure to acknowledge their generosity.

For this edition, I would particularly like to thank Christine Cardone, our Executive Editor, for her warmth, enthusiastic and unflagging commitment to the book, her patience, and efficiency. I would also like to thank Brad Bushman, Donal Carlston, Eli Finkel, Jack Dovidio, and Matthew McGlone, who generously reviewed chapters and made wise suggestions about how to improve them.

Joshua is indebted to Carol Tavris for expert editing and constant inspiration, and to Stacey, Eliana, and Leo Aronson for their love, support, and patience. We are also grateful to Jeff and Spencer Tweedy. The following students and research assistants made valuable contributions and have our sincere thanks: Joshua Adler, Paige Alenick, Rotem Blatt, Christina Crosby, Rayna Epstein, Madison Katz, Jessica Mar, Kaya Mendelsohn, Scott Mengebier, Ashley Panookin, Ella Quinlan, Angela Spears, Zachary Williams, and Kathy Yu.

Additionally, we would like to extend thanks to William Dragon for his work on the instructor resources and the professors who reviewed the eleventh edition and provided feedback for this revision: Kristin J. Anderson (University of Houston—Downtown), Fred Bryant (Loyola University—Chicago), Brad J. Bushman (The Ohio State University & VU University—Amsterdam), Donal E. Carlston (Purdue University), John F. Dovidio (Yale University) William Dragon (Cornell College), Eli Finkel (Northwestern University), Judy Ho (Pepperdine University), Alison E. Kelly (University of North Dakota), Matthew McGlone (University of Texas at Austin), Anjali Mishra (Northern Arizona University), Brandy Moore (Texas A&M University—Texarkana), Marcus D. Patterson (University of Massachusetts at Boston), and Michael J. Tagler (Ball State University).

The Social Animal

Man is by nature a social animal; an individual who is unsocial naturally and not accidentally is either beneath our notice or more than human. Society is something in nature that precedes the individual. Anyone who either cannot lead the common life or is so self-sufficient as not to need to, and therefore does not partake of society, is either a beast or a god.

Aristotle
Politics, c. 328 BC

Saul Steinberg, *Untitled drawing*, ink on paper.
Originally published in *The New Yorker*, November 1, 1958.
© The Saul Steinberg Foundation / Artists Rights Society (ARS), New York

What Is Social Psychology?

As far as I know, Aristotle was the first serious thinker to call our species "the social animal." Of course he was right, but what does that mean? A host of other creatures are "social," from ants and bees to monkeys and apes. What is unique about the human social animal? And what is unique about the field of social psychology, which studies our puzzling, creative, and infuriating species?

I have been a social psychologist all of my professional life — and before I entered this field or even knew what it was, I was an amateur social psychologist, eager to understand the mysteries of human behavior. As a Jewish boy growing up in the 1940s in the blue-collar town of Revere, Massachusetts, I wondered why some Catholic kids taunted me with anti-Semitic slogans and occasionally roughed me up. My son Joshua, who struggled in elementary school in the 1960s, wondered why some kids thrive in the classroom and others are suffocated by its competitiveness and regimentation. These early experiences, which caused both of us great pain, are also what drew us to the exciting field you are going to study in this book: a field that offers a scientific understanding of human social life and, more important, ways to improve it.

There are many definitions of social psychology, but before I get to the one I prefer, let me offer some concrete examples of the human social animal in action:

A college student named Sam and four of his acquaintances are watching a senatorial candidate make a speech on television.

Sam is favorably impressed; he likes the female candidate better than the opposing male candidate because he thinks she is sincere. After the speech, one of the other students asserts that she was turned off by the female candidate and considered her to be a hypocrite. All of the others are quick to agree with this student. Sam feels puzzled and a trifle distressed. Finally, he mumbles to his acquaintances, "I guess she didn't come across as sincere as I would have hoped."

A 10-year-old girl avidly consumes two bowls of Wheaties each morning because Michael Phelps, the Olympic swimming champion, is pictured on the box, implying that he owes his athletic prowess, in part, to eating that brand of cereal.

A shopkeeper who has lived his entire life in a small town in Montana has never had any contact with real, live Muslims, but he "knows" they are un-American, disloyal, and likely to be terrorists.

Charlie, a high-school senior, has recently moved to a new city. He used to be popular, but not anymore. Although the kids at school are civil, they have not been particularly friendly. He feels lonely, insecure, and unattractive. One day during lunch period, he finds himself at a table with two female classmates. One is warm, intelligent, and vivacious; he has been daydreaming about her for weeks, longing for an opportunity to talk to her. The other young woman is not nearly as appealing. Charlie ignores the vivacious woman of his dreams and begins an earnest conversation with her companion.

On December 4, 2016, Edgar Welch, a 28-year-old man from North Carolina, went into Comet Ping Pong, a wildly successful pizza restaurant in Washington, D.C., and fired three shots with a rifle. No one was injured. Welch told police that he had read online that the restaurant was harboring child sex slaves and that he wanted to see for himself if they were there. He surrendered after he found no evidence for his belief, which had been generated by a conspiracy theory that went viral during the presidential election season. A white supremacist Twitter account had claimed that the New York City Police had discovered a pedophilia ring linked to members of the Democratic Party, and that somehow Comet Ping Pong was at the center of it. The story was widely circulated by fake news websites. Welch later said that he regretted what he did but that he continued to believe the conspiracy theory.

Kaya was asked in second grade to name her favorite subject. "Math," she wrote on the questionnaire. One year later, her third-grade class was assigned a similar exercise. This time the questionnaire asked, "What is your *least* favorite subject?" She wrote, "Math." In one year, Kaya had gone from a confident, excited student of mathematics to someone who dreaded it.

On April 20, 1999, the corridors of a sparkling suburban high school in Littleton, Colorado, reverberated with the sound of gunshots. Two Columbine High School students armed with assault weapons and explosives went on a rampage, killing a teacher and several of their fellow students. They then turned their guns on themselves. After the smoke had cleared, fifteen people were dead (including the shooters) and twenty-three were hospitalized, many with severe wounds. In the nearly twenty years since the Columbine High School massacre, hundreds of American adolescent boys have committed equally horrifying mass shootings at schools. What was once unthinkable has become commonplace.

Steve, a college senior, is a cautious, even conservative, driver; he could be the star of a safe-driving video—when he is alone in the car. However, whenever two or three of his buddies are with him, Steve's behavior gets riskier: When he sees the light turn yellow a half block away, he often hits the accelerator, hoping he can get through the intersection before the cross traffic moves.

In 1939, Oskar Schindler, a greedy German businessman, joined the Nazi party and set out to profit from the destruction of Jews during the barbaric reign of Hitler's Third Reich. After exploiting the labor of Jewish inmates at Auschwitz for several years, Schindler had a change of heart and began to use his factory as a way to save more than one thousand Jews from death. In doing so, he risked his life and spent all of his wealth to save others, a story told in the book and Oscar-winning movie, *Schindler's List.* Emerging from the theater after watching this movie, my son Joshua was approached by a panhandler asking for spare change. Contrary to his habit of ignoring people looking for handouts, Joshua, still a financially strapped student, reached into his pocket, pulled out all the bills, and without counting or examining them, gave them to the panhandler.

Douglas McCain grew up in Minnesota, played basketball in high school, and wanted to be a rapper. Friends remember him as a "goofball," a "really nice guy," and a "good person." So they were shocked when, at age thirty-three, McCain joined ISIS, the militant terrorist group, and died in the Middle East, waging war against his own country. Thousands of other apparently ordinary young men and women from Western countries have also left their homes to fight and die in Syria and Iraq as Islamic jihadists.

In the 1940s, when I was in elementary school, I had a close African American friend named George Woods. At the time, George referred to himself as a "colored boy" and confided to me that he, like many black children at the time, felt inferior to his white friends.[1] He had many reasons for this feeling, starting with the direct experiences of prejudice that the dominant white community inflicted on him. But George's feelings of inferiority also came from indirect sources, such as the portrayal of African American adults in radio and television as naïve children — lazy, illiterate, but rather cute. If films had black male actors at all, they were portrayed only as a stereotypical "colored man," usually a chauffeur or menial worker, who was often made the butt of ugly jokes. Imagine what George felt while watching these racist films in the company of his white friends. He never told me how he felt, though.

Things change. George Wood's grandchildren, growing up in the twenty-first century, live in a different world than he did. He would never have envisioned that one day black actors would be cast in serious roles and win Academy Awards; that segregation and discrimination would be illegal; or that black people would be able to enter all professions, including the presidency of the United States. Yet we should not be complacent in the belief that changes move in a linear, humanistic direction. George Wood's grandchildren may not face the same degree and flavor of bigotry endured by their grandfather, but racial prejudice continues. Most African Americans know the experience of "shopping while black," which means being followed by salespeople who question their credit, suspect they will steal something, or even deny them service. Young black males in particular continue to be victims of "driving while black" — being stopped for trivial reasons or even for no reason — and "walking while black," as when sixteen-year-old Trayvon Martin was stalked and killed by a neighborhood watch captain named George Zimmerman.[2] When Zimmerman noticed a tall black teenager wearing a hoodie, he saw a possibly armed-and-dangerous criminal, not what Trayvon actually was: a normal high school student walking home from a convenience store with an iced tea and a bag of Skittles.

Defining Social Psychology

The examples all illustrate social psychological situations. As diverse as they seem to be, they contain a common factor: *social influence*.

The opinion of Sam's friends on the merits of the senatorial candidate influenced Sam's judgment (or at least his public statement regarding that judgment). The Olympic champion's influence on our Wheaties-eating youngster was intentionally designed to get her to convince her parents to buy Wheaties. The Montana shopkeeper was not born with an unflattering stereotype of Muslim people in his head; somebody, somehow, put it there. Steve's riskier driving was certainly influenced by the presence of his friends, but how? Kaya's transformation from math lover to math hater is not uncommon, particularly for girls in America, where math has been traditionally seen as both an endowed talent and a "boy thing." Charlie's ignoring the woman of his dreams has something to do with how he was feeling about himself and his assumption about which woman was less likely to reject him. Rejection is among the most painful experiences for human beings, and it can cause all kinds of self-defeating and destructive behaviors, from overeating to violence—as it did in the school shooting at Columbine. The presence and example of other people, in the flesh or in movies like *Schindler's List*, can inspire positive emotions and generosity, as when it led my normally frugal son to give all of his precious cash to a panhandler.

Social psychology also tackles some of the most disturbing questions that plague society, from racism and other forms of prejudice to the success of terrorist groups like ISIS in recruiting young people, many who have no spiritual or family connection to Islam. What forces persuade them to leave their homes and families and become suicide bombers? The answers involve age, personality dynamics, social identity, persuasion tactics, and other powerful factors you will learn about as this book unfolds. You will see that ISIS takes advantage of many of the same influence strategies used by great coaches to create winning sports teams and by successful elementary-school principals to lift the achievement of their students. Understanding people's social motivations can be used for good, for evil, for winning reality TV competitions—for anything in which social influence matters, which is pretty much everything.

Our definition of **social psychology**, therefore, is the scientific study of the influence of the real, imagined, or implied presence of others upon our thoughts, emotions, beliefs, and behavior—and of how we influence others.

How are we influenced? Why do we accept influence or, put another way, what's in it for us? What are the social motives that make us susceptible to what others think, say, and do? What factors increase or decrease the effectiveness of social influence? Which ones increase or decrease the permanence of the effects of social influence? Can the same principles be applied equally to our opinion of a senatorial candidate as to the school subjects that young children prefer? How does one person come to like another? Is it through these same processes that we choose Wheaties over granola? How does a person develop prejudices against an ethnic, religious, or racial group? Is prejudice akin to liking but in reverse, or does it involve an entirely different set of psychological processes?

Many people are interested in questions like these. Because we all spend a good deal of our time interacting with other people—being influenced by them; influencing them; being delighted, amused, saddened, disgusted, frustrated, and angered by them—it is in our nature to develop hypotheses about why people do what they do. In that sense, everyone is an amateur social psychologist. Although most amateurs test these hypotheses to their own satisfaction as they interact with others, these casual "tests" lack the rigor and impartiality of careful scientific investigation.

To be sure, sometimes the results of scientific research correspond with what most people already believe to be true. This is not remarkable; conventional wisdom is usually derived from shrewd observations that have stood the test of time. But sometimes that conventional wisdom leads us astray. Indeed, when you are reading the results of the research discussed in this volume, you may occasionally find yourself thinking, "That's obvious—why did they spend time and money to 'discover' that one? My grandmother could have told me that." Maybe she could have, but it's also likely that you are acting on the **hindsight bias,** which refers to our tendency to overestimate our powers of prediction once we know the outcome of a given event. This is precisely why it is so easy to be a Monday morning quarterback and why we say "Hindsight is twenty–twenty." Numerous studies have demonstrated this bias, from predicting the outcomes of elections ("I always knew he'd win, even if the polls didn't say so") to predicting how a given social psychology experiment will turn out ("Oh, please, it was obvious the participants would obey those cruel instructions"). In fact, social psychological findings seem far more obvious to college students who've been told what happened in a study than to students asked to *predict* what will happen.[3] Everything is clearer in hindsight.

Social psychologists conduct research because many of the things we think we know to be true turn out to be false, or more nuanced than we originally thought, when subjected to investigation. For example, it seems reasonable that people who are threatened with punishment for doing something forbidden, illegal, self-defeating, or fattening might eventually stop, and the more severe the punishment, the more likely they will be to comply. After all, they would now associate the activity with fear or pain. But when tested empirically, this assumption turns out to be dead wrong. It is those who are threatened with *mild* punishment who develop a dislike for the forbidden activity; people who are severely threatened, if anything, are even more drawn to the forbidden activity. Likewise, most of us, from our own experience, would guess that, if we overheard someone saying nice things about us (behind our backs), we would tend to like that person—all other things being equal. This turns out to be true. But what is equally true is that we tend to like that person even more if some of the remarks we overhear are anything but nice. We will explain more about these phenomena in later chapters.

In the goal of understanding the social animal, professional social psychologists have an advantage over most amateur social psychologists. Although, like the amateurs, we usually begin with an observation, we do not stop there. We do not need to wait for things to happen so that we can observe how people respond; we can make things happen. We can conduct an experiment in which we subject scores of people to particular events (for example, a severe threat or a mild threat; overhearing nice things or overhearing a combination of nice and nasty things). Moreover, we can do this in situations in which everything can be held constant, except the particular factors being investigated. We can then draw conclusions based on data that are more precise and numerous than those available to the amateur, who must depend on observing events that occur randomly and under circumstances in which many things are happening at once.

Nearly all the data presented in this book are based upon experimental evidence. That's why we want you to understand what constitutes an experiment in social psychology, along with the advantages, disadvantages, ethical problems, excitements, headaches, and heartaches that are associated with the adventure of research. The final chapter in this book, "Social Psychology as a Science," will give you that understanding. You can read it first, or last, or at any point on your journey through the book—whenever your interest in how social psychologists do their work is piqued.

People Who Do Crazy Things Are Not Necessarily Crazy

Social psychologists examine the way people make sense of and behave in social situations. Occasionally, these situations create pressures that can cause people to behave in ways that you could classify as abnormal, even crazy. When I say "people," I mean very large numbers of people. To my mind, these labels are often just name-calling; they do little to increase our understanding of human behavior. It is much more useful to try to understand the nature of the situation, the often complex processes operating to produce the behavior we observe. This brings me to Aronson's first law:

People who do crazy things are not necessarily crazy.

Let us take, as an illustration, the man who went into Comet Ping Pong with a rifle, intending, as he said, to "self-investigate" the presence of kidnapped children. Was he crazy? If he really wanted the truth, why not accept the investigations of the police departments, FBI, and other reliable sources that had thoroughly debunked the allegations? If he were crazy, so were the thousands of others who bought into the conspiracy belief, many of whom sent Comet Ping Pong and other restaurants they thought were part of "the ring" vicious threats, harassing owners and customers. The owner of Comet Ping Pong told the *New York Times* that "From this insane, fabricated conspiracy theory, we've come under constant assault. I've done nothing for days but try to clean this up and protect my staff and friends from being terrorized." What draws people to believe "insane" conspiracy theories—and why do they cling to that belief despite solid evidence to the contrary? Later in this book, we will examine the processes that produce these attitudes and the tendency to stick by them no matter what. We'll also see how we might counteract them.

One central discovery of social psychology is that people are prone to explain unpleasant behavior by assigning personality traits to the perpetrator, such as "psychotic," "sadistic," or "evil." Most people—particularly those of us from Western cultures—do this spontaneously, without intention or conscious awareness, as a way of organizing and categorizing information and satisfying a need to feel in control of events. This *dispositional* view of human actions refers to the assumptions that people who do crazy things have a personality disposition to be crazy, people who do stupid things must be stupid, only evil people do evil things, people who do nice things are nice, and so on. It's appealing to think this way because it helps us mentally separate those bad people who do bad things from the rest of us "nice people." This belief may comfort us when we think about unpleasant behavior, because, as nice people, *we* would never do such a thing.

Yet that assumption is often a mistake, an oversimplification, and we pay a price for it, as you will see in Chapter 2. Dispositionalism can make us smug about our own invulnerability to pressures that could induce *us* to behave stupidly, crazily, or cruelly. It moves the focus off of improving situations and onto a narrow approach to fixing people: Is a manager worried about employees who steal? Let's give everyone a personality test to try to diagnose who will steal in the future, and never mind whether our employees are stealing because they feel overworked, resentful, and underpaid. Are we worried about students who might become violent? Let's give everyone a personality test and try to predict which of the unhappy or bullied kids we identify *might* erupt one day, and let's not ask questions about the world in which those kids struggle every day.

Of course, I am not saying that psychosis doesn't exist. Some personality traits and mental illnesses do affect people's behavior. Nor am I saying that all people are the same and respond exactly as crazily to the same social pressures. What I *am* saying is that some situations can cause a surprisingly large proportion of us "normal" adults to behave in unexpected, unappetizing, and sometimes *abnormal* ways. It is of paramount importance to understand what is going on in those situations that can produce unpleasant or destructive behavior.

An illustration may be useful. What kind of person murders their own child? Crazy? Desperate? Evil? Surely there must be something psychologically wrong with the brain or character of such a person. In 1977, the Reverend Jim Jones, a charismatic leader of the People's Temple in San Francisco, convinced his followers to uproot their lives and move to Guyana in South America to establish a humanistic paradise—a utopian community where people of different racial backgrounds could live in harmony. When, in 1978, the existence of the group was threatened by a congressional investigation, Jones decided to end the crisis by asking the group to perform a "revolutionary act": killing their children and then themselves. Vats of poison were prepared, and amid only scattered shouts of protest or acts of resistance, mothers and fathers administered the fatal mixture to their infants and children, drank it themselves, and laid down to die.

When one person kills their own child, it's reasonable to ask if they are mentally ill. When 613 parents murder their children in one place, we are forced to look beyond mental conditions and personality traits and consider the nature of the situation that caused them to do this. Of course, we could call them crazy and feel complacent that we would never do what they did. However, before these people moved to Guyana, none of their neighbors, friends, or relatives would have thought of them as anything other than ordinary, sensible people who belonged to a supportive, tightly knit church community. The "Jonestown massacre," as it became known, is a reminder of the often powerful yet frequently hidden role of social influence in determining what human beings think, feel, and do.

Helping us appreciate this more complex *situational view* of human behavior—the many ways social context influences what we do—is *the* central contribution of social psychology, one whose value I hope will become apparent in the pages that follow.

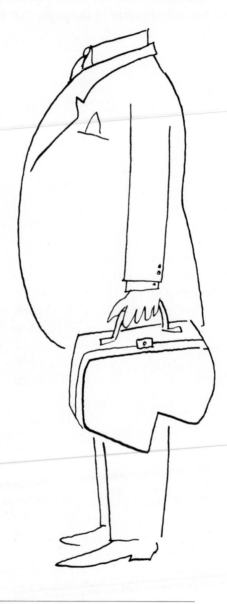

Saul Steinberg, *Untitled drawing*, ink on paper.
Originally published in *The New Yorker*, August 29, 1953.
© The Saul Steinberg Foundation / Artists Rights Society (ARS), New York

2

Social Cognition

During the Middle Ages it was not uncommon for European pedestrians to be hit with human waste as they walked down the street. City dwellers at the time would occasionally empty their chamber pots — containers full of urine and excrement — by hurling the contents out the window into the street below. The sewage would sit there, breeding pestilence and disease, until street cleaners hauled it away, often for use as fertilizer. To the modern mind, this system seems gross and senseless, especially when you learn that earlier civilizations, like the Greeks, Romans, and the Mayans, had developed far better systems — with indoor plumbing and even flushable toilets.

Why trade indoor plumbing for a chamber pot? People at the time were convinced of many things that were simply not true: that nudity was sinful, that an unclothed body left one vulnerable to attack by evil spirits, and that evil spirits made people sick.[1] Daily bathing, made famous by the Romans in their beautiful public baths, was discouraged and replaced by washing the hands and face and other publicly viewable parts of the body. These superstitions had two notable effects. First, nearly everything and everyone smelled awful. As one writer described it, "The peasant stank as did the priest, the apprentice as did his master's wife; the whole of the aristocracy stank, even the king himself stank, stank like a rank lion and the queen like an old goat, summer and winter."[2] Second, indoor baths eventually fell into disrepair and citizens lost the skills needed to maintain plumbing. So the primitive sewer systems and chamber pots were, for a time, the best solution to a self-inflicted problem. It would take several hundred years for the "spirit" theory of disease to yield to science, which identified microbes as the invisible culprits that make people sick.

My point here is not to explore the inner workings of the medieval mind, nor to describe modern advances in health and hygiene. Instead, I tell you this story to raise a larger question: to what extent do we moderns behave like the users of chamber pots centuries ago? Every generation can look back at the foolishness of its forebears and find plenty of reasons to feel smug. In the Victorian era, the same doctors who would have chuckled at the thought of people being afraid of bathing and ghosts nevertheless believed the nonsense of their own time. Medical journals warned that women (but not men) who read novels were at risk of becoming sick, infertile, and even insane![3]

We human beings like to see ourselves as rational animals. (We smugly call ourselves *homo sapiens*, after all: Humans the Wise.) But we are capable of holding on to many unwise beliefs — and we suffer for it. Millions of people still refuse to believe the overwhelming scientific evidence that human beings are causing global warming and massive climate change. "It's a hoax perpetrated by the Chinese," some say, or "Sure, the earth is warming, but not because of anything people do." As a result, glaciers have continued to melt, sea levels have continued to rise, storms have become more frequent, insect-borne diseases are proliferating, and thousands of people die each year from these changes. In the United States, thousands of people still deny the overwhelming scientific evidence that vaccines for children do not cause autism, and many parents have refused to vaccinate their young children. As a result, fatality rates from measles and whooping cough have risen among unvaccinated populations; once thought to be eradicated, these deadly diseases are making a comeback.

A major area within social psychology is **social cognition**, the study of how people come to believe what they do; how they explain, remember, predict, make decisions, and evaluate themselves and others; and why these processes so frequently produce errors. Although humans can rightfully claim to be the most adaptive, intelligent, and successful species on the planet, we are nonetheless maddeningly prone to misunderstandings, conflict, error, and the kinds of biases that gave us the chamber pot long ago and the denial of climate science and vaccines today.

This chapter will tell the story of our "social brains," which, over eons of evolution, have created a great paradox and dilemma of human life. Evolution endowed us with brains that became well adapted to life in small hunter-gatherer groups, providing us with efficient cognitive shortcuts, biases that made life easier and safer, and dispositions to cooperate and care for one another. Yet as we survey today's complex, interconnected, multicultural planet, we can see how those very mechanisms often backfire, leading us to make bad decisions, stay stuck in our biases, and fight with one another out of prejudice and hatred.

If you think that we use our powers of reason to determine the truth, you are in for frustration when you see how immune to facts people become when they disagree with you. Much of the time, we use reason, facts, and critical analysis not to *form* our opinions but to *confirm* what we already see, feel, or believe. As the novelist Anaïs Nin put it, "We don't see things as they are; we see them as *we* are."[4] To a great extent, how we make sense of the world depends on a combination of our intuitions, our personalities and ways of perceiving the world, and a set of fundamental social motives.

Cognitive and social limitations are built into the ways our minds work, but if we learn to recognize them, we can avoid being enslaved by them. We can begin to think a little better, make smarter decisions, and organize our lives more intelligently. I hope this chapter will help you think about yourself and your fellow humans with a bit more humility and compassion — qualities that will bring us closer to being true *homo sapiens*.

Evolution and the Biased Brain

For centuries, philosophers have held that human cognition is completely rational: All individuals attempt to do their best to be right, to hold correct beliefs, and to maximize their pleasure while minimizing their pain.

One of the primary proponents of this view was Jeremy Bentham (1748–1832), who wrote that people decide the moral status of their behavior or choices — what's good or bad, right or wrong — by creating a happiness calculation.[5] Let's say I am in the market for a car. In determining the make and model to buy, I would add up the pleasures each brand would bring (sporty design, comfortable interior, powerful engine) and subtract the pain (the monthly payments that will strain my budget, the high cost of frequent fill-ups). I would then select the car that brings me the most pleasure with the least amount of pain. For Bentham, it was the role of governments and economic systems to ensure "the greatest happiness for the greatest number." Others agreed; Bentham's notion became one of the foundational ideas of modern capitalism.

Do ordinary people think this way? Sometimes, sure. Many of us adopt Benjamin Franklin's advice about how to make wise decisions—by writing down their pros and cons. However, that method requires that the person has accurate, useful information and the mental resources to think rationally. But these conditions do not often exist in everyday life. Why? For two reasons.

First, no one gets a "God's-eye" view of the world—a perspective that is all-knowing and free from bias. Take that car purchase. I don't know all the facts about the car's pros and cons to begin with, and I have heard some bad stories about car dealers and their tactics. Further, my view of the car is limited; what I know about it comes primarily from advertisers, who are motivated to exaggerate its positive features, and from what I learned on the internet. I have little experience with the actual car—a 10-minute test drive as opposed to long-term driving in hazardous weather conditions. If something as common as a car purchase can be fraught with missing and misleading information, imagine the difficulty people have when it comes to making more monumental decisions, such as whether or not to get married (or break up!) or what kind of work to choose.

Second, even when data are both available and reliable, I simply do not have the time to conduct a full-scale analysis of every problem I encounter. Suppose I go ahead and spend 10 hours doing research and weighing alternatives for that car. But in the meantime I have a dozen other decisions to make: What am I doing for lunch? How should I revise my lecture notes? Which job candidate is best to hire? Does my daughter really need those expensive braces on her teeth? I can't possibly spend hours and hours listing the pros and cons of every decision I have to make in a day, and neither can you.

That's why most of us are **cognitive misers**: We seek ways to conserve cognitive (mental) energy and simplify complexity. We take shortcuts and use rules of thumb. We ignore some information to reduce our cognitive load; we overuse other information to keep from having to search for more; or we just go with our initial intuitions and accept a less-than-perfect alternative because it is good enough.[6] The strategies of the cognitive miser may be efficient, and sometimes our intuitions can lead to good decisions. But if unchecked, these strategies invite serious errors.

How Thinking About Thinking Has Evolved Although psychologists have made enormous progress in the past few decades, nobody yet fully understands how or why brains produce conscious experience, or how the brain gives rise to a sense of self. When describing things we don't fully understand, we turn to metaphors; we compare things we don't understand to things we do understand. Metaphors can be helpful, but if embraced uncritically, they can also be misleading.

Whenever people have attempted to explain how the mind works, they've used metaphors derived from the technology of their day. Plato famously described the human psyche as a charioteer steering a chariot pulled by two horses, one horse representing reason, the other desire. In the 1800s, the brain was compared to a telegraph and in the 1900s to a telephone switchboard. With the advent of computers, psychologists began to describe the functions of the mind as being comparable to a Mac or PC. Just like a computer, the human brain is said to *store* and *retrieve* memories; departures from rational thinking are often described as "bugs" in an operating system, or the result of our "limited processing capacity," or a reduction in "cognitive bandwidth" due to stress.[7]

The computer supplies a handy vocabulary for describing certain brain functions and limitations, yet our brains don't really store memories or process information in the same way that computers do. Moreover, because computers do not worry about the future, fear death or rejection, experience joy, sorrow, jealousy, or any other emotion, the mind-as-computer metaphor is ultimately an incomplete and unsatisfying account of mental life.

One long-standing metaphor turns out to have been particularly misleading: John Locke's portrait (in the 1600s) of the mind as a *tabula rasa* or *blank slate*. This metaphor portrays our minds, personalities, and traits as shaped entirely by learning and experience, the way one would draw upon a blank sheet of paper. It lasted for centuries, being enthusiastically embraced in the 1900s by psychoanalytic and behaviorist traditions in psychology. If you are shy, in this view, it is because of experiences with your parents, and the rewards and punishments you received, *made* you shy. John Watson, the founder of behaviorism, went so far as to claim that with sufficient control over the environment and the right combination of rewards and punishments, he could shape a randomly selected healthy baby into virtually anything: a doctor, lawyer, beggar, or thief.[8] Although Watson did manage to train a baby to become frightened by the sight of a bunny, thankfully he never attempted the longer experiment of turning them into beggars or thieves.

This extreme, you-can-become-anything view of human malleability lingers in today's society, but it has faded among psychologists in light of the scientific evidence on genetic predispositions. Identical twins who are separated at birth and raised in different families nonetheless reveal a striking similarity in mannerisms, behavior, habits, attitudes — even political views; and siblings who grow up in the same family do not become more alike in personality.[9] Babies enter the world with a mind that has had a great deal of preprogramming, with a temperament, a readiness for learning language and culture, and even innate expectations of how the physical and social world works. Paul Bloom and his associates[10] have found that babies as young as three months of age who watch a brief puppet show will later reach out for the puppet whose behavior was helpful rather than hostile. This fascinating research suggests that we come preprogrammed with moral intuitions and the ability to make moral distinctions long before our first playdate.

Metaphorically, then, our minds are more like sketches than blank pages. Experience doesn't create us from scratch; it elaborates on what's already there, revises it, and colors it in with personal, cultural, and social influences. Nature and nurture interact to make us who we are. Let's look now at what nature has given us.

The Hunter-Gatherer Mind and Human Universals According to evolutionary psychology, the brain is an organ that has been shaped and programmed by evolution, adapted to challenges that faced our biological hunter-gatherer ancestors in their foraging way of life for hundreds of thousands of years.[11] Evolution rewarded traits and tendencies — including intelligence, physical strength, sex drive, and risk taking — that allowed our ancestors to survive long enough to pass on their genes to their children. Most social psychologists now embrace this perspective, which has shed enormous light on the way we understand the human mind.

Consider the fascinating discovery that the anthropologist Robin Dunbar[12] made while he was delving into the grooming habits of primates: he found a strong relationship between the size of an animal's group and the size of the animal's neocortex. The *neocortex* is the part of the mammalian brain that evolved last and houses many of its advanced functions. In humans it makes up over three-fourths of the brain's volume, and within its many folds lie the regions responsible for higher-order processes, such as self-awareness, conscious thought, problem solving, self-control, and language. The especially large size and complexity of the neocortex, and the abilities it gave early humans, enabled us to form larger cooperative groups than other mammals and transmit our knowledge through culture.

Dunbar discovered that our brain size appears to set a limit of about 150 people with whom we can have stable, meaningful relationships; human communities function optimally when they do not exceed this number by much. Group life confers tremendous advantages, like food sharing and protection, but it also imposes cognitive challenges, like learning and remembering important information about members of a group—who is apt to steal your food or your mate. It takes a big brain to house all the information about other group members and the variety of ways they act. That's why, when tribes of hunter-gatherers grew larger than 150 members or so, group life became more difficult and stressful, and the tribes tended to splinter into smaller ones.

Has modern life changed this reality? It would be reasonable to assume that with media and technology we could easily enlarge our social circle far beyond this natural limit, now that we can reach thousands of others with a post or a tweet. Still, here's the question: How many of your online friends or followers do you actually have *meaningful interactions* with at any given point in time? It turns out that few people have two-way communications with more than 150 people. That limit holds true even in the era of Facebook and Twitter, despite the fact that we do appear to derive some self-esteem from having hundreds or even thousands of friends or followers.[13]

A useful implication of knowing the 150-person limit is that human organizations function better when they don't get too large—when they can operate like *communities* rather than *bureaucracies.* Small schools have lower rates of violence and absences, better relationships, and higher-quality learning than larger, impersonal schools do.[14] Being mindful of the nature and limitations of our evolved hunter-gatherer minds provides ways of optimizing our lives and institutions.

The long process of evolution has produced other *human universals*—traits, behavioral tendencies, motivations, and emotional systems that all humans manifest regardless of their culture. In all societies (and among our closest nonhuman relatives, the chimpanzees) certain facial expressions indicate the basic emotions of fear, happiness, anger, sadness, disgust, and surprise. People prefer close kin over distant kin and prefer distant kin to strangers. People live in family units, where the males are older than their female mates. On average, males are more physically aggressive than females, and most activities are divided by gender, with women doing more childcare. All societies have some form of religion, lists of taboo words, and norms of conduct. In all societies, people make toys for children, tell stories and myths, make music, engage in malicious gossip, and practice age-related rites of passage. The existence of such universals points to the centrality of group life for the survival of our species. These adaptations exist everywhere because they facilitated living in groups—and living in groups was critical to our survival.

The impact of the evolutionary view of the human mind cannot be overstated. Only in the last twenty or so years have social scientists fully accepted the argument that many of our illogical, maladaptive tendencies and motivations—as well as generous, compassionate, and touching ones—are rooted in their survival value from the era when we lived in small groups of hunter-gatherers. But the same fictions, errors, and departures from rationality that served us well as hunter-gatherers can get us into trouble in today's complex, multicultural world. The rules of the game have changed, but our evolutionary predispositions have not.[15]

Because we have always needed other human beings to survive, we evolved to be extremely social and group oriented—good team players like bees, but also good competitors like chimpanzees. We are wired to connect, cooperate, conform, and harmonize with members of our group, but also to compete to gain resources and status within our group. We are wired for prejudice and aggression, to be wary of and hostile toward outsiders and those whom we perceive as threats. Our brains developed rapid mental processes to alert us to danger, to decide quickly who was friend or foe, and to ready us to fight with or flee from perceived enemies. These tendencies helped keep us alive when we fought with stones and clubs, but over the millennia the human tendency to see the world in tribal, us-and-them terms has laid the foundation for conflict, political division, hatred, and war.[16]

The Brain's Built-In Biases As you see, many of our mental quirks and glitches are not just foolish or random mistakes, nor are they flaws in the design of our brains. The human brain was designed to work efficiently, but some quirks and biases emerged along the way. A characteristic one is the **bias blind spot**, the belief that we are more objective and less biased than most other people. We are biased to think we aren't biased! This blind spot arises from the fact that many of our beliefs operate *implicitly*, hidden beneath conscious awareness. When we see our own behavior, we know the context and can make excuses for it; we know what we feel, after all. But when we see others' behavior, we miss the full context. That's why it is easy to see hypocrisy in others but not in ourselves. The same politician who is busy condemning another politician for having an affair might be having one of his own right there in his office. Our bias blind spot allows us to explain away our own hypocritical actions easily ("He's an immoral bastard, but I'm entitled to have this affair because I'm under a lot of stress").[17]

Worse yet, we are subject to *naïve realism*, the propensity to believe that our subjective interpretation of reality *is* reality. *We* see things as they really are; those other folks are biased. This belief makes it easier to think that anybody who doesn't share our perspective is misguided, ignorant, selfish — or evil. History demonstrates, all too often and tragically, how much easier it is for people to commit acts of hatred and cruelty if they are certain that they are absolutely right and others are wrong.[18]

Of all the mind's biases, the **confirmation bias** is central to how we see the world and process information: We notice, remember, and accept information that *confirms* what we already believe, and tend to ignore, forget, and reject information that *disconfirms* what we believe. In an experiment by Mark Snyder and William Swann,[19] female college students were told that the person they were about to meet was either an extrovert (outgoing, warm, and friendly) or an introvert (reserved, cool, and aloof). They then were asked to prepare a set of questions that they would like to ask this person to get to know him or her. What types of questions did they ask? Students who thought they would meet an extrovert were more likely to ask questions that confirmed their expectation, such as "What do you do to liven up a party?" and "In what situations are you most talkative?" Those who expected to meet an introvert were likely to ask questions like "In what situations do you wish you could be more outgoing?" and "What things do you dislike about loud parties?" Notice that whatever the respondent answers, the questioners' hypothesis about the person is likely to be confirmed. That is, a person who isn't especially introverted or extroverted will appear to be extroverted when they answer the first set of questions and introverted when they answer the second set.

The confirmation bias helps explain why people cling tenaciously to debunked beliefs. They look for any scrap of evidence to support their wish to be right, so they do not have to "change their minds." In our evolutionary past, this bias would have been adaptive, leading our forebears to have an "if it works, stay with it" strategy. But in the modern world, sometimes that strategy can lead us into dark alleys and dead ends.

The Egocentric Bias Human beings are a social species, but we are also egocentric: We tend to place ourselves in the center of our own universes. That's why people remember new information better when they can apply it to themselves than if they think it only affects other people.[20] If they are working in groups, they tend to focus on and recall their own performance better than the performance of their teammates. And when people play an active role in generating information, they recall that information better than when they receive it passively.

You can see the **egocentric bias** in yourself if you have ever felt absolutely sure that the entire world has seen that pimple on your face or is gossiping about the bad hair day you're having. Many teenagers dread going to school if they suddenly have a flaw that they are sure "everyone will notice." Social psychologists have found, however, that such worries are usually greatly exaggerated. People feel as though the social spotlight shines more brightly on them than it actually does, a bias Thomas Gilovich and his associates named the **spotlight effect**.[21] In one experiment, college students were asked to wear an attention-arousing T-shirt—one with a large picture of Barry Manilow on it—and then enter a room full of other students.

Later, the participants imagined that about half of their peers had seen and reacted negatively to their shirt, but in reality only about 20 percent had even noticed it.

We may feel we're in the spotlight when imagining how others see us, but we also feel that we notice and observe others more than they notice and observe us—a form of egocentrism that's called the *cloak of invisibility illusion*. For example, students in an experiment who sat in a waiting room with a stranger later erroneously estimated having paid a lot more attention to the stranger than they believed the stranger paid to them. Participants consistently reported this sense of invisibility—unless they were wearing a T-shirt provided by the experimenter, this time one emblazoned with a large picture of Pablo Escobar. The moral of the story is that it is very difficult to move beyond our own perception of reality when we're estimating how others see things.

The egocentric bias can lead us to uncritically accept flattery and falsehoods. The great showman P.T. Barnum is credited with saying, "There's a sucker born every minute," and his name now applies to a common psychological phenomenon. The *Barnum Effect* refers to the fact that when people are given vague, all-purpose descriptions of themselves that could apply to almost anyone, they usually say "Incredible! That's me *exactly!*" This effect helps explain why so many people mistakenly believe in the accuracy of astrology, fortune telling, and even some pop-psych personality tests.[22] Suppose I were to examine your astrological chart and tell you, "You are quite reserved in unfamiliar social situations. You view life with a mixture of optimism and pessimism. You have an open mind but can take a firm stand when the situation calls for it." Would you think me a particularly talented reader of the stars and your own personality? A moment's reflection will tell you that this description fits almost everyone. But because of our tendency to think egocentrically, most of us will feel it is a perfect description of us.

Why Bad Is Stronger Than Good A curious feature of the evolved human mind is that it is oriented toward negativity: We tend to focus more on potential threats than blessings, a tendency often called the **negativity bias**. We are quicker to find angry faces in a crowd than smiling ones. Negative interactions at the office are far more influential than positive ones, and employees are likely to remember their boss's negative statements and behaviors more than their positive ones. Negative feedback has a more powerful emotional impact than positive feedback. Bad news is shared more readily and frequently than good news.[23]

People who win money in a lottery will enjoy a spike in happiness but eventually return to their pre-lottery happiness "set-point."[24] The same thing happens after losing money, failing a test, or other negative events: We adapt to the new circumstances and our feelings return to baseline. But consistent with evolutionary theory, interviews with lottery winners and accident victims show that, on average, it takes longer to return to baseline after bad experiences than after good ones. Roy Baumeister and his colleagues found that negative events typically have more power than positive ones. It is evolutionarily adaptive, they concluded, for *bad to be stronger than good*, because animals with a heightened alertness to danger, pain, failure, or other negative experiences would have been more likely to survive threats and consequently would have better odds of passing along their genes.[25]

This evolved negativity bias is yet another reason that we aren't always the rational animals economists have supposed. For example, from an economic point of view, it makes sense for me to mourn the loss of $50 just as much as I would celebrate a gain of $50. After all, it's the same amount of money. Yet experiments repeatedly show that the distress that participants feel when they lose money tends to be greater than the joy they feel gaining the same amount of money.[26] When given a choice, people are more likely to try to avoid loss than to try to achieve gains, a phenomenon known as **loss aversion**.

By framing choices to emphasize losses, researchers and policy-makers can influence people's behavior and decision-making.[27] In a field experiment I did with two of my students, Mark Costanzo and Marti Gonzales,[28] we used loss aversion to get people to invest in insulation for their homes. In one condition, after examining each home, energy experts gave each homeowner a detailed description of how much money they could be *saving* each year on heating bills by insulating. In the other condition, auditors provided the same information but informed the homeowners of how much money they were *losing* every day—that doing nothing was akin to throwing money out the window. Homeowners in the "loss" condition were twice as likely to invest the money to insulate their homes as those in the "save" condition.

Understanding the negativity bias shows us a way out of it. Although some of us won the temperamental lottery and are endowed with a happy disposition, the rest of us need to actively seek out the positive in life, exposing ourselves to beauty, small pleasures, and goodness in others, precisely because it is not our automatic tendency to do so.[29] We can learn to focus on the things we are grateful for and do kind things for others, habits that offset the negativity bias by generating satisfaction.[30]

The Mind's Two Thinking Systems   The human mind is divided according to two forms of processing: automatic and controlled. **Automatic processing** refers to the unconscious (*implicit*) and involuntary operations that guide most of our behavior: well-learned associations or routines that our mental systems perform effortlessly, without awareness. This is the kind of thinking that animal brains have been doing for half a billion years — fast, efficient responses to sensory input. We can perform many automatic operations at once, which is why experienced drivers can drive without consciously paying attention to all the countless adjustments and decisions they are making (checking the rearview mirror, being alert for *other* drivers who are texting, etc.). When we read simple bits of text on a page, detect anger in a friend's voice, complete the phrase "salt and ___," or categorize a person by their race, gender, or age, we are engaged in automatic processing.

Controlled processing, by contrast, is the conscious (*explicit*) effort we make in dealing with novel problems, such as learning to drive, solving complex math problems, trying to remember the name of a movie, or answering a question like "Why do you love your boyfriend?" This kind of thinking is evolutionarily more recent, and it is tied to the development of language. It is slower and *sequential* — we process one thought after another rather than several in parallel. In his influential book *Thinking, Fast and Slow*, the Nobel prize–winning psychologist Daniel Kahneman[31] describes these two systems and spells out the implications of their operation for a wide range of psychological phenomena.

Most decisions involve a two-step process. Our automatic system first produces a quick-and-dirty assessment of reality — an intuition, a feeling, an unthinking preference. Then, if we are motivated and if we have access to valid information, we use more controlled or deliberate thinking to modify the initial impressions. We do this all the time—for example, when deciding whether an idea is as useful as we intuitively assumed, whether a situation is safe or dangerous, or whether our neighbor is being thoughtless or intentionally malicious.

Because controlled processing demands more time, focus, effort, and energy than automatic thinking, it is prone to fatigue and distraction, and therefore we are attracted to shortcuts. When this happens, our first impressions and impulses may go uncorrected. Moreover, unlike automatic processing, controlled processing cannot do two things at once. This is why so many studies have shown that, despite what you egocentrically believe about your own abilities, it is impossible to multitask effectively.[32] (When you are trying to text and drive, one of those actions is going to fail.) Human beings are usually pretty proud of our controlled-processing skills, but Jonathan Haidt[33] estimates that our conscious reasoning—"the stream of words and images of which we are fully aware"—represents only about 1 percent of our thinking. The other 99 percent occurs outside of awareness, but that's the percentage, he argues, that actually governs most of our behavior.

By understanding how evolution has shaped our cognitive processes, we can approach social problems with greater understanding. We turn now to some social characteristics of our minds that are of special relevance.

Evolution and the Social Brain

I've always been fascinated by how fascinating other people are. We all are, actually. No one needs to be bribed into indulging in gossip, even gossip about people they will never meet. In fact, we pay to do it: the magazine with the largest readership and the most advertising revenue in America is *People*, a publication that shares the details of lives of celebrities—strangers we may feel we know, but with whom we have no relationship. People pay for *People* even when they can indulge their gossip quotient on the internet 250 times a day.

Another marker of how our brains are wired to be social is how readily we interpret things in human terms. People frequently see faces in unlikely places: on the surface of the moon, on potato chips, on a slice of toast, or famously, on a cinnamon bun, which showed the alleged face of Mother Teresa. We connect random stimuli into meaningful patterns, and much of the time those patterns involve people, most likely because people are on our minds.[34]

In a classic demonstration of this tendency, Fritz Heider and Marianne Simmel[35] showed college students a brief animated film in which a few geometric shapes move around the screen, in and around a large rectangle, in randomly determined ways. The students were simply instructed to watch the movie and "write down what happened." One of the thirty-four movie watchers described the film literally: "A large solid triangle is shown entering a rectangle. It enters and comes out of this rectangle, and each time the corner and one-half of one of the sides of the rectangle form an opening." That guy was on his own. Nearly everyone else read more into it, telling a story about people, like this one:

> A man has planned to meet a girl, and the girl comes along with another man. The first man tells the second to go; the second tells the first, and he shakes his head. Then the two men have a fight, and the girl starts to go into the room to get out of the way and hesitates and finally goes in. She apparently does not want to be with the first man. The first man follows her into the room after having left the second in a rather weakened condition leaning on the wall outside the room. The girl gets worried and races from one corner to the other in the far part of the room.

This was in response to seeing a film about rectangles and triangles! Our minds are rarely satisfied with reporting the world as it appears. When asked what happened, we make up stories readily and automatically. We go beyond the information given to attribute human intentions, motives, and personalities—even to geometric figures, inanimate objects, and increasingly in today's world, robots. We treat R2-D2, Siri, and Alexa as if they were human.

For another window on your social brain, think about this: Where does your mind go when it goes *wandering*? Where is it wandering to? What do you think about when you are "off task"? The **default mode network** is a set of interacting brain regions that are active when not directed to a task or focused on the outside world. This network is also active when we're explicitly thinking about people. That is why, when our minds wander, they typically wander to social matters: plans we're making with friends, memories of loved ones, conflicts with a partner, sexual fantasies about all kinds of people, or problems caused by other people. We see human stories in everything because people are never far from our thoughts.[36]

A lesson here is that if you want to sell a product, get children interested in mathematics or history, or motivate your best friend to get help for that drinking problem, tell them a story about a *person*—or get them to tell one. In an experiment led by David Hamilton,[37] two groups of college students read statements about everyday human behaviors, but each group received a different set of instructions. One group was instructed to remember the information because they would be tested later for recall; the other group was told to form an overall impression of what the person who was doing these things was like. This second group was not warned about the recall rest. What happened? The impression-formation group remembered more facts than those who were trying to memorize facts for the recall test. Thinking in "people terms" improves memory because when a task is framed around people, the default mode network gets involved, which in turn helps store the memories.

Why Social Pain Hurts So Much "My heart is broken." "My feelings are hurt." Despite the obvious differences between a broken heart and a broken leg, the fact that human beings talk like this suggests that *social pain*—the sting of rejection, humiliation, or insult—hurts like physical pain. Think of a time when you were rejected or publicly shamed. It's likely you felt this physically, a twisting feeling in your gut, perhaps, or hotly flushed cheeks.

It may be hard to believe this when you are suffering after a breakup, but the ability to feel social pain had survival value for early humans.[38] Our large brains require big heads to house them, which means that human babies must be born relatively immature, while their heads can fit through the birth canal. They are unable to feed or fend for themselves while their brains and bodies develop outside the womb. Therefore they must stay close to caregivers for food and protection, and this kind of connection to others remains critical throughout life to ensure safety and access to resources. Emotional pain served the purpose of making sure people cared when social connections were broken or at risk; individuals untouched by separation or rejection wouldn't have lasted long.

Naomi Eisenberger and Matthew Lieberman[39] scanned the brains of college students with functional magnetic resonance imaging (fMRI)—a procedure that identifies active brain regions by tracking blood flow—while each student played a game of three-way cyberball catch with two other players. At one point the two other players would exclude the scanned person from the game, no longer tossing her the ball. The fMRI revealed a pattern of activation in the excluded student's brain parallel to that seen when people endure pinpricks, electric shock, or other experimentally induced physical pain.

This result suggests that the mental system involved with human connectedness attached itself to the system already involved with signaling physical pain. It explains why insults, shunning, and name-calling are no less serious than physical injury. Children who are rejected or teased in school can suffer severe and enduring effects; in fact, many adults remember experiences of rejection in childhood much more vividly than physical punishment.[40]

The Us–Them Thinking of Tribal Minds Evolution has shaped our minds to be *tribal*, exquisitely tuned to categorizing other individuals as part of *us* or part of *them*. As soon as we see an unfamiliar person, we instantly put them in a box: Are you dangerous? Do you have hostile intent? Are you attractive? Are you competent? Are you cold and rejecting or warm and inviting?[41] Ultimately, we ask: Are you one of us or one of them?

It doesn't take much to engage us–them thinking. My son Josh loves to tell the story that many years ago, when he and his three siblings were kids, they often competed with one another for my wife's and my attention or for the last piece of pizza, or argued about whose turn it was to empty the dishwasher; but mostly it was just four kids pursuing their own interests and agendas. Yet outside the house, on a family vacation or in some unfamiliar place, they were transformed into part of a *team*, a family united by an us-against-the-world feeling. An old Bedouin proverb says, "Me against my brother, my brother and I against my cousin, and all of us against the stranger." This proverb perfectly captures how our tribal minds divide the world into gradations of us and them.

In a classic line of research, Henri Tajfel[42] explored the effects of dividing objects and people into groups. A Polish Jew who fought for the French army against the Nazis and ended up in a German prisoner-of-war camp, Tajfel developed a keen interest in social identity; later, when he became a social psychologist, he developed **social identity theory**, which described how our most important memberships in religious, political, regional, national, or occupational groups (e.g., Baptist, Muslim, Jewish? Texan or Hoosier? Firefighter or nurse?) feed a sense of belonging and self-worth and shape our thinking about people in and beyond our group.

Tajfel's research revealed that once we divide people into groups, our minds automatically lead us to exaggerate the differences between *us* and *them*, rather than notice similarities. Whereas we tend to see people in our group—**the ingroup**—as a collection of unique individuals, we tend to see those in the **outgroup** as more alike—"they're all the same," people often say, or "they all look alike to me." In fact, "they" often do look alike. That is a common perceptual glitch: white people who evaluate a photo array of faces will have more trouble distinguishing them from one another if the faces are Asian or black than if they are white. Asians have precisely the same trouble distinguishing between the faces of blacks or whites. You can imagine how this bias might impair accurate eyewitness identification: White eyewitnesses are significantly more likely to mistakenly confuse one black person for another.[43]

We are also far more charitable in judging members of our own group than when judging "them." We not only see people in our group as being more varied; we see our group as being better and more deserving. This *ingroup bias* confers feelings of pride and esteem: We distort our perceptions of the world so that our group looks better than others, and we feel better because we are part of it.

Favoring our own group may seem perfectly reasonable given that we often choose to be in the group based on real differences in tastes, values, beliefs, and political ideology. Yet human beings are so naturally inclined to divide the world into *us* and *them* that ingroup bias emerges even when group membership is based on differences that are trivial, even meaningless. Tajfel[44] randomly divided complete strangers into groups labeled "Group X" or "Group W." These strangers never interacted during the study, and their actions were completely anonymous, yet they behaved as if those who shared their meaningless label (X or W) were their good friends or close kin. In study after study, on the basis of group assignment alone, participants prefer those who share their label; they rate them as having a more pleasant personality and more likely to produce better work than people assigned a different label. They even allocate more money and rewards to those in their "group."

Why are we so ready to discriminate so much on the basis of so little? Because it's in our DNA. For hunter-gatherers, it paid to be vigilant for differences between members of their own tribe, who might be competitors, and for outsiders, who would likely be attackers. Coalition formation, the grouping of individuals into teams, comes naturally when there is a shared purpose that also benefits each member. Cohesion among our own tribe or team was highly adaptive because we shared resources and enjoyed the group's protection against constant external threats.

Unfortunately, we often let our group membership do our thinking for us. Geoffrey Cohen and his colleagues[45] recruited a large number of self-identified liberals and conservatives and asked them to evaluate proposals for two welfare reform programs: one a generous program and the other a more austere program that provided fewer benefits to welfare recipients. As expected, liberals preferred the generous plan and conservatives favored the more stringent one. Next, a separate group of liberals and conservatives looked at the same plans, which were labeled as having been proposed either by Democrats or Republicans. This time, group membership completely trumped the content of the proposal: Liberals preferred the plan they thought came from Democrats and conservatives preferred the plans they thought came from Republicans—regardless of the actual content they read. Objective policy content had *no effect whatsoever* on the judges. Notably, this "party over policy" effect was as strong among people who were knowledgeable about welfare issues as it was among people who were not. Moreover, participants insisted they formed their attitude *logically*, based on the policy alone, even though it was clear that their preferences were driven by group affiliation.

Turn on the news and listen to political pundits defending their party's candidate or position, and you will see this phenomenon play out repeatedly. (Many Republicans in Congress spent years opposing Barack Obama's Affordable Care Act, even though it was almost entirely based on a successful program implemented in Massachusetts by Mitt Romney—a Republican.) Read through the comments thread of any politically biased news story, and you'll see the same thing: the reflexive devaluation by *us* of any ideas coming from *them*.

Such biases emerge whenever teams or groups have competing interests, as shown in another classic study of partisanship among fans in a football game between Princeton and Dartmouth. The game is remembered as the roughest and dirtiest in the history of either school. Sometime after the game, Albert Hastorf of Dartmouth and Hadley Cantril of Princeton[46] visited both schools and showed films of the game to students. The students were instructed to be completely objective while watching the film and to write down each infraction of the rules—how it started and who was at fault. As with Cohen's political partisans, there was a big difference in the way students at each university viewed this game: each side saw their fellow students as victims rather than perpetrators of illegal aggression. Moreover, this was no minor distortion. Princeton students saw fully twice as many violations on the part of the Dartmouth players as the Dartmouth students saw.

Cognitive scientists Steven Sloman and Philip Fernbach[47] argue that we literally think in groups rather than as rational individuals, especially in today's complex world, where we need the expertise of others for almost everything we do. It may take a tribe to raise a child, but it also takes a tribe to cure a disease or get to the moon or design a self-driving car. From an evolutionary perspective, relying on the knowledge of others has worked well for human beings—except, of course, when it doesn't.

Tribal thinking is natural, but is it inevitable? Not necessarily. Our history is replete with shifting alliances and attitudes rooted in us–them distinctions. An ally we think is terrific one year can become an enemy or competitor next year, or vice versa. As Daniel Yudkin and Jay Van Bavel point out,[48] such shifts provide hope that we needn't resign ourselves to a future of tribalism. We can train ourselves to correct our hardwired automatic impulses toward treating *us* as friends and *them* as threats. In experiments, if group members are given the time and motivation to apply reason and deliberation—to think about whether it was fair to punish a member of an outgroup—they were less apt to discriminate or act unfairly.[49]

The Central Social Motives

Human beings have many universal physical needs for survival, but we also have certain basic *social* motives that shape our thinking, emotions, and relationships. All human beings pursue social motives to varying degrees, as dictated by their culture, their individual personalities, and the details of the situation. When these motives are satisfied, we tend to feel good; when they are frustrated or when circumstances place them in conflict, we feel stressed, unhappy, and even less than human. Susan Fiske, a pioneer in social cognition research, has identified a core group of these motives.[50]

Belonging Of all the motives that govern social life, the most important is **belonging**: our desire for stable, meaningful connections with others.[51] We long to fit in; as we saw earlier, even a mild dose of exclusion during a game of cyberball with two unseen strangers sets off alarms in our brains akin to those of physical pain. College students who recalled episodes of exclusion, or who were excluded during a brief game in the laboratory, later rated themselves as "less human" than students who were not led to feel excluded.

This root social motive is the reason that long periods of involuntary isolation are not only unpleasant; they are also psychologically damaging, generating depression, anxiety, and self-destructive impulses. The suicide rate is many times higher among prisoners kept in solitary confinement than among the total prison population; it's truly the cruelest of punishments.[52] Craig Haney, who has studied prisoners who have been kept for years in total isolation, observed that "they are not sure that they exist and, if they do, exactly who they are."[53]

On a less extreme level, feeling socially disconnected can cause people to lose the ability to regulate their emotions and control their attention, behavior, and impulses. Rejected, isolated students tend to do worse on tests, eat more junk food, and behave more aggressively than do students who feel part of a group.[54] A threatened or diminished sense of belonging also changes the way people process and interpret information, at once making them more open to interaction with others but also more cautious of rejection — and thus hypersensitive to other people's behavior.[55] It's as if they say to themselves, "I really want to be accepted by this group, but I'll keep an eagle eye out for signs they don't want me."

The need to belong fosters conformity and smooth relationships and generates many of our customs. Consider music. Why has every known culture developed some form of song, dance, rhythm, or melody? Is it a byproduct of evolution with no special value? Given music's universality, that answer is unlikely. Rather, music exists everywhere because of its power to organize individuals into a coordinated group or team in a way that nothing else quite can, transmitting information about a group's mood or intended purpose to many people at once. Think of tribal war drums or military marches, which bring soldiers into order and prepare them for battle. Think of how college fight songs at sporting events pump up and organize thousands of individual spectators into a unified crowd. Think of how concertgoers sway in synchrony with the music, and how all of us can be moved to tears or laughter or dancing by our favorite songs. Music is essential because it connects us, emotionally, with others.[56]

Understanding Others and Predicting Accurately Human beings have a strong motive to be accurate in how we read and understand people and situations, accurate enough to navigate the world safely and in a way that optimizes our relationships. We want to be able to predict what will happen and make sense of the things that do happen. When this sense-making motive is frustrated, the uncertainty we feel can be unnerving; when a situation is stable and certain, we can prepare, adapt, and move on. Uncertainty keeps us in limbo, unable to brace ourselves for what's coming. Indeed, we feel better knowing for sure that something bad *is* coming than suspecting that something bad *might* happen.

In one study,[57] participants played a video game while connected to a shock generator and a monitor of their stress levels. They received a mild but painful shock on their hand each time they turned over a digital rock and found a digital snake beneath it. As some players continued, they got better at predicting which rocks had snakes hiding under them, and thus they could predict when they would get a shock; they couldn't avoid the shock, but they knew when it was coming. But for some players the odds of finding a snake kept changing, so the shocks remained unpredictable. Players who were certain that they were going to find a snake had significantly lower stress levels than those who were uncertain.

Control Certainty, even unhappy certainty, satisfies a third strong social motive: the *need for control*, the feeling that we have the autonomy and competence to direct our own actions and make things happen. A sense of control contributes to our well-being because it gives us feelings of initiative and competence to get things done. The sensation that we lack control is unpleasant and, in the long run, unhealthy. Bruce McEwen[58] has found that humans and other primates who are on the lower rungs of social hierarchies—who have relatively little control over their lives, and who can be pushed around by a larger, more dominant monkey or by a boss—tend to suffer the most stress-related illness and die significantly earlier than their higher-status peers.

For many people, a sense of control is so central to well-being that they act as though they have control when they don't. They are more reluctant to part with a lottery ticket if they have chosen their own numbers, for instance, and they believe shaking the dice vigorously in a game of craps will yield higher numbers.

A Need to Matter Human beings have a strong motive to feel that they are worthy, have social status in their community, and have positive reputations. They want their lives to *matter*—whether it's to one other person, to their families, or to the world; Fiske calls this a motive for "self-enhancement." Indeed, how much we admire ourselves is directly related to how we think we are valued by others.[59] This motive expresses itself in many ways, from trying to improve ourselves, to improving our communities, to becoming active in politics, to displaying wealth and signs of status, to performing small acts of kindness. Conversely, when people feel that they don't matter—when they feel that society doesn't care if they live or die, if the jobs that gave them stability and meaning are gone—the result can be despair or angry protest. To take one example only, the Black Lives Matter movement began as a cry by the African American community to get the white majority to understand that their lives and safety are as important as white lives.[60]

Trust As social animals, we cannot survive without trusting other people. Although evolution endowed us with the negativity bias—"the bad is stronger than the good" effect—we are highly motivated to trust that the world is safe, benevolent, and fair. We want to feel that others will ensure our safety, treat us with kindness, and provide us with resources. Despite the risks of making ourselves vulnerable by trusting, we generally do expect that others—particularly those similar to us—will not do us harm. As with all the social motives, people differ in how much they trust others and the world, partly because of their individual temperamental dispositions and partly because of their early childhood experiences. But we are so inclined to trust that we feel surprised, angered, and hurt when other people cheat or deceive us. Trusting others makes interactions simpler and more pleasant; it frees us from worry that others are out to get us or that they will gossip about us if we reveal our genuine selves. The Victorian novelist George Eliot expressed this well when she wrote, "What loneliness is lonelier than *distrust*?"

As we do with the other social motives, we often distort our view of the world to satisfy our desire for trust and maintain our underlying faith in a benevolent world. If you, or someone you know, has been robbed, raped, attacked, or suffered other trauma, you know how disorienting this experience is—because, in addition to the shock and pain of the event, it temporarily wrecks the assumption that the world is safe, just, and fair. Our trust has been shattered. In a common but unfortunate attempt to feel better and assure ourselves that such a thing could never happen to us, we may resort to *blaming the victim*, trying to find reasons that the victim did something to invite such treatment.[61]

A Concluding Word on Social Motives Throughout this book, you will see how an understanding of these social motives provides a lens through which to view social cognition and behavior. We do our best work when we feel that we belong, when we can predict results, when we are free to make choices and be in control, when we get to do work that makes us feel useful, and when we trust our loved ones and colleagues.[62] Therefore, when people believe things that aren't true, or do things that seem crazy, it's often the case that these core motives have been warped in some way.

In Chapter 1, I raised the question of why middle-class teenagers with no particularly deep connection to religious fundamentalism would leave their homes to join a terrorist group. Who in their right mind would seek pleasure by leaving a stable home to join ISIS, quite possibly to become a suicide bomber? Arie Kruglanski, an expert on terrorism, has found several commonalities among terrorists, and three central motives stand out.[63] First, they have an intense desire to *belong*, to be part of a larger group that provides them with an identity and purpose. Second, they have a high need for *certainty*, order, and structure; the black-and-white dogma of fundamentalist groups provides them with clear answers—with the certainty they crave in an uncertain world. Third, belonging to a terrorist group resolves their feeling that their lives are trivial and meaningless; it provides them with significance, an intense feeling that their lives *matter*.

I want to emphasize that most human beings find ways to fulfill these universal needs in ways compatible with living peaceably in their societies. But for those who feel marginalized and alienated, the need to belong and to matter can be more precious than life itself.

Perceiving and Explaining Our Social Worlds

Every day of our lives, we seek to explain a great variety of events: Why are the North Koreans behaving so erratically? Why did that attractive person across the room ignore me? How come I did so poorly and you did so well on the recent essay assignment? Our explanations are often rational and accurate, but they are also vulnerable to bias and inaccuracy.

Attributions and Explanations: Why Do People Do What They Do? In the mid-twentieth century, Fritz Heider and Harold Kelley argued that people think like "naïve scientists."[64] They might not test their hypotheses about behavior as systematically as professional scientists do, but they try to understand why other people act as they do. In this goal, they make **causal attributions**: They want to know what caused Joe to be mean or Jim to be generous. Do these guys always behave selfishly or generously, or did the situation influence their actions?

Let's say you and a friend are walking across campus when you see your classmate Margaux kissing Scott. "Why is she doing that?" your friend asks you. "I thought she *hated* him." According to **attribution theory**, people make one of two kinds of causal explanations before they answer: One explanation has to do with the person's typical personality (a **dispositional attribution**); the other has to do with the situation the person is in (a **situational attribution**). Does Margaux go around kissing almost everyone at the drop of a hat? If so, you would probably conclude that she kissed Scott because she is a highly affectionate person. That is a dispositional attribution: You are inferring that a person is behaving in a particular way because of something *internal* to that person, such as a personality trait or motive.

But suppose you learn that almost *everybody* kisses Scott. Now you might infer that Margaux kissed Scott because Scott is a kissable guy—a situational attribution for her behavior. Finally, if Margaux kisses only Scott and no one else kisses Scott, the distinctiveness of the kissing is likely due to some special relationship between them; you will probably conclude that either they are in love or Scott has done something especially deserving of a kiss.

This kind of attributional analysis can be extremely useful and can help us with far weightier decisions than determining why one person kisses another. Teachers must figure out why students struggle. Juries must decide a defendant's innocence or guilt. Nations must decide how to respond to the provocations of other nations. In all such cases, the attributions that we make will have powerful consequences. For that reason, social psychologists have identified a number of influences on our attributions and explanations:

the fundamental attribution error, self-fulfilling prophecies, and *self-serving biases.*

The Fundamental Attribution Error The term **fundamental attribution error** refers to a human tendency to overestimate the importance of personality or dispositional factors relative to situational or environmental influences when describing and explaining why people do what they do.[65] If you try to explain why your classmate has stopped studying and is coasting through classes, you will probably reach for a reason in his or her personality: "She's gotten lazy" or "He's not as smart as I thought." As a result, though, you may come to believe that your classmate just is that way consistently, rather than temporarily suffering from an external problem, such as a parent's illness.

One critical aspect of the situation is the social role we happen to be playing at any given time. A clever experiment by Lee Ross, Teresa Amabile, and Julia Steinmetz illustrates how we underestimate the power of roles in explaining behavior.[66] They set up a quiz show format in which they randomly assigned participants to one of two roles: (1) a questioner, whose task was to prepare difficult questions for (2) a contestant, whose task was to answer them. An observer watched this simulated quiz show and then estimated the questioner's and the contestant's general knowledge. Try to put yourself in the role of the observer. What do you see? You most likely will see one very smart, knowledgeable person and one rather dimwitted, ignorant person. But notice how these two roles constrain the behavior of the participants. The questioner will strive to come up with difficult questions based on esoteric knowledge: "In what baseball park did Babe Ruth hit his second-to-last home run?" "What is the capital city of Lithuania?" and "What is the date of Thomas Jefferson's death?"

By simply *asking* these questions, the questioner looks smart. The poor contestant is faced with answering them and is bound to miss plenty of them, making him or her look a little dumb. And that is exactly what Ross and his colleagues found. The observers felt that the questioners were far more knowledgeable than the contestants. However, since everyone was randomly assigned to their roles, it is extremely unlikely that all of the questioners were *actually* smarter and more knowledgeable than all of the contestants. And here is the kicker: Even though the observers *knew* that the participants had been randomly assigned to these roles, they nonetheless failed to acknowledge the impact of these social roles in making their judgments about the quiz show participants. They fell smack into the trap of attributing what they saw to personal dispositions.

The fundamental attribution error has consequences in our personal, romantic lives, too. If your partner does something thoughtless, for example, you could make a dispositional attribution ("My partner is an inconsiderate slob; we need to break up") or a situational attribution ("My partner must be under incredible pressure at work; we need a vacation"). Guess which attribution leads to happier relationships?

Attributions also underlie beliefs about social issues and their solutions. Many Americans regard a person using food stamps at a supermarket as being unwilling to work: "If she just tried harder, she could get a job." Or they might say a convicted burglar "must be a terrible, heartless human being." Both descriptions could be accurate, but they blind us to the possibility that we are making the fundamental attribution error. Many factors other than personality traits can explain why a person is poor or commits a crime, including lack of job opportunities, illiteracy, an economic recession, or growing up in a dysfunctional family.

I am not saying that criminals shouldn't be held accountable for their actions. And I am definitely not saying that dispositional factors such as laziness, heartlessness, or viciousness don't exist. They do! But focusing on personal rather than situational factors will result in different policies for reducing poverty and crime. The attribution "this criminal is inherently evil" will lead us to support policies of spending more money on prisons and doling out longer, crueler prison sentences. Perceiving the causes of crime as due largely to unemployment, poor role models, and illiteracy will result in policies like increased spending for better schools and tax credits to businesses that invest in poverty-stricken areas.

At the very least, our knowledge of the fundamental attribution error should alert us to the possibility that our attributions may not always be correct. By directing us to consider situational forces, it reminds us that we ourselves might be caught in situations that cause us to behave badly. We should take seriously the motto of the English Protestant reformer John Bradford: "There, but for the grace of God, go I."

Attributions for Success and Failure – and the Self-Fulfilling Prophecy Of all the attributions we make, those about success and failure are among the most important, because they affect our sense of control. When children have trouble in school or fail their tests, the explanations they tell themselves and others about the reasons will determine whether they continue to fail—or eventually succeed.

When we make dispositional attributions for performance, we locate the cause inside of us, blaming success or failure on our personalities, abilities, or effort. When we make situational attributions for the same thing, we locate the cause in the difficulty of the task or the conditions under which the task was performed. If you fail a math test, you can conclude that your failure was caused by something internal, in you (*"I'm* bad at math"; *"I* didn't try hard enough") or external ("The *test* was unbelievably hard or tricky"; "The *room* was so noisy I couldn't focus").

Over time, people develop a habitual pattern of explaining their successes and failures, and this pattern—called their **explanatory style**—affects their sense of control and emotional well-being.[67] People who have a pessimistic explanatory style are relentlessly gloomy, because they think that the cause of their troubles permeates their lives, can't be changed, and will haunt them forever ("I'm just awful at everything, and nothing I do will ever change that"). People who have an optimistic explanatory style attribute unfortunate events to causes that are external, situational, and within their control: "Yeah," they might say, "I blew that particular math test, but I can study harder next time and get better. Besides, that was a really hard test, and I did well on my other exams."

You can see how these attributions can lead to full-fledged narratives that set us up for future success or failure. The mechanism creates a **self-fulfilling prophecy**, which occurs when we act on our initial attribution of our behavior and then behave in a way to confirm it: "I failed that test, so I'm stupid. Therefore I won't study. Therefore, I will fail. See? I told you I was stupid." But we could also create a positive self-fulfilling prophecy: "I failed that test, so clearly I didn't work hard enough. Therefore, I will study harder and make sure I understand the material. Therefore, I will do better. See? I told you I could."

Self-fulfilling prophecies apply to our attributions about other people, too: We think they are stupid, so we treat them as if they are stupid, and then they behave in ways to fulfill our prophecy that they are stupid. In a classic experiment that illuminated this sad cycle, Robert Rosenthal and Lenore Jacobson[68] planted a false stereotype in the heads of schoolteachers, and the resulting attributions that the teachers made about their students influenced how well the children did. In this study, the experimenters first gave an IQ test to all the children in an elementary school. After the tests were scored, 20 percent of the children from each class were chosen at random. The teachers were informed that the test had indicated that these students were "bloomers," on the verge of making significant intellectual gains over the coming year. This completely false information gave the teachers a positive expectation about some of their students. Then the researchers simply sat back and watched. At the end of the year, they administered the IQ test again.

Overall, all the children made considerable IQ gains over the year, yet those labeled as "bloomers" made significantly larger gains than the children not labeled bloomers. Apparently, the teachers, believing that the bloomers would bloom, paid more attention to them, treated them more respectfully, and made the children feel more confident of their abilities. In turn, the children fulfilled the teachers' positive expectations.

This effect was primarily found in first and second grades, which suggests that children are particularly susceptible to their teachers' expectations of them when they are new to school and their academic self-concepts are still forming. In later grades, the score differences were smaller or nonexistent. However, for students belonging to minority groups, the impact of teacher expectations was larger and spanned more grades, suggesting that minority status leaves children especially sensitive to the way their teachers treat them.[69]

The Effects of Context on Social Judgments

A basic principle of social cognition is that *all judgment is relative; how we perceive and think about a person or an event depends on its social context.* "Social context" is a pretty big term, though, so here I want to explore some ways that the outside world gets into our minds and influences the way we make decisions and explain behavior.

Contrast Effects and Social Comparisons An object can appear to be better or worse than it is, depending on what we compare it with. Most salespeople implicitly understand this, and some act on it. Let me take you house shopping with a real estate agent. The first stop is a tiny two-bedroom house sitting on a smallish lot. The house needs a new coat of paint; the interior is in disarray; the linoleum in the kitchen is buckling; the living room carpet is worn and smells bad. When the realtor tells you the asking price, you are stunned: "Holy cow! They want that much for this place? Who'd be dumb enough to pay so much for this shack?" Certainly not you, and probably not anyone else. Now the agent takes you to an average-looking house. How do you suppose that viewing that dilapidated house first might influence your evaluation of the second one? Right you are. The dilapidated house is a *decoy*, designed to influence your perception of the next ones.

On most restaurant wine lists, you'll typically find a wide price range for each variety of wine. Let's say there are four merlots, at $14, $35, $70, and $170 per bottle. Although the restaurant may not sell much of the $170 wine, its existence makes the other wines look cheaper by comparison. And because most people don't want to appear cheap by ordering the least expensive bottle on the list, the strategic placement of the outrageously pricey decoy allows the restaurant to jack up the price of the second- and third-cheapest bottles, charging you a good deal more than they are worth.[70]

The principle behind the use of such decoys is the **contrast effect**, a change in how good something looks to you in contrast to a similar item. In contrast to the overpriced shack, the average-looking house with the average price is a great find; in contrast to a $170 bottle of wine, the pricey $70 dollar bottle seems just right. When any object is contrasted with something similar but not as good (or as pretty, or as tall, or as inexpensive), it is judged to be prettier, taller, or a better bargain than would normally be the case. In Jonathan Swift's classic novel *Gulliver's Travels*, the hero, a man of normal height, was regarded as a giant when traveling among the residents of Lilliput but a dwarf when traveling among the actual giants of Brobdingnag.

Contrast effects can be strategically used to great effect. A used-car dealer may place an old clunker on the lot to improve the appearance of the autos in its immediate vicinity. A presidential candidate may select a vice-presidential running mate of lesser stature to enhance the positive perception of his or her own presidential qualities. Often we do not pay much attention to the influence of context, much less question the validity of the alternatives presented. This enhances the power of "context makers," such as politicians, advertisers, and sales agents: The context they create influences our perceptions and judgments, lulling us into decisions that we might not otherwise make.

Important judgments we make about *ourselves* can also be influenced by contrast effects. One of the most potent sources of information about ourselves is **social comparison**, the process by which we evaluate our abilities, achievements, attitudes, and other attributes by comparing ourselves to others. Depending on whom we compare ourselves to, the results can be informative, comforting, inspiring, or deflating. That's why many high school valedictorians experience a dip in self-esteem when they arrive at an elite college and find themselves surrounded by other former high school valedictorians. No longer the smartest kid around, they can feel unintelligent merely by being average in the new context.[71] Similarly, when young women look at images of models in the media, they later rate themselves as less attractive than if shown images of more average-looking women.[72] And many people suffer from the "Facebook blues," the vague depression that follows from checking on friends and learning how perfect their lives are — or seem to be with all those vacations they take, the cute puppies they have, their perfect families, the parties, etc.[73]

Sonja Lyubomirsky once observed that social comparisons are primarily to blame for feelings of inadequacy and discontent. No matter how good your situation, after all, there will always be someone who can provide an unfavorable contrast — someone with a stronger body, more athletic skills, more Facebook friends, a bigger paycheck, or a larger yacht. Social comparisons cannot be avoided; they arise automatically and effortlessly. When she compared the social cognitions of happy and unhappy people, Lyubomirsky found that the happiest people evaluate themselves not by paying attention to what other people are doing but by tuning into and consulting their own internal standards of success.[74] We can also avoid painful comparisons with others by cultivating what Carol Dweck calls a **growth mindset**, the belief in the human ability to grow and the commitment to self-improvement. We can, she says, learn to see other people as sources of inspiration and knowledge rather than as opportunities to feel inadequate.[75]

Schemas and Priming The human effort to make sense of the world and explain other people's actions often runs into a wall of ambiguity, and faced with ambiguity, people will come up with different stories about what's going on. What influences the stories they tell?

As cognitive misers, we are prone to organize and retrieve information by way of **schemas**, mental models of the world. Schemas can be stereotypes, categories, expectations, attitudes, and mindsets. While most of us within a culture have shared schemas, every individual develops habitual leanings in the way they construe social information. Our memories, feelings, and beliefs about *ourselves* and the world eventually form an integrated whole. Thus, some of us see the world through rose-colored glasses (as we saw, they have an optimistic explanatory style), while others see it in hostile or depressive terms. These schemas about ourselves lead us to interpret the world around us in characteristic and consequential ways.

Schemas can be activated through **priming**, the use of subtle cues that direct our thinking. A classic study by Tory Higgins, William Rholes, and Carl Jones illustrates the role of priming in the formation of impressions about other people.[76] In their experiment, college students participated in two apparently different research projects: one on perception and one on reading comprehension. The first experiment served to prime different trait categories; some of the students were asked to remember a list of positive traits (adventurous, self-confident, independent, and persistent), and the others were asked to remember a list of negative traits (reckless, conceited, aloof, and stubborn). Five minutes later, as part of what they were led to believe was an unrelated study of reading comprehension, students read a paragraph about a fictitious person named Donald and answered questions about him.

The paragraph was ambiguous. It described Donald doing things that, depending on your point of view, could be interpreted as either adventurous or reckless (e.g., skydiving), either self-confident or conceited (he believes in his abilities), either independent or aloof (he doesn't rely on anyone), and either persistent or stubborn (he doesn't often change his mind). The students then described Donald in their own words and rated how much they liked him. When the students had been primed by reading negative traits, they characterized Donald in negative terms and saw him as less likeable than when they had been primed to think in positive categories.

Most of the time, reality is like the Donald story: open to interpretation. Priming studies demonstrate that recent events or cues in the current environment can color our perceptions in predictable ways. In one study, police officers and juvenile probation officers read a story about a teenager whose race was unspecified, but who was alleged to have committed a crime. Half of the officers had been unobtrusively primed with words related to black people ("homeboy," "Harlem") and the other half to neutral words. The first group judged the child to be older, more culpable, and more likely to get into trouble, and they recommended harsher punishment for him. Simply activating a racial schema set these professionals up to be biased in regarding the teenager as a troublemaker.[77]

Stories covered in the media also "prime" viewers to regard them as the most serious issues of the day.[78] By making certain issues and concepts mentally accessible, the media set the public's political and social agendas. As political scientist Bernard Cohen[79] observed, "The mass media may not be successful much of the time in telling people *what to think*, but it is stunningly successful in telling its readers *what to think about*."

The Power of the Primacy Effect Another way that the social context affects what people think is deceptively simple but quite effective. "Put your best foot forward" turns out to be excellent advice; the things we learn first about a person are especially influential. In an early experiment, Solomon Asch[80] had college students read descriptive sentences such as the following, and then rate the person described in each sentence.

   a. Steve is intelligent, industrious, impulsive, critical, stubborn, and envious.

   b. Steve is envious, stubborn, critical, impulsive, industrious, and intelligent.

The two sentences contain exactly the same information about Steve; however, the first option puts the positive traits first, whereas the second option puts them last. Students rated Steve more positively when he was described with the first sentence. This is called the **primacy effect**, referring to the fact that early information has more influence than later information. When you describe yourself on social media or on a job or graduate school application, the words you use *first* can say as much about you as *which* words you use. Naturally, primacy effects can be misleading; what people learn first about you in real life may not be the most important things about you. Yet what comes first in the narrative they hear about you often determines how they respond to you. Thus, if you write in a job application that physics was your favorite subject in college, the employer is likely to come away with a somewhat different picture of you—scientific, studious, maybe a little nerdy—if you reveal this fact early in the essay rather than at the end.

The primacy effect has been corroborated many times in different ways. In experiments by Edward Jones and his colleagues,[81] participants observed an individual taking an intelligence test consisting of 30 items. In each case, the person answered 15 of the 30 questions correctly. However, sometimes the person started out "hot"—answering a lot of questions correctly at the beginning—and then declined in performance; at other times, the person started out slow, answering only a few questions correctly at first, and then answering most of the final items correctly. The students who started out "hot" were rated as being more intelligent than those who started out slowly, despite the fact that all of them answered the same number of questions correctly.

Of course, sometimes we are not simply sitting back, passively observing the people we are judging; we are interacting with them and actively influencing them, and we may have motives that shape our perceptions. Teachers judge the intelligence of their students, but they are also teaching and influencing those whom they are judging. An interesting exception to the primacy effect was discovered in an experiment by Joshua Aronson and Edward Jones,[82] in which college students coached performers who were trying to solve a set of anagrams. Half of the coaches were promised a reward if they could raise their performers' scores; the other coaches were promised a reward for improving their performers' ability to solve anagrams so that they would do better on anagrams in the future. During the coaching session, the performers followed a script. Half did extremely well at the beginning and then declined; the others started slowly and then improved. The total score was identical;

only the pattern differed. Those coaches who were motivated to maximize their performer's *score* rated them as more intelligent when their early performance was good. That's the primacy effect at work: They wanted to help their students to do well and, after the first few trials, concluded that their students were intelligent—regardless of their later performance. But those coaches who were motivated to improve their performers' ability to solve anagrams rated as more intelligent those who started poorly but ended up doing well. In other words, they were more impressed with increases in performance than with a fast start.

Such findings suggest that if teachers are invested in the long-term development of their students (rather than focused on how well they will do on the next test), they should resist making a snap judgment based on a first impression. The Aronson and Jones experiment demonstrates that primacy effects are not inevitable, particularly if we are motivated to pay careful attention. But the tendency toward cognitive miserliness means that first impressions form quickly and endure.

Navigating Our Social Worlds: Heuristics and Memories

As I noted at the beginning of this chapter, we often rely on automatic processing—our intuition—to make sense of the flood of information that comes our way. To help us do this efficiently, our minds usually rely on **heuristics**, mental operations that provide rules of thumb that guide problem solving and making judgments.[83] Heuristics require little conscious thought; we go through life, mindlessly applying them to the issue at hand. Usually, they are efficient shortcuts, but as with all human cognitive skills, sometimes they lead us astray.

Let's look at three of the most common heuristics: the *representativeness heuristic*, the *availability heuristic*, and the *affect heuristic*.

The Representativeness Heuristic When we focus on surface similarities to make inferences, we are using the **representativeness heuristic**. We know that high-quality products are often costly; therefore, if something is expensive, we infer that it's better than something cheaper. My friend Oliver will always choose an expensive wine, assuming that he will like it better than a less costly one.

He is using only one source of information (price) from among the many others that he might have focused on.

Similarly, when choosing a cereal, we're apt to rely on its packaging to infer how healthy it is. *Lucky Charms* comes in a red box adorned with a cartoon leprechaun sprinkling sugar that looks like twinkling stars over pink and purple marshmallow bits. But *100 Percent Natural Granola* comes in a box featuring a bowl of light brown cereal set against a wood-grain background with stalks of unprocessed grains, and its name says "natural." Is it healthier than *Lucky Charms*? No.[84] *Consumer Reports* found that young rats, which have nutritional requirements remarkably similar to those of humans, thrived on a diet of *Lucky Charms*, whereas a diet of *100 Percent Natural Granola* actually stunted their growth. The fine print on the box accurately reported all of its unhealthy contents, but the packaging itself falsely *represented* the contents as being healthy. That's the representativeness heuristic in action.

The Availability Heuristic   The **availability heuristic** is the tendency to predict the likelihood of an event, or judge how risky it is, based on how easy it is to bring specific examples to mind. Do more people in the United States die from shark attacks or from falling airplane parts? Do more people die from fires or drowning? Who kills more Americans, terrorists or toddlers? The overwhelming majority of people answer that deaths from shark attacks and fires are more common than deaths from falling airplane parts and drowning. Yet both answers are wrong. And despite the widespread fear of terrorism in America, current statistics show that people are far more likely be fatally shot by a toddler than to die in a terrorist attack. The wrong answers, however, are more "available" in our minds, because of the vivid images we have seen or can imagine of scary sharks, terrorists, and fires. Whatever comes to mind most readily will intuitively feel more likely to occur, even if these events are rare. We mistake their availability in memory for their frequency in the world. Shark attacks may be rare, but they are terrifying and easy to visualize.

Priming can increase the images that are available to us. If you ask people to estimate the number of violent crimes committed each year in the United States, you will get very different answers, depending on how much media they consume and what shows they watch. TV news is often based on the mantra "If it bleeds, it leads"—the latest disaster, shooting, or other tragedy will start the show. Because crime and violence play such a dominant role in the media, often gruesomely depicted at that, viewers' cognitive availability of crime increases. That's why people who consume crime dramas and television news tend to vastly overestimate the crime rate. The more they watch, the more fearful they become.[85]

The availability heuristic also affects how we see ourselves and the things we believe. If we can remember and process information fluently or easily, it seems "truer" to us than if we have to struggle to assess its veracity. In a simple demonstration, people who read arguments printed in a clear, easy-to-read font were more likely to believe what they read than those who read the same words printed in a blurry, hard-to-read font.[86] Statements that rhyme or "roll off the tongue" are judged to be truer than statements that say the same thing but are less felicitous.[87]

And the more familiar we are with a statement or idea, the more available it is to us. Simply hearing a statement repeated over and over—even the basest lie—makes it more familiar to people, increasing their belief that if it is familiar, it must be true. The availability heuristic is usually benign and often useful, but it has a dark disadvantage when it leads us to decide what is true and right not based on a claim's logical merit but on its ease of retrieval: an unintended hazard of the internet is that everything from conspiracy claims to pseudoscientific medical advice, endlessly repeated, can flourish unchecked. As William James said in 1890, "There is nothing so absurd that it cannot be believed as truth if repeated often enough." This observation was implemented by the Nazi propaganda machine and became known as the Big Lie.

The Affect Heuristic   Do I like this person? How do I feel about that idea? Our feelings are valuable sources of information so when we tap into our feelings to shape our evaluations of people or ideas, we are using an **affect heuristic**. If you're in a bad mood, you are likely to evaluate a job candidate more negatively than if you're in a happy mood. If something makes you aware of your good or bad mood before you make the judgment, however, your mood is less likely to influence your appraisal.[88]

Our enduring feelings about people influence how we judge their actions. Anthony Pratkanis once asked college students to identify which of two statements about former president Ronald Reagan was true:

   a. Reagan maintained an A average at Eureka College.

   b. Reagan never achieved above a C average at Eureka College.

Few students actually knew what Reagan's college grades were; their answers depended on their feelings about him. Students who liked Reagan were more likely to think he was an A student; those who disliked him believed he was a C student. This phenomenon is sometimes called the *halo effect*, a bias in which a favorable or unfavorable feeling colors specific inferences and future expectations about a person. We likewise look inward and consult our feelings to predict how others will act. If we don't know the people involved, we usually assume that they will feel as we feel and do as we do, and that they will agree with us on any issue.

The affect heuristic can be beneficial—for example, by allowing us to act quickly in an uncertain or dangerous situation. But it can also mislead us by preventing us from accurately assessing risk. One ingenious field study looked at how people in France responded to the "mad cow" crisis that occurred years ago. (Mad cow disease affects the brain and can be contracted by eating meat from contaminated cows.) Whenever newspaper articles reported the dangers of "mad cow disease," beef consumption fell during the following month. But when news articles, reporting the same dangers, used the technical names of the disease—Creutzfeldt-Jakob disease and bovine spongiform encephalopathy—beef consumption stayed the same. The alarming label caused people to reason emotionally and to overestimate the danger. And after all, the image of a "mad cow"—that placid creature running amok!—is highly "available" cognitively. But during the entire period of the supposed crisis, only six people in France were diagnosed with the disease.[89]

When Do We Use Heuristics? Fortunately, we do not have to rely on cognitive shortcuts. When buying cereal, we can carefully read the ingredients on the cereal box or consult the web; when we vote, we can carefully reason about an issue and study the record and accomplishments of a politician; and we can strive to avoid the confirmation bias by gathering evidence from impartial sources we don't normally rely on. By being aware of how these heuristics can cause us to make wrong choices, we can take steps to counteract them. Psychologists have identified several conditions under which we are more likely to rely on heuristics rather than rational decision making:[90]

- when we don't have time to think carefully about an issue;

- when we are so overloaded with information that it becomes impossible to process the information fully;

- when the issues at stake are not very important to us;

- when we lack the required knowledge for making a reasoned decision; and

- when we let our emotions and wishful thinking get in the way.

Mental Time Travel: Biases in Predicting the Future and Recalling the Past

Sometimes it seems that human beings spend half their time thinking about the past and the other half imagining the future. Either way, we make mistakes.

Constructive Prediction   Predicting how certain outcomes will make us feel determines the goals we set and the risks we are willing to take. Indeed, whenever we seek to get something (whether it is a sandwich, a job, or a divorce), we are essentially making a bet that getting it will make us happy, or at least happier. Yet we often make predictions about ourselves that are dead wrong.[91] We overestimate the emotional impact of future events and how long our reactions will last, whether the events are positive or negative.

In one study, college students were asked how happy or unhappy they imagined they would feel after being randomly assigned to live in a dorm they thought was "desirable" or "undesirable." The students predicted that their dorm assignments would have a huge impact on their overall level of happiness and that being assigned to an undesirable dorm would essentially wreck their satisfaction for the whole year. In fact, one year later, everyone had nearly identical levels of happiness no matter where they were living. Perhaps the undesirable dorms turned out, unexpectedly, to have cool people living in them? No. The students had focused on the wrong factors when forecasting their future feelings of happiness; they had placed far more importance on what the dorm looked like and on its location than on its inhabitants. But, in fact, it's people who make a place fun or unpleasant to live in, and all of the dorms had likable people in them. Because the students could not foresee this, or how much they would like their new dormmates, they mispredicted their future happiness.[92]

Why do we mispredict? One reason is that we adjust to both happy and sad events in our lives, but we fail to recognize our powers of adjustment when we mentally construct what our futures will look and feel like. Another reason is that when we imagine the future, we tend to focus only upon the event in question and fail to consider all the other things that will undoubtedly occur at the same time to take the sting out of failure or to dilute our happiness. So we imagine that marriage, winning the lottery, or becoming famous will keep us giddy with happiness for a long time, or that losing a job or being jilted will devastate us forever, despite the fact that the pleasure or pain these events bring will fade with time.

Our inability to forecast the future can cause trouble, especially when we make plans way in advance. "What was I thinking when I thought it would be a good idea to take three science classes in the same semester? I'm drowning in work here!" When viewed from today, the future looks different from the present, in much the same way that objects look smaller from a distance. We imagine the future at an abstract level, and we are more concerned with how *desirable* our prediction is than with how *feasible* it is. From a distance, you might think it sounds like a great idea to take three science classes in the same semester and get a big jump ahead on your major, but you are probably not thinking of how hard that might be, logistically and pragmatically. In a study conducted by Nira Liberman and Yaacov Trope,[93] students were more likely to make a decision about whether or not to attend a concert based on how much they thought they would enjoy the concert rather than on how feasible attending the concert would be. (Could they afford the tickets? How difficult would it be to get there?) This disregard for feasibility leads to ineffectual planning. When you make plans, you can save yourself a lot of grief if you are mindful of the human tendency to construe the future as rosier than the present.

Reconstructive Memory People love to believe that memories are accurately embedded or buried somewhere in the mind and can be recalled through drugs or hypnosis. Unfortunately, there's no exact recording of past events in our memories that we can access with a rewind button nor, to use that incorrect computer metaphor, are they digitally encoded. On the contrary, remembering is a **reconstructive process**. Our memories are most strongly influenced not by what actually happened *in the past* but by what we are thinking about those events *in the present*. We recreate our memories from bits and pieces of actual events filtered through and modified by our notions of what might have been, what should have been, or the way we would like things to have been.

Our memories are undergoing constant revision, and they are influenced by what other people tell us about the past event, by photos, and by hearsay. Elizabeth Loftus, a prominent cognitive psychologist, has conducted a fascinating program of research on **reconstructive memory**,[94] investigating how suggestive questioning, with the most subtle of words, can influence memory and subsequent eyewitness testimony. In one of her experiments,[95] Loftus showed people a film depicting a multiple-car accident. After the film, some were asked, "About how fast were the cars going when they smashed into each other?" Others were asked the same question, but the word *smashed* was replaced by the word *hit*. Those who were asked about smashing cars, as opposed to hitting cars, estimated that the cars were going significantly faster. Moreover, a week after seeing the film, they were more likely to state, erroneously, that there was broken glass at the accident scene. In another study, Loftus showed students a series of slides depicting an accident involving an automobile and a pedestrian.[96] In a critical slide, a green car was shown driving past the accident. Immediately after viewing the slides, half of the students were asked, "Did the *blue* car that drove past the accident have a ski rack on the roof?" The other half were asked this same question but with the word *blue* deleted. Those who were asked about the "blue" car were more likely to claim incorrectly that they had seen a blue car. A simple word change in the question had altered their memories.

Autobiographical Memory Memory is not only reconstructive when it involves quick, snapshot-like events, such as the details of an automobile accident, but also when it involves something more enduring, such as our own history. Major distortions occur over time, and these revisions of autobiographical memory are not random. Rather, we construct memories to fit the picture we have of ourselves. Thanks to the confirmation bias, we are more likely to recall memories that confirm our belief.

For example, when people have a narrative of their childhoods as having been unhappy, any events that violate that picture (say, that great family vacation at Disney World) will be more difficult to recall than events that support it. If they have good relationships with their parents now, their childhood memories will be sweeter than they felt at the time (say, they forget how really mad they were at their parents for not being allowed to go to Disney World with a childhood friend). Over the years, as people seek out memories that confirm their current beliefs about their parents and reject and forget those that "don't fit," their memories become increasingly coherent and less accurate. In this manner, all of us rewrite our personal histories. It is not necessarily that we are lying about our past; it is simply that we misremember in a way that fits with our schemas.[97]

Elizabeth Loftus has carried this line of research a step further. She has shown that it is possible—indeed, relatively easy—to plant false memories of childhood experiences in the minds of young adults merely by having a close relative talk about these events as fact.[98] For example, if a young man's older sister said to him, "Remember the time when you were five years old and you got lost for several hours at the University City shopping mall? And you went into a panic—and an old man tried to help you? When we discovered you, you were holding the old man's hand and crying." Within a few days of hearing such a story, most people will have incorporated that planted false memory into their own history, will have embroidered it with details ("Oh, yeah, the old man who helped me was wearing a flannel shirt"), and will be absolutely certain that it happened—when, in fact, it didn't.

One of the striking findings in this research is how the affect heuristic can be immensely misleading when it comes to memories. People can feel absolutely confident that planted memories are real, and be absolutely wrong. In study after study, confidence in a memory turns out to be a poor guide to its authenticity.[99]

I find one aspect of autobiographical memory is especially useful to students. Recall the discussion of the egocentric bias? There's a lesson in here for you: One of the best ways to recall material from this book is to relate it to your personal experiences—to think how it applies to you.

Living with the Cognitive Miser Within

I don't want you to come away from reading this chapter with the impression that human beings are wholly and hopelessly irrational. The take-home message is that we are born with the ability to be both irrational *and* rational, and that even our biases can be adaptive. Being a cognitive miser brings us an array of benefits, but these benefits come with a price tag: a somewhat distorted picture of yourself and the world. As long as sticking with our initial way of seeing things and making decisions doesn't get us into big trouble, our cognitive miserliness can get us through the day with maximum efficiency and minimal effort.

Steve Jobs, the legendary founder of Apple, was said to have had a "reality distortion field" that enabled him to see and remember things as he wished, including a faith in his ability to make "insanely great" products that people would stand in line for.[100] Without his optimism, combined with creativity and relentless perfectionism, Apple might have folded before developing the iPhone, which made Apple the world's most valuable company. But the same "reality distortion field" that kept Jobs innovating also led him to delay medical treatment for his pancreatic cancer, which was diagnosed at an early, treatable stage. He believed that he could cure it with a vegan diet. He could not.

For me personally, one of the most fascinating aspects of the social animal is the need to see ourselves as good, smart, and sensible people—and to observe how this need frequently leads us to do things and adopt beliefs that are neither good nor smart nor sensible. The human tendency for self-justification is so important and multifaceted that it deserves a chapter all to itself. I turn to that chapter now.

Saul Steinberg, *Untitled drawing*, ink on paper.
Originally published in *The New Yorker*, February 16, 1963.
© The Saul Steinberg Foundation / Artists Rights Society (ARS), New York

Self-Justification

Picture the following scene: A young man named Sam is being hypnotized. The hypnotist gives Sam a posthypnotic suggestion, telling him that, when the clock strikes 4:00, he will (1) go to the closet, get his raincoat and galoshes, and put them on; (2) grab an umbrella; (3) walk eight blocks to the supermarket and purchase six bottles of bourbon; and (4) return home. Sam is told that, as soon as he reenters his apartment, he will "snap out of it" and be himself again.

When the clock strikes 4:00, Sam immediately heads for the closet, dons his raincoat and galoshes, grabs his umbrella, and trudges out the door on his quest for bourbon. There are a few strange things about this errand: (1) it is a sunshiny day without a cloud in the sky; (2) there is a liquor store half a block away that sells bourbon for the same price as the supermarket eight blocks away; and (3) Sam doesn't drink.

Sam arrives home, opens the door, reenters his apartment, snaps out of his trance, and discovers himself standing there in his raincoat and galoshes, with his umbrella in one hand and a huge sack of liquor bottles in the other. He looks momentarily confused. His friend, the hypnotist, says, "Hey, Sam, where have you been?"

"Oh, just down to the store," Sam says.

"What did you buy?"

"Um ... um ... it seems I bought this bourbon."

"But you don't drink, do you?"

"No, but ... um ... um ... I'm going to do a lot of entertaining during the next several weeks, and some of my friends do."

"How come you're wearing all that rain gear on such a sunny day?"

"Well ... actually, the weather is quite changeable this time of year, and I didn't want to take any chances."

"But there isn't a cloud in the sky."

"Well, you never can tell."

"By the way, where did you buy the liquor?"

"Oh, heh, heh. Well, um ... down at the supermarket."

"How come you went that far?"

"Well, um ... um ... it was such a nice day, I thought it might be fun to take a long walk."

People are motivated to justify their own actions, beliefs, and feelings. When they do something, they will try, if at all possible, to convince themselves (and others) that it was a logical, reasonable thing to do. There *was* a good reason that Sam did those silly things—he was hypnotized. But because Sam was unaware of the posthypnotic instructions and because it was difficult for him to accept the fact that he was capable of behaving in a nonsensical manner, he went to great lengths to convince himself (and his friend) that there was a method to his madness, that his actions were perfectly sensible. As we saw in Chapter 2, much of our behavior is governed by factors of which we are unaware. Then, when pressed to explain our actions, we attempt to construct a story that makes sense but at the same time satisfies our desire to look good to ourselves and to others. That's the essence of **self-justification**.

Let's say you are in the midst of a natural disaster, such as an earthquake. All around you, buildings are toppling and people are getting injured and killed. You're scared. Do you need to seek a reason or justification for your fear? Certainly not. The evidence is all around you; the injured people and the devastated buildings are ample explanations for your fear. But suppose the earthquake occurred in a neighboring town. You felt the tremors, and you're hearing stories of the damage that occurred there. You are frightened, but you are not in the midst of the devastated area; neither you nor the people around you have been hurt, and no buildings in your town have been damaged. Would you need additional reasons to explain why you are nonetheless scared? Yes. Much like our hypnotized friend in the raincoat and galoshes, you would be motivated to make sense of your feelings. Because you see nothing to be afraid of in the immediate vicinity, you would be inclined to generate reasons for being scared out of your wits.

This example is not hypothetical; it actually occurred in India. In the aftermath of an earthquake, investigators collected and analyzed the rumors being spread among those living where the earthquake had hit and those living nearby. What they discovered was startling: Jamuna Prasad,[1] an Indian psychologist, found that people living in the neighboring villages away from the epicenter—that is, those who could feel the tremors but were not in imminent danger—began spreading rumors of impending doom: A flood was rushing toward them; February 26 would be a day of deluge and destruction; another severe earthquake would erupt on the day of the lunar eclipse; a cyclone would strike within a few days; and other unforeseeable calamities were on the horizon.

Why in the world would people invent, believe, and communicate such stories? Were these people masochists? Were they paranoid? Clearly, spreading rumors about coming disasters would not encourage people to feel calm and secure. One explanation is that the people were terribly frightened, but because they lacked ample justification for this fear, they invented their own—which spared them feeling foolish. After all, if a cyclone is on the way, isn't it perfectly reasonable that I should be wild-eyed with fear? This explanation was bolstered by Durganand Sinha's study of rumors.[2] Sinha investigated the rumors spread in an Indian village in the wake of a disaster of similar magnitude. The major difference between the situation in Prasad's study and the one in Sinha's study was that the people studied by Sinha had directly experienced the destruction and witnessed the damage. They were scared, but they had good reasons to be; they had no need to seek additional justification for their fears. Thus, their rumors contained no prediction of impending disaster and no serious exaggeration. Indeed, if anything, the rumors were comforting, such as one that predicted (falsely) that the water supply would be restored in a short time.

The Theory of Cognitive Dissonance

Inspired by these findings, Leon Festinger developed a powerful theory of human motivation that he called the theory of **cognitive dissonance**.[3] It is a remarkably simple theory but, as we shall see, the range of its application is enormous. Festinger described cognitive dissonance as a state of tension that occurs when an individual simultaneously holds two cognitions (ideas, attitudes, beliefs, opinions) that are psychologically inconsistent. Two cognitions are dissonant if the opposite of one follows from the other. Because the experience of cognitive dissonance is unpleasant, people are motivated to reduce it; this is analogous to the processes involved in reducing such drives as hunger or thirst—except that, here, the driving force arises from cognitive discomfort rather than physiological need. To hold two ideas that contradict each other is to flirt with absurdity, and as the existentialist philosopher Albert Camus observed, humans are creatures who spend their lives trying to convince themselves that their existence is not absurd.

How do we convince ourselves that our lives are not absurd? That is, how do we reduce cognitive dissonance? We do this by changing one or both cognitions in such a way as to render them more compatible (more consonant) with each other or by adding more cognitions that help bridge the gap between the original cognitions.

Let me give you an example that is, alas, all too familiar to many people. Suppose a person loves to smoke cigarettes and then sees an anti-smoking message. The smoker experiences dissonance: The cognition "I smoke cigarettes" is dissonant with the cognition "Cigarette smoking is a major cause of lung cancer and is unhealthy for many other reasons." The smartest and most efficient way for this person to reduce dissonance is to give up smoking. The cognition "Cigarette smoking causes cancer" is consonant with the cognition "I do not smoke."

But for most people it is not easy to give up smoking. Imagine Sally, a long-time smoker. What will she do to reduce dissonance? In all probability, she will try to work on the other cognition: "Cigarette smoking causes cancer." Sally might attempt to make light of evidence linking cigarette smoking to disease, comforting herself with the thought that medical science is imperfect. After all, she might say, aren't scientists always changing their minds about what's good for you? She might seek out intelligent people who smoke and, by so doing, convince herself that if Debbie, Nicole, and Larry smoke, it can't be all that harmful. Sally might switch to an ultra-light or organic brand and delude herself that it's healthier. Finally, she might add cognitions that are consonant with smoking in an attempt to make the behavior less absurd in spite of its danger. She might enhance the value she places on smoking, deciding that smoking is not only pleasurable but essential for relaxation: "I may lead a shorter life, but it will be a more enjoyable one." Or she might try to make a virtue out of smoking by developing a romantic, devil-may-care self-image, flouting danger by smoking.[4] Sally can justify her behavior by cognitively minimizing its danger or by exaggerating its importance in her life. She can find relief by modifying an existing attitude, by constructing a new one, or by doing a little of both. All of these efforts reduce dissonance by downplaying the absurdity of courting disease.

In 1964, about half of the American population smoked cigarettes. With the release that year of the Surgeon General's report, which alerted the public to the dangers of smoking, a survey was conducted[5] to assess people's reactions to the new evidence linking smoking with cancer. Nonsmokers overwhelmingly believed the health report; only 10 percent doubted smoking caused the disease. Smokers, however, disparaged the report. Forty percent of the heavy smokers doubted a link had been proven. They were also more apt to rationalize their habit: More than twice as many smokers as nonsmokers agreed that life is full of hazards and that both smokers and nonsmokers get sick.

Smokers can also reduce dissonance by minimizing the extent of their habit. Another study of people who smoked between one and two packs of cigarettes a day found that 60 percent considered themselves to be "moderate" smokers; the remaining 40 percent considered themselves to be heavy smokers.[6] How can we explain these different self-perceptions? People who considered themselves moderates were more aware of the harmful long-term effects of smoking than were those who called themselves heavy smokers. The moderates apparently reduced dissonance by convincing themselves that smoking one or two packs a day isn't really all that much. *Moderate* and *heavy* are, after all, subjective terms.

Now imagine the plight of cigarette smokers who know they are heavy smokers, know that smoking is harmful, and so try to stop smoking but fail. What do these people do?

To find out, Rick Gibbons and his colleagues[7] studied heavy smokers who attended a smoking cessation clinic, quit smoking for a while, but then relapsed. Did they simply swallow hard and prepare to get sick and die? Not at all. Instead, they reduced dissonance in a different way: by convincing themselves that smoking isn't as bad as they originally thought. Likewise, a study that tracked the progress of 135 students who made New Year's resolutions supports this observation.[8] Individuals who broke their resolutions — to quit smoking, lose weight, or exercise more — initially felt bad but, after a short time, succeeded in downplaying the importance of the resolution.

Smokers, of course, have only their own health to worry about (and that of secondhand smokers they might live with). But what if you are one of the top executives of a major cigarette company and therefore in a situation of maximum commitment to the sales of cigarettes all over the world. If it is true that cigarette smoking causes cancer, then in a sense, you are partially responsible for the illness and death of millions of people. This realization would produce a painful degree of dissonance. Your cognition "I am a decent, kind human being" would be dissonant with your cognition "I am contributing to the early death of millions of people." To reduce this dissonance, you must try to convince yourself that cigarette smoking is safe — not an easy task given that you are frequently confronted with anti-smoking rhetoric and accusations that you are evil. You must also refute the mountain of scientific evidence documenting a link between cigarettes and disease. Moreover, to bolster your disbelief in the evidence, you might smoke a pack or two a day yourself. If your need is great enough, you might even succeed in convincing yourself that cigarettes are good for people. Thus, to see yourself as wise, good, and right, you take action that is stupid, wrong, and detrimental to your own health.

This analysis sounds so fantastic that it's almost beyond belief — almost. In 1994, Congress conducted hearings on the dangers of smoking. At these hearings, the top executives of every major tobacco company admitted they were smokers and brazenly argued that cigarettes are no more harmful or addictive than playing video games or eating Twinkies! In a subsequent hearing in 1997, James J. Morgan, president and chief executive officer of Philip Morris, the leading U.S. cigarette manufacturer, said that cigarettes are not pharmacologically addictive. "Look, I like gummy bears and I eat gummy bears. And I don't like it when I don't eat gummy bears," Morgan said. "But I'm certainly not addicted to them."[9]

It is possible that Morgan was lying. But I think what he said is more complicated than that. My guess is that, over time, people like Morgan begin to believe their own lies, in an effort to deceive *themselves*.[10]

People's self-deceptions can even lead directly to their self-destruction. In 1997, thirty-nine members of Heaven's Gate, an obscure religious cult, were found dead at a luxury estate in Rancho Santa Fe, California, participants in a mass suicide. Several weeks earlier, a few members of the cult had walked into a specialty store and purchased an expensive high-powered telescope so that they might get a clearer view of the Hale-Bopp comet and the spaceship they fervently believed was traveling behind it. They were convinced that when the comet got close to Earth, it would be time to rid themselves of their "earthly containers" (their bodies) by killing themselves, so that their essence could be picked up by the spaceship. A few days after buying the telescope, they brought it back to the store and politely asked for a refund. When the manager asked why, they complained that the telescope was defective: "We found the comet all right, but we can't find the spaceship that's following it." Needless to say, there was no spaceship. But if you are so convinced of the existence of a spaceship that you're ready to die to ride on it, and yet your telescope doesn't reveal it, then obviously there must be something wrong with the telescope!

The members of Heaven's Gate may have had a tragically misguided conviction, but they illuminate a central scientific contribution of dissonance theory: Not unlike members of cults, whenever we feel a strong allegiance to a religion, political party, charismatic leader, or ideology, we too are capable of coming up with all kinds of distortions of the evidence when those loyalties are challenged by facts. Lenny Bruce, a perceptive comedian and social commentator (who almost certainly never read about cognitive dissonance theory), had the following insight into the 1960 presidential election campaign between Richard Nixon and John F. Kennedy:

> I would be with a bunch of Kennedy fans watching the debate, and their comment would be, "He's really slaughtering Nixon." Then we would all go to another apartment, and the Nixon fans would

say, "How do you like the shellacking he gave Kennedy?" And then I realized that each group loved their candidate so that a guy would have to be this blatant—he would have to look into the camera and say: "I am a thief, a crook, do you hear me? I am the worst choice you could ever make for the presidency!" And even then his following would say, "Now there's an honest man for you. It takes a big guy to admit that. There's the kind of guy we need for president."[11]

More than fifty years later, presidential candidate Donald Trump marveled at the same unconditional loyalty of his own supporters: "I could stand in the middle of Fifth Avenue and shoot somebody and wouldn't lose any voters, okay? It's, like, incredible."[12]

Dissonance Reduction and Irrational Behavior

Cognitive dissonance results from the clash of two fundamental motives: our striving to be right, which motivates us to pay close attention to what other people are doing and to heed the advice of trustworthy communicators; and our striving to believe we *are* right (and wise, and decent, and good). Sometimes our motivation to *be* right and our motivation to believe we *are* right work in the same direction: We seek information (say, about the risks of smoking) and pay attention. But the theory of cognitive dissonance predicts that more often we seek information and then ignore it if we don't like what we learn (and keep smoking). Understanding dissonance explains why so much of human thinking is not rational, but *rationalizing*. No matter how smart they are, people who are in the midst of reducing dissonance are so involved with convincing themselves that they are right that they frequently end up behaving irrationally. By "irrational," I mean their maladaptive behavior can prevent them from learning essential facts or from finding real solutions to their problems.

In the laboratory, researchers have amply demonstrated the irrationality of people's efforts to reduce dissonance. Suppose you have strong feelings about whether or not the death penalty deters people from committing murder. I now give you a series of arguments on both sides of the issue; some of those arguments are plausible and others are silly. Which arguments will you remember best? If you are thinking rationally, you should remember the plausible arguments best and the implausible arguments least, regardless of your own position. But what does dissonance theory predict? A silly argument that supports your own position arouses some dissonance because it raises doubts about the wisdom of that position or the intelligence of people who agree with it. Likewise, a sensible argument on the other side of the issue also arouses some dissonance because it raises the possibility that the other side might be smarter or more accurate than you had thought — or, God forbid, that they might be right. Because these arguments arouse dissonance, we try not to think about them. Dissonance theory predicts that people will remember the plausible arguments agreeing with their own position and the *implausible* arguments agreeing with the *opposing* position.[13]

In one of many studies that demonstrated this phenomenon, Charles Lord, Lee Ross, and Mark Lepper[14] selected several Stanford University students who opposed capital punishment and several who favored it. They showed the students two research articles that discussed whether the death penalty tends to deter violent crimes. One study confirmed and the other study disconfirmed the existing beliefs of the students. If these students were perfectly rational, they might conclude that the issue is a complex one, and accordingly, the two groups of students might move closer to each other in their beliefs about capital punishment. But dissonance theory predicts that they would distort the two articles, clasping the confirming article to their bosoms and hailing it as brilliant confirmation of their belief, while finding methodological or conceptual flaws in the disconfirming article and refusing to be influenced by it. This is precisely what happened. Indeed, rather than coming closer in their beliefs after being exposed to this two-sided presentation, the students disagreed with each other more sharply than they did beforehand. This process probably accounts for the fact that, on issues like politics and religion, people who are deeply committed will almost never come to see things our way, no matter how powerful and balanced our arguments are.[15] This study illuminates the state of polarized political discourse in America today.

The theory of cognitive dissonance explains why a good deal of people's behavior is not rational — and why, from inside, they think it is. If you ask the hypnotized young man why he wore a raincoat on a sunny day, he'll come up with an answer he feels is sensible; if you ask the vice president of Philip Morris why he smokes, he'll give you a reason that makes sense to him — he'll tell you how good it is for everyone's health to have a stress buster. If you ask participants in the death-penalty experiment why they remembered one particular set of arguments rather than others, they will insist that the evidence against their position is flawed.

It goes without saying that we are all capable of behaving rationally. But my point is that we are all capable of behaving irrationally when we need to reduce dissonance. We will see both sides of human behavior over and over as we discuss some of the wide ramifications of our need for self-justification. Let us begin with the decision-making process, a process that shows humans at their most rational and their most irrational in quick succession.

Dissonance as a Consequence of Making a Decision

Suppose you are about to make a decision about buying a new car. This involves a significant amount of money, so it is, by definition, important. After looking around, you are torn between getting a sports utility vehicle and an all-electric model. Each has advantages and disadvantages. The SUV would be convenient; you can haul things in it and sleep in it during long trips, and it has plenty of power, but it gets atrocious mileage and is not easy to park. The electric car is less roomy, you can't drive long distances in it, and you are concerned about its safety, but it is less expensive to buy and operate, it is more fun to drive, and you've heard it has a pretty good repair record. My guess is that *before* you make the decision, you will seek as much information as you can. Chances are you will go online and sample reviews of the various makes and models. Perhaps you'll confer with friends who own an SUV or an electric car. You'll probably visit the dealers to test-drive the vehicles to see how each one feels. All of this predecision behavior is perfectly rational.

Now you make a decision: You buy the all-electric car. What happens next? Your behavior will begin to change; no longer will you seek objective information about all makes of cars. Chances are you will spend more time talking with other owners of your car. You will begin to talk about its small carbon footprint and how far it goes on a charge. My guess is that you will not be spending any time thinking about the fact that you can't sleep in your new car. Similarly, your mind will skim lightly over the fact that driving your new little car can be hazardous in a collision and that the brakes are not very responsive.

How does your change of mind come about? Following a decision — especially a difficult one or one that involves a significant amount of time or money — people almost always experience dissonance. They do because their choice is seldom entirely positive and the rejected alternatives are seldom entirely negative. In this example, your cognition that you bought an electric car is dissonant with your cognition about any deficiencies the car may have. Similarly, all the positive aspects of the other cars that you thought about buying are dissonant with your cognition that you didn't buy one of them. A good way to reduce such dissonance is to seek out exclusively positive information about the car you chose and avoid negative information about it. Accordingly, I would predict that a person who had recently bought a car will begin to read advertisements selectively, reading more ads about his or her car *after the purchase* than people who have not recently bought the same model. Moreover, owners of new cars will tend to steer clear of ads for other makes of cars. And that is just what researchers found in a study of ad readership.[16] Today, of course, thanks to social media, people do not have to work hard to get information that is consonant not only with what car they just bought but also what idea they now believe — and avoid any information that is dissonant.

People do not always need help from Madison Avenue to gain reassurance; they can do a pretty good job of reassuring themselves. An experiment by Jack Brehm[17] demonstrates how they do this. Posing as a marketing researcher, Brehm showed several women eight different appliances (a toaster, an electric coffee maker, a sandwich grill, and the like) and asked that they rate them in terms of how appealing each appliance was. As a reward, each woman was told she could have one of the appliances as a gift, and she was given a choice between two of the products she had rated as being equally desirable. After she chose one, it was wrapped up and given to her. Several minutes later, she was asked to rate the products again. After receiving the appliance of her choice, each woman rated its appeal somewhat higher and decreased the rating of the appliance she had had a chance to own but rejected.

Again, making a decision produces dissonance: Cognitions about any negative aspects of the preferred object are dissonant with having chosen it, and cognitions about the positive aspects of the unchosen object are dissonant with not having chosen it. To reduce dissonance, people cognitively spread apart the alternatives. That is, *after making their decision*, the women in Brehm's study emphasized the positive attributes of the appliance they decided to own while deemphasizing its negative attributes; for the appliance they decided not to own, they emphasized its negative attributes and deemphasized its positive attributes.

The tendency to justify our choices is not limited to consumer decisions. In fact, research has demonstrated that similar processes can even affect our romantic relationships and our willingness to imagine becoming involved with other partners. In a study conducted by Dennis Johnson and Caryl Rusbult,[18] college students were asked to evaluate the probable success of a new computer dating service on campus. Participants were shown pictures of individuals of the opposite sex, who they believed were applicants to the dating service. They were then asked to rate the attractiveness of these applicants, as well as how much they believed they would enjoy a potential date with him or her—a possibility that was presented in a realistic manner. The results of this study were remarkably similar to Brehm's findings about appliances: The more heavily committed the students were to their current romantic partners, the less attractive they found potential new partners. In a subsequent experiment, Jeffry Simpson and his colleagues[19] also found that those in committed straight relationships saw opposite-sex persons as less physically and sexually attractive than did those who weren't in committed relationships. In addition, they showed that this effect holds only for "available others"; when shown individuals who were somewhat older or who were of the same sex, people in committed straight relationships did not lower their attractiveness ratings of the strangers. In short: no threat, no dissonance; no dissonance, no diminishing their appeal.

Whether we are talking about appliances or romantic partners, once you have made a firm commitment, you will tend to focus on the positive aspects of your choices and downplay the appeal of the alternatives.

Is Dissonance Reduction Conscious? As we saw in Chapter 2, most of us aren't good at predicting how quickly we will adjust to negative events. Now I can tell you why: because people are unaware of how successfully they will reduce dissonance. Given that they have successfully done so in the past, why aren't they aware that they will do so in the future? The answer is that the process of reducing dissonance is largely unconscious. People don't sit down and say, "I guess I will reduce some dissonance now." For example, what happens when the person you love dumps you? Over time, you will come to see the person as less lovable—perhaps even as an insufferable narcissist—and come to believe that you deserve better or are better off alone. This process is effective precisely because it happens below the level of conscious awareness and without intention. Unfortunately, this invisibility makes dissonance both effective and forgettable. Because the process is unconscious, we do not realize that it will protect us from pain in the future.

What would have happened at the end of the classic movie *Casablanca* if Ingrid Bergman did not rejoin her Nazi-fighting hero husband but instead remained with her lover Humphrey Bogart in Morocco? Would she, as Bogart tells her in a famously heart-wrenching speech, have regretted it—"maybe not today, maybe not tomorrow, but soon, and for the rest of your life"? Or would she forever regret leaving Bogart behind at the rainy airport? I suspect that the answer to both questions is no; Bogart was eloquent but wrong. She might have regretted whichever choice she made for today or for tomorrow, but soon (and for the rest of her life) she would have convinced herself that she had made the best decision.[20] This is not to say we never have regrets. But given the countless decisions we make in our lives, it is remarkable how seldom we have them—thanks to our ability to reduce dissonance.

Is Dissonance Universal? How universal is the experience of cognitive dissonance? Is it something that is experienced mostly by Americans, or is it part and parcel of the human condition? It is impossible to answer that question definitively, because dissonance experiments have not been done everywhere. But I can say this: Although most of the research has been done in North America, the effects have been shown to exist in every part of the world where research has been done.

And that research has been extensive. Cognitive dissonance theory has been supported by thousands of studies, some in related fields such as cognition and neuroscience—and even primatology. In some respects, monkeys are like those homemakers faced with choices between appliances: Offered a choice between two differently colored boxes of treats, they are likely to stay with the one they pick, even when another option comes along. This research suggests that there is an evolutionary benefit to postdecision dissonance, if it led our forebears to stick with a tried-and-true option and reject something new but untested (which, in our species' past, could be risky or dangerous).[21]

Humans, who contributed the "cognitive" part to cognitive dissonance, also display cognitive justifications at a very early age.[22] A friend of mine took her three-year-old to the park and gave her some stickers to play with. Another child approached them. "Wouldn't you like to offer some of your stickers to that other little girl?" my friend asked. The child thought for a while and said, "That little girl doesn't *like* stickers, Mommy." Dissonance reduction at age three! She gets to see herself as a good little girl *and* keep all of her stickers.

In support of the argument that the experience of dissonance is universal, Eddie Harmon-Jones and his colleagues[23] have used fMRI technology to monitor neural activity in specific areas of the brain while people were experiencing various kinds of dissonance: rating their preferences for things they had chosen and those they had rejected, arguing that the uncomfortable scanner experience was actually quite pleasant, or being confronted with unwelcome (dissonant) information. The areas of the brain that are activated during dissonance include highly specific areas within the prefrontal cortex, the site prominently involved in planning and decision-making. And in a study of people who were trying to process dissonant or consonant information about their preferred presidential candidate, Drew Westen and his colleagues[24] found that the reasoning areas of the brain virtually shut down when a person is confronted with dissonant information and the emotion circuits of the brain light up happily when consonance is restored. As Westen put it, people twirl the "cognitive kaleidoscope" until the pieces fall into the pattern they want to see, and then the brain repays them by activating circuits involved in pleasure. It seems that the feeling of cognitive dissonance can literally make your brain hurt.

Dissonance operates in almost every part of the world, but it does not always take the same form, and the *content* of the cognitions that produce it may differ across cultures. For example, in less individualistic societies than ours, dissonance-reducing behavior might take a more communal form.[25] In such cultures, we would be more likely to feel dissonance when their behavior shames or disappoints *others* than when they need to justify *personal* misbehavior. This is just what the Japanese social psychologist Haruki Sakai[26] found in his experiments. In Japan, many people will vicariously experience dissonance on the part of someone they know and like—and they will change their attitudes to conform to those of their dissonance-reducing friends. Moreover, the Japanese justified their choices when they felt others were observing them while they were making their decision, but not when they were making decisions privately; this pattern was reversed for Americans.[27] The perceived privacy or public visibility of the choice being made interacts with culture to determine whether dissonance is aroused and the choice needs to be justified.

The Importance of Irrevocability

A key characteristic of the examples we have discussed is the relative *irrevocability* of the decision—the person's inability to undo it. This needs some explaining. As we saw, while you are thinking tentatively about buying a car or making another decision, you don't need to expend effort trying to convince yourself of the wisdom of your choice. But once you decide and you can't go back, it all changes.

Some direct evidence for the importance of irrevocability comes from a study of the cognitive gyrations of gamblers at a race track. The race track is an ideal place to scrutinize irrevocability, because once you've placed your bet, you can't go back and tell the nice person behind the window you've changed your mind. Robert Knox and James Inkster[28] simply intercepted people who were on their way to place $2 bets. They had already decided on their horses and were about to place their bets when the investigators asked them how certain they were that their horses would win. Because they were on their way to the $2 window, their decisions were not irrevocable. The investigators collared other bettors just as they were leaving the $2 window, *after* having placed their bets, and asked them how certain they were that their horses would win. Typically, people who had just placed their bets gave their horses a much better chance of winning than did those who were about to place their bets. But, of course, nothing had changed except the finality of the decision.

Moving from the racetrack to the Harvard campus, Daniel Gilbert[29] tested the irrevocability hypothesis with students interested in learning photography. He told them to shoot a roll of film and print two of the photographs, rating them and choosing one to keep. Some students had the option to exchange photographs within a five-day period, while others were told their first choice was final. Gilbert then contacted them two, four, and nine days later, to see if their feelings about the photographs had changed. Those who made their final choice on the first day liked their choice more than those who had the option of exchanging photographs. Again, once a decision is irrevocable, people get busy making themselves feel good about the choice they made. And thus, they frequently become more certain that they have made a wise decision once there is nothing they can do about it.

Although the irrevocability of a decision always increases dissonance and the motivation to reduce it, sometimes people feel dissonance even when technically they could get out of the decision. Years ago, Robert Cialdini[30] demonstrated how this works by temporarily joining the sales force of an automobile dealer. (Cialdini did lots of imaginative field studies in social psychology, and this was one of his most fun.) That's how he identified a common and successful ploy called **lowballing**, or *throwing the customer a lowball*. It works like this: A customer goes to a car dealer prepared to pay $19,300 for their dream car—a price advertised as an incredible bargain. The dealer, smiling, says, "I'll go you one better," and offers the customer the car for $18,942. Excited by the bargain, the buyer agrees to the deal and writes out a check for the down payment, happily anticipating driving home in that shiny new car. Alas, 10 minutes later, the dealer returns with a forlorn look on his face; it seems, he says, that he made a calculation error, and the sales manager caught it. The price of the car is actually $19,384. What will the buyer do? The customer can get this car cheaper elsewhere, so the decision to buy this one is not irrevocable. And yet far more people in this situation will go ahead with the deal than if the original asking price had been $19,384—even though the reason for purchasing the car from this dealer (the bargain price) no longer exists.

What is going on in this situation? There are at least three important things to notice. First, while the customer's decision to buy is certainly reversible, there is an implicit commitment created by the act of signing a check for a down payment. Second, this commitment triggered the anticipation of a pleasant experience: driving out with a new car. To have the anticipated event thwarted (by not going ahead with the deal) would have produced dissonance and disappointment. Third, although the final price is higher than the salesman said it would be, it is only slightly higher than the price somewhere else. Under these circumstances, the customer says, in effect, "Oh, what the hell. I'm already here; I've already filled out the forms—why wait?" Lowballing rarely applies nowadays when people buy cars, as the internet has made people smarter and more informed consumers. But it applies in many other situations when we are not so informed, as in replacing an expired cell phone contract with a new one that promises a great bargain.

The Decision to Behave Immorally How can an honest person become corrupt? Conversely, how can we get a person to be *more* honest? One way is through the dissonance that results from making a difficult decision. Suppose you are enrolled in a tough biology course. Your grade will hinge on the final exam you are now taking. The key question involves some material you know fairly well—but, because of anxiety, you draw a blank. You are sitting there in a nervous sweat. You look up, and lo and behold, you happen to be sitting behind a woman who is the smartest person in the class (who also happens, fortunately, to be the person with the most legible handwriting). You glance down and notice she is just completing her answer to the crucial question. You know you could easily read her answer if you chose to. What do you do? Your conscience tells you it's wrong to cheat—and yet, if you don't cheat, you are certain to get a poor grade. You wrestle with your conscience. Regardless of whether you decide to cheat or not, you are doomed to experience dissonance. If you cheat, your cognition "I am a decent, moral person" is dissonant with your cognition "I have just committed an immoral act." If you decide to resist temptation, your cognition "I want to get a good grade" is dissonant with your cognition "I could have acted in a way that would have ensured a good grade, but I chose not to."

Suppose that, after a difficult struggle, you decide to cheat. How do you reduce the dissonance? Before you read on, think about it for a moment. One way to reduce dissonance is to minimize the negative aspects of the action you have chosen and maximize the positive aspects—much the same way the women did after choosing an appliance in Jack Brehm's experiment. In this instance, the most efficient way to reduce dissonance would be to change your attitude about cheating. If you cheat, you will adopt a more lenient attitude. Your reasoning might go something like this: "Cheating isn't so bad under some circumstances. As long as nobody gets hurt, it's really not very immoral. Anybody would do it. Therefore, it's a part of human nature—so how could it be bad? Since it is only human, those who get caught cheating should not be severely punished but should be treated with understanding."

But suppose that, after a difficult struggle, you decide not to cheat. How would you reduce dissonance—that is, make your action consonant with your belief? Once again, you could change your attitude about the morality of the act, but in the opposite direction. To justify giving up a good grade, you must convince yourself that cheating is a heinous sin, one of the lowest things a person can do, and that cheaters should be found out and severely punished.

The essential thing to remember here is that two people acting in these two different ways could have started out with almost identical attitudes. Their decisions might have been a hairsbreadth apart: One came within an ace of resisting but decided to cheat, while the other came within an ace of cheating but decided to resist. Once they have made their decisions, however, their attitudes toward cheating will diverge sharply as a consequence of their decisions.

These speculations were put to the test by Judson Mills[31] in an experiment with sixth-graders. Mills first measured their attitudes toward cheating. He then had the children participate in a competitive exam with prizes being offered to the winners. The situation was arranged so that it was almost impossible to win without cheating; also, it was easy for the children to cheat, thinking they would not be detected. As you might expect, some of the students cheated and others did not. The next day, the sixth-graders were again asked to indicate how they felt about cheating. In general, those children who had cheated became more lenient toward cheating, and those who resisted the temptation to cheat adopted a harsher attitude toward cheating.

To visualize the Mills experiment as it applies to you, imagine yourself at the top of a pyramid. As you go through life, you will face many decisions that will require you to step off that pyramid in one direction or another: what to major in, whether to go along with friends who are doing something illegal or unethical or not rock the boat, whether to stay in a romantic relationship or leave, whether to believe some conspiracy claim or check it out on Snopes.com or PolitiFact. The minute you take a step in one direction or the other, however, you will feel dissonance—and now you will be motivated to justify what you did to reduce it. That justification, in turn, makes it harder for you to change your mind, even when you should. By the time you are at the bottom of the pyramid, you will be very far apart from those who faced the same dilemmas but who made a different decision and stepped off the pyramid in the opposite direction. And you will have convinced yourself that your decision was absolutely, positively the right one, and that those people who slid down on the other side are idiots or crooks. (And how do you think they feel about you?)

The pyramid metaphor is also useful in helping us understand how attitudes and behavior can change through the process of **entrapment**, or how people can start off making a small, impulsive decision and, over time, find themselves a long way from their original goals and intentions. The process underlying entrapment has been explored under controlled experimental conditions. Suppose you would like to enlist someone's aid in a massive undertaking, but you know the job you have in mind for the person is so difficult and will require so much time and effort, that the person will surely decline. What should you do? One possibility is to get the person involved in a much smaller aspect of the job, one so easy that he or she wouldn't dream of turning it down. This action serves to commit the individual to "the cause." Once people are thus committed, the likelihood of their complying with the larger request increases.

This phenomenon was demonstrated by Jonathan Freedman and Scott Fraser,[32] who attempted to induce homeowners to put up a huge sign in their front yards, reading "Drive Carefully." Because of the ugliness and obtrusiveness of this sign, most residents refused; only 17 percent complied. A different group of residents, however, was first "softened up" by an experimenter who got them to sign a petition favoring safe driving. Because signing a petition is an easy thing to do, virtually all who were asked agreed to sign. A few weeks later, a different experimenter went to each resident with the obtrusive ugly sign reading "Drive Carefully." This time, more than 55 percent of these residents allowed the sign to be put up on their property. Thus, when individuals commit themselves in a small way, the likelihood increases that they will commit themselves further in that direction.

This process of using small favors to encourage people to accede to larger requests has been dubbed the **foot-in-the-door technique**. It is effective because having done the smaller favor provides justification in advance for agreeing to do the larger favor. Similar results were obtained by Patricia Pliner and her associates.[33] When they asked people to make a small donation to the American Cancer Society, 46 percent agreed. But when, a day earlier, they had induced a similar group of people to wear a lapel pin publicizing the fund-raising drive, and then approached them the next day for a contribution, approximately twice as many agreed. Entrapment through self-justification can thus be used for altruistic, socially admirable goals—but also for devastating, self-defeating ones, as we will see at the end of this chapter.

The Psychology of Insufficient Justification

Attitude change as a means of reducing dissonance is not limited to post-decision situations. It can occur in countless other contexts, including every time a person says something he or she doesn't believe or does something foolish or immoral. Of course, in a complex society, we occasionally find ourselves saying or doing things we don't completely believe. Does this always lead us to change our minds? No. I will choose a simple example: Joe enters the office and sees that his law partner, Joyce, has hung a perfectly atrocious painting on the wall of the office they share. He is about to tell her how awful he thinks it is when she says proudly, "How do you like the painting? I did it myself."

"Very nice, Joyce," Joe answers. Theoretically, Joe's cognition "I am a truthful person" is dissonant with the cognition "I said that painting was nice, although it really is unbelievably ugly." Whatever dissonance might be aroused by this inconsistency can easily and quickly be reduced by Joe's cognition that it is wrong to hurt other people: "I lied so as not to hurt Joyce; why should I tell her it's ugly? It serves no useful purpose." This is an effective way of reducing dissonance because it completely justifies Joe's action. In effect, the justification is situation-determined. We call this **external justification**.

But what happens if there is not ample justification in the situation itself? In such cases we need to create **internal justification**, a change in attitude used to justify behavior. If you do or say something that is difficult to justify *externally*, you will attempt to justify it *internally* by making your attitudes more consistent with what you did or said.

These speculations have been investigated scientifically in several experiments, notably a classic study by Leon Festinger and J. Merrill Carlsmith.[34] These investigators asked college students to do a boring and repetitive series of tasks: packing spools in a tray, dumping them out, and then refilling the tray over and over, or turning rows and rows of screws a quarter turn and then going back and turning them another quarter turn. The students did these mindless activities for a full hour. The experimenter then induced them to lie about the task—specifically, by telling a young woman (who was waiting to participate in the experiment) that the task she would be performing was interesting and enjoyable. Some of the students were offered $20 for telling this lie; others were offered only $1. After the experiment was over, an interviewer asked the liars how much they enjoyed the tasks they had done earlier in the experiment. How do you suppose the students who had been paid $20 for lying replied? They rated all that spool packing and screw turning as dull. This is not surprising—those tasks *were* dull. But what about the students who had been paid only $1 for lying? They rated the task as enjoyable. In other words, people who received abundant external justification for lying told the lie but didn't believe it, whereas those who told the lie *in the absence* of external justification moved in the direction of believing that what they said about the task was true. We call this result the *"saying is believing" paradigm*, because under these circumstances, people will come to believe their own statements. If you want to get a person to change an attitude, get them to do or say something counter-attitudinal and underpay them for it.

Research on this idea has extended beyond relatively unimportant attitudes like the dullness of a task. Attitude change has been shown on a variety of more serious issues in which people argue for a position that is exactly the opposite of the one they believe in. Arthur R. Cohen[35] conducted an experiment with Yale students immediately after a student riot in which the New Haven police had overreacted, clubbing and arresting protesters. The students (who were sure the police had behaved badly) were asked to write a strong and forceful essay in support of police. The experimenters paid students anything from a meager fifty cents to a full $10 for writing the brief essay. Later they were asked to indicate their true feelings about the New Haven Police. The results were perfectly linear: The *less* they were paid for writing in support of the police, the *more* liking for the police they expressed later. Saying had become believing, but mainly if they hadn't been well paid for what they said.

Thus, dissonance theory predicts that we begin to believe the things we say—but only if we don't have enough external justification for saying them. The smaller the bribe used to get you to give a speech, the more likely it is that you will feel the need to justify delivering it by convincing yourself that the things you said were true.

This mechanism is so powerful that it not only helps explain how attitudes change; it can affect the way we experience basic physiological drives. Imagine that our friend Sam is induced to commit himself to a situation in which he will be deprived of food or water for a long time or in which he will be given electric shocks. If Sam doesn't have a good external reason for doing this, he will experience dissonance. His cognitions concerning his hunger pangs, his parched throat, or the pain of electric shock are each dissonant with his cognition that he volunteered to go through these experiences and is not getting much in return. To reduce this dissonance, Sam convinces himself that the hunger isn't so intense, or the thirst isn't so bad, or the pain isn't so terrible.

Such self-persuasion is not as surprising or difficult as it might seem. Although hunger, thirst, and pain all have physiological bases, they also have a strong psychological component. That is why suggestion, meditation, hypnosis, placebo pills, the bedside manner of a skillful physician, or some combination of these can reduce people's perceived pain. Experimental social psychologists have shown that, under conditions of high dissonance arousal, ordinary people, with no special skills in hypnosis or meditation, can accomplish the same things for themselves.

For example, Philip Zimbardo[36] subjected his study participants to intense electric shocks. Half were in a high-dissonance condition—that is, they were induced to commit themselves to volunteer for the experience and were given little external justification. The other half were in a low-dissonance condition—they had no choice in the matter, giving them plenty of external justification. People in the high-dissonance condition reported feeling less pain than those in the low-dissonance condition. Even their physiological response to pain (as measured by the galvanic skin response) was somewhat less intense, and the pain did not interfere as much with the tasks they were performing. Thus, not only did they report less pain than the low-dissonance group, but objectively, they were less bothered by it.

Similar results have been shown for hunger and thirst. Jack Brehm[37] reported a series of experiments in which people were deprived of either food or water for long periods. Like Zimbardo's participants, some had low external justification for going through this unpleasant experience, whereas others had high external justification. In separate experiments on hunger and thirst, Brehm found that high-dissonance participants said they were less hungry (or thirsty) than low-dissonance participants who were deprived of food (or water) for the same length of time. Again, this was no mere verbal report. After the experiment, when all of the participants were allowed to eat (or drink) freely, those in the high-dissonance condition consumed less food (or water) than those in the low-dissonance condition.

What Constitutes External Justification? Monetary gain or a forced requirement to do something is not the only form of external justification. People can be persuaded to say or do things that contradict their beliefs or preferences if they are enticed by other rewards, such as praise or the desire to please. Furthermore, most of us would probably agree to do something that we otherwise wouldn't do if a good friend asked us to do it as a favor. To take a far-fetched example, suppose a friend asked you to eat an unusual food she or he had recently learned to prepare in an "exotic foods" cooking class. And just to make things interesting, let's say the food in question was a fried grasshopper. Now, imagine the reverse situation: that someone you didn't like asked you to sink your teeth into a fried grasshopper.

Okay, are you ready? Assuming you went ahead and ate the grasshopper, under which circumstance do you think you would enjoy the taste of it more: when asked to eat it by a good friend or by someone you didn't like? Common sense might suggest that the grasshopper would taste better when recommended by a friend. After all, a friend is someone you can trust and, hence, would be a more credible source of information than someone you didn't like. But think about it for a moment: Which condition involves less external justification? Common sense notwithstanding, the theory of cognitive dissonance would predict that you would come to like eating grasshoppers more if you ate one at the request of someone you *didn't* like. Your cognition that eating a grasshopper is repulsive would be at odds with the fact that you just ate one. But if it was *your friend* who made the request, you would have enough external justification for having eaten it—you pleased someone you like. But you would not have much external justification for munching on a grasshopper if you did it at the request of someone you didn't like. In this case, how could you justify your contradictory behavior to yourself? Simple: Start liking grasshoppers—"Gee, they're pretty tasty critters after all." Philip Zimbardo and his colleagues[38] had an army officer instruct a group of reservists to eat grasshoppers, rating their liking for them before and after tasting them. Reservists found the grasshoppers significantly tastier if the officer who asked them to eat it acted like a jerk rather than behaving in a friendly and likable manner.

Insufficient Punishment   One clear form of external justification for behaving a certain way is knowing you'll be punished if you don't. We know that if we exceed the speed limit and get caught, we will pay a fine, and if it happens too often, we will lose our licenses. So we learn to obey the speed limit when police are in the vicinity. Schoolchildren know that if they cheat on an exam and get caught, they could be humiliated by the teacher and severely punished. So they learn not to cheat while the teacher is in the room watching them. But does the threat of punishment teach people not to speed or cheat? I don't think so. I think it teaches them to try to avoid getting caught. The use of threats of harsh punishment as a means of getting someone to refrain from doing something he or she enjoys doing requires constant vigilance. It would be much more efficient and would require much less restraint if, somehow, people could enjoy doing the things that contribute to their own health and welfare and to the health and welfare of others. If children enjoyed *not* beating up smaller kids or *not* cheating or *not* stealing from others, then society could relax its vigilance and punitiveness. It is extremely difficult to persuade people (especially young children) that it's not enjoyable to beat up smaller people. But it is conceivable that, under certain conditions, they will persuade *themselves* that such behavior is not enjoyable.

Picture the scene: You are the parent of a five-year-old boy who enjoys beating up his three-year-old sister. You've tried to reason with him, but to no avail. So, to protect the welfare of your daughter and to make a nicer person out of your son, you begin to punish him for his aggressiveness. As a parent, you have at your disposal a number of punishments that range from extremely mild (a stern look) to extremely severe (a hard spanking, forcing the child to stand in the corner for two hours, and depriving him of TV for a month). The more severe the threat, the more likely that the boy will mend his ways while you are watching him. But he will probably hit his sister again as soon as you turn your back.

Suppose instead you threaten him with a mild punishment. In either case (under the threat of severe or mild punishment), the child feels dissonance. He is aware that he is not beating up his little sister, and he is also aware that he would really, really like to beat her up. When he has the urge to hit his sister and doesn't, he asks himself, in effect, "How come I'm not beating up my little sister?" Under a severe threat, he has a ready-made answer in the form of sufficient external justification: "I'm not beating her up because, if I do, that giant over there (my father) is going to spank me, stand me in the corner, and keep me from watching TV for a month." The severe threat has provided the child ample external justification for not hitting his sister while he's being watched.

The child in the mild-threat situation feels dissonance, too. But when he asks himself, "How come I'm not beating up my little sister?" he doesn't have a good answer because the threat is so mild that it does not provide abundant justification. The child isn't doing something he wants to do — and while he does have some justification for not doing it, he lacks complete justification. In this situation, he continues to experience dissonance, but he can't reduce it by simply blaming his inaction on a severe threat. The child must find a way to justify the fact that he is not aggressing against his little sister, and the best way is to try to convince himself that he really doesn't like to beat his sister up, that he didn't want to do it in the first place, and that beating up little kids isn't fun anyway. The less severe the threat, the less external justification; the less external justification, the greater the need for internal justification. Allowing people the opportunity to construct their own internal justification can help them develop a permanent set of values.

To test this idea, I designed an experiment at the Harvard University nursery school in collaboration with Merrill Carlsmith.[39] First, we asked five-year-old children to rate the desirability of several toys. Then we told each child not to play with the toy they had rated as particularly appealing. We threatened half of the children with mild punishment for transgression: "I would be a little angry." We threatened the other half with more severe punishment: "I would be very angry; I would have to take all of the toys and go home and never come back again; I would think you were just a baby." After that, the kids were left alone to play with all the toys. All the children resisted the temptation to play with the forbidden toy.

On returning to the room, the children again rated how much they liked all the toys. The results were both striking and exciting. Those children who had been threatened with *mild* punishment now found the forbidden toy less attractive than before. Lacking adequate external justification for refraining from playing with it, they succeeded in convincing themselves that they hadn't played with it because they didn't really like it. But the forbidden toy remained just as appealing to the children who were threatened with severe punishment. They continued to rate the forbidden toy as highly desirable; indeed, some even found it more desirable than they had before the threat. The children in the severe-threat condition had good external reasons for not playing with the toy—"that big man is going to be very angry with me"—and therefore had no need to find additional reasons; consequently, they continued to like the toy.

Jonathan Freedman[40] extended these findings and dramatically illustrated the permanence of the phenomenon. He used as his "crucial toy" an irresistible battery-powered robot that scurried around, hurling objects at a child's enemies. The other toys were sickly by comparison. Naturally, all of the children preferred the robot. He then asked them not to play with that toy, threatening some children with mild punishment and others with severe punishment. Then he left the school and never returned. Several weeks later, a young woman came to the school to administer some paper-and-pencil tests to the children. The children didn't know that she was working for Freedman or that her presence was in any way related to the toys or the threats that had occurred earlier. But it just so happened that she was administering her test in the same room Freedman had used for his experiment—the room where the same toys were casually scattered about. After she gave the children her test, she asked them to hang around while she scored it, suggesting, offhandedly, that they might want to amuse themselves with those toys someone had left in the room. The overwhelming majority of the children who had been mildly threatened weeks earlier refused to play with the robot; they played with the other toys instead. But the majority of the children who had been severely threatened went straight to the robot. Freedman's severe threat was not effective in inhibiting subsequent behavior—but one mild threat inhibited behavior as much as nine weeks later.

What Is Insufficient Justification?   Throughout this section, I have referred to situations in which there is *insufficient* external justification and to those with an *abundance* of external justification. These terms require some clarification. In the Festinger-Carlsmith experiment, all of the participants did, in fact, agree to tell the lie, including all of those paid only $1. In a sense, then, $1 was *adequate*—that is, sufficient to induce the participants to tell the lie; but it wasn't enough to prevent them from feeling foolish. To reduce their feelings of foolishness, they had to reduce the dissonance that resulted from telling a lie for so paltry a sum. This entailed additional bolstering in the form of convincing themselves that it wasn't completely a lie and the task wasn't quite as dull as it seemed at first; as a matter of fact, when looked at in a certain way, it was pretty interesting. In the grasshopper experiment, a friend was *sufficient* to persuade people to try eating the insect, but because they did it for a friend, that wasn't enough reason to like it. In the forbidden toy experiment, threats were *sufficient* to get the kids to avoid playing with the toy, but only the mild threat succeeded in making them not want to.

It would be fruitful to compare these results with Judson Mills's data on the effects of cheating among sixth-graders. Recall that, in Mills's experiment, the decision about whether to cheat was almost certainly a difficult one for most of the children. This is why they experienced dissonance, regardless of whether they cheated or resisted temptation. What do you think would happen if the rewards to be gained by cheating were large? You might predict that large rewards would make cheating more tempting, and therefore more children would cheat. But if the gains for cheating were astronomical, those who cheated would undergo little attitude change. Much like the college students who lied in Festinger and Carlsmith's $20 condition, those children who cheated for a substantial reward would have less need to reduce dissonance, having been provided with an *abundance* of external justification for their behavior.

In fact, Mills included this refinement in his experiment, and his results supported the hypothesis: Those who cheated to obtain a small reward tended to soften their attitude about cheating more than those who cheated to obtain a large reward. Moreover, those who refrained from cheating in spite of the temptation of a large reward—a choice that would create a lot of dissonance—hardened their attitude about cheating to a greater extent than those who refrained in the face of a small reward. This was just as predicted.

These results might be surprising to you. Some of my students used to wonder why cognitive dissonance theory always predicts the opposite of what seems to be common sense. But when you understand the theory, those predictions make a lot of sense. By and large, if you want someone to do something just once (or refrain from doing it), while you are standing there watching them, then by all means provide them with the largest incentive (or the most severe punishment) you can deliver. If you offer that person a million dollars to say that the North Korean dictator is a great humanitarian, or if you put a gun to their head and threaten to pull the trigger six times, chances are that person will say what you want—but they won't believe it. But if you want that person to develop a set of values or beliefs that they will act on even when you aren't there, then offer the person the smallest award that will bring about the behavior you want. That gets them to do the work of persuading themselves, which ensures that they will continue to do those things (or refrain from doing those things) for years after you have left the room.

Dissonance, the Self-Concept, and Self-Esteem

I now want to highlight a major departure from Festinger's original theory, one that has been embedded in some of the examples of dissonance I've already mentioned. In the experiment by Festinger and

Carlsmith, the original statement of dissonance went like this: The cognition "I believe the task is dull" is dissonant with the cognition "I said the task was interesting." Years later, I went on to reformulate the theory in a way that focuses more attention on the way people conceive of themselves.[41] I demonstrated experimentally that dissonance is most painful, and we are most motivated to reduce it, in situations in which the self-concept is threatened—when we have done something that violates our view of ourselves. True, "I said X" is dissonant with "I don't believe X," but for me, the crucial element is that I have misled people. The cognition "I have told people something I don't believe" is dissonant with my self-concept that "I am a good person of integrity."

As this reformulation would predict, people are less likely to cheat if they have a self-concept of being honest—not being "a cheater"—and when that self-concept is invoked. In one experiment, some students read instructions that highlighted their identity ("Please don't be a cheater"), whereas others read instructions that highlighted the action ("Please don't cheat"). They were then given the opportunity to cheat, by claiming money they weren't entitled to from the experimenter. The "Please don't be a cheater" group was far less likely to cheat, because that would have created dissonance with their self-concept of being honest. The second group, which was asked to simply refrain from the behavior of "cheating," claimed more than twice as much unearned money as people who were asked not to be "cheaters." This difference occurred in a face-to-face situation as well as when it was done privately online.[42]

Understanding the pain of dissonance when the self-concept is involved helps us sympathize with individuals who suffer when two central aspects of their identity conflict. In one study, for example, researchers wondered how gay men who strongly identified with their Christian church dealt with pronouncements from their ministers that the Bible prohibits homosexuality and that God hates gay people. One way to resolve dissonance would be to change their behavior—to try to suppress their sexual attraction to other men, change their church denomination, or even give up their religion altogether. But those who decide to stay in their church can resolve dissonance by saying that the Bible emphasizes compassion and love, and by emphasizing the shortcomings of the minister; for example, they might say, "It's not my religion that promotes anti-gay prejudice and this interpretation of the Bible; it's the narrow-mindedness of this particular preacher."[43]

The Importance of Self-Esteem Who do you think feels the greatest dissonance after doing something cruel, foolish, or incompetent: a person with high self-esteem or low self-esteem? The answer is the people with the highest self-esteem. They experience the most dissonance when they behave in ways that are contrary to their high opinion of themselves, and they will work harder to reduce it than will those with average levels of self-esteem.[44] In contrast, when people who have low self-esteem commit an incompetent or unethical action, they do not feel as much dissonance, because the cognition "I've done an awful thing" is consonant with their self-concept, which is the cognition "I'm a loser; I often do awful things." Psychopaths are fairly immune from dissonance caused by behaving badly, because the cognition "I just treated that person in a cold and heartless way" is consistent with "I'm really good at manipulating all those stupid people who can't see through me."[45] One of the great advantages of my modification of cognitive dissonance theory is that in taking into account the self-concept of the psychopath and people with low self-esteem, it enhances the precision of predictions made by the theory.

My reformulation of dissonance theory, however, was primarily based on my assumption that most people want to preserve their good feelings about themselves. If they do something cruel or thoughtless or incompetent, their self-esteem is threatened—because it makes them feel that they *are* cruel, thoughtless, or incompetent. In the thousands of experiments inspired by the theory of cognitive dissonance, the clearest results were obtained in those situations in which a person's self-esteem was threatened.

I tested this idea in collaboration with David Mettee.[46] We predicted that, given the opportunity to cheat during a card game, individuals with a low opinion of themselves would be more likely to cheat than individuals who had a high opinion of themselves. We predicted that, if people receive a temporary blow to their self-esteem (e.g., if they are jilted by their lover or flunk an exam) and thus feel low and worthless, they are more likely to cheat at cards, kick their dog, or do other ignoble things. As a function of feeling they are low people, individuals will commit low acts.

In our experiment, we temporarily modified the self-esteem of college students by giving them false information about their personalities. After taking a personality test, some were given positive feedback and told the test indicated that they were mature, interesting, deep, and so forth. Another group received negative feedback and told the test indicated that they were relatively immature, uninteresting, rather shallow, and the like.

Immediately afterward, they all played a gambling game that had no apparent relation to the personality inventory. They were allowed to bet money and were told they could keep whatever they won. In the course of the game, they were given a few opportunities to cheat in a situation where it seemed impossible to be detected. The situation was arranged so that if a student decided *not* to cheat, she would certainly lose, whereas if she decided to cheat, she would be certain to win a sizable sum of money. The students who had previously received information designed to lower their self-esteem cheated to a far greater extent than those who had received the high self-esteem information. The control group—those receiving no information—fell exactly in between.

These findings suggest that parents and teachers should be alert to the potentially far-reaching consequences of their own behavior as it affects the self-esteem of their children and students. If high self-esteem can serve as a buffer against dishonest behavior and promote desirable behavior, then it might seem reasonable to do everything possible to help individuals learn to respect themselves. In support of this idea, Geoffrey Cohen and his associates[47] found that African American children received significantly higher grades if, at the beginning of the school year, their feelings of self-esteem were bolstered by classroom assignments that made them focus on their personal strengths and values.

We must be cautious in generalizing from these results. Strengthening self-esteem is unlikely to produce positive effects if it is done in an artificial or superficial way, or if the person's self-esteem is not grounded in reality.[48] Moreover, it's important to separate healthy *self-esteem* from *narcissism*, having a false sense of grandiosity and superiority to others. A person with healthy, realistically grounded self-esteem, when given constructive criticism, says, "Why, thank you!" This is not so for narcissists.

Roy Baumeister, Brad Bushman, and Keith Campbell[49] found that when narcissists are threatened by criticism, they often aggress against their critics, in an attempt to get even and restore their threatened self-image. They asked participants to write an essay and then hand it to a partner to criticize. After receiving the criticism, the participants were given the opportunity to express hostility against their partners by blasting them with an unpleasant noise, at whatever decibel level they chose. The people who turned the noise-maker up to the highest levels were those who had scored high on measures of both self-esteem and narcissism and whose inflated opinion of themselves had been threatened. Christina Salmivalli and her colleagues[50] suggest that this syndrome, "high narcissistic self-esteem," is not genuine high self-esteem at all; rather, it is paper-thin and self-aggrandizing and based on feelings of insecurity. This is the kind of self-esteem you find in schoolyard bullies, while youngsters with genuinely high self-esteem are more secure and do not engage in bullying. Indeed, they try to defend the bully's victims.

We are now in a position to state a general principle about dissonance and the self-concept: Dissonance effects are greatest when:

(1) people feel personally responsible for their actions,

(2) people's actions conflict with a central aspect of their self-concept,

(3) people's actions have serious consequences, and

(4) the action is irrevocable; a person can't take it back.

Under those four conditions, people will feel the most dissonance; and the greater their dissonance, the more their attitudes will change. The fact that dissonance is aroused whenever the self-concept is challenged has many interesting ramifications. Let us look at some of them.

The Justification of Effort

If we suffer to get something, chances are we will like it better than if it came more easily. And if that something isn't attractive, we may have to do some creative work to justify our efforts.

Suppose you are a college student who decides to join a fraternity. To be admitted, you must pass an initiation; let us assume it is a rather severe one that involves effort, pain, or embarrassment. After successfully completing the ordeal, you are admitted to the fraternity. When you move into the fraternity house, you find that your new roommate has some bad habits: He borrows money and forgets to repay you, he leaves dirty laundry on your bed, and he uses your stuff without asking. An objective person would see him as an inconsiderate slob. But you are not an objective person; your cognition that you went through hell to get into the fraternity in order to live with an inconsiderate slob is dissonant with your view of yourself as a rational, intelligent person who makes good decisions. To reduce dissonance, you will try to see your roommate and your experience in the most favorable light possible. Again, there are constraints imposed by reality—no matter how much pain and effort you went through, there is no way an inconsiderate slob can become Prince Charming—but, with a little ingenuity, you can convince yourself that he isn't so bad. What some people might call sloppy, for example, you might call laid back. Because he's so nice and casual about material things, it's certainly understandable that he would borrow and stain your best jacket and forget about the $50 he owes you.

Prince Charming he isn't, but he's certainly tolerable. Contrast this viewpoint with what your attitude would have been had you made no investment of effort: Suppose you had moved into a regular campus dormitory and had been assigned the same guy with same bad habits. Because you neither chose this room, nor made any investment to get it, you would feel dissatisfaction but no dissonance; because you feel no dissonance, you have no need to see your roommate in the best possible light. You could quickly write him off as an inconsiderate slob and try to make arrangements to move out.

These speculations were tested in a classic experiment that I did more than five decades ago with my friend Judson Mills.[51] In this study, college women volunteered to join a group that would be meeting regularly to discuss various aspects of the psychology of sex. The women were told that if they wanted to join, they would first have to go through a screening test designed to ensure that everyone admitted to the group could discuss sex freely and openly. This instruction served to set the stage for the initiation procedure. One-third of the women were assigned to a severe initiation procedure, which required them to recite aloud a list of obscene words. One-third of the students underwent a mild procedure, in which they recited a list of words that were sexual but not obscene. The final one-third of the participants were admitted to the group without undergoing an initiation. Each participant was then allowed to listen in on a discussion being conducted by the members of the group she had just joined. Although the women were led to believe the discussion was a live, ongoing one, they actually listened to a prerecorded discussion, designed to be as tedious and as bombastic as possible. Afterward, each participant was asked to rate the discussion in terms of how much she liked it, how interesting it was, how intelligent the participants were, and so forth.

The results supported our predictions: The women who made little or no effort to get into the group did not enjoy the discussion much. They were able to see it for what it was: a dull and boring waste of time. Those who went through a severe initiation, however, succeeded in convincing themselves that the same discussion was interesting and worthwhile.

Other investigators, using different kinds of unpleasant initiations, have gotten the same results as we did. For example, Harold Gerard and Grover Mathewson[52] conducted an experiment similar in concept to the Aronson-Mills study, except that the participants in the severe-initiation condition were given painful electric shocks instead of a list of obscene words to read aloud. Those who underwent a series of severe electric shocks to become members of a group liked that group better than those who underwent a series of mild electric shocks.

I am not asserting that people enjoy painful experiences — they do not; nor am I saying that people enjoy things because they are associated with painful experiences. What I am saying is that if a person goes through a difficult or a painful experience in order to attain some goal or object, that goal or object becomes more attractive — a process called the **justification of effort**. If, on your way to a discussion group, a flowerpot fell from a ledge and you got hit on the head, you would not like that group any better; but if you *volunteered* to get hit on the head by a flowerpot in order to join the group, you would definitely like the group better.[53]

The biologist Robert Sapolsky[54] describes a medical phenomenon that took place in the twentieth century that nicely demonstrates the justification of effort. At that time, some Swiss physicians believed that they could slow down the aging process by injecting men with testosterone. As Sapolsky put it:

> Thus, a craze developed of aged, moneyed gentlemen checking into impeccable Swiss sanitariums and getting injected daily in their rears with testicular extracts from dogs, from roosters,

from monkeys. By the 1920s, captains of industry, heads of state, famous religious leaders—all were doing it, and reporting wondrous results. Not because the science was accurate, but because if you're paying a fortune for painful daily injections of extract of dog's testicle, there's a certain incentive to decide you feel like a young bull. One big placebo effect.

In most dissonant situations, there is more than one way to reduce dissonance. In the initiation experiment, for example, the women convinced themselves that the group was interesting. Is this the only way they could have reduced dissonance? No. Another way of making sense of the effort we've expended is to revise our memory of the past—that is, to misremember what things were like *before* we suffered or worked hard.

In an experiment by Michael Conway and Michael Ross,[55] one group of students participated in a study-skills course that promised more than it delivered; another group of students signed up but did not participate. Whether or not they took the course, all students were asked to evaluate their study skills. After three weeks of useless training, the students wanted to believe that their skills had improved, but the objective data showed that they had not; they were still doing just as poorly in their coursework. How could they reduce dissonance between "I worked hard to improve" and "I didn't"? This was done by misremembering how bad their skills were before they took the course and underestimating the skills they had before they enrolled. Students who signed up but did not participate showed no such self-justifying behavior; their recollections of earlier self-evaluations were accurate. This study may explain why people who spend time and money to get in shape may feel satisfied even if they don't fully succeed. They may not be able to convince themselves that they reached their goals, but they can overestimate the progress they did make by distorting their memories of how out of shape they were before they went into training. Conway and Ross call this self-justifying technique "getting what you want by revising what you had."

The Justification of Cruelty

I have repeatedly made the point that we need to convince ourselves that we are decent, reasonable people. Now suppose you did something that seriously, unambiguously harmed an innocent person:

You posted a rumor about a friend that turned out to be untrue, or you texted your romantic partner a spontaneous but nasty insult. Your cognition "I am a good person" would be dissonant with your cognition "I've hurt another person." If the harm is obvious, then you cannot reduce the dissonance by changing your opinion of what happened and blithely telling yourself that you've done no harm. In this situation, the most effective way to reduce dissonance would be to maximize the culpability of the victim of your action—by telling yourself that the victim deserved what he or she got, either because he did something to bring it on himself or because she was a bad person.

This mechanism might operate even if you did not directly harm the victim but disliked the person and were hoping that harm would befall him. For example, during a peaceful protest march in 1970 against the Vietnam war—a war that was creating as deep a political and cultural polarization across the country as we see today—four students at Kent State University were shot and killed by members of the Ohio National Guard. Nine others were wounded and one paralyzed for life. Quickly, rumors spread—even before there was Twitter: The slain women were pregnant (and therefore, by implication, sexually promiscuous); the dead students were crawling with lice; the victims were so ridden with syphilis that they would have been dead in two weeks anyway, and so on. These rumors were preposterous and totally untrue. Why were the townspeople so eager to believe and spread them? It is impossible to know for sure, but my guess is that it was for reasons similar to the reasons rumors spread among the people in Indian towns following the earthquake: The rumors were comforting.

Picture the situation: Kent is a conservative small town in Ohio. Many of the townspeople were infuriated by the radical behavior of some of the students. Some were probably hoping the students would get their comeuppance, but death was more than they deserved. In such circumstances, any information that put the victims in a bad light helped to reduce dissonance by implying that it was, in fact, a good thing that they died, or at least an inevitable thing, considering how sinful and diseased they all were. Several members of the Ohio National Guard stoutly maintained that the protesters *deserved* to die, and a local high-school teacher went so far as to state that "anyone who appears on the streets of a city like Kent with long hair, dirty clothes, or barefooted deserves to be shot." That opinion, she added, applied even to her own children.[56]

Although few people were as extreme in their condemnation of the victims as the high-school teacher, just about everyone can be influenced, under certain conditions, to justify cruelty committed against innocent victims. That's why it is essential for the social psychologist to step back from the helter-skelter of the real world (temporarily) and test predictions in the more controlled world of the experimental laboratory. Ideally, if we want to measure attitude change as a result of dissonance, we should know what the attitudes were *before* the dissonance-arousing event occurred.

Such a situation was produced in an experiment conducted by Keith Davis and Edward Jones.[57] They asked students, one at a time, to watch a young man (a confederate of theirs) being interviewed and then describe their general opinions of him. Next, the students were instructed to provide the confederate with a prearranged analysis of his shortcomings as a human being. After telling him things they knew were certain to hurt him—that they thought he was shallow, untrustworthy, and boring—they convinced themselves that he deserved to be insulted this way; why, he really *was* shallow and boring. Their opinion of him had become much more negative than it was prior to saying the hurtful things to him directly. This shift in views of their victim occurred even though all participants were aware that the other student had done nothing to merit their criticism and that they were just responding to the experimenter's instructions.

An experiment by David Glass[58] had a similar result. In this study, when induced to deliver a series of electric shocks to other people, individuals who considered themselves good and decent people denigrated their victims as a result of having caused them this pain. This result was strongest among people with high self-esteem. If I'm just a person with low self-esteem who believes I'm always hurting other people's feelings, then causing others to suffer does not introduce much dissonance; therefore, I have little need to convince myself that they deserved it. Here's the irony: It is precisely because I think I am such a nice person that, if I do something that causes you pain, I must convince myself you are a rat. Because nice guys like me don't go around hurting innocent people, you must have deserved every nasty thing I did to you.

One condition, however, limits the justification of cruelty: the capacity of the victim to retaliate. If the victim is able and willing to retaliate at some future time, then a harm-doer feels that equity will be restored and thus has no need to justify the action by denigrating the victim. In an experiment by Ellen Berscheid and her associates,[59] college students volunteered for an experiment in which each of them delivered a painful electric shock to a fellow student; as expected, each participant belittled the victim as a result of having delivered the shock. But half the students were told there would be a turnabout—that is, the other students would be given the opportunity to shock *them*. Those who were led to believe their victims would be able to retaliate had less dissonance to reduce, and hence had no need to belittle their victims to convince themselves that the victims deserved it.

This research has serious implications: It shows that people do not perform acts of cruelty and come out unscathed. When we are engaged in a war in which, through our actions, many innocent people are being killed, we might try to blame the victims to justify our complicity—especially civilian victims who can't retaliate. A sad, though universal, phenomenon is that all cultures are inclined to **dehumanize** their enemies by calling them cruel names and regarding them as "vermin," "animals," "brutes," and other non-human creatures. During World War II, Americans called the Japanese "Japs" and portrayed them as sneaky and diabolical; during the Vietnam War, American soldiers referred to the Vietnamese as "gooks"; during the wars in Iraq and Afghanistan, American soldiers began referring to the enemy as "ragheads" because of the turbans or other headdresses that many Arabs and Muslims wear. The use of such language is a way of reducing dissonance: "I am a good person, but we are fighting and killing these other people; therefore, they must deserve whatever they get, because they aren't fully human like us." But once we have succeeded in doing that, watch out, because dehumanization makes it easier to hurt and kill "subhumans" than to hurt and kill fellow human beings. Thus, reducing dissonance in this way increases the likelihood that the atrocities we are willing to commit now will justify our committing more of them over time.[60]

People often justify other acts, besides the violence of warfare, that can feed hostility and discrimination. Just to take a wild example, imagine you live in a society in which poor children, many of whom are blacks and Latinos, have been blocked from attending first-rate public schools. Instead, they have been given a second-rate and often stultifying education. As a consequence, these children become less educated and less motivated than middle- and upper-class white children, ending up doing poorly on achievement tests. Such a situation provides a golden opportunity for civic leaders to justify the status quo and, hence, to reduce dissonance. "You see," they might say, "those kids are stupid and unteachable (because they perform poorly on the achievement tests); see how clever we were when we decided against wasting our hard-earned tax dollars, trying to provide them with a high-quality education." This self-fulfilling prophecy provides a perfect justification for further neglect of those less advantaged. John Jost and his colleagues[61] have studied this phenomenon, which they call *system justification*: Many people who were born into the highest levels of society, who have the greatest wealth and power, justify that position by believing they are entitled to it by virtue of their superior abilities and native talent, whereas all those poor and struggling people are just too unable or unmotivated to succeed. As the football coach Barry Switzer once said, "Some people are born on third base and go through life thinking they hit a triple."

In the final analysis, as I keep repeating, people are accountable for their own actions. Not everyone dehumanizes their opponents, or people who are economically worse off than they, or even their nation's enemies. But dissonance theory identifies the mechanism at the heart of dehumanization—the reason so many people resort to it to preserve their opinion of themselves as right, moral, and good. There is good news in this research. Because dehumanization is rooted in a desire to feel better about ourselves in the face of misfortunes of others, expressing our negative feelings—disgust, sorrow, shock, terror—that the victim's plight inspires eliminates our need to dehumanize them.

Consider an experiment conducted by Kent Harber and his associates.[62] Participants watched a disturbingly violent and graphic bar scene from *The Accused*, in which a young woman called Sarah flirts and dances with one of the men, who becomes more aggressive in sexually groping her. She tries to stop him, with increasing fear, but he pins her down and rapes her; other bar patrons join the assault, as she struggles desperately against them. The scene clearly portrays Sarah as an unwilling victim, but it also shows her drinking heavily, wearing revealing clothing, and dancing provocatively. Nothing she does remotely justifies the brutality of what is done to her, but for viewers inclined to "blame the victim," her dress and actions give them ammunition. Afterward, participants were asked to write their evaluation of what they had seen. The "suppression" group was instructed to suppress their feelings and write only about factual details, such as what people were wearing. Participants in the "disclosure" group were told to freely express their deepest thoughts and feelings about their assigned movie. A week later, everyone evaluated Sarah. Had she shown bad judgment, could she have done more for herself, was she sympathetic and likeable, was she irresponsible, was she moral, was she someone participants could identify with, had she brought her difficulties on herself? The answers were combined into a measure of blaming. The more distress the viewers acknowledged and expressed, the less they blamed the victim. In contrast, those instructed to suppress their emotions blamed Sarah more readily.

Victim blaming, it would appear, is rooted in our need to justify ourselves and our attitudes toward those less fortunate, or who are victims of crime, poverty, or tragic events. Remarkably, it can sometimes be avoided by recognizing, and expressing, our own distress and human feelings, before it turns into something more unsavory.

The Psychology of Inevitability

George Bernard Shaw was hard hit by his father's alcoholism, but he tried to make light of it. He once wrote, "If you cannot get rid of the family skeleton, you may as well make it dance."[63] In a sense, dissonance theory describes the ways people have of making their skeletons dance—of trying to make the best of unpleasant outcomes. This is particularly true when a situation arises that is both negative and inevitable.

And what situation is more negative and inevitable for little kids than having to eat vegetables they hate? In one experiment, Jack Brehm[64] got children to volunteer to eat a vegetable they had previously said they disliked a lot. Afterward, he led half the children to believe they could expect to eat much more of that vegetable in the future; the remaining children were not so informed. The children who were led to believe it was inevitable that they would be eating the vegetable in the future succeeded in convincing themselves that the vegetable was not so bad. In short, the cognition "I dislike that vegetable" is dissonant with the cognition "I will be eating that vegetable in the future." To reduce the dissonance, the children came to believe the vegetable was really not as noxious as they had previously thought.

John Darley and Ellen Berscheid[65] showed that the same phenomenon works with people as well as vegetables. In their experiment, college women volunteered to participate in a series of meetings in which each student would be discussing her sexual behavior and sexual standards with a woman she didn't know. Before beginning these discussions, each participant was given two folders. Each folder contained a personality description of a young woman who had supposedly volunteered for the same experience; the descriptions contained a mixture of pleasant and unpleasant characteristics. Half of the participants were led to believe they were going to interact with the young woman described in folder A, and the remaining participants were led to believe they were going to interact with the one described in folder B. Before meeting these women, the participants were asked to evaluate each of them on the basis of the personality descriptions they had read. Those who felt it was inevitable that they were going to share their intimate secrets with the young woman described in folder A found her much more appealing than the one described in folder B, whereas those who believed they had to interact with the young woman described in folder B found *her* much more appealing. The knowledge that one is inevitably going to be spending time with another person enhances the positive aspects of that person — or at least deemphasizes his or her negative aspects.

People tend to make the best of something they know is bound to happen. Just as with vegetables, inevitability makes the heart grow fonder. Deemphasizing the negative is an adaptive strategy when what's in store is a disliked vegetable or meeting a new person, but sometimes such a strategy can prove disastrous. People who live on the West Coast, especially Californians, for example, know that one of these days a big earthquake will hit. Rational people would no doubt acknowledge the danger and work to prepare by learning all they can about it and by taking safety precautions, right? Nope. Even among well-educated people, a typical response to an inevitable catastrophe is to do nothing to prepare for it. Darrin Lehman and Shelley Taylor[66] interviewed 120 undergraduates from UCLA and found that, although they all knew about the earthquake threat, only 5 percent had taken any safety precautions (such as locating the nearest fire extinguisher); only one-third knew that the best action to take during a quake is to crawl under a desk or other heavy piece of furniture; and not one respondent had taken preparatory measures recommended by experts.

Coping styles, however, varied as a function of the students' living situation. Students living in seismically unsafe residence halls were more likely than those living in relatively safe residence halls to cope with the impending disaster by refusing to think about it or by minimizing the expected damage. But if you're pretty sure that there's going to be an earthquake, how can you justify continuing to live in an unsafe residence hall? Easy—you deny that there's ever going to be an earthquake and refuse to think about it. Self-justifying responses to dangerous and inevitable events can be comforting in the short run. But when they keep us from taking steps to enhance our safety, such responses can, in the long run, prove deadly.

Perhaps you have noticed the curious difference between the responses of children facing a disliked vegetable or college students facing an inevitable interaction with another person, on the one hand, and the responses of UCLA students to the threat of an impending earthquake, on the other hand. In the former situations, people accept the inevitable and embrace attitudes stressing the positive aspects of the unavoidable event. The latter situation, however, involves confronting a highly probable event that is life-threatening and largely uncontrollable. It would be stretching the limits of the human imagination to redefine a major earthquake as desirable—or as anything less than a catastrophe. And we can't prevent earthquakes; the best we can hope for is to respond adaptively to one, with no guarantee that safety measures will really save us. Thus, the nature of our response may depend on whether we believe preventive steps will genuinely increase our sense of control over the inevitable. If such steps seem futile, then the prospect of expending effort will only serve to increase our feeling of dissonance even further. Under such circumstances, we are likely to justify not taking safety measures by denying the probability of the potential disaster or vastly underestimating its magnitude.

Can you see where this is going? Scientists have reached an international consensus that global warming poses a major threat to the planet, yet many Americans remain unconcerned by it or think climate change is a "hoax." Dissonance theory suggests that if scientists want to motivate people into taking immediate action on global warming, it will be vital to also convince them that doing something about it is within their control. Simply stoking up their fears is likely to make them either deny its existence or actively disregard the scientific evidence.

Practical Applications of Dissonance Theory

One of the reasons the theory of cognitive dissonance has attracted enormous interest and inspired so much research is its ability to explain and predict people's behavior that defies common sense. Moreover, dissonance theory accounts for many phenomena, ranging from how rumors are spread to how people change their attitudes and behaviors, from practicing safer sex to the reduction of racial prejudice. Beyond its power to help us understand and predict, a theory is of particular value if it can be practically applied in ways that benefit people. I turn now to some notable applications of the theory.

Condoms and Conservation As we saw in the case of earthquake preparedness (or, rather, lack of it), one way of remaining oblivious to dissonance is by steadfastly refusing to pay close attention to what we are doing. In the 1980s, nearly 17,000 Americans died in the AIDS epidemic, and hundreds of millions of dollars were spent on AIDS-prevention campaigns in the mass media. Although these campaigns were reasonably effective in conveying information about how the disease was transmitted and the importance of condoms for safe sex, they were not nearly as successful in preventing people from engaging in risky sexual behavior. Sexually active college men were aware that AIDS was a serious problem, but only a small percentage used condoms regularly. When asked to explain why, they offered the familiar reasons: Condoms were inconvenient, unromantic, and reminded them of disease. (People generally don't like to think of death when they are preparing to make love.) Thus, as researchers have consistently discovered, people will delude themselves—in this case, believing that, while AIDS is a serious problem, they themselves are not at risk.[67] If the mass media have been ineffective, is there anything that can be done to shake people out of their denial?

During the height of the AIDS epidemic, my students and I developed a method for convincing men to use condoms by using a variation of the "saying is believing" paradigm discussed earlier. In the typical "saying is believing" experiment, individuals are asked to make a speech advocating a point of view that runs counter to their own opinion. This arouses dissonance; dissonance is then reduced by changing their attitude to bring it more into line with their speech. I wondered how this paradigm could be applied to the AIDS epidemic.

As a researcher, here is the problem I faced: When it came to practicing safe sex, almost everybody knew what they *should* do but hardly anyone wanted to do it. So how do you get men to experience dissonance by making an argument favoring the use of condoms when they already believe that using condoms is a good idea? It's a dilemma. And then we hit upon a solution: Because men were insulating themselves from dissonance via the mechanism of denial, the experimenters would cut through this denial by confronting them with their own hypocrisy. This method was so successful that it came to be called the "hypocrisy paradigm." It rests on the fact that almost all of us are on a personal quest for integrity.

We began by asking college students to compose a speech describing the dangers of AIDS and advocating the use of condoms "every single time you have sex."[68] Every student was more than willing to do it, because every one of them believed it was a good idea for sexually active men to use condoms. (Well, other guys, anyway.) In one condition, the students merely composed the arguments. In another condition, after composing the arguments, the students were asked to record their argument on a videotape that would be played to an audience of high-school students as part of a sex-education class. Prior to making the speech, half of the students in each condition were made mindful of their own past failures to use condoms by making a list of the circumstances in their own lives when they found it particularly difficult, awkward, or "impossible" to use condoms.

Essentially, then, the participants who made a video for high-school students, after having been made mindful of their own reluctance to use condoms, were in a state of high dissonance. We had made them aware of their own hypocrisy in preaching behavior to high-school students that they themselves were not practicing. To avoid feeling like hypocrites and maintain their self-esteem, they would need to start practicing what they were preaching. And that is exactly what we found. Students in the hypocrisy condition were far more likely to purchase condoms (on display on a table outside the experimental room) than in any of the other conditions. Furthermore, several months later, a large proportion of the students in this condition reported that they were using condoms regularly.

The hypocrisy paradigm has been used to attack other problems as well, such as the problem of water conservation. Women in public shower rooms at the University of California were approached and asked to sign a petition and lend their name to the effort of persuading people to take short showers. After signing the petition, their name was pasted onto a sign that read: "TAKE SHORT SHOWERS. IF I CAN DO IT, SO CAN YOU!" After adding their name to the sign, some of the students were asked to think of all the times they had failed in the past month to take short showers, which highlighted the dissonance between their preaching and their practicing. Later these women were (unobtrusively) observed and timed in the shower room. Those who had been made mindful of their hypocrisy took significantly shorter showers. This kind of self-persuasion technique can be used whenever we would like to get people to do more of what they already agree is a good thing to do, such as exercising, studying, recycling, using sunscreen—you name it.[69]

Shedding Light on the Power of Cult Leaders Dissonance theory has shown itself to be useful as a way of increasing our understanding of events that totally confound our imagination—like the enormous power that cult leaders like Jim Jones (the massacre at Jonestown, Guyana) and Marshall Herff Applewhite (the group suicide of the Heaven's Gate cult) have had over the hearts and minds of their followers. Let us focus on the Jonestown massacre described in Chapter 1. How could a single individual have such power that, at his command, hundreds of people would kill their own children and themselves? The tragedy at Jonestown is too complex to be understood fully by a single explanation. But one clue does emanate from the foot-in-the-door phenomenon discussed earlier: Jim Jones extracted his followers' trust in him one step at a time. Indeed, close scrutiny reveals a chain of ever-increasing commitments on the part of his followers.

Let us start at the beginning. It is easy to understand how a charismatic leader like Jones might extract money from the members of his church. Once they have committed themselves to donating a small amount of money in response to his message of peace and universal brotherhood, they have stepped off the pyramid in his direction—and will feel the need to justify their decision to give him money. Therefore, he is able to request and receive more. Next, he induces people to sell their homes and turn over the money to the church. Soon, at his request, several of his followers pull up stakes, leaving their families and friends, and start life anew in the strange and difficult environment of Guyana. There, not only do they work hard (thus increasing their commitment by justifying all that effort, time, and money), but they also are cut off from potential dissenting opinion, inasmuch as they are surrounded by true believers. Then Jones begins to take sexual liberties with several married women among his followers, who acquiesce, if reluctantly. Finally, as a prelude to the climactic event, Jones induces his followers to perform a series of mock ritual suicides as a test of their loyalty and obedience. Thus, in a step-by-step fashion, the members' commitment to Jim Jones increases. Each step in itself is not a huge leap from the one preceding it, but the last step is a far cry from the first one.

Dissonance on the World Stage

Dissonance in our everyday lives is mostly benign, helping us get along with our decisions and choices with a minimum of misery or regrets. But, as the Jonestown story shows, it is impossible to overstate the potential dangers posed by our susceptibility to the need to reduce dissonance.

Suppose a madman has taken over your country and has decided to eradicate all members of your religious group. But you don't know that for sure. What you do know is that your country is being occupied, that the leader of the occupation forces does not like your religious group, and that occasionally members of your faith are forced to move from their homes and are kept in detention camps. What do you do? You could try to flee your country; you could try to pass as a member of a different religious group; or you could sit tight and hope for the best. Each of these options is extremely dangerous: It is difficult to escape or to pass and go undetected; and if you are caught trying to flee or disguising your identity, the penalty is immediate execution. Yet deciding to sit tight could be disastrous if it turns out that your religious group is being systematically annihilated. Let us suppose you commit yourself to sitting tight, turning your back on opportunities to try either to escape or to pass. Such a life-or-death decision naturally produces a great deal of dissonance. To reduce dissonance, you convince yourself that you made a wise decision, that although people of your religious sect are made to move and are being treated unfairly, they are not being killed unless they break the law. This position is not difficult to maintain because there is no unambiguous evidence to the contrary.

Suppose that, months later, a respected man from your town tells you that, while hiding in the forest, he witnessed soldiers butchering all the men, women, and children who had recently been deported from the town. I predict that you would try to dismiss this information as untrue; you would convince yourself that the reporter was lying or hallucinating. If you had listened to the man who tried to warn you, you might have escaped. Instead, you and your family are slaughtered.

Fantastic? Impossible? How could anyone not take the respected man seriously? Yet the events I just described are an accurate account of what happened in 1944 to the Jews in Sighet, Hungary.[70]

The processes of cognitive distortion and selective exposure to information have been crucial factors in the wars in Vietnam and Iraq (as well as in many other wars). In a thought-provoking analysis of the Pentagon Papers, a secret Department of Defense study of American political and military involvement in Vietnam that was eventually leaked to the public, Ralph White showed how dissonance blinded our leaders to information incompatible with the decisions they had already made. As White put it, "There was a tendency, when actions were out of line with ideas, for decision-makers to align their ideas with their actions." Lyndon Johnson's decision to continue to escalate the bombing of North Vietnam was made at the price of ignoring crucial evidence from the CIA and other sources that bombing would not break the will of the North Vietnamese people but, quite the contrary, would only strengthen their resolve. White wrote:

> It is instructive, for instance, to compare [Secretary of Defense Robert] McNamara's highly factual evidence-oriented summary of the case against bombing in 1966 ... with the Joint Chiefs' memorandum that disputed his conclusion and called the bombing one of our two trump cards, while it apparently ignored all

of the facts that showed the opposite. Yet it was the Joint Chiefs who prevailed.[71]

Presidents of both political parties have overlooked evidence they didn't want to accept. Lyndon Johnson did so in the Vietnam War; George W. Bush did so in the Iraq war. In 2003, Bush wanted to believe that Iraqi leader Saddam Hussein possessed weapons of mass destruction (WMDs) that posed a threat to Americans. This led him and his advisors to interpret the information in CIA reports as definitive proof of Iraq's WMDs, even though the reports were ambiguous and contradicted by other evidence. President Bush's interpretation provided the justification to launch a preemptive war. He was convinced that once our troops entered Iraq they would find these weapons.[72]

After the invasion of Iraq, when asked "Where are the WMDs?" administration officials said that Iraq is a big country in which the WMDs were well hidden, but asserted that the weapons would be found. As the months dragged on and still no WMDs were found, the officials continued to assert that they would be uncovered. Why? Because the administration officials were experiencing enormous dissonance. They had to believe they would find the WMDs to justify the decision to start a war; otherwise, Iraq had posed no immediate threat to the United States. Finally, officials concluded that there were no such weapons. Even George Bush finally admitted it in his memoir.[73]

Now what? American soldiers and Iraqi civilians were dying every week, and hundreds of billions of dollars were being drained from the U.S. Treasury. How did President Bush and his staff reduce dissonance? They did so by adding new cognitions to *justify* the war. Suddenly, we learned that the U.S. mission was to liberate the nation from a cruel dictator and bestow upon the Iraqi people the blessings of democratic institutions. To a neutral observer, that justification was inadequate (after all, there are a great many brutal dictators in the world). But to Bush and his advisors, who had been experiencing dissonance, the justification seemed reasonable, indeed essential.

Many of Bush's critics believed that he was deliberately trying to deceive the American people. We cannot be certain what was going on in the president's mind, but what we do know, based on more than 50 years of research on cognitive dissonance, is that he and his advisors succeeded in deceiving themselves. They convinced themselves that invading Iraq was worthwhile even in the absence of WMDs.[74]

How can a leader avoid falling into the self-justification trap? Historical examples show us that the way out of this process is for a leader to bring in skilled advisors from outside his or her inner circle, because the advisors will not be caught up in the need to reduce the dissonance created by the leader's earlier decisions. As the historian Doris Kearns Goodwin[75] pointed out, it was precisely for this reason that Abraham Lincoln chose a cabinet that included several people who disagreed with his policies about how best to end slavery.

Let's return to the Vietnam War for a moment. Why did the Joint Chiefs make the ill-advised decision to increase the bombing, escalating a war that was unwinnable? They were staying the course, justifying earlier actions with identical or even more extreme ones. Escalation of this sort is self-perpetuating. From Jonestown to war, once a small commitment is made, the stage is set for ever-increasing commitments. The behavior needs to be justified, so attitudes are changed; this change in attitudes influences future decisions and behavior. It's the large-scale version of the foot-in-the-door technique, but at a life-and-death level of importance. Once a European Jew had decided not to pass and allowed himself to be identified as a Jew, the decision was irrevocable; he could not easily pretend to be a Gentile. Once Pentagon officials intensified the bombing of North Vietnam, they could not undo it. The flavor of this kind of cognitive escalation is nicely captured in an analysis of the Pentagon Papers by the editors of *Time* magazine:

> Yet the bureaucracy, the Pentagon Papers indicate, always demanded new options; each option was to apply more force. Each tightening of the screw created a position that must be defended; once committed, the military pressure must be maintained.[76]

Living with the Rationalizer Within

Why is it so hard to apologize when we make a big mistake or hurt a friend—and mean it? Dissonance theory provides the answer: because we don't really mean it. We are so busy justifying our actions that we privately feel we did nothing wrong at all: "The other person started this." "The other person insulted me." "The other person made me cheat." "Yeah, what I did wasn't so great, but the *other* guy's behavior was way worse." That's why, when people are forced to apologize, what they say usually rings hollow: "If I offended anyone ..." Of course you did! That's why we want you to apologize! Only by stepping back and recognizing how prone we are to rationalizing and justifying ourselves can we take the first step to being able to apologize and really mean it—and thereby maintain healthy relationships.

Near the beginning of this chapter, I made the point that people are capable of rational, adaptive behavior, as well as dissonance-reducing behavior. Let's return to that issue. If individuals concentrate their time and effort on protecting their egos, they will never grow. To grow, we must learn from our mistakes. But if we are intent on reducing dissonance, we will not admit to our mistakes. Instead, we will sweep them under the rug or, worse still, turn them into virtues. The memoirs of presidents are full of the kind of self-serving, self-justifying statements that are best summarized in the words of former President Lyndon Johnson, who escalated the war in Vietnam with disastrous consequences for both countries: "If I had it all to do over again, I would not change a thing."[77]

On the other hand, people do frequently grow and learn from their mistakes. How? Under what conditions? Ideally, when I make a mistake, I should look at what I did in a nondefensive manner and, in effect, say to myself, "Okay, I blew it. What can I learn from the experience so that I will not end up in this position again?" I can increase the probability of being able to do this in the following ways:

- Through a greater understanding of my own defensiveness and dissonance-reducing tendencies.

- Through the realization that doing something foolish, immoral, or hurtful does not necessarily mean that I am an irrevocably foolish, immoral, or cruel person; cheating on one occasion doesn't inevitably make me a "cheater," unless I keep justifying what I did.

- Through the development of enough ego strength to acknowledge and learn from errors in myself.

Of course, it is far easier to list these procedures than it is to accomplish them. How do we get in touch with our defensiveness and dissonance-reducing tendencies? How can we come to realize that good people like ourselves can occasionally do something at work or in love that is misguided or immoral? It is not enough to understand dissonance abstractly or superficially; to fully use this knowledge, a person must consciously practice it. We will take a closer look at this process in Chapter 8, where we will examine the advantage of authenticity and nondefensive communication in our relationships.

Saul Steinberg, *Untitled drawing*, ink on paper.
Originally published in *The New Yorker*, April 24, 1965.
© The Saul Steinberg Foundation / Artists Rights Society (ARS), New York

4

Conformity

Suddenly somebody began to run. It may be that he had simply remembered, all of a moment, an engagement to meet his wife, for which he was now frightfully late. Whatever it was, he ran east on Broad Street (probably toward the Maramor Restaurant, a favorite place for a man to meet his wife). Somebody else began to run, perhaps a newsboy in high spirits. Another man, a portly gentleman of affairs, broke into a trot. Inside of 10 minutes, everybody on High Street, from the Union Depot to the Courthouse, was running. A loud mumble gradually crystallized into the dread word "dam." "The dam has broke!" The fear was put into words by a little old lady in an electric car, or by a traffic cop, or by a small boy; nobody knows who, nor does it now really matter. Two thousand people were abruptly in full flight. "Go east!" was the cry that arose east, away from the river, east to safety. "Go east! Go east!" A tall spare woman with grim eyes and a determined chin ran past me down the middle of the street. I was still uncertain as to what was the matter, in spite of all the shouting. I drew up alongside the woman with some effort, for although she was in her late fifties, she had a beautiful, easy running form and seemed to be in excellent condition. "What is it?" I puffed. She gave a quick glance and then looked ahead again, stepping up her pace a trifle. "Don't ask me; ask God!" she said.[1]

Although comical, this story from the great humorist James Thurber's autobiography is an apt illustration of people conforming. One or two individuals begin running for their own reasons; before long, everyone is running. Why? Because others are running. In Thurber's story, when the runners realized that the dam hadn't broken after all, they felt pretty foolish. And yet how much more foolish would they have felt if they hadn't conformed and the dam had actually burst?

Is conformity good or bad? In its simplest sense, this is an absurd question. Still, words carry evaluative meaning. Thus, in American culture to be called an individualist or a nonconformist evokes an image of a lone cowboy standing on a mountaintop with a rifle slung over his shoulder, the breeze blowing through his hair as the sun sets in the background. To call someone in this culture a conformist is an insult; the term evokes an image of a person who mindlessly follows others: business executives in formal suits; teenagers adopting the dress, talk, and mannerisms of their friends; people coming to believe some doomsday prediction or conspiracy theory because "everyone they know" does. Everyone can summon an image of a conformist, and it is rarely a flattering one.

One consequence of the fact that we are social animals is that we live in a state of tension between values associated with individuality and values associated with conformity. We have synonyms for these words that bring to mind very different images. For individualist or nonconformist we can substitute the word *deviant*; for conformist we can say *team player*. Somehow, deviant no longer evokes the lone cowboy; likewise, team player doesn't suggest the conforming white-collar worker, teenager, or conspiracy theorist. Our culture is likewise ambivalent about conformity (team playing) and nonconformity (deviance). For example, one of the bestsellers of the 1950s was a book by (then-future President) John F. Kennedy, called *Profiles in Courage*, in which he praised several politicians for their courage in resisting political pressure to conform. To put it another way, Kennedy was praising deviant and bad team players who lacked the ability to harmonize with their parties or constituents. These nonconformists earned Kennedy's praise, but at the time of their actions, their colleagues were generally far from pleased—indeed, most were angry at what they saw as "betrayal" and failing to follow party line. Nonconformists make for interesting stories precisely because they are frequently treated so badly by the people around them. As much as we may admire them in history or in movies, in our daily transactions we tend to prefer the conformist.

This observation receives strong support from a number of classic experiments in social psychology. In one by Stanley Schachter,[2] groups of male students met to discuss the case history and decide the fate of a teenager who had been arrested for breaking the law. After reading the case, each group was asked to discuss it and to come to an agreement regarding the young man's punishment on a scale ranging from "very lenient treatment" to "very harsh treatment." A typical group consisted of nine participants, six of whom were genuine and three of whom were paid confederates of the experimenter. The confederates took turns playing one of three roles that they had carefully rehearsed in advance: the *modal* person, who took a position that conformed to the average position of the real participants; the *deviant*, who took a position diametrically opposed to the general orientation of the group; and the *slider*, whose initial position was similar to the deviant's but who, in the course of the discussion, gradually "slid" into a modal, conforming position.

Which participant do you think was most liked? The rebel? Not at all. It was the man who conformed most to the group norm; the deviant was liked least. Moreover, patterns of communication changed predictably: Early on in the discussion, the group spent considerable time trying to talk the deviant into accepting their point of view. But when it became clear the deviant wouldn't budge, the others largely ignored him, essentially cutting him out of the group discussion. In a follow-up experiment, Arie Kruglanski and Donna Webster[3] found that nonconformists are especially disliked if they voice their dissent near a deadline, when groups are feeling the pinch to come to closure, than if they voice dissent earlier in the discussion.

Thus, the data indicate that at least in decision-making groups, we tend to like conformists better than nonconformists. This preference is not irrational. The inclination to harmonize with others by sacrificing personal wishes conferred a tremendous evolutionary advantage for our species; our ability to work in teams and transmit culture allowed humans to thrive. We can laugh at Thurber's mob running from a flood that wasn't, but we should also marvel at the mechanism at work: Like a flock of birds in the park, startling a single bird will spread quickly and the entire flock flies away. That conformist reflex was undoubtedly crucial in our hunter-gatherer past; indeed, nonconformity can be disastrous. Suppose I suddenly decide I am fed up with being a conformist. So I hop in my car and start driving down the left-hand side of the road—not a terribly smart or adaptive way of expressing my rugged individualism and not very fair to you if you happen to be driving toward me (conformist-style) on the same street.

Yet as adaptive as our conformist nature can be, history is marked by events in which the tendency to do as others do leads to tragedy, from post-game riots at soccer matches to Adolf Hitler's throngs of fanatics shouting "*Sieg heil*" in unison. But conformity occurs not only in mindless crowds but also among close-knit groups, whose members ought to know better. In his memoirs, Albert Speer, one of Hitler's top advisers, described the circle around Hitler as one of total conformity—deviation was not permitted. In such an atmosphere, even the most barbarous activities seemed reasonable because the absence of dissent, which conveyed the illusion of unanimity, prevented any one adviser from entertaining the possibility that other options might exist. Speer wrote:

> In normal circumstances, people who turn their backs on reality are soon set straight by the mockery and criticism of those around them. In the Third Reich there were not such correctives. On the contrary, every self-deception was multiplied as in a hall of distorting mirrors, becoming a repeatedly confirmed picture of a fantastical dream world, which no longer bore any relationship to the grim outside world. In those mirrors I could see nothing but my own face reproduced many times over.[4]

Closer to home, consider the White House staffers and top-level advisers involved with former president Richard Nixon in the Watergate cover-up. Here, men in high government office—many of whom were attorneys—perjured themselves, destroyed evidence, and offered bribes without an apparent second thought. This was due, at least in part, to the closed circle of single-mindedness that surrounded the president in the early 1970s. This single-mindedness made deviation virtually unthinkable until the circle had been broken. Once it was, several high-ranking advisers seemed to view their illegal behavior with astonishment, as if it were performed during some sort of bad dream. Nixon's White House lawyer, John Dean, put it this way:

> When you picked up the newspaper in the morning and read the new cover story that had replaced yesterday's cover story, you began to believe that today's news was the truth. This process created an

atmosphere of unreality in the White House that prevailed to the very end. If you said it often enough, it would become true. When the press learned of the wiretaps on newsmen and White House staffers, for example, and flat denials failed, it was claimed that this was a national security matter. I'm sure many people believed that the taps were for national security; they weren't. That was concocted as a justification after the fact. But when they said it, you understand, they really believed it.[5]

Sometimes the need to conform will even silence an individual's certain knowledge of a forthcoming disaster. On January 28, 1986, the space shuttle *Challenger* exploded a few seconds after lifting off. Seven astronauts, including a much beloved schoolteacher named Christa McAuliffe (who had won a contest to become the first civilian in space), perished in a fireball of smoke and flames. Somehow the decision had been made to go ahead with the launch despite strenuous objections and warnings from engineers about defective O-rings at the joints of the booster rockets. The administrators at the National Aeronautics and Space Administration (NASA), who made the ultimate decision to launch, were neither ignorant of the danger nor cavalier about the lives of the astronauts. Nor were the makers of the defective booster rockets. Yet, amid the pressures for NASA to go forward with the highly anticipated launch, decision-makers with dissenting opinions—which turned out to be correct—were either converted to the majority position or were excluded from the conversation altogether, much like the deviants in Stanley Schachter's experiment.

Let's take stock. What do Hitler's inner circle, Nixon's close advisers, and NASA administrators have in common, aside from the fact that they made terrible decisions? Each was a relatively cohesive group isolated from dissenting points of view. When such groups are called upon to make decisions, they can fall prey to what Irving Janis called **groupthink**,[6] a way of thinking that occurs in cohesive groups in which the members' need for agreement overrides their ability to realistically assess a course of action and its alternatives. Groups engaging in this maladaptive decision-making strategy typically perceive themselves as invulnerable; they're blinded by optimism. And this optimism grows when dissent is discouraged. In the face of conformity pressures, group members may come to doubt their own reservations and refrain from voicing them, much like our hypothetical friend Sam from Chapter 1, who concealed his true opinions after learning that his debate-watching companions unanimously disagreed with him.

By citing these examples, I do not mean to suggest that individuals who make bad decisions should be let off the hook because conformity comes naturally to humans. Rather, I am arguing that it is vital to appreciate the power and the psychological workings of conformity, so that we might reduce it when it is maladaptive—when the crowd is wrong. It is only through digging deeper and trying to understand these processes that we can have any hope of improving the way people make decisions and reducing the frequency of future calamities.

What Is Conformity?

Conformity can be defined as a change in a person's behavior or opinions as a result of real or imagined pressure from another person or group of people. As evolutionary theory would predict, it begins early—in infancy—and has neurological underpinnings.

The Biology of Conformity You can appreciate how fundamental conformity is to our species by looking at how early in life we start to copy one another. Although we are not born mimics,[7] babies learn early through social interaction to respond in kind to the faces in front of them,[8] and, indeed, will often pay more attention to a face that mirrors their own facial expressions than to one that does not.[9]

When people talk to each other, they often mirror one another's nonverbal behaviors and mannerisms, a phenomenon called the *chameleon effect.* Tanya Chartrand and John Bargh[10] had students discuss a set of photographs with a confederate who, at regular points during the interaction, either touched his face or shook his foot. Students paired with the face-touching partner touched their own faces significantly more often during the interaction; those paired with the foot-shaking partner were more likely to shake their own foot. In another session, the confederates either subtly mirrored the posture and mannerisms of the study participant—for example, by crossing their legs, touching their faces, or fiddling with their hair—or they did not. After this interaction, participants rated their partners, liking the chameleons more than the non-chameleons. This finding suggests that we mimic others because doing so both reflects and engenders feelings of closeness, creating a sort of "social glue."[11] People who are especially skilled at changing their perspective, seeing the world through other people's eyes, are better chameleons—and thus better liked.[12] But mimicry has to be done naturally; intentional efforts to mimic other people in order to win favor can backfire.[13] It did for Hillary Clinton, who was criticized for adopting a Southern drawl (and saying "Y'all") when she campaigned in the South.[14]

Although many animals imitate others of their kind, humans are exceptionally prone to it. Some neuroscientists attribute this fact to *mirror neurons*, highly specialized brain cells that are activated both when we perform an action and when we witness another person performing the same action. Think of how you cringe when you see a comedian bombing on stage, or wince when witnessing another's pain. Mirror neurons enable empathy but certainly do not guarantee it: They turn off when people are looking at individuals they dislike or who have less power and status than they do.[15]

One of the major functions of the mirror system is that it facilitates **social learning**, the process by which we learn by observing. Experiments led by Daniel Haun[16] found that toddlers will copy the behaviors of their peers, even if it means ignoring prior learning and losing a reward. Toddlers in one study were given a ball and puzzle box with three ball-sized holes in it, and they learned quickly that putting the ball in a specific hole (e.g., the middle one) earned them a piece of chocolate. After this learning phase, each child joined a group of other toddlers who had learned to get their chocolate by dropping their ball into a different hole (e.g., the left one). During this second phase, the toddlers continued getting chocolate for putting the ball into the same hole as before, but many tended to conform to their peers instead, abandoning their learning—and the chocolate—in favor of conforming to the children who had learned a slightly different rule. When the same experiment was conducted with chimps and orangutans, also highly social animals, they did not show these conformist tendencies; they stuck with the behavior that maximized their own rewards. Once again we see how, in humans, the impulse to conform can trump a personal preference—even for chocolate.

Subtle Influences on Conformity Most acts of conformity occur without any sense that "pressure" is being applied. For example, laugh tracks on television comedies are so ubiquitous that we scarcely notice them, yet the information they convey—that other people find something funny—profoundly influences our own response to that same something.

In 1984, in a famous episode in American politics, the 73-year-old president, Ronald Reagan, was facing difficulties in his bid for reelection. Already the oldest president in American history, there was widespread concern that Reagan was too old for the demands of the job. His much younger opponent, Walter Mondale, had been vice president and a popular senator; he had experience, as well as youth and vigor. Yet Reagan defeated Mondale in a landslide. How did Reagan reassure voters and win so decisively? Partly, with humor—notably, a zinger he delivered during their second debate, when asked if he might not be too old to be president: "I will not make age an issue in this campaign," Reagan said. "I'm not going to exploit, for political purposes, my opponent's youth and inexperience." The audience, including Mondale, laughed and applauded at Reagan's ironic wit, and many voters changed their mind about Reagan at that moment, apparently reassured by this and other rehearsed jokes that he was still mentally fit to serve.

Many years later, in a clever experiment, Steven Fein and his colleagues[17] played tapes of the famous debate to college students who had never heard of it or seen it before. (They were babies at the time it aired.) In a baseline condition, they presented the debate just as people saw it in 1984. In a second condition, he removed two of Reagan's most humorous lines, including the age-and-inexperience joke. In the third condition, he left the funny lines in but removed the audience laughter and applause. After watching, participants rated their liking for both candidates and assessed who had done a better job in the debate. Both changes to the original tape made a difference: Eliminating Reagan's jokes altogether was enough to completely erase the perception that Reagan won the debate. But it wasn't the jokes by themselves that were crucial. When observers heard Reagan's jokes without the audience reaction, most of them thought Mondale won; with the laughter included, they thought Reagan won! No direct pressure was needed, just other people laughing. A good deal of conformity proceeds this way; social cues in the environment tell us what others are feeling or thinking or doing, which in turn influences what we feel and think and do.

Let's return to our friend Sam, the hypothetical college student. Recall that Sam was watching a senatorial candidate on television and was favorably impressed by her sincerity. However, the unanimous opinion of his friends that the candidate was insincere put a lot of social pressure on him, and he acceded—verbally, at least—to their opinion.

Even this little story raises interesting questions: (1) What causes people to conform to group pressure? Specifically, what's in it for Sam? (2) What was the nature of the group pressure? Specifically, what were Sam's acquaintances doing to induce conformity? (3) Did Sam revise his opinion of the candidate during that brief but unsettling period when he learned that all his fellow students disagreed with him? Or did Sam hang on to his original opinion and only modify what he said about the candidate? If he changed his opinion, was it permanent or just for that evening?

Unfortunately, because Sam is a hypothetical character we are unable to ask him. Moreover, it's doubtful that even a flesh-and-blood Sam could give us an accurate accounting, because not only are humans limited in their ability to explain their own behavior with much accuracy,[18] there are simply too many factors in this situation. We don't know how confident Sam was in his initial opinion; we don't know how well he knew or how much he liked the people with whom he watched the candidate's speech; we don't know whether Sam considers himself to be a good judge of sincerity or whether he considers the others to be good judges of sincerity; we don't know whether Sam is generally a strong person or a wishy-washy person; nor do we know how much willpower Sam has left after a day of studying—and so on.

What we can do is conduct experiments in which people face dilemmas like Sam's and where we have the ability to control and vary the factors we think might influence conformity. A great many studies in social psychology have done this, beginning with early research by Muzafer Sherif and Solomon Asch.

Sherif's and Asch's Classic Experiments If you are in a dark room and you stare at a fixed point of light from a distance, after a while the light will appear to move, a visual illusion called the *autokinetic effect*. Muzafer Sherif[19] harnessed this illusion to study how perceptions are socially influenced. He had college students sit in a dark room, watch a point of light, and then, each time it "moved," report how far. Each student did this alone for several trials, and after several trials, settled on a reliable distance, usually between two to six inches. Then they were put in the dark room in small groups and asked to repeat the task, this time reporting their estimates out loud. Sherif noticed a strong effect of the presence of others: Nearly everyone's own judgments started to move in the direction of the group average. For example, if I typically saw the light move two inches when I was on my own, but my groupmates tended to see it move six inches, I would now start reporting around four inches of movement. Likewise, those who originally saw more movement would report seeing less after hearing my opinion. What's more, the change stuck. After being exposed to a group's opinions, members were tested again, and their answers continued to reflect the group's influence on their own judgments. Sherif later found that he could reliably shape the group norm by having his confederates give arbitrary estimates. So long as the deviation from the actual norm wasn't too large, he could steer the group in whichever direction he wanted.

Estimating how much a point of light is moving has a built-in ambiguity. Some years later, Solomon Asch wanted to see what would happen when the object of judgment was unambiguous.[20] What if you were judging not an optical illusion but an obvious fact right in front of your eyes? Asch predicted that conformity would plummet.

Put yourself in the following situation: You have volunteered to participate in an experiment on perceptual judgment. You enter a room with six other participants. The experimenter shows all of you a straight line (line X) next to three other lines for comparison (lines A, B, and C). Your job is to judge which of the three lines is closest in length to line X. The judgment strikes you as being ridiculously easy.

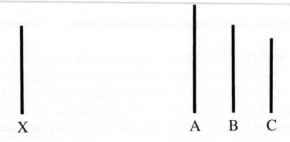

X   A   B   C

It is perfectly apparent to you that line B is the correct answer, and when your turn comes, you will say that B is the one. But it's not your turn. You are second to last. The young man whose turn it is looks carefully at the lines and says, "Line A." Your mouth drops open and you look at him quizzically. "How can he believe it's A when any fool can see that it's B?" you ask yourself. "He must be either blind or crazy." Now it's the second person's turn to respond. He also chooses line A. You begin to feel like Alice in Wonderland. "How can it be?" you ask yourself. "Are *both* of these people blind or crazy?" But then the next person responds, and he also says, "Line A." You take another look at those lines. "Maybe I'm the only one who's crazy," you mutter inaudibly. Now it's the fifth person's turn, and he also judges the correct line to be A. Finally, it's your turn. "Why, it's line A, of course," you declare. "I knew it all the time."

This is the conflict that Asch created in his experiment. As you might have guessed, the individuals who preceded you were in his employ and had been instructed to agree on an incorrect answer. The perceptual judgment itself was incredibly easy; when people were asked to judge the lines when they were alone, they made almost no errors. Indeed, the task was so easy, and the correct line was so obvious, that Asch himself firmly believed that there would be little, if any, yielding to group pressure. But his prediction was wrong. When faced with the fact of all of their fellow students agreeing on the same incorrect responses in a series of 12 judgments, approximately three-quarters of the participants conformed at least once by responding incorrectly. Over the entire spectrum of judgments, an average of 35 percent conformed to the incorrect judgments.

Asch performed his experiments in the middle of the twentieth century. Although the results were powerful, it is tempting to dismiss his findings on the grounds that American college students are different now. With the advent of computers and the internet you might think we have grown more sophisticated and therefore much less susceptible to this kind of group pressure—not so. Over the years, the Asch experiment has been successfully replicated many times. In an especially striking demonstration on national television (*Dateline*, in fact), Anthony Pratkanis[21] repeated the experiment precisely as Asch had run it 50 years earlier. The participants in this *replication* were also college students, many of whom considered themselves nonconformists. The results were almost identical to Asch's.

However, there are some cultural differences in the tendency to go against the group. One is nicely illustrated by this contrast in folk wisdom: In America, people say, "The squeaky wheel gets the grease" (meaning, "Speak up! Be heard!"); in Japan they say, "The nail that sticks up gets pounded down" (meaning, "Don't deviate from your group"). In their analysis of 133 experiments using the Asch procedure in 17 different countries, Rod Bond and Peter Smith[22] found that conformity is more prevalent in collectivist societies, which explicitly value group harmony (like Japan and China), than in individualistic societies (like the United States and France).

Nevertheless, for human beings anywhere, resisting group pressure is very difficult, and the pain of nonconformity shows up not only on their faces but also in their neurological activity. Gregory Berns and his associates[23] replicated Asch's procedures while monitoring participants' neural activity with functional magnetic resonance imaging (fMRI). These scans indicated a major difference between participants who resisted group pressure and those who yielded. Those who resisted showed heightened activity in the amygdala, a region of the brain associated with pain, fear, and emotional discomfort, showing that going against the group induces neural signals of physical pain,[24] just as we saw that social rejection does.[25]

The situation created by these experiments is especially intriguing because, unlike many situations in which we tend to conform, there were no explicit constraints against individuality. More often, the sanctions against nonconformity are unequivocal. For example, I have always hated to wear ties, and the world has finally caught up with me—nowadays ties are rarely required. But in the 1960s, when I was a young professor, dress codes were more formal. This meant that if I went out for an evening's celebration at a fancy restaurant, the maître d' would politely (but firmly) inform me that if I didn't put on the tie they offered, then no table. So I could put on the tie and eat in the restaurant or I could leave, open-necked and comfortable but hungry. In this case as in many others, the negative consequences of nonconformity are made explicit. Likewise, Janis found in his studies of groupthink that one or two people typically step forward to enforce the norms of the group. These self-appointed *mindguards*, as Janis called them, encourage conformity and consensus. Much like the maître d' in the restaurant, mindguards make it clear that if you want to be included, you'll need to comply with the norms of the group.

But in Asch's experiment and in the case of Sam and his friends, the situations were much more subtle. In these situations, there were no explicit rewards for conformity, no explicit punishments for deviance, and no mindguards prodding deviants toward agreement, just people reporting what they saw in a matter-of-fact way. Why, then, did Asch's participants conform?

Motives for Conformity: Belonging Versus Getting Information There are two primary reasons for conformity: because other people are sources of valuable information; or because being too different from others is uncomfortable, and conformity secures our place within a group by signaling our similarity and ideological kinship. The former reason is *informative*: People become convinced in the face of the unanimous majority that their own opinions are wrong for some reason. The other is *normative*: People "go along with the crowd," while inwardly believing their initial judgments are correct, in order to be accepted by the majority or to avoid being disliked by them for disagreeing. The behavior of the individuals in Asch's experiment, and in others where judgments are straight-forward, seemed to be largely a matter of going along to avoid the sense of exclusion. We can infer this from the fact that everyone gave their honest opinion about the line match when they were allowed to respond privately.

At the same time, in many situations we conform to the behavior of others because as physical reality becomes increasingly uncertain, people rely more and more on "social reality."[26] That is, other people's behavior is the best available guide to understanding what's going on. In such cases, conformity is especially likely to result in shaping our opinions and perception of reality, as with students in Sherif's experiments and in the scene recalled by Thurber at the beginning of this chapter. If other people are doing it, it must be the right thing to do.

An example should clarify this distinction between normative and informative conformity. Years ago, I was in an unfamiliar building when I needed to use the toilet. Following the sign for "Restrooms," I found the usual two doors, but someone had removed the specific designations, so I could not distinguish the men's room from the women's. Quite a dilemma—I didn't dare guess for fear of entering the women's bathroom and being embarrassed, or embarrassing (or frightening) any woman who was in there. As I stood waiting in discomfort, hopping from one foot to the other, the door on my left opened and out strolled a guy. With a sigh of relief, I went in, conforming because I had the right information.

Much of the time, other people are an excellent source of information, and conforming satisfies our needs for both accuracy and belonging. Phoning your mother on Mother's Day, going with your friends to work at a homeless shelter at Thanksgiving, and studying hard to do well on an exam are all things that people do and that are right to do. Sometimes, however, we are like the students in Asch's experiment; our need to be right is in conflict with our need to belong. If you were a participant in that experiment and you initially believed that the correct answer was line B, then saying so might satisfy your desire to be correct—but it might also violate the expectations of your peers, and they might think you odd. Choosing line A might win you the acceptance of the others, but unless you became convinced that they were correct, it would violate your desire to be right.

This fundamental predicament—between being right or trying to please the group—lies at the heart of some of our greatest failings. Every year in Joshua's social psychology class, students write anonymously about their most regrettable acts of conformity, acts they would undo if they could travel back in time. Year after year, a striking number of students confess to having bullied, teased, or humiliated another person, for no reason other than the implied or actual approval of their peers. "I knew I was destroying this kid," one student wrote, describing having mercilessly teased a "funny-looking boy" one night at summer camp. "I could hear him trying not to cry. He was lying a couple of bunks away from me, in the dark, pleading for us to stop calling him the name we'd given him: *monk*, short for monkey. But I just kept going, egged on by the laughter. I can still hear it—them giggling while I ruined this poor kid's life … I've never forgiven myself for that." Another student regretted refusing to speak to his mother for a month in the eighth grade after she'd tried to save money by getting a less expensive shirt without the Abercrombie logo prized by eighth graders at the time. "I can't believe how much I *hated* my mom for that," he wrote. "The absence of a little moose on my shirt, and I wanted to *kill* her." Another student regretted witnessing a murder and never telling the police. "In my neighborhood we just didn't talk to the police," he said. "That was the norm."

Despite what social psychology students say when prompted to recall past acts of conformity, most of us believe that *we* are motivated primarily by a desire to be correct whereas *others* are motivated primarily by a desire to please the group. When people unobtrusively observe an Asch-like conformity experiment, they typically underestimate how much they would conform and overestimate how often others will.[27]

As we have seen, sometimes conformity is induced by fear of violating norms, other times by information that clarifies ambiguity. But it is not always easy to distinguish between them. Often the conforming behavior is identical; the key element that differentiates them is the presence or absence of a punitive agent. Imagine that, in the mythical nation of Freedonia, it is considered gracious for guests to belch after eating, as a way of showing the host that they enjoyed the meal. Suppose you didn't know this, and you were visiting the home of a Freedonian dignitary in the company of some diplomats from the U.S. State Department. If, after the meal, these diplomats began to belch, chances are you would belch, also. They are providing you with valuable information: Conform to belching to do the right thing. But suppose you were in the same home in the company of some rude and brawny young men who were introduced to you as members of the Freedonian Olympic heavyweight wrestling team. If these behemoths belched after their meal, you might not go along; you would probably consider this an act of bad manners. However, if they glared at you for your failure to follow suit, you might indeed belch, too — not because of the information they supplied but because you feared rejection or even a broken nose for refusing to be a good sport by going along with their boorish behavior.

Conformity resulting from the observation of others for the purpose of gaining information about proper behavior tends to have more powerful ramifications than conformity in the interest of being accepted or of avoiding punishment. I would argue that, if we find ourselves in an ambiguous situation where we must use the behavior of other people as a template for our own behavior, we are likely to repeat our newly learned behavior, without a cue, on subsequent similar occasions. This would be the case unless, of course, we later received evidence that our actions had been inappropriate or incorrect. Thus, now suppose you are invited back to the home of the Freedonian dignitary for dinner, but this time you are the only guest. The question is, do you or don't you belch after the meal? If you had belched after the first meal at his home because you realized it was the proper thing to do (as would have been the case had you dined in the company of the diplomats), you would be quite likely to belch when dining alone with the dignitary. However, if you had belched the first time out of fear of rejection or punishment (as would have been the case had you dined in the company of the wrestlers), you would almost certainly not belch when you are the lone guest.

Factors That Increase or Decrease Conformity

What about Sam? Was he convinced by his fellow college students that his preferred senatorial candidate was a phony, or did he simply go along with their judgment in order to be accepted? To answer such questions, it's helpful to consider the factors that influence conformity and that can also be used to prevent groupthink.

The Prestige and Prevalence of Models When we are unclear about what is going on in a situation, we are particularly likely to conform to people whose behavior provides the most reliable information. Say you live in a town where jaywalking is rare and frowned upon, but you really want to save a few seconds by crossing in the middle of a busy road. Field experiments show that you are more likely to do it if you follow a jaywalker who is well dressed rather than poorly dressed.[28]

On a broader level, popular writer Malcolm Gladwell[29] suggests that major social trends often change dramatically and suddenly through the mechanism of conformity when respected and well-connected people happen to be in the right place at the right time. When a video goes viral, a trend becomes "epidemic," or a brand of shoes all of a sudden becomes the must-have item of apparel, it is often because of one or two individuals who are connected to vast social networks (e.g., thousands of Instagram or Twitter followers). They begin wearing the cool new thing, which leads others to crave the cool new thing, and soon a critical mass or "tipping point" is reached and the trend explodes. Influential people needn't be experts; they are simply people who seem to be in the know, or who, like the Kardashians, are famous for being famous. Nowadays, of course, the big connectors are people whose tweets or social media posts reach massive audiences, many of whom may retweet or repost them through their networks, who in turn retweet them through theirs.

When large numbers of people are doing something, it is especially informative. Where should I eat? Log on to Yelp to see what the crowd thinks. What should I read? See what's trending on Amazon. Which food truck is the best? I'll bet on the one with the longest line of customers. So long as the crowd's judgments are independent from one another—as with the collection of strangers who submit reviews to Yelp—the crowd can provide a far better estimate of what is true and good than our own private guesses.[30]

Unanimity In face-to-face group situations, like the one investigated by Asch, one of the crucial factors that determines whether a person will conform is whether everyone else shares an opinion. The actual number of people in that "everyone else" group need not be very high to elicit maximum conformity; people will conform to group pressure about as often when the unanimous group consists of only 3 other people as when it consists of 16. But when unanimity is broken, so is the pressure to conform. Even a single ally who sees it your way releases you from that pressure; conformity drops sharply in such cases.[31] In fact, even if the unanimity is broken by someone who gives a different *wrong* answer (answering that the correct line is C while the rest of the group responds with A), the presence of a fellow dissenter sharply reduces conformity, and the participant is likely to give the correct response: line B. It only takes one dissenter to seriously diminish the power of the group to induce conformity.[32]

Commitment Conformity to group pressure can also be decreased by inducing a person to make some sort of commitment to his or her initial judgment. Picture yourself as an umpire at a major-league baseball game. There is a close play at first base and you call the runner out—in the presence of 50,000 fans. After the game, the three other umpires approach you, and each says that he thought the runner was safe. How likely are you to alter your judgment? Compare this with a situation in which each of the three umpires calls the runner safe and then it is your turn to make a judgment. Such a comparison was made in an experiment by Morton Deutsch and Harold Gerard,[33] using the Asch paradigm. They found that when participants had made no prior commitment to a line choice, some 25 percent of the responses conformed to the erroneous judgment of the majority. But when the individuals had publicly committed themselves before hearing the judgment of the other "umpires," fewer than 6 percent of their new responses were conformist.

Accountability Suppose you're in a group problem-solving discussion and others are pressuring you to agree with their decision. In addition, suppose that you knew that, at the end of the meeting, you would need to justify your decision to the other members of the group. What effect do you think that might have on your thinking? Research has shown that under most conditions, this kind of accountability would increase your tendency to conform.[34]

But what happens if you were also given instructions stressing the importance of being as accurate as possible? To answer that question, Andrew Quinn and Barry Schlenker[35] put people through a procedure aimed at producing conformity to a poor decision. Before the conformity aspect of the experiment began, the experimenters did two things: (1) they got half of their participants thinking about the importance of being as accurate as possible, while getting the other half thinking about the importance of cooperation; and (2) they told half of the participants in each of those two conditions that, after they made a decision, they would need to explain their reasoning to the group. The people who showed the most independence and made the best decisions were those who were oriented toward being accurate and had to explain their nonconformity to the very people whose influence they resisted. They behaved more independently than those who were oriented toward being accurate but were not held accountable. What this suggests is that most people will go along to get along—unless they know that they will be held accountable for a dumb, compliant decision.

Self-Esteem and Security Generally speaking, people who have low self-esteem are more likely to yield to group pressure than those with high self-esteem.[36] If they are led to believe that they have little or no aptitude for the task at hand (like judging the lengths of lines), their tendency to conform increases. If they are given the opportunity to have prior success with a task—and thereby feel secure in their abilities—they are far less likely to conform than those who walk into the situation cold.[37]

Similarly, how secure we feel in a given group determines how free we feel to deviate from its norms. If our friend Sam had felt sure that he was liked and accepted by the people watching the debate with him, he would have been more likely to voice disagreement than if he felt insecure in his relationship with them. To demonstrate this phenomenon, James Dittes and Harold Kelley[38] recruited college men to join a prestigious group and subsequently informed them that the members could remove any participant, at any time, in the interest of efficiency. The group then got into a discussion of juvenile offending. Periodically, the discussion was interrupted and each member was asked to rate every other member's value to the group. After the discussion, each member was shown how the others rated him; in actuality, the members were given prearranged false feedback. Some members were led to believe they were well liked and accepted, and others were led to believe they were not terribly popular. Each member's degree of conformity was measured by the opinions he subsequently expressed in further discussion and by his vulnerability to group pressure during the performance of a simple perceptual task. Those who were led to feel only moderately accepted were more likely to conform to the norms set by the others than were those who were led to feel totally accepted. Once we've earned a secure place in the group, we relax and express our opinions more freely.

Age As we have seen, even toddlers reflexively conform to what their peers are doing. This is how we learn many things, including our patterns of speech and accents.[39] But conformity pressures are most intense for young people between the ages of 10 and 25. Until then, the brain's self-control systems—which govern planning, thinking about the future, assessing risk, and suppressing impulses—are still developing. What adults have observed about adolescents since time immemorial turns out to be true: Teenagers become very different people in one another's company—often to their detriment and health. Compared to adult drivers, teenage drivers are more than three times as likely to be in an accident if passengers are in the car.[40] Laurence Steinberg and his associates[41] found that young adults were more likely to interpret risky behaviors—running a red light, using drugs and alcohol, shoplifting, and so on—as "exciting" rather than "dangerous" if they were with their peers at the time. Pleasure centers in the brain are activated when peers are present, and without a fully developed prefrontal cortex to impose self-control, young people show a greater tendency to commit hazardous, foolish actions. As one expert on teen violence put it, "The stupidest creature to ever walk the face of the earth is an adolescent boy in the company of his peers."[42] Perhaps, but adolescent girls are not far behind. Abigail Baird[43] has found that if a popular girl in an adolescent peer group expresses an opinion—even a crazy one—her peers will frequently find a way to talk themselves into agreeing with her position. In one study, teenage girls were asked if it was a good idea to go swimming in the ocean if a shark had been spotted in the area. Individually, all the girls were adamant in their thinking—no way would they go in. But in groups, when Baird had the dominant girl answer the question by suggesting that it could be an exciting adventure, the other girls would start agreeing with her, constructing rationalizations for swimming with sharks.

The Nature of the Group A group is more effective at inducing conformity if (1) it consists of perceived experts, (2) its members are of high social status (for example, the popular kids in a high school), or (3) its members are alike in a significant way, such as age, occupation, political ideology, race, or ethnicity. Thus, Sam would be more likely to conform to the pressure exerted by his acquaintances if he thinks they are experts in politics and in making judgments about human sincerity. He would be more likely to yield to their views if they have higher status and he wants to be part of their circle. He would be more likely to conform to his fellow students than, say, to a group of 10-year-old children, a group of construction workers, or a group of Portuguese biochemists. Finally, he will be more likely to conform if he is in a racially homogenous group than a racially diverse one. When white male college students were exposed to the unanimous (but erroneous) judgments of three peers in an Asch-like judgment task, they were more conforming when all three peers were white than when a person of another race was in the group. You might anticipate a real-life benefit of that finding: namely, that racial diversity can discourage groupthink.[44]

Groups that we belong to and identify with—our **reference groups**—both reflect and shape our identities and behaviors. Often, when we change reference groups, we change our behavior and attitudes as well in order to conform. For example, students who move to a new school or find new friendship groups within a school tend to become more like the group they have joined; their academic efforts and achievements rise or fall to conform to their new peers. "Do they work hard? I will too." "Do they think school-work is boring and not worth doing? I agree."[45] Likewise, students who move from politically conservative families to much more liberal environments when they go to college will often become more liberal in their attitudes, unless they maintain close connections with their more conservative reference group at home.[46]

Christian Crandall[47] discovered an especially pernicious effect of group conformity when he examined the body image and eating patterns of women in two college sororities. Each sorority differed in its collective attitudes about the ideal female body image and whether binge eating and purging was a desirable way to maintain it. The powerful reference group of the sorority exerted pressure on its members to have the "right" body type (how thin to be) and the right behavior (how much bingeing was cool). The more the women hewed to the group ideal of looks and behavior, the more popular they were. Thus, if you were in a sorority where everyone thought you should be thin and yet eat a lot, you'd be more popular if you binged and purged.

Social Norms

Our discussion of conformity strongly suggests that people form their ideas about what is socially appropriate behavior in a given setting or within a community by observing what other people are doing. The power of that perceived norm over their own beliefs and actions depends on the extent to which they perceive the norm to be universally endorsed, and the extent to which they care about the situation or the community involved. A norm might simply be **descriptive**, reflecting our knowledge about *what most people do* in a given situation. Some norms are **injunctive**, specifying what people *should do*, often through explicit directives, such as signs prohibiting smoking, cell phone use, or littering.

Institutions frequently want to create norms without making an outright demand. Many years ago, during one of California's recurrent droughts, it turned out that only 6 percent of the students at my university's field house were conforming to the request to take short showers, as the university was requesting. In the previous chapter I wrote about the "hypocrisy paradigm" we used to get people to conserve water. This time, my students and I[48] conducted a simple field experiment aimed at inducing students to shorten their showers by leading them to believe that their peers were shortening theirs.

We enlisted the aid of a few male students who acted as role models and observers. Not wanting people to conform out of a fear of disapproval or punishment, we set up the experiment in the following way: Our role model entered the shower room at the university's athletic center when it was empty, went to the far end, turned his back to the entrance, and turned on the shower. As soon as he heard someone enter the shower room, he would turn off the shower, lather up his body with soap, and then briefly rinse off, just as signs posted nearby requested. He'd then leave the room without so much as glancing at the student who had entered. As he left, another student (our observer) entered and surreptitiously noted whether the subject of our investigation followed suit by turning off the shower while soaping up. We found that 49 percent of the students conformed, and when two students simultaneously modeled the appropriate behavior, conformity zoomed to 67 percent! Thus, in an ambiguous situation, other people can induce us to conform by behaving in ways that let us know what "most people" do in that situation.

Let's look at the norms regarding littering. Suppose, as you approach your car in the parking lot of the local library, you notice that someone has stuck one of those annoying fliers under your windshield wiper. So you remove it and, without thinking, crumple it up. The crucial question: Do you throw it on the ground or shove it into your pocket so that you can drop it in a trashcan later? The answer: To a large extent, it depends on what you think others would do in this setting. In their field experiment, Robert Cialdini and his associates[49] placed fliers under the windshield wipers of a number of cars and waited to observe what people did when they returned to their cars. Sometimes, an accomplice of the experimenters walked past them as they left the library, stooped down, picked up a discarded fast-food bag that was lying in the street, and placed it in a trashcan. In the control condition, no bag was lying on the ground; the accomplice simply walked past the people who were headed toward their cars. In that situation, when the people got to their car and noticed the flier, 37 percent threw it on the ground. In the food-bag modeling condition, only 7 percent threw it on the ground.

In a parallel experiment,[50] researchers eliminated the role model and instead manipulated the appearance of the parking lot—by littering it with fliers, leaving only a single piece of paper on the ground, or having it be completely clean. Which condition made people least likely to litter? When the ground was covered in paper, the majority of the drivers simply followed suit—probably thinking, "After all, if no one cares about the cleanliness of the parking lot, why should I?" But they were least likely to litter if a single piece of paper lay on the ground nearby than if the parking lot was completely clean. Why might this be? The one piece of crumpled paper reminds us of the injunctive norm against littering—and shows us that the vast majority of people are following the norm of keeping the lot clean. If the parking lot is free of litter, most people probably do not even think about the norm and therefore are more likely to litter mindlessly.

In another set of experiments, Kees Keizer and his associates[51] took this reasoning a step further, to show that when environmental cues suggest that most people are disregarding the rules, bad behavior and norm-breaking are encouraged. Keizer's team left a large envelope hanging part way out of a public mailbox in an urban area of a city in the Netherlands, as though someone had hurriedly—and unsuccessfully—tried to mail the letter. A €5 bill showed through the address window in the envelope. Would passersby who saw it push the envelope into the mailbox, or would they steal the envelope with the money? The answer depended on a critical detail manipulated by the experimenters: Sometimes the mailbox had graffiti on it and there was litter strewn about the area; sometimes the mailbox and surrounding area were clean. In the clean-mailbox condition, only 13 percent of the passersby stole the envelope. With the graffiti and litter, 27 percent of the passersby stole the letter. (Still a low number—but this was, after all, in the Netherlands!) You may recognize this setup as a test of the "broken windows theory," which holds that when the environment sends the message that people don't care, the disorder spreads to human behavior.[52] People seem to say to themselves, "Oh, what the hell. If others are going to behave irresponsibly, I might as well, too."

To summarize, people take their cues from others and typically feel uncomfortable when they deviate from the norms of the group they belong to, especially if they value or identify with the group. In many situations (such as the Asch situation) the norms are well-defined (everyone thinks line A is longer). In other situations, people have no idea about the norms and are forced to infer them from others' actions, which is why the fellow in the shower room, the guy picking up a piece of litter, or the presence of graffiti can be so influential. A number of researchers have used the power of norms to get people to change behavior, sometimes with dramatic success. For example, signs in hotel rooms urging guests to reuse their towels work better when they explicitly say that "most other guests in this room have reused theirs."[53] Informing hikers in a national park that very few people broke the rules against collecting petrified wood reduced the incidence significantly more than signs that only asked people not to remove the wood.[54]

The Uninvolved Bystander as Conformist

Our tendency to conform can also prevent us from taking action when people need our help. In 1964, the *New York Times* ran a shocking story, one that left a major legacy in the history of social-psychological research. A young woman named Kitty Genovese was stabbed to death near her home in Queens, New York. It was a tragic event, but not an especially newsworthy one for New Yorkers at a time when murder rates were much higher than they are today. What made the Genovese case distinctive was that, according to news reports at the time, 38 of her neighbors came to their windows at 3:00 a.m. in response to her screams of terror—and remained at their windows watching in fascination for the 30 minutes it took her assailant to complete his grisly deed. The *New York Times* claimed that no one came to her assistance; no one so much as lifted the phone to call the police until it was too late.[55]

The story, which turned out to be exaggerated for the sake of sensational headlines,[56] nonetheless articulated many people's deep fears of crime and of social alienation. It produced a rash of speculations and handwringing about the apathy of people who live in cities. What's wrong with them? Why would they turn their backs on a neighbor in distress? Maybe the onlookers were sleepy or dazed. After all, people are hardly in full control of their mental faculties at three o'clock in the morning. Perhaps, but it was in broad daylight that a two-year-old girl was run over by two vans in Foshan, China. For the next seven minutes, more than a dozen people, recorded by an impassive security camera, walked or bicycled past her, doing nothing. Eventually, a woman pulled the little girl to the side of the road and she was taken to a hospital, where she died soon thereafter.

Why didn't these bystanders rush to help? To begin with, interviews conducted with the bystanders in the Genovese murder revealed them to be anything but nonchalant—they were horrified.

Something other than apathy was at play in their apparent unresponsiveness.

The Genovese murder launched extensive research designed to identify reasons that a person might fail to intervene when a stranger is in trouble. One reason is cultural norms.[57] Were you to travel the globe dropping pens, faking illness, or pretending to be blind, you would tend to receive more assistance from people in Latin countries, which place a higher value on *simpático*, the willingness to offer help to others, than in the United States. You're also more likely to get help in places where the pace of life is slower and there are fewer demands on a passerby's attention. Research led by Robert Levine[58] found helpfulness to be lowest in big crowded cities like New York, where people walk quickly and confront abundant distractions; they need to notice your distress before they can respond to it.

A second reason for failing to intervene is that even when people do notice someone in trouble, they may fail to identify it as an emergency. John Darley, Bibb Latané, and their colleagues[59] hypothesized that a victim is less likely to get help if many people are watching his or her distress. Their nonintervention is an act of conformity to how other people were defining the reasonableness and appropriateness of helping or not helping. What's the appropriate way to think or feel about what's going on right now? As we have seen, what other people are doing is often the clearest guide.

Suppose you encounter a woman lying with a broken leg on a busy street. She is clearly in pain. What else do you see? You see scores of people walking past the woman, glancing at her, and continuing on their way. How will you define the situation? You may conclude that it's inappropriate for you to intervene. Perhaps it's not serious; perhaps she's intoxicated; perhaps the whole thing is being staged for a reality show. "After all," you say to yourself, "if she's really in trouble, she will have used her cell to call 911. Or someone else would have. And why aren't any of these other people doing anything?" Thus we might predict that the very presence of a lot of other people, rather than increasing the likelihood that *someone* will help, actually decreases the likelihood that *anyone* will help.

This is an interesting conjecture, but is it true? To find out, Bibb Latané and Judith Rodin[60] conducted an experiment constructed around a woman in distress. A young woman asked 120 male college students to fill out a questionnaire. She then retired to the next room, saying she would return when the students finished.

A few minutes later, she staged an accident. The students heard the sound (from a hidden tape recording) of the young woman climbing a chair, followed by a loud scream and a crash, as if the chair had collapsed and she had fallen to the floor. They then heard moaning and crying and the anguished statement, "Oh, my God, my foot, I ... I can't move it. Oh ... my ankle ... I can't get this thing off me." The cries continued for about a minute and gradually subsided.

The question, of course, was whether the participants would come to the woman's aid. The important variable in the experiment was whether the young men were alone in the room. Of those who were alone, 70 percent offered to help her; of those who were sitting in the room with a stranger, only 20 percent offered help. Thus, the mere presence of another bystander tends to inhibit action, a phenomenon called the **bystander effect**. When interviewed subsequently, the unhelpful participants who had been in the room with another person said they had concluded that the accident probably wasn't serious, at least in part because of the inactivity of their partner.

Another reason, besides conformity, that bystanders may fail to intervene is the **diffusion of responsibility**: Even if people conclude that the event is a genuine emergency, the awareness of other witnesses diffuses the responsibility felt by any one person. To test this idea, Darley and Latané[61] arranged an experimental situation in which people were placed in separate rooms but were able to communicate with one another by microphones and earphones. They could hear one another but not see one another. The investigators then played a recording imitating the sounds of an epileptic seizure on the part of one of the participants. In one experimental condition, each person was led to believe that he or she was the only one who overheard the seizure; in other conditions, each person was led to believe that one or more people had also heard it. Those who thought they were the only listener were far more likely to leave their room and try to help than were those who thought others were listening, too. As the number of people listening increased, individual responsibility was diffused among them, and the likelihood of offering assistance decreased.

Other factors can enter the calculation of whether to help a stranger, including seemingly trivial ones, as John Darley and Daniel Batson[62] illustrated. They enlisted divinity students at Princeton

Theological Seminary, ostensibly for the purpose of recording a speech. Each student practiced his talk in one room; then he was instructed to walk to another building, where his presentation would be taped. At this point, some of the students were told they were late for their appointment and were hurried out. Others were told they were on time, and the rest that they had time to spare. On their way to the other building, the students encountered an apparent victim slumped in a doorway, with head down and eyes closed, coughing pathetically. More than half of these future ministers who were early or on time stopped to assist the victim, but only 10 percent of those who thought they were late for their appointment offered help—even when the speech they were to deliver included the parable of the Good Samaritan! Apparently the students were too distracted by their lateness and their mission to define the situation as enough of an emergency to get involved.

The ease with which people can be led to not intervene projects a rather grim picture of the human condition. But that is not the full picture. Camping in Yosemite National Park many years ago, my family and I heard a man's voice cry out. No one in our tent could be certain whether it was a cry of pain, surprise, or joy. Maybe someone was horsing around? Maybe a fellow camper was being attacked by a bear? What we saw when we left the tent was heartening. From all over the area, myriad flickering lights were converging on a single point. These were lanterns and flashlights being carried by dozens of campers running to the aid of the man who had screamed. It turned out that his scream had been one of surprise caused by a relatively harmless flare-up in his gasoline stove. The other campers seemed almost disappointed when they learned their help wasn't needed. They trudged back to their tents and, I assumed, dropped off to sleep immediately.

I, however, couldn't sleep, puzzled by the contradiction between what had just happened and the bystander effect. Why had these campers behaved so differently? In what way were the situations different? There were at least two factors operating in the campground that were either not present or present only to a small degree in the situations previously discussed. One is reflected in my use of the term "our fellow campers." Specifically, a feeling of "common fate" or mutuality may be engendered among people sharing the same interests, pleasures, hardships, and environmental conditions of a closed environment like a campground, a stronger feeling of mutuality than exists among people who are merely residents of the same country, county, or city. A second factor is that there was no escape from the face-to-face aspect of the situation: In a big city, people can walk away from a stranger in trouble; the participants in the Darley-Latané experiments were not in a face-to-face relationship with the victim, and they knew they could escape from the environment in a short time. In the campground, we were all there together; the campers were going to have to face squarely the next morning whatever they had allowed to happen the night before. It seems that, under these circumstances, individuals are more willing to take responsibility for one another.

Of course, I'm speculating. The helpfulness of the campers at Yosemite is not conclusive because it was not part of a controlled experiment. One of the major problems with observational data like these is that the observer has no control over who the people in the situation are. Perhaps campers, by nature or experience, are kinder, gentler, more thoughtful, and more humane than urban dwellers. Perhaps they were Boy Scouts and Girl Scouts as children—hence their interest in camping—and in scouting, they were taught to be helpful to other people.

One of the reasons for doing experiments is to control this kind of uncertainty, and indeed, a subsequent experiment by Irving Piliavin and his associates[63] supported my speculations about the campground experience. In their experiment, an accomplice of the experimenters staggered and collapsed in a New York City subway car, in the presence of several other people. The "victim" remained stretched out on the floor of the train, staring at the ceiling. This scene was repeated 103 times under a variety of conditions. The most striking result was that, a large part of the time, people spontaneously rushed to the aid of the victim, especially when he was made to seem obviously ill; in more than 95 percent of the trials, someone offered help immediately. Even when the victim had been given a liquor bottle to carry and was made to reek of alcohol, he received immediate help on 50 percent of the trials. Unlike the behavior of the participants that Darley and Latané dealt with, the helping behavior of the people on the subway train was not affected by the number of bystanders. People helped just as often and just as speedily on crowded trains (where there could have been a diffusion of responsibility) as they did on virtually empty trains. Although the people in the New York subway were in an environment as unlike Yosemite National Park as could be, the subway and the campground had two things in common: (1) people had the feeling of sharing a common fate, and (2) they were in a face-to-face situation with the victim from which there was no immediate escape.

Today, after decades of research on bystander apathy and bystander intervention, we have a better idea of the influences on both of these responses. A meta-analysis of the many studies done since the first identification of the bystander effect offers cause for optimism: In truly dangerous, *unambiguous* emergencies—a child is drowning; people are being shot at by a deranged gunman in a school, movie theater, or street; or a terrorist attack—people are more likely to intervene to help, and in fact are often spurred to do so by the presence of others. Indeed, they will rush in to help in stunningly generous ways, sometimes risking their own safety.[64] After the terrorist bombing at the Boston marathon in 2013, many bystanders actually ran *into* the most dangerous area to help survivors.

What conditions make apathy or altruism more likely? The sense of a "common fate" is clearly activated, and they are in face-to-face situations with victims. When these conditions are lacking, individuals make a quick, often unconscious assessment of whether or not they should get involved: Is the situation really serious? Does it require my personal intervention? Will helping be difficult or costly for me? Will my help benefit the victim? Can I easily leave? Your response to the situation will depend on your answers to each of these questions.

Pluralistic Ignorance

Norms even govern our inner emotions and how and when we are expected to express them (or suppress them). Most people conform to the *display rules* of demonstrating sadness at funerals, happiness at weddings, and affection toward relatives. What if we don't actually feel sad, happy, or affectionate? Acting out an emotion we do not really feel because we believe it is socially appropriate is called *emotion work*.[65] Sometimes emotion work is a normative job requirement. Flight attendants, servers in restaurants, and customer-service representatives must put on a happy face to convey cheerfulness, even if they are privately angry about a rude or drunken customer. Bill collectors must put on a stern face to convey threat, even if they feel sorry for the person they are collecting money from.[66]

Conforming to display rules may smooth out our social interactions, but our use of others to define situations for us can be especially problematic where strong feelings are involved that people are afraid to show—or are trying to conform to what is expected of them. People often consider it uncool to reveal certain emotions in public, so we try to appear less fearful, worried, depressed, anxious, or sexually aroused than we really are. For example, from the blasé looks on the faces of patrons of strip clubs, one might *never* guess that they were sexually aroused or even interested. Similarly, the proverbial visitor from Mars might not realize the anxiety of the adult patients in a dentist's waiting room by observing the impassive looks on their faces. Thus, it can be misleading to judge the seriousness of a situation by looking to others' emotional expressions, because people often hide their true feelings behind a poker face.

This can create a situation that social psychologists call **pluralistic ignorance**, the collective belief in a false norm created by the ambiguous behavior of others. The classic setting to see pluralistic ignorance in action is the college classroom. Imagine that your professor has just explained an extremely complicated concept. She turns to the class to check to see if everyone understands. "Any questions? Anyone not get this?" she asks. As a matter of fact, *you* don't get it, and you sure would appreciate some further explanation. You glance around the room nonchalantly to see if you are alone in your confusion and find nothing but the nonchalant expressions of your classmates. They make you worry that you alone are confused, and this raises the stakes of your raising your hand to admit you don't get it. In reality, many of your classmates are having the same experience, partly from looking at *your* blank face. Pluralistic ignorance can be a serious barrier to classroom effectiveness, yet it is overcome easily with technology that allows students to answer anonymously in real time to potentially embarrassing questions like "Anyone not get this?"

Binge drinking on college campuses is also promoted by pluralistic ignorance, because students must infer norms from the (often drunken) behavior of their peers. And that norm creates serious problems: Two out of three college students who consume alcohol engage in binge drinking, not infrequently to blacking out, which causes nearly 1,800 deaths each year and leads to other high-risk behaviors, such as unsafe sex and sexual assault.[67] Yet surveys show that most college students believe that they themselves are more uncomfortable drinking heavily than their peers are—so of course they drink more in order to match their perceived norm. What to do? Dale Miller and Deborah Prentice[68] have found that merely giving students accurate information about their fellow students' alcohol consumption and their true (negative) feelings about binge drinking reduced conformity—and lowered the rate of drinking. A similar study assigned first-year students to either a peer-oriented discussion, which made them aware of pluralistic ignorance, or an individual-oriented discussion, which focused on making decisions about drinking. Four to six months later, students in the peer-oriented condition reported drinking significantly less than did students in the individual-oriented condition; the strength of the drinking norm had been weakened.[69] Change the perceived norms and people's behavior follows suit.

Pluralistic ignorance can literally be a killer. For example, despite a general drop in homicide over the past decade, black Americans are nearly eight times as likely as white Americans to be murder victims; gang-related homicide in urban areas remains stubbornly high. In his breakthrough approach to reducing the murder rate among urban gangs, the legendary criminologist David Kennedy[70] spent hundreds of hours getting to know the young men. The police had described them as "heartless, fearless, sociopaths," so Kennedy was surprised when he learned, by interviewing the gang members, that most of them were scared, hated the violence, and wanted normal lives. "They talked very tough when they were in groups, and that's why the cops would think they were sociopaths," Kennedy wrote, "but when I'd get them alone, they'd confess they were scared to death. To show fear in front of your gang members is dangerous, so everyone looks around and thinks they alone hate the life." Kennedy and his team began their intervention by confronting this pluralistic ignorance, which Kennedy described as the condition where "everybody in a group believes that everybody in the group believes something that nobody in the group believes." By bringing the police and gang members together and unveiling their actual feelings of horror and despair about what was going on, they were able to begin a process that substantially reduced gang violence and the homicide rate in several major cities.[71]

Levels of Conformity

Thus far, I have been describing two motives for conformity: whether a person is motivated by the desire to fit in and belong, or by a need to be correct. Let us move beyond these simple distinctions to a more complex and useful classification, distinguishing among three levels of conformity: *compliance*, *identification*, and *internalization*.[72]

The term **compliance** best describes the behavior of a person who is motivated by a desire to gain reward or avoid punishment. Typically, the person's behavior is only as long-lived as the promise of reward or the threat of punishment. You can get a rat to run a maze efficiently by making it hungry and placing food at the end of the maze. A ruthless dictator could get a percentage of his citizens to swear their allegiance by threatening them with torture if they don't comply or by promising to feed and enrich them if they do. Remove the threat of punishment or the benefits of riches, however, and the citizens will cease showing allegiance to the dictator. Compliance is the least enduring and has the least effect on the individual, because the person's behavior changes as soon as the rewards or punishments change.

The term **identification** describes a level of conformity brought about by an individual's desire to be like the group or role model they admire. In identification, as in compliance, we do not behave in a particular way because such behavior is intrinsically satisfying; rather, we do it because it puts us in a satisfying relationship with the person or persons with whom we are identifying. Identification differs from compliance in that we do come to believe in the opinions and values we adopt, although we may not believe in them very strongly. Thus, if we find a person or a group appealing in some way, we will be inclined to let that person or group influence us by adopting their values and attitudes.

I think of this as the good-old-Uncle-Harry-and-Aunt-Harriet phenomenon. Suppose you have an uncle and aunt who are warm, dynamic, and exciting; ever since you were a young child, you loved these elders and wanted to grow up to be like them. By the time you are in college, you have incorporated their political beliefs—left, right, or center—into your own, not because you have examined those beliefs carefully or acquired them through your own experience, or even because you were rewarded for adopting (or punished for not adopting) their views. Rather, their opinions have become part of your belief system because you love those relatives so much and want to be like them.

This phenomenon occurs often when we encounter the opinions of people we like or admire—even relative strangers. Geoffrey Cohen and Michael Prinstein[73] asked high school students to participate in online chat room discussions with one another. One of the topics being discussed was what students would do if offered marijuana at a party. In one condition, the participants were led to believe that they were chatting with two popular and admired classmates from their school. In the other, these classmates were identified as students of merely average popularity. When the teenagers believed they were chatting with the popular classmates, they were far more likely to adopt their opinions. If the admired classmates said they would smoke the marijuana, the participants tended to agree that they would do so as well; if the admired classmates said they would refuse the marijuana, so did the participants. Unlike the kind of conformity in the Asch experiment, which was merely compliance, the influence here was durable; it was evident even later when participants were asked to give their opinions about marijuana in private.

Continuous reward or punishment is not necessary for identification. You can identify with someone who isn't present at all; you just need to want to be like that person. If your aunt and uncle move to a different city and months (or even years) go by without your seeing them, you will continue to hold beliefs similar to theirs as long as (1) they remain important to you, (2) they still hold the same beliefs, and (3) their beliefs are not challenged by counter-opinions that are more convincing to you. Conversely, your beliefs can be changed if your relatives change their political beliefs, or if you find other people who are more important to you and who profess different beliefs. In that case, you may change your mind because you are now more strongly identifying with your new reference group.

Finally, the **internalization** of a value or belief is the most permanent level of conformity. The motivation to internalize a belief is the desire to be right. If we admire someone whom we perceive to be trustworthy and to have good judgment, we accept the belief that he or she advocates and integrate it into our system of values. Once we have internalized a belief and made it our own, it becomes independent of its source and will become extremely resistant to change—as we saw in the discussion of self-justification in the previous chapter.

Internalization is therefore the most permanent level of conformity precisely because the motivation to be right—and to believe that we are right—is a powerful and self-sustaining force that does not depend upon constant surveillance in the form of agents of reward or punishment, as does compliance, or on our continued esteem for another person or group, as does identification.

Any specific action may be rooted in compliance, identification, or internalization. Let us look at a simple piece of behavior: obedience to speed limits. Most people conform to the speed limit to avoid paying a penalty if they are caught. That's compliance; they are obeying the law. If the police were told to stop enforcing the law, many people would exceed the speed limit. But some would continue to obey because, let's say, Dad always stressed the importance of obeying traffic laws, and they admire their dad and want to drive the way he does. Their reason for conforming is identification. Finally, people might conform to the speed limit, whether or not Dad or the police are nearby, because they are convinced that speed laws are good, that obeying such laws helps to prevent accidents, and that driving at a moderate speed is a sane and reasonable form of behavior. Their reason for conforming is internalization.

Obedience as a Form of Compliance

Acts of compliance are almost always ephemeral. This does not mean they are trivial. People can commit an act only once or twice, but it might have far-reaching consequences, as Stanley Milgram demonstrated in a classic series of studies of obedience.[74] His studies, first done in the early 1960s, became world famous, with books written and films made about them, because their message was not entirely what people wanted to hear.

Picture the scene in his initial experiment: Forty men volunteer for a project advertised as a study of learning and memory. But this is just the cover story; actually, it is a study of the extent to which people will obey authority. When the volunteer appears at the lab for his appointment, he is paired with another man, and a somewhat stern experimenter in a technician's coat explains that they will be testing the effects of punishment on learning. The exercise requires one person, the "learner," to memorize a list of word pairs on which the other person, the "teacher," will test him. The two men draw slips to determine their roles; the actual participant draws the role of teacher. He is led to a "Shock Generator," which has an instrument panel with a row of 30 toggle switches, calibrated from a low point of 15 volts (labeled "Slight Shock") and extending through levels of moderate and higher shocks (labeled "Danger—Severe Shock") to a high of 450 volts (labeled, ominously, XXX). By throwing the successive switches, the teacher will deliver an increasingly intense shock each time the learner fails to answer correctly. Then the teacher follows the experimenter and the learner into the next room, where the learner is strapped into an electric chair apparatus and attached by electrodes to the Shock Generator. In response to the learner's inquiry about his mild heart condition, the experimenter reassures him, "Although the shocks can be extremely painful, they cause no permanent tissue damage."

In actuality, the learner knows that he needn't worry. He is an accomplice of the experimenter, and the drawing to assign roles has been rigged so that he will play the role of the learner and the real participant will be the teacher. The learner never receives any jolt of electricity, but the teacher has no reason to doubt that the man in the next room is wired to the Shock Generator that he operates. He has even experienced a sample shock himself (from a 45-volt battery inside the machine), he hears the learner react as if he is really being hurt, and he is convinced that the shocks are extremely painful.

As the exercise begins, the learner responds correctly several times but makes mistakes on a few trials. With each error, the teacher throws the next switch, supposedly administering a shock of increased intensity. With the fifth shock, at 75 volts, the victim begins to grunt and moan. At 150 volts, he asks to be let out of the experiment. At 180 volts, he cries out that he can't stand the pain. As the shock levels approach the point labeled "Danger—Severe Shock," the teacher hears the learner pound the wall and beg to be released. But this, of course, does not constitute a correct response, so the experimenter instructs the teacher to increase the voltage and deliver the next shock by throwing the next switch. At 300 volts, the learner stops responding altogether.

The participants in this experiment were a random sample of businessmen, professionals, white-collar workers, and blue-collar workers in Connecticut. What percentage of them continued to administer shocks to "XXX" at the very end of the experiment? How long would you have continued? Before the experiment began, Milgram posed these questions to 40 psychiatrists at a leading medical school. The psychiatrists predicted that most participants would quit at 150 volts, when the victim first asks to be freed. They also predicted that only about 4 percent would continue to shock the victim after he stopped responding, and that fewer than 1 in 100 would administer the highest shock on the generator.

The psychiatrists were completely wrong. The great majority of the participants—some 67 percent—continued to administer shocks to the maximum level, although some of them required prodding from the experimenter (who had been instructed to say only "The experiment requires that you continue"). The obedient individuals did not continue administering shocks because they were sadistic or cruel. Indeed, when Milgram and Alan Elms later compared people's scores on a series of standardized personality tests, they discovered no differences between those who were fully obedient and those who successfully resisted the pressure to obey.[75] Nor were obedient people insensitive to the apparent plight of the learner. Some protested; many sweated, trembled, stuttered, and showed other signs of tension. Some burst out in fits of nervous laughter. But they continued to obey to the very end.

This behavior is not limited to American men living in Connecticut. Wherever the Milgram procedure has been tried, it has produced a significant degree of obedience. Several replications of the experiment[76] have demonstrated that people in Australia, Jordan, Spain, Germany, and the Netherlands react in much the same way as the men in Milgram's original experiment, and women are just as obedient as men.[77] A replication of the basic Milgram procedure conducted in 2007 by Jerry Burger shows that high levels of obedience in the Milgram experiment are not artifacts of a bygone era; modern Americans are every bit as susceptible to being led to shock an innocent victim as were their counterparts in Milgram's time—nearly 60 years ago.[78]

Real-World Implications — and Limitations — of the Milgram Experiment

Milgram's unwelcome and controversial message was that an astonishingly large proportion of people will cause pain to other people when an authority figure orders them to obey. It is difficult to read about these studies without applying them to the world outside the experimental laboratory, for example by noticing some similarity between the behavior of the teachers in Milgram's experiment and the blind obedience of the Nazi officers who obeyed orders to exterminate millions of innocent people who were not "pure Aryans." At his trial for crimes against humanity, conducted when Milgram was doing his studies, Adolf Eichmann justified his actions by claiming he was a good bureaucrat, merely obeying orders issued by his superiors in the Nazi regime.

During the Iraq war, American soldiers guarding Iraqi prisoners of war subjected them to torture and humiliation in the notorious Abu Ghraib prison.[79] Although military leaders were quick to blame this behavior on a few "bad apples"—and court-martialed them—the facts suggest that Abu Ghraib was another instance of obedience to authority. The soldiers who tortured their prisoners claimed that they were just following orders. Milgram's obedient participants likewise had many justifications for their behavior: It wasn't *their* fault, they kept saying; they were only doing their job. One man, when questioned after the session, replied, "I stopped, but he [the experimenter] kept going."

As provocative as these comparisons are, we should be cautious lest we overinterpret Milgram's results. Given that 67 percent of the participants complied with the experimenter's command, some commentators have suggested that perhaps most people would have behaved as Adolf Eichmann did had they found themselves in a similar situation. This may be true, but we should also notice some important points of difference. Because each man in Milgram's study freely consented to participate, he had every reason to assume that the learner had also volunteered. Accordingly, it is likely that he felt that they were both obligated to avoid disrupting the experiment. Moreover, each participant faced the demands of the experimenter alone. Just as conformity dropped in the Asch experiment with the presence of one dissenter, the proportion of fully obedient people in a variation of the Milgram paradigm dropped to just 10 percent when they were joined by two fellow teachers who defied the experimenter's orders to continue.

Also, in most of Milgram's studies, the authority figure issuing the orders was a scientist in a prestigious laboratory at Yale University, and his cover story credits the experiment as being an investigation of an important scientific question. The participants naturally assumed that the experimenter (wearing a white lab coat, no less) at a highly respected institution like Yale would be a responsible, benevolent professional. Surely he would not issue orders that would result in the death or injury of a human being as a part of his experiment. Indeed, when Milgram moved the study from Yale University to a suite of offices in industrial Bridgeport, a few miles away, full obedience dropped to 48 percent. Removing the prestige of Yale University considerably reduced the degree of obedience.

Of course, 48 percent is still a high figure. Would even fewer people have obeyed if the person conducting the experiment were not a scientist or another legitimate authority figure? Milgram addressed this question in another version of the study, in which the scientist-experimenter was replaced at the last minute by a non-authoritative substitute. This time only 20 percent delivered the full set of shocks, demonstrating that for most people, only legitimate authority can command high obedience, not just any person assuming the role of authority.

Finally, the physical proximity of the authority figure also plays a role in whether people obey. Milgram found that when the experimenter was out of the room and issued his orders by telephone, the number of *fully* obedient participants dropped to below 25 percent. Moreover, released from the close scrutiny of the experimenter, several of the people who continued to administer shocks *cheated*; they administered shocks of lower intensity than they were ordered to—and never bothered to tell the experimenter that they had deviated from the proper procedure. I regard that finding as their touching attempt to respond to the demands of legitimate authority while at the same time minimizing the pain they inflict on others. It reminds me of Dunbar, a character in Joseph Heller's classic World War II novel *Catch 22*. Dunbar is ordered to bomb villages in Italy. Unwilling either to rebel openly or to harm innocent civilians, he drops his bombs over empty fields close to the Italian villages designated as his targets.

Dunbar's sensitivity to the potential victims of his bombs is especially poignant given the distance and anonymity afforded by his position high in the sky above the villagers; the operators of drones in today's warfare are even more removed from their victims. Vividly witnessing the suffering of others makes it more difficult to continue inflicting pain upon them. Indeed, Milgram found in subsequent studies that the farther teachers were from the learner, the more willing they were to obey the commands of authority. When teachers actually saw the learner, only 40 percent continued to deliver painful shocks, compared with 67 percent who merely heard the learner's cries of agony. Similarly, when teachers were required to physically force the learner's hand down onto the shock plate—instead of using the remote Shock Generator—the rate of obedience dropped to 30 percent. Still, proximity cannot explain all of the results. After all, 30 percent of Milgram's participants continued to deliver shocks to their victims, even when doing so required physical contact.[80]

In a set of experiments conducted in the Netherlands, Wim Meeus and Quinten Raaijmakers[81] explored the issue of obedience and distance in a slightly different manner. In addition to successfully replicating the original Milgram procedure, they tried a new approach. They asked people to obey by making a series of increasingly negative remarks about an applicant's performance on a test that would determine whether he or she would be hired for a job. The participants were convinced that they were harming the person, but the harm would not be manifested until some future time, when they would not be present to witness the consequences of their obedience. Obedience in these situations was much higher than in the direct replication of the Milgram experiment; in this version, more than 90 percent of the participants continued to obey to the very end of the series.

Although the Milgram studies, like the atrocities that took place during the Holocaust, Vietnam, and Iraq, and continue today in the countless other wars that plague our planet, certainly underscore the fallibility of human nature in the face of pressures to conform, the extremity and exotic nature of these studies can lull us into thinking that destructive obedience is beyond the realm of everyday life. After all, when was the last time someone asked you to deliver deadly shocks to a kindly stranger with a heart condition or hide a family of Jews in your basement? But if we look around, we can see that many of us, whether we recognize it or not, are in positions where conforming to the wishes of a group or people in authority will have serious consequences for others.

To take but one example, for the past two decades, American public schools have been under increasing pressure to improve students' academic performance. Legislation called "No Child Left Behind" (now called "Every Student Succeeds") mandated that all schools make progress every year, to be measured by standardized tests. If you attended public school in the last 15 years, you probably were aware to some degree of the pressure your school was under;

the law mandated that unless a school demonstrated improvement in student test scores, it would be shamed or punished. Faced with this situation, many teachers and administrators sought to raise their students' scores one way or another to please the authorities. In some cases they did so by eliminating recess and increasing class time or narrowing the curriculum and making classes more about test prep than the joy of learning or discovery. Some teachers even cheated, correcting wrong answers on student tests.

Julian Vasquez-Heilig and Linda Darling-Hammond[82] found that many educators went beyond these measures in order to comply with pressure from above, sometimes in ways that were devastating to children. Some schools would cook up rationales to suspend underperforming black and Latino students days before the test, so that their low scores would not figure into the school average; others would expel such students or "encourage" them to drop out. In a particularly diabolical maneuver, some schools promoted low-scoring ninth graders to the eleventh grade (thus conveniently evading the tenth-grade test). Hopelessly over their heads, the students would invariably flounder and then drop out of the eleventh grade. What a mockery these instances were of "No Child Left Behind" and "Every Student Succeeds."

These strategies may seem less cruel than administering electric shocks, but when we consider that 30 percent of black male high school dropouts will end up in prison and potentially marked for life as failures, we can appreciate the relevance of Milgram's findings for our most ubiquitous institution. Indeed, one of Jerry Burger's fully compliant participants gave this chilling response when asked if she was surprised that she had followed Burger's orders to the end, delivering the maximum level of shock to the learner: "I guess I'm not completely surprised," she said. "After all, I'm a teacher."

A Note on the Ethics of the Milgram Experiments The Milgram experiment generated considerable debate at the time, and it continues to this day. It is certainly true that in their quest for knowledge, experimental social psychologists occasionally subject people to some fairly intense experiences. These procedures raise ethical problems, which I will discuss more fully in Chapter 9. Here, I want to make two points: First, it is the responsibility of all experimenters to protect their participants from harm.

The experimenter must take steps to ensure that participants leave the experimental situation in a frame of mind that is at least as sound as it was when they entered the experimental situation. This frequently requires post-experimental **debriefing** procedures that sometimes need more time and effort than the main body of the experiment. The vast majority of Milgram's participants, especially those who went all the way, felt they had learned something deeply important about themselves.

But perhaps the great message of the Milgram experiments lies precisely in the discomfort it generates and the reactions of people who think, "I would never do that." Every year in our social psychology classes, before discussing Milgram's findings, Joshua and I have asked students how far they think they would go. Every year, some 99 percent of the 250 to 300 students say that they would *not* continue to administer shocks after the learner began to pound on the wall. They are always confident that *they* would defy the experimenter's instructions. But once, many years ago in a class of 300 students, I asked for the usual show of hands of those who thought they might obey fully. One hand slowly rose. It belonged to a Vietnam veteran who had obeyed an order that, in retrospect, he knew would be considered a war crime. He understood that he was capable of doing what Milgram's participants had done.

This brings me to my second point, which is that social psychologists are obligated to use their research skills to advance our knowledge and understanding of human behavior for the ultimate aim of human betterment. They face a dilemma when their general ethical responsibility to society conflicts with their more specific ethical responsibility to each individual experimental participant. That conflict is greatest when they are investigating such issues as conformity, obedience, and helping, because the more important the issue, the more likely it is that a participant will feel uncomfortable, anxious, or upset—but in exchange, the greater the potential benefit for the individual's self-knowledge and for society.

Countering Conformity

Most of the time, the human tendency to conform to social norms and to our reference groups keeps societies functioning. And obviously it is adaptive, most of the time, for people to obey the laws, regulations, and requirements of their jobs and governments. But while social psychologists study these necessary activities of the "social animal," they also want to understand the conditions under which people resist conformity and obedience, sometimes at risk of their lives.

After all, if everyone simply conformed to the opinion of majorities, and if everyone obeyed unjust, discriminatory laws or commands to carry out illegal acts, there would be little progress in society. Rosa Parks refused to sit at the back of the bus. Joseph Darby blew the whistle on his fellow soldiers at Abu Ghraib who were committing acts of torture. Mark Felt, the government insider who came to be known as "Deep Throat," told reporters about the criminal cover-up in the Nixon White House. And the fact that most Americans now support once-unpopular ideas like gay and interracial marriage shows that minority positions can prevail under certain conditions. What are they?[83]

- If the people holding a minority view express their position consistently, with confidence, conviction, and dogged persistence

- If the minority used to agree with the majority position but changed their minds

- If the minority is willing to compromise, even just a bit

- If group members who are in the majority are motivated to make an *accurate* decision rather than a quick one

Under such conditions, the majority can be moved to think more deeply about the issue and consider its merits, rather than mindlessly going along, conforming to the norms and beliefs of the crowd. But these factors are rarely enough if we are on our own; we need allies to move others. After all, without an ally it is hard to resist the kind of social pressure (such as the threat of rejection and punishment) that sways most of us. To be the lone representative of a group or an opinion is hard even for esteemed experts. Sandra Day O'Connor, the first female Supreme Court Justice, endured many years as the only woman on the court, an experience she described as "asphyxiating." When she was joined on the court some years later by Ruth Bader Ginsberg, she described the change as "night and day."[84] Empowered by the presence of a single ally reduces the pressure immensely, increases the currency of our convictions, and reduces the tendency of others to write us off as an outlier. When dissenters have enough allies, they can move the majority to broaden their thinking and envision new solutions to old problems. As the anthropologist Margaret Mead once said, "Never doubt that a small group of thoughtful, committed, organized citizens can change the world; indeed, it's the only thing that ever has."

Saul Steinberg, *Untitled drawing*, ink on paper.
Published in Steinberg, *The Labyrinth*, 1960.
© The Saul Steinberg Foundation / Artists Rights Society (ARS), New York

5

Mass Communication, Propaganda, and Persuasion

Every day you are subjected to hundreds of people trying to sell you a product, a trip, or an idea; persuade you they're right; convince you to vote their way; make you angry about some injustice; make you afraid of some outside danger; or seduce or charm you into doing what they want. And every day you are subjected to thousands of ads that you can't escape any more than you can escape breathing. Ads interrupt what you're reading online; pop up in the margins of websites; are on every purchase; precede most television; and are on every gas pump, ATM, and bus bench.

Of all the rapid changes in modern life, nothing compares with the rapid evolution in technology and the way we use it to entertain ourselves, communicate, and influence others—and the way others influence us through what comes at us though our televisions, computers, smartphone screens, and other media. This chapter will therefore begin with a look at the current landscape of mass communication and its effects on its consumers. I will then focus on **persuasion**, which occurs when communication from one person changes the opinions, attitudes, or behavior of another person.

How easy is it to persuade a person? The answer depends in part on whether we are dealing with opinions or attitudes. An **opinion** is what a person believes to be true: It is my opinion that eating vegetables is good for me, that wearing seat belts reduces traffic fatalities, and that it's important to take vitamins every day. Such opinions are primarily cognitive; that is, they take place in the head rather than in the gut. They are also transient; they can be changed by good evidence to the contrary. Thus, if I'm presented with an excellent review of the research showing me that multivitamin supplements are useless at best and harmful at worst (as is the case, by the way[1]), I'm likely to change my opinion on that issue.

But suppose a person believes that a vegetarian diet is unhealthy and unnatural, or that a requirement to wear seat belts is an illegitimate intrusion on a driver's freedom, or that vitamins saved a friend's life? These "opinions" are no longer purely cognitive. It is almost certain that there are strong feelings embedded in them, along with an evaluation as to whether the subject is good or bad. An opinion that includes an emotional and an evaluative component is called an **attitude**. Compared with opinions, attitudes are extremely difficult to change—as we will see when we discuss the complex attitudes called prejudices. As you read the discussion of influence tactics in this chapter, you might want to keep this difference between opinions and attitudes in mind. What is an easily changeable opinion to one person might be a deeply entrenched attitude to another.

We have already seen how susceptible people are to social influence, but here I will explore how this susceptibility depends on the particular kinds of tactics aimed at us, identifying the social psychological triggers that make us more likely to say yes. Sometimes, however, we can also be maddeningly resistant to persuasion, as when we try to use facts to change a child's mind about bedtime or change a friend's mind about politics. How are we persuaded? Why do we sometimes yield to persuasion and sometimes not?

Effects of the Modern Media Landscape

It is mind-boggling to ponder the changes that technology brings to nearly everything we do—even the way we walk. Just 10 years ago, we moved through the world as humans have for millennia: upright, eyes surveying the environment for potential danger or opportunities, or just to enjoy the view. Then, in 2007, the iPhone appeared and people everywhere suddenly began walking while staring down at their smartphone screens, doing anything from watching cartoons to conducting business meetings. I marvel at the inconceivability of it, the fact that these computers fit inside our pockets but have more computing power and functionality than the room-sized behemoths that NASA utilized to send astronauts to the moon.

We use our phones for everything: getting updates on news; writing; consulting our calendars; getting directions; doing research; making reservations for restaurants, air travel, and hotel rooms; shopping; or selecting from an infinite number of entertainment options on Spotify, Netflix, or YouTube—immediately. This versatility only partly explains why most people who own a smartphone spend more than 25 percent of their waking hours with their eyes glued to its screen. Much of that time they are interacting with others,[2] evaluating hundreds of potential romantic partners a day, or reading the latest thoughts from virtually anyone—our friends, professors, favorite musicians, even the president of the United States—and replying to them. We can comment upon and share any video, photo, or piece of music throughout our social network. On websites that allow comments, we can entertain ourselves by conversing with, arguing with, consoling, and celebrating our friends. We can harass, troll, or pass judgment on complete strangers 24 hours a day.

Because these advances have fundamentally reshaped how we transact the business of our lives, many people are concerned about how our immersion in media affects our social interactions and well-being. Technology has improved social relations in some cases and worsened them in others. For example, until recently, if you were an African American man, hailing a taxi was often a demoralizing experience; fearing trouble, taxi drivers would often not stop for men with dark skin. Then Uber arrived, an app that allows anyone with a credit card and smartphone to have a driver pick them up anywhere, anytime. For every benefit an app might provide, however, cell phone technology has enabled some unfortunate human tendencies, such as cyberbullying, sexting, and stalking.[3]

Distraction Millions of people are literally addicted to their smartphones, which like any drug, create an unending hunger for stimulation. Smartphones behave much like slot machines, doling out intermittent rewards in the form of alerts, news, tweets, and texts, all of which keep people continually checking for the next hit of social connection.[4] Steve Jobs, who gave us the iPhone and iPad, refused to give these devices to his own children because he understood their addictive nature. One observer pointed out, "It seemed as if the people producing tech products were following the cardinal rule of drug dealing: never get high on your own supply."[5] As a result of the constant, sometimes obsessive focus on our phones, we are distracted from our surroundings, the people around us, and the tasks we are trying to accomplish. Cell phone addiction is highest in adolescents and associated with both depression and lower performance in school.[6] If that weren't bad enough, smartphone addiction hurts innocent bystanders too: More than 30 percent of adults and 40 percent of adolescents admit to texting while driving, which demonstrably impairs driving and increases the risk of deadly crashes.[7]

Even when we're not actively using our phones, our reliance on them means that their mere presence frequently takes a toll on our attention. In one experiment led by Bill Thornton,[8] college students took a test composed of a series of difficult or easy cognitive tasks. Half of these test takers were asked to put their phones away during the test; the others were asked to keep their phones close by on the table in order to answer an upcoming survey about its features. Although no one had trouble with the easy problems, the students who took the test with a phone in view performed about 20 percent worse on the difficult problems than students who stowed their phones out of sight.

A similar experiment showed how this distractedness can also spoil our face-to-face interactions.[9] Pairs of strangers were introduced to one another and got acquainted by taking turns talking about interesting and meaningful recent events in their lives. In one condition, the experimenter left his cell phone on the table near them; in the other condition, the experimenter left his notebook in the same spot. After the conversation, the participants rated their interaction and their partner. As in the earlier study, the cell phone was disruptive; when it was present in the room, people saw their partners as being less understanding and trustworthy and thought it less likely that spending more time together could lead to a friendship. Other similar studies find that the presence of a cell phone during social interactions reduces eye contact, engagement, empathic concern for the partner, and enjoyment of the conversation.[10]

Social Skills Deficits

The average American spends about 10 hours a day staring at a screen: five hours watching television and about five on their smartphone.[11] This means that the average American child spends more time immersed in electronic media than with parents or in school. You've probably heard your parents and professors say something like,

"In my day, we talked to each other, told stories, made up games, and ran around outside. Today, a birthday party is just a bunch of kids in the same room, sitting around eating cake and looking at their phones. I worry about what this does to their social skills."

Are their worries justified? Apparently so. Yalda Uhls and her colleagues[12] measured the social abilities of school children, examining similar students from the same school, who on average spent about 4.5 hours a day consuming media on their phones. First, all of the students were tested on their social skills; specifically, they were shown pictures of faces expressing different emotions (fear, anger, sadness, happiness) and were asked to identify the emotion the person was feeling in each picture. Then, half of the students were sent to a five-day summer camp that allowed no cell phones or other devices. The rest stayed home with their electronics. After the five days, all of the children were tested again, revealing a significant improvement in social intelligence among the children who were phoneless for five days. Although electronics — including videogames — can be powerful tools for learning,[13] it seems that nothing beats good old face-to-face interactions for learning to read and how to interact with others. In addition to robbing us of opportunities to develop social skills, heavy immersion in social networking sites can encourage people to become more self-centered and narcissistic, and to believe that fame, wealth, and popularity matter more than friendship, generosity, and community.[14]

That's not the whole story, of course. Clearly, there are pros and cons to our immersion in the digital world. It's instructive to remember that just about every new form of media was greeted with apprehension about its effects on the hearts and minds of the young. Socrates lamented the invention of books, which he said would promote "forgetfulness." When comic books were introduced in the 1930s, parents were warned that comics would turn their children into juvenile delinquents (unlike books, which were considered good for young minds). Radio, television, computers, texting, Google, and Powerpoint — all have been accused of making us lazy, less intelligent, shortening our attention spans, and ruining our social lives.[15] Yet our cognitive abilities actually grew over the decades that television, comic books, and other technologies flourished, and the crime rate among teenagers declined.[16] Technologies will continue to proliferate and change the way we live, and the best response is not to bemoan this fact, but to learn to use our devices intelligently and in moderation. Studies have identified the psychological and emotional benefits of turning off e-mail and Twitter when people study or work, of having face-to-face conversations without a phone on the table, and taking walks in nature, looking up at the sky and trees.[17]

In addition to how *much* we use media, *how* we use it makes a difference, too. A key determinant of whether immersing ourselves in social media elevates us or depresses us is how actively we participate. Do you passively look at other people's profiles, scrolling through without communicating? Or do you comment, like, and post your own news and pictures? It's the more passive use—*lurking*—that is most likely leave us feeling down, left out, and unhappy that our lives seem much less exciting than the lives of our friends. To enjoy social media optimally, we need to respond to others; just as in real life, we need to participate. By actively participating when we are online, and by being mindful and proactive about the addictive potential of our gadgets, we can reap considerable benefits and joys without crowding out or distracting us away from valuable offline experiences.[18]

Persuasion

We live not only in an age of mass communication, but also in an age characterized by attempts at mass *persuasion*. Everywhere we look, someone is trying to educate us; convince us to buy a product or donate to a cause; or persuade us to vote for a candidate or subscribe to some version of what is right, true, or beautiful. This aim is most obvious in advertising. Manufacturers of nearly identical products (aspirin, toothpaste, or detergent, for example) spend vast amounts of money to persuade us to buy the product in *their* package.

But influence through the mass media needn't be as blatant as an ad. Let's look at something that claims to be objective: the network news. Are the newscasters *trying* to sell us anything? With a few exceptions, no, but those who produce television news exert a powerful influence on our opinions simply by determining which events are given exposure and how much exposure they are given. What factors determine their selection? The primary one is the need to attract viewers. News is a form of *entertainment*. When those in charge of news programming decide which news events to cover—from the thousands of stories that occur every day at a local, national, and international level—and then which to present to the public, they make their decisions, in large part, on the entertainment value of the material. It's much more compelling to watch images of a flooded city (cars washed away, people floating on fallen trees) than of people building a levee to prevent flooding; it is not nearly as exciting to watch a construction project. And yet a city's decision to build a levee may be more important news.

Just as action events such as football games are more entertaining on television than quiet events such as chess matches, it is more likely that riots, bombings, earthquakes, massacres, and other violent acts will get more air time than stories about people working to prevent violence. Thus, newscasts tend to focus on the violent or destructive behavior of terrorists, murderers, protesters, strikers, police, or out-of-control celebrities because action makes for more exciting viewing than does a portrayal of people behaving in a peaceful, orderly manner.[19] Moreover, the most violent stories are usually reported earliest in the broadcast—especially on local news programs—creating the message that the violent stories were the essential news of the day. As reporters put it, "If it bleeds, it leads."

Such coverage obviously presents a distorted picture of the world. In trying to entertain us, the news media unwittingly lead us to believe that people behave far more violently now than ever before. As we saw in discussing the availability heuristic in Chapter 2, people estimate the frequency of events by how easily they come to mind. When the media bombard viewers with bad news about crime and terrorism, people will overestimate the prevalence of violence and disaster. This bias both reflects and reinforces our evolved tendency to attend to what is threatening—the "bad is stronger than good" phenomenon. Little wonder that 60 percent of people surveyed in a Gallup poll said they believed that crime and murder are on the rise in America, when in fact, crimes of all kind have been steadily declining for 25 years.[20] This false perception may cause people to be unhappy, fearful, and depressed about the state of society and may ultimately affect how they vote, their attitudes about other groups and other nations, and their desire to visit major urban centers. (As one resident in a rural Idaho town said to a visiting New Yorker, "Why would I go to New York? It's full of gangs killing each other.")

Of course, some violent events do warrant extensive coverage. Following the terrorist attack of September 11, 2001, most Americans sat glued to their TV sets because they wanted to know what was happening, and they needed reassurance that the situation was under control. They watched the collapse of the Twin Towers hundreds of times as the news channels gave that event round-the-clock coverage. How can we be sure that is what citizens wanted to see? In the two weeks following the attack, the number of people who tuned in to CNN jumped 667 percent. The *New York Times* sold a quarter of a million more newspapers on September 12 than it did on September 10.[21]

It is good to be informed, and the media play a crucial role in keeping us informed. However, there can be a downside to this kind of exposure, as well. Whether it is intentional or not, repeated vivid imagery of this sort shapes attitudes and opinions. The constant images of the collapsing Twin Towers, as well as the repetition of bellicose slogans on news channels ("The War on Terror," "America Under Attack!", "America Fights Back!"), contributed to the arousal of intense emotions in viewers and thus reduced the likelihood of any real debate about how America should respond. Instead, the proposal to declare war on Iraq (a nation that had nothing to do with the destruction of the Twin Towers) sailed through Congress with hardly a murmur of opposition, a war that most Americans later came to see as a terrible blunder.[22]

This is a social psychology book, not a political treatise. What I am suggesting is that, in a democracy, major decisions—like whether to go to war—benefit from rational public debate. Strong emotions, such as those stirred up by the news media, often get in the way of rational decision-making. As Hermann Goering, one of Adolf Hitler's top aides, said before being sentenced to death at Nuremberg, "The people can always be brought to do the bidding of the leaders ... all you have to do is tell them they are being attacked and denounce the peacemakers for lack of patriotism and exposing the country to danger. It works the same in any country."[23]

Media Contagion The media also exerts its power through a phenomenon known as **emotional contagion**, which occurs when one person's emotional behavior triggers similar emotions and behaviors in observers. When you go into a drugstore to buy pills of any kind, there will be a safety cap on the bottle. Want to know why? In the fall of 1982, seven people in the Chicago area died after taking Extra Strength Tylenol capsules laced with cyanide. This event, both tragic and bizarre, was widely publicized; even in those pre-internet days, the story was ubiquitous. You couldn't turn on the TV or radio or pick up a newspaper without learning about the Tylenol poisonings. The effects of this prominent coverage were immediate: Similar poisonings were reported in cities across the country involving the contamination of mouthwash, eyedrops, nasal spray, soda pop, and even hot dogs. Dramatically billed as "copycat poisonings," these stories, in turn, received widespread media attention, creating a spiral of even more stories. Many people panicked, seeking medical aid for burns and poisonings when they suffered from no more than common rashes, sore throats, and stomachaches. False alarms outnumbered verified cases of product tampering by seven to one.[24] Because these events occurred just prior to Halloween, worried officials in scores of communities banned trick-or-treating, fearing that many individuals might mimic the murders by contaminating children's candy.

The initial Chicago poisonings were almost certainly the work of one person, who has never been identified or caught. But the belief caught hold that the wave of poisoning constituted "an epidemic without a cure," in the words of one news service,[25] and was itself the symptom of a "sick" society, a country going "crazy." Many newspapers found themselves in the ironic position of first sensationalizing the poisoning incidents and then sensationalizing the subsequent critical comments of media experts discussing the disastrous consequences of such publicity.

A few years later, four teenagers in New Jersey made a suicide pact and then carried out their plan. Within a week of this multiple suicide, two teenagers in the Midwest were found dead under similar circumstances. Media reports spotlighted the confusion and grief surrounding teenage suicide, with many feature stories about it—and that very coverage triggered some vulnerable, depressed teens to consider suicide a solution for their own unhappiness. Sociologist David Phillips and his colleagues[26] tracked fluctuations in teenage suicides by comparing suicide rates before the stories with rates after the stories; the more coverage devoted by major television networks to suicide, the greater the subsequent increase in suicides among teenagers. Suicides are particularly likely to spike when a celebrity commits suicide, both because their example generates more publicity and because they are more potent agents of influence. When depressed individuals learn that someone famous has taken their life—beloved figures like Marilyn Monroe, Kurt Cobain, or Robin Williams—they begin to think seriously of doing the same thing, especially if they feel an emotional link or psychological connection to the celebrity.[27] That's why suicide prevention researchers have found that when media stories avoid emphasizing or glamorizing suicide, and don't make it seem like a simple or inevitable solution for people who are at risk, the contagion effect is reduced.[28]

I am not suggesting that the media should not report sensational events like the Tylenol poisoning or celebrity suicides. And I'm not suggesting that the news media are *trying* to foster violence or suicide. Rather, I am underlining the obvious fact that their selective emphasis puts the media in the position not only of reporting events but of determining subsequent ones. The more media attention an event gets, the more "contagious" it becomes, and the higher the likelihood that others will be inspired to follow suit.

In today's 24/7 news cycles, sometimes the role of the media in reporting an event becomes more newsworthy than the event itself. (It wasn't always this way; there was a time in American history when news stations didn't have "breaking news" every five seconds.) Today, when a significant event happens, newscasters not only report on it, but they report on all the people analyzing it and commenting on it, and then their comments often become newsworthy. In its circularity, this phenomenon reminds me of a brand of table salt that was popular when I was a kid. On the box of table salt was a picture of a little girl holding up a box of the table salt, on which there was a picture of a little girl holding a box of salt, on which there was a picture of a little girl holding a box of salt, and so on. On 24-hour cable news channels like CNN, MSNBC, and FOX, the need to fill the hours of air time with news and analysis has made this sort of redundant exercise commonplace.

Effectiveness of Media Appeals

What about intentional persuasion? How credible and effective are obvious attempts to package and sell products (toothpaste, aspirin, presidential candidates) through the mass media? They must work; why else would corporations and political parties spend hundreds of millions of dollars a year trumpeting their products?

Most of us have seen children being seduced by toy commercials that artfully depict the drabbest toys in an irresistible way. A child watching the Disney Channel, Nickelodeon, or the Cartoon Network is also inundated with fast-paced ads for cereal, junk food, and candy, which use familiar characters, promotional offers, and the promise of fun to persuade kids to get their parents to buy them the products presented in commercials. It works.[29] More than 90 percent of preschool children asked for toys or food they saw advertised on television, according to a survey of their mothers.[30] Two-thirds of mothers in another study reported hearing their very young children sing advertising jingles they learned from television.[31] And experiments show that when young children are given a choice of candy bars, they are significantly more likely to choose one that they saw during an advertisement or during the show itself.[32]

Most children catch on after a time; my own children eventually developed a healthy skepticism about the truthfulness of these commercials. Indeed, one survey[33] found that by the sixth grade, only 12 percent of children believed that television commercials told the truth all or most of the time; by the tenth grade, only 4 percent felt the ads were truthful most of the time. And by the time they are adults, the overwhelming majority of viewers believe that advertisements contain untruthful arguments. The more educated that viewers are, the more skeptical they are, and that skepticism leads them to believe that they are immune to persuasion. If only the mere fact of knowing that a communicator is biased protected us from being influenced by the message! Unfortunately, just because we *think* we are immune to persuasion does not necessarily mean we *are* immune. Indeed, our sense of immunity can make us more susceptible to persuasion of all kinds.[34]

In the case of many consumer products, the public tends to buy a specific brand for no reason other than that it is heavily advertised. The headache-remedy business is an excellent example of our susceptibility to TV ads even when we know they are biased. A well-known brand of aspirin (let's say "Brand A") advertises itself as 100 percent pure aspirin; the commercial goes on to say that government tests have shown that no other pain remedy is stronger or more effective than Brand A. What the maker doesn't bother to mention is that the government test showed that no brand was any weaker or less effective than any of the others, because all of them were straight aspirin. In other words, all tested brands were equal—except, that is, in price. For the privilege of popping Brand A, consumers pay approximately three times the price of an equally effective but unadvertised version. Another product proclaims it uses the special (unnamed) ingredient "that doctors recommend."

By reading the label, we discover the mystery ingredient to be good old inexpensive aspirin.

Such blatant attempts at mass persuasion seem pitifully obvious. Yet tremendous numbers of consumers set aside their skepticism even though they "know" the message is an obvious attempt to sell a product. Why? When we are dealing with identical or very similar products, mere familiarity with the brand name can make a huge difference. Robert Zajonc[35] showed that, all other things being equal, the more familiar an item is, the more attractive it is, even if the item is just a silly nonsense word. We prefer faces we've seen 10 times to equally attractive faces we've seen only five times,[36] we prefer words that contain the same letters as those in our names,[37] and we prefer pictures of ourselves that are backward (and thus match the familiar view of our faces that we see in the mirror every day), whereas our friends prefer the non-mirror image of our faces (which *they* are accustomed to seeing).[38] Unless there is something inherently noxious about a stimulus, the more we are exposed to it, the more we will tend to like it.

Suppose I walk into a supermarket looking for laundry detergent. I go to the detergent section, and I am staggered by the wide array of brand names. Because it doesn't matter too much to me which one I buy, I reach for the most familiar one—and, chances are, it is familiar because I've heard and seen the name advertised over and over again. If this is the case, then sudden increases in television exposure should produce big changes in familiarity and, perhaps, in sales. And they do. Several years ago, the Northwestern Mutual Life Insurance Company conducted a nationwide poll to find out how well the public recognized its name. It came out thirty-fourth among insurance companies. Two weeks later the company repeated the poll. This time it came out third in name familiarity. What caused this amazing leap from obscurity to fame? Two weeks and $1 million worth of advertising. Familiarity does not necessarily mean sales, but the two are frequently linked—as evidenced by the fact that A&W Root Beer boosted its share of the market from 15 percent to 50 percent after six months of television advertising. The primary function of many commercials is to get the name of the product firmly planted in our heads, which is why the product's name is repeated often while the competitor's product is rarely named. This availability of the advertised brand can suggest to us its superiority to the brand that comes to mind less easily. Then, once we buy the product and find that we like it, we develop brand loyalty. So although we rarely feel consciously influenced by advertising—we don't leap out of our chairs and rush to the supermarket to get that root beer—it can initiate a longer-term process that indirectly gets us to buy heavily advertised products later, when we have a choice.[39]

Is voting for a presidential candidate the same kind of decision as choosing an insurance company, root beer, or brand of aspirin? The answer is sometimes. Sometimes candidates who spend the most on advertising receive the most votes,[40] but this happens primarily when they spend early in the campaign to define themselves against their opponents, and therefore establish the "narrative" of the campaign.[41] Commercials on TV are especially effective when the campaign centers on a highly charged issue that arouses strong emotions in voters. For a compelling illustration, let's travel back to the 1988 presidential campaign between George H. W. Bush and Michael Dukakis, former governor of Massachusetts, which featured what is now one of the most iconic political attack ads in history. In the summer of 1988, Bush trailed far behind Dukakis in the race for the presidency. Many observers were convinced that Dukakis's lead was insurmountable. Within a few short months, however, the lead had all but evaporated, and on election day, Bush won handily. A number of political analysts credit Willie Horton with playing a major role in this turnaround. Indeed, *Time* magazine referred to Willie Horton as "George Bush's most valuable player."[42]

Who was Willie Horton? He was not one of Bush's advisors, nor was he a major financial contributor to the Bush campaign. Indeed, the two men had never met. Willie Horton was a convicted felon who had been released from a Massachusetts prison before the end of his term as part of a furlough program. (Furloughs are temporary, approved leaves of absence from prison for medical, religious, or educational purposes.) While on furlough, Horton escaped to Maryland; there, he raped a woman in front of her male companion, whom he had wounded and tied to a chair—a disgusting story, to be sure. Michael Dukakis was governor of Massachusetts when Horton's furlough was granted. Claiming that Dukakis was "soft on crime," Bush ran a series of television ads showing the mug shot of a scowling Willie Horton and depicting criminals going in and out of prison through a revolving door. These ads struck a chord with many Americans, who were frightened of street crime and who believed that the criminal justice system favored criminals at the expense of victims. Moreover, the fact that Willie Horton was black, and that his victims were white, was not lost on most white viewers.[43]

How did Dukakis fight back? With facts and figures—he pointed out that Massachusetts was only one of many states with furlough programs and that even the federal government (of which Bush was a member) furloughed inmates from its prisons. In addition, he noted, furlough programs were highly effective. The year before, 53,000 inmates received more than 200,000 furloughs, and only a small percentage got into trouble.[44] Dukakis also pointed out that, typically, furloughs were granted to convicts who were near the end of their terms, and that the furloughs were intended to orient them to the outside world. He insisted that the whole issue was a contrivance—that, if elected, George Bush had no intention of changing the furlough system.

Are you getting bored yet? So were the voters. If Michael Dukakis had put a social psychologist on his staff, he would have received better advice. When people are scared and angry, facts alone are neither reassuring nor convincing.[45] Information can be effective, but only if it is tied to solutions to problems the voters are deeply concerned about. In the 1992 and 1996 presidential elections, candidate Bill Clinton (apparently having learned a lesson from the Dukakis campaign) kept the attention of the American people focused on one overriding issue—the state of the economy—and did not allow himself to be sidetracked by emotional issues.[46]

In most American elections, the most successful candidates are those who target strong emotions: fear of crime, disgust at the idea of gay marriage or unisex bathrooms, anger at government bailouts of failed banks, fear of climate change, anger at immigrants for stealing jobs from hardworking Americans, and so on. Candidates have a harder time when they attempt a more reasoned approach, such as explaining the complex economic rationale for bailouts or international trade agreements. The 2016 presidential campaign—arguably the most vulgar in American history—took this focus on fear, anger, and other negative emotions to a new level. At one point, Donald Trump accused Hillary Clinton of being a dangerous criminal who would destroy the country, allow illegal immigrants to take American jobs, admit terrorists, send American jobs to China, and take away people's guns to boot. He called her a "nasty woman" and intimated that if elected, he would put her in jail. Clinton attacked back hard, mostly by using facts and figures to dispute Trump's allegations. By the end of the campaign, both candidates were demonized to the point that many voters were motivated less by love of their own candidate than by hatred, fear, or disgust for their candidate's monstrous opponent.

Education, Propaganda, or Fake News?

What is the difference between propaganda and education? The *American Heritage Dictionary of the English Language* defines *propaganda* as "the systematic propagation of a given doctrine" and *education* as "the act of imparting knowledge or skill." We can all agree that aspirin ads are propaganda, designed intentionally to mislead consumers into believing that a product with a brand name is better than a generic. "Selling" a candidate, however, blurs the line. Political consultants display their candidate in a favorable manner, which could conceivably be considered an attempt to *educate* the public on the policies and virtues of the candidate. But as we saw, their efforts often dismiss factual information in favor of promoting a "given doctrine." And what about high-school history textbooks that intend to "impart knowledge"? What knowledge, and from whose point of view? As the old saying goes, "History is written by the victors," and until relatively recently, the contributions made by women, blacks, and other minorities to the American story were almost invisible in such books. The fact that school boards around the country still fight furiously over what a history or biology book "should" say illustrates the thin line between education and propaganda.

In practice, whether a person regards a particular course of instruction as educational or propagandistic depends, to a large extent, on his or her moral values and ideology. When my children were in high school, they were required to watch a film about drug abuse, which mentioned that many hard-core narcotics users began their addiction by smoking marijuana. I'm certain that most school officials regarded the presentation of this fact as a case of "imparting knowledge," but most recreational marijuana users regarded it as "the systematic propagation of a given doctrine"—the belief that marijuana invariably leads to the use of harder drugs. Or consider the topic of sex education in the schools as viewed by evangelical Christians or by supporters of Planned Parenthood: One side would regard its teachings about sex as "education" and the other side's as "propaganda." This is not to say that all communications are drastically slanted and one-sided. Rather, when we are dealing with emotionally charged issues upon which people disagree, it is virtually impossible to construct a communication that people on both sides would agree is fair and impartial.

This issue has become thornier with the rise of cable news and the internet, which allow us to choose our preferred sources of "information." If you are conservative, you most likely get your news from right-leaning sources like Fox News or websites with a right-wing view of the world. If you are liberal, you most likely get your news from MSNBC or correspondingly left-wing websites. In addition, many of us get our news from social networks like Facebook, which further guarantees that what we see is the result of a filtering process that gives us more of what we already believe. Algorithms generated by our clicking patterns feed our interests and filter out content we find offensive or boring. But the biggest filter is social: When we see mainly what others in our social network see and "like," we are less likely to encounter stories that might challenge, broaden, or change our established worldview. The result is what the internet activist Eli Pariser calls the "filter bubble," the personalized universe of information that makes it into our social media feeds and therefore gets our attention.[47] Black and white, religious and secular, liberal and conservative, old and young, urban and rural—each "bubble" has its own interests and attitudes. The filtering process ensures that we will marinate in news and ideas that we "like," with the result that our belief systems are reinforced and others are attacked and ridiculed. And because the filter does this invisibly, we think we are seeing reality instead of a carefully curated version of it.

We also think it was always this way—but it wasn't. In 1968, most Americans got their TV news from Walter Cronkite, a veteran war reporter who, as anchor of the CBS evening news, was widely considered the most trusted man in America. That year, Cronkite famously changed the course of history when, during his evening newscast, he shared his opinion that the Vietnam war was unwinnable. Because most Americans—right and left—trusted Cronkite, their attitudes shifted and public support for the war eroded. It is impossible to imagine a news anchor wielding such broad influence today.[48]

Today, anyone with a computer can be a blogger or even start a web-based newspaper or magazine, creating and distributing news with little or no editorial oversight. This capability has led to a proliferation of propaganda in the form of "fake news"—false stories packaged as true. During the 2016 election, a photo of Donald Trump went viral on the internet, emblazoned with a quote purportedly from years earlier about his presidential ambitions: "If I were to run, I'd run as a Republican. They're the dumbest group of voters in the country. They believe anything on Fox News. I could lie, and they'd still eat it up. I bet my numbers would be terrific." Because this statement felt true to liberals, and echoed sentiments that Trump actually did say, most liberals believed it; despite its being false and repeatedly debunked, the quote continued to circulate on the internet for over a year.[49] An equally false claim also went viral within right-wing circles, alleging that the Democratic candidate, Hillary Clinton, was helping operate a sex trafficking network out of a pizza parlor in Washington, D.C. As we saw in Chapter 1, the pizza parlor endured constant harassment and death threats from irate citizens. One such citizen traveled from North Carolina to investigate and ended up shooting several rounds into the restaurant with an assault rifle.

Fake news demonstrates an unsettling fact about modern persuasion: Because it comes from so many (often unknown) sources and is so easy to package and share as real news, more than ever people rely on their existing ideas and their social network to determine what to believe. Such an environment encourages the human tendency to categorize information as *education* if we agree with its implications or as *propaganda* if we do not.

Two Major Routes to Persuasion

When confronted with a persuasive argument, do we think deeply about it or do we accept it without much thought? This question underlies much of our understanding of persuasion. As we saw in Chapter 2, automatic thinking processes allow us to move through the world without thinking too much. According to Richard Petty and John Cacioppo,[50] we are inclined to think deeply about an issue if it is one that is relevant to us and if we have the required expertise. In these circumstances, we tend to give the argument careful scrutiny. But sometimes, even if the issue is important, we may not process an argument carefully because we are distracted or tired, we lack the knowledge to evaluate it critically, or the communication is presented in a way that lulls us into acceptance.

Petty and Cacioppo argue that there are essentially two ways that people are persuaded—*centrally* or *peripherally*. The **central route to persuasion** involves weighing arguments and considering relevant facts, thinking about issues in a systematic fashion, and coming to a decision. In contrast, the **peripheral route to persuasion** is less direct; rather than weighing and considering the strength of arguments, the person responds to simple, often irrelevant cues that suggest the rightness, wrongness, or attractiveness of an argument without giving it much thought. For example, people who consider the strength of arguments about how to reduce prison recidivism are taking the central route; those who get scared and angry by the image of Willie Horton are taking the peripheral route. Likewise, if you decide to buy a particular laptop because you've read about its user-friendliness, processing speed, memory, and data storage, you are being moved by the logic of the argument. This is the central route. But if you decide to buy the laptop because your favorite entertainer endorses it, you are being moved by issues irrelevant to the product. This is the peripheral route. Few persuasive appeals are purely central or peripheral; most contain elements aimed at both modes of processing.

Lawyers and politicians often combine central arguments and peripheral cues. In 1995, the murder trial of O. J. Simpson riveted the nation; millions of viewers tuned in to see the Hall of Fame running back and his "dream team" of lawyers fight the charges that Simpson had brutally murdered his ex-wife and her friend. In 2016, this story and the trial were retold in an award-winning series, *The People v. O.J. Simpson: American Crime Story*, and in the documentary *O.J.: Made in America*. In one of the most dramatic moments of the trial, the prosecutor asked Simpson to try on the bloodstained gloves worn by the murderer. Simpson struggled to get the gloves on, but they appeared to be too tight. Simpson's lead attorney, Johnnie Cochran, wasted no time in coming up with a memorable line, and in so doing, added a persuasive peripheral cue to the jury. Cochran said, "If it doesn't fit, you must acquit." The statement was persuasive, but not because of the argument's logic—after all, it is certainly possible to commit murder wearing tight gloves, and leather gloves will shrink if soaked in water (or blood). But Cochran's statement resonated because when people are evaluating the quality of an argument, they can be influenced by the way it is phrased. In Cochran's case, his rhyme gave the statement a ring of truth. Matthew McGlone[51] demonstrated our susceptibility to such tactics. He found that college students were more persuaded by unfamiliar aphorisms that rhyme ("woes unite foes") than the same ideas presented in nonrhyming form ("woes unite enemies"). The peripheral route to persuasion can be surprisingly subtle — yet surprisingly effective.

In recent years, choosing the right words (even if they don't rhyme) has become a science. Politicians and advertisers hire researchers to set up focus groups and conduct surveys to test terms, phrases, and names to see which ones fly best with the public they hope to reach. For example, most Americans are in favor of what used to be called the "estate tax," a tax on individuals when they inherit immense wealth from their parents. Public opinion about the estate tax changed when it was renamed by a clever political consultant named Frank Luntz. Luntz's research[52] suggested that people could be turned against the tax law if politicians began referring to it as a "death tax," which conjures the image of being unfairly penalized for dying.

Politicians and political action groups routinely give policies nicknames that belie the genuine content of the legislation, depending on whether they want it to succeed or fail. The Affordable Care Act (ACA) of 2010 nearly failed when a politician charged that a provision in the bill would allow doctors and insurance companies to decide the fate of patients with terminal illnesses. In their attack on the bill, opponents started calling these decision-making meetings "death panels," implying that strangers could decide, as one congressman put it, "to pull the plug on Grandma." In reality, the provision merely required that insurance companies pay for consultation between patients and their doctors to consider options for terminally ill patients — a far cry from the image evoked by the term "death panel." Moreover, the ACA itself was given a disparaging title by its opponents, which reduced its popularity: Obamacare. Far more Americans approved of the Affordable Care Act than approved of Obamacare, although it was the same program.

In 2001, the United States Department of Agriculture approved a meat additive called "lean finely textured beef," intended to stretch out packages of ground beef without increasing its fat content. When ABC News questioned the use of the paste-like additive, which is put in 70 percent of the ground beef supply in America, it referred to the substance as "pink slime." Imagine the public reaction! Petitions to eliminate the substance from school lunches and supermarkets were circulated, and despite its safety,[53] the producers lost customers. Eventually they sued ABC News for over a billion dollars. True or false, the pictures that pop into our heads influence our beliefs, feelings, and behaviors, and these images often depend on the specific words we use to label them. Words conjure powerful images and emotions that can overwhelm our consideration of the facts.

To sum up, if your aim is to persuade, you need to know how important the issue is to your audience and how well informed they are. If they are knowledgeable and motivated, you will need to include strong, logical arguments in your persuasive appeal. If they don't care about the issue or cannot comprehend it fully, you will need to persuade them by using high-quality peripheral cues that you attach to the message. That might work for a short while, but if you want your persuasive message to stick, experiments suggest that persuasion that gets people to process arguments systematically is much more likely to endure than persuasion based solely on peripheral cues.[54]

Let's turn now to the three key factors that can increase the effectiveness of a communication or persuasive attempt: (1) the source of the communication (who says it), (2) the nature of the communication (how he or she says it), and (3) the characteristics and mindset of the audience (to whom he or she says it). Put another way: Who says what to whom? We will look at each of these separately.

The Source of the Communication

It seems pretty clear that we are most likely to be persuaded by people whom we trust. But what determines trust?

Credibility Many years ago, I saw the poet Allen Ginsberg on a late-night talk show. Ginsberg was among the most popular poets of the so-called Beat Generation; his poem "Howl" had scandalized the literary establishment in the 1950s. On the talk show, Ginsberg was at it again: Having just finished boasting about his homosexuality (which at that time was shocking to most Americans), he was talking about the generation gap — how young and old misunderstand one another. The camera panned in. He was fat, bearded, and looked a trifle wild-eyed (was he stoned?); long hair grew in unruly patches from the sides of his otherwise bald head; he was wearing a tie-dyed

T-shirt with a hole in it and a few strands of beads. Although he was talking earnestly—and, in my view, sensibly—about the problems of the young, the studio audience was laughing. They were treating him like a clown. It dawned on me that, in all probability, the vast majority of the people at home, lying in bed watching him, could not possibly take him seriously—no matter how sensible his message and no matter how earnestly he delivered it. His appearance was overwhelming the audience's reaction. The scientist in me longed to replace the wild-eyed Ginsberg with a well-dressed Ivy League professor and have him move his lips while Ginsberg said the same words off camera. My guess is that, under these circumstances, Ginsberg's message would have been well received.

No need. Similar experiments have already been done. Indeed, speculations about the effects of prestige on persuasion are ancient. Earlier than 300 years B.C., Aristotle, the world's first published social psychologist, wrote:

> We believe good men more fully and more readily than others: this is true generally whatever the question is, and absolutely true where exact certainty is impossible and opinions are divided ... It is not true, as some writers assume in their treatises on rhetoric, that the personal goodness revealed by the speaker contributes nothing to his power of persuasion; on the contrary, his character may almost be called the most effective means of persuasion he possesses.[55]

It took some 2,300 years, but Aristotle's observation was finally put to a scientific test by Carl Hovland and Walter Weiss.[56] They asked large numbers of people to evaluate a claim that building nuclear-powered submarines was a feasible undertaking. (This experiment was done in 1951, when harnessing nuclear energy for such purposes was merely a dream.) Some were informed that the argument was made by a highly credible person, namely J. Robert Oppenheimer, a nationally known and highly respected atomic physicist; others were informed that the same argument came from a source with low credibility, namely *Pravda*, the official newspaper of the Communist Party in the then Soviet Union—a publication infamous for its lack of objectivity and truthfulness. Almost everyone who believed that the communication came from Oppenheimer changed their opinions, believing more strongly than they had in the feasibility of nuclear submarines. Very few of those who read the identical prediction attributed to *Pravda* shifted their opinions.

This phenomenon has been repeatedly confirmed by other experimenters using a wide variety of topics and attributing the messages to a wide variety of communicators. A judge in the juvenile court is better than most people at swaying opinion about juvenile delinquency, a famous poet can sway opinion about the merits of a poem, and a medical journal can sway opinion about whether antihistamines should be dispensed without a prescription. What do the physicist, judge, poet, and medical journal have that *Pravda* didn't have? What makes the difference in their effectiveness? Aristotle said we believe "good men," by which he meant people of high moral caliber. Hovland and Weiss use the term *credible*, which removes the moral connotations present in the Aristotelian definition. The famous physicist, judge, and poet are credible; they are not necessarily good, but they are both *expert* and *trustworthy*. It makes sense to allow yourself to be influenced by communicators who are trustworthy and who know what they are talking about. It makes sense for people to be influenced by J. Robert Oppenheimer when he is voicing an opinion about nuclear power, and it makes sense for people who are evaluating the quality of a poem to be influenced by a great poet.

But not everyone is equally influenced by the same communicator. Indeed, the same communicator may be regarded by some people as possessing high credibility and by others as possessing low credibility. Moreover, certain peripheral attributes of the communicator may loom large for some members of the audience; such attributes can make a communicator either effective or ineffective.

This phenomenon was demonstrated in an experiment I did with Burton Golden[57] in which sixth-grade children listened to a speech extolling the usefulness of arithmetic. The man giving the talk was introduced either as a prize-winning engineer from a prestigious university or as someone who washed dishes for a living. As you might expect, the engineer was far more effective at influencing the youngsters' opinions than the dishwasher was—hardly surprising or even interesting. But in addition, we varied his race. In some of the trials the communicator was white, and in others, black. Several weeks prior to the experiment, the children (all of whom were white) had filled out a questionnaire designed to measure their degree of prejudice against black people. The results were striking: Among those children who were most prejudiced against blacks, the black engineer was *less* influential than the white engineer, although both delivered the same speech. Moreover, among those children who were least prejudiced against blacks, the black engineer was *more* influential than the white engineer. You might think that, in a purely rational world, a prestigious engineer should be able to influence sixth-graders about the importance of arithmetic regardless of the color of his or her skin, but as you have been learning throughout this book, this is not a purely rational world. Depending upon the children's racial attitudes, they were either more influenced or less influenced by a black engineer than by an otherwise identical white engineer.

This behavior hardly seems adaptive. If the quality of your life depends on the extent to which you allow a communication about arithmetic to influence your opinion, the expertise of the communicator would seem to be the most reasonable factor to heed. To the extent that other factors (such as skin color) decrease or increase your susceptibility to persuasion, you are behaving in a maladaptive manner. But advertisers bank on your irrationality in this respect, counting on irrelevant factors to increase a spokesperson's effectiveness — a cute little gecko to sell you insurance! Frequently, such peripheral cues are the only aspects of the communicator the viewer sees. For decades, ever since the 1950s, the marketers of Wheaties have had famous athletes on their cereal boxes, all enthusiastically endorsing their product: decathlon champions Bob Richards in the 1960s and Bruce Jenner (now Caitlin Jenner) in the 1970s; gymnast Mary Lou Retton in the 1980s; and later such star athletes as Alex Rodriguez, Michael Phelps, and LeBron James. Apparently, whoever is in charge of selling Wheaties to the masses is convinced that athletes are better than some learned professor of nutrition at being effective communicators.

Is this conviction justified? Will people be influenced by an ad just because a prominent sports personality is involved? Even if we admire the skill such athletes display on the playing field, can we trust them to tell us the truth about the products they endorse? After all, we all know that the sports star peddling a particular brand of breakfast cereal or athletic shoes is getting paid handsomely for his or her endorsement. My guess is that most of us would be quick to say, "No way. I'm not going to eat Wheaties or buy Nikes just because LeBron *says* he eats Wheaties and favors Nikes. Maybe *other* people might be persuaded to run out and buy something just because a sports figure tells them to, but I certainly wouldn't trust even my favorite player's advice on how to spend my hard-earned cash." But can people predict their own behavior? Before you answer, let's take a closer look at the factor of trust.

Clearly, trust is important in determining whether a communicator will be effective. For example, perhaps the crucial reason the prejudiced sixth-graders in the Aronson and Golden experiment were less influenced by the black engineer than by the white engineer was that they did not trust black people. If this is true, then if we could offer the audience independent evidence that a person is trustworthy, that person should become more persuasive.

How might communicators make themselves seem trustworthy to us? One way is to argue against their own self-interest. If people have nothing to gain (and perhaps something to lose) by convincing us, we will trust them and they will be more effective. An illustration may be helpful. Suppose a habitual criminal, a recently convicted smuggler and peddler of heroin, is giving a talk on the abuses of the U.S. judicial system. Would he influence you? Probably not. Most people would regard him as untrustworthy, outside the Aristotelian definition of a good man, because he has a vested interest in criticizing the system that is punishing him. But suppose he is arguing that the criminal justice system is too lenient on people like him—that criminals almost always beat the rap if they have a smart lawyer, and that even if criminals are convicted, the sentences normally meted out are too soft. Would his argument influence you now?

I'm certain it would. Elaine Walster, Darcy Abrahams, and I[58] presented college students with a newspaper clipping of an interview between a news reporter and Joe "The Shoulder" Napolitano, who was identified as a mobster and hit man. (We made up his name.) In one experimental condition, Joe "The Shoulder" argued for stricter courts and more severe sentences. In another condition, he argued that courts should be more lenient and sentences less severe. We also ran a parallel set of conditions in which the same statements were attributed to a respected public official. When Joe "The Shoulder" argued for more lenient courts, he was totally ineffective; in fact, he caused the participants' opinions to change slightly in the opposite direction. But when he argued for stricter, more powerful courts, he was extremely effective—as effective as the respected public official delivering the same argument.

This study demonstrates that Aristotle was not completely correct. A communicator can be an unattractive, immoral person and still be effective, as long as we believe that he or she has nothing to gain (and perhaps something to lose) by persuading us. Why was Joe "The Shoulder" so effective in our experiment? When people argue against their own self-interest, we infer that the truth of the issue is so compelling that they sincerely believe what they are saying. When Patrick Reynolds, who inherited millions of dollars from the R. J. Reynolds Tobacco Company, which was founded by his grandfather, took a strong public stand against smoking and encouraged victims of smoking-related illnesses to file lawsuits against tobacco companies, no one disputed his sincerity![59] And when John Robbins, heir to an enormous fortune from his father's Baskin-Robbins ice cream company, wrote a best-selling vegan diet book that advocated eliminating dairy products, his argument influenced countless readers. When we argue against our interests, people listen.

Another way to increase trustworthiness is to create a situation where people do not think you are trying to persuade them. Many years ago, the brokerage firm E. F. Hutton produced a series of highly successful television commercials. The commercial opens with a shot of two people engaged in private conversation in a noisy, crowded restaurant. When one person begins to pass on some stock advice from E. F. Hutton, a sudden hush falls over the room and everyone—waiters, diners, busboys—is straining toward the speaker to overhear the tip. "When E. F. Hutton talks," says the announcer, "people listen." (You can see this vintage ad on YouTube.) The implication is clear: Everyone in the restaurant is getting in on advice that wasn't intended for them, and the information is all the more valuable as a result. When communicators are not *trying* to influence us, their potential to do so increases.

This is exactly what Elaine Walster and Leon Festinger[60] discovered when they staged a conversation between two graduate students in which one of them expressed his expert opinion on an issue. An undergraduate was allowed to overhear their conversation. In one experimental condition, participants knew that the graduate students were aware of their presence in the next room; therefore, they knew that anything being said could conceivably be intentionally designed to influence their opinion. In the other condition, the situation was arranged so that participants believed the grad students were unaware of their presence in the next room. In this condition, the participants' opinions changed significantly more in the direction of the opinion expressed by the grad students.

After all, they knew what they were talking about—and weren't trying to change anyone's mind.

Attractiveness and Similarity Where do these findings leave LeBron James urging us to eat Wheaties or wear Nikes? It's obvious that he is *trying* to influence us. Moreover, he is operating in his own self-interest; Wheaties and Nike are paying him and other famous athletes huge amounts of money to hawk their products. That fact alone should make them less trustworthy. But does it make them less effective? Not necessarily.

First, we tend to like and trust people whom we find attractive, so unless we are actively processing the fact that they are being paid to endorse a product, we may be persuaded peripherally.[61] Second, even though we may not *trust* the sincerity of the endorsers, that does not mean we don't buy the products they endorse. Attractiveness and likability are powerful factors in persuasion, even if a source lacks expertise or has something to gain from persuading us. Judson Mills and I[62] did an experiment demonstrating that a beautiful woman—simply because she was beautiful—could have a major impact on the opinions of an audience on a topic wholly irrelevant to her beauty, and further, that her impact was greatest when she openly told the audience she wanted to influence them. Alice Eagly, Shelly Chaiken, and colleagues[63] carried out experiments that not only replicated our finding that more likable communicators are more persuasive but went on to show that we expect beautiful people to think the way we do. No wonder they can persuade us!

We associate the attractiveness of the communicator with the desirability of the message. We are influenced by people we like and with whom we perceive similarities. When we like the communicator, we behave as though we were trying to please that person by changing our opinions—but only about trivial issues. Athletes and celebrities can influence our cereal choices, and beautiful women and handsome men can get us to agree with them on an abstract topic, whether or not we are willing to admit it. But it is unlikely that they could influence us to support an issue on which we strongly disagree with them, such as gun control or abortion.

Finally, we might ask: Who is more trustworthy, communicators who state their case with certainty or with apprehension? In most cases people trust the confident speaker rather than one who hems and haws; they take confidence as an indicator of expertise and truthfulness. However, if we suspect flimflam—if we are made aware of the likelihood that someone is trying to persuade us to believe something or buy something out of an ulterior motive ("This magic tonic is *guaranteed* to improve your grades!")—that extreme confidence can rouse our suspicions.

To summarize, communicators who are most likely to influence us are those we regard as being both expert and trustworthy. That said, their trustworthiness and effectiveness can be increased if:

- they take a position that seems opposed to their self-interest.

- they do not seem to be trying to influence our opinion.

- they are especially attractive and appealing—at least where our opinions and not our deep-seated attitudes are concerned.

- they are confident in their assertions, because confidence increases their credibility, unless we have reasons to doubt their motives.

The Nature of the Communication

Communications themselves differ, and how they differ can determine their effectiveness. Here I want to consider five dimensions along which they vary: (1) Is a communication more persuasive if it is designed to appeal to the audience's reasoning ability or if it is aimed at arousing the audience's emotions? (2) Are people more swayed by a communication if it is tied to a compelling personal experience or if it is bolstered by a stack of unimpeachable statistical evidence? (3) Does the communication resonate with the audience's way of seeing themselves, that is, with their basic identity? (4) Should the communication present only one side of the argument or should it also present the opposing view? (5) What is the relationship between the effectiveness of the communication and the discrepancy between the audience's original opinion and the opinion advocated by the communication?

Logical Versus Emotional Appeals As I said earlier, when Donald Trump was campaigning for president, he ran on an emotionally charged platform: fear of immigrants and terrorists and other mysterious foreigners who are coming to get us. He said they are rapists and murderers and bad people. Just as Dukakis could not prevail with his statistics on the success of furlough programs, Clinton could not counter Trump's alarms, which resonated with many sections of the country that were fearing demographic and economic changes. And as we saw in describing the results of the emotion-laden political ads featuring Willie Horton in the Bush-Dukakis campaign, we might suspect that emotional appeals—especially those that generate fear—will be more effective than reasoned ones. Why and when does fear work, and when might it backfire?

Years ago, I was living in a community that was about to vote on whether to fluoridate the water supply as a means of combating tooth decay. The proponents of fluoridation launched an information campaign that seemed logical and reasonable, with statements by noted dentists describing the benefits of fluorides and discussing the evidence on the reduction of tooth decay in areas with fluoridated water, as well as statements by physicians and other health authorities that fluoridation has no harmful effects. The opponents of fluoridation used a much more emotional counterargument, passing out leaflets with a picture of an ugly rat, along with the statement, "Don't let them put rat poison in your drinking water." The referendum to fluoridate the water supply was soundly defeated.

This story does not prove conclusively that fear appeals are superior, because it was not a scientifically controlled study. We have no idea how people would have voted on fluoridation if no publicity were circulated, nor do we know whether the antifluoridation circular reached more people or whether it was easier to read than the proponents' literature. In one early study of voting preferences, George Hartmann[64] demonstrated that individuals who received a *primarily* emotional message voted for the candidate endorsed by the message more often than did people who received a *primarily* logical message.

I emphasize the word *primarily* for good reason: It defines the major problem with research in this area—namely, that there are no foolproof, mutually exclusive definitions of *emotional* and *rational*. In the fluoridation illustration, most people would probably agree the antifluoridation pamphlet was designed to arouse fear; yet it was not entirely illogical, because it is indeed true that the fluoride used in minute concentrations to prevent tooth decay is also used in massive concentrations as a rat poison. On the other side, presenting the views of professional people is not entirely free from emotional appeal; it's comforting to know that physicians and dentists endorse the use of fluorides.

Because, in practice, operational distinctions between *logical* and *emotional* are difficult to draw, some researchers have turned to an equally interesting and far more researchable problem: the problem of the effect of various *levels* of a specific emotion on opinion change. Suppose you wish to arouse fear in the hearts of your audience as a way of getting them to change their minds. Would it be more effective to arouse just a little fear, or should you try to scare the hell out of them? If your goal is to convince people to drive more carefully, without texting, would you be more effective if you showed them films of the broken and bloody bodies of victims of highway accidents, or would you be more effective if you soft-pedaled your communication—showing crumpled fenders, discussing increased insurance rates due to careless driving, and pointing out that people who drive carelessly may have their driver's licenses suspended?

Common sense is no help here. On the one hand, it suggests that a good scare will motivate people to act; on the other hand, it argues that too much fear can interfere with a person's ability to pay attention to the message, to comprehend it, and to act upon it. We've all believed, at one time or another, that "it only happens to the other guy—it can't happen to me." That's why some people continue to drive and text or to insist on driving after they've had a few drinks, even though they know better. Perhaps this is because the risks of accidents are so alarming that people put them out of their minds. Thus we might predict that if a communication really frightens us, we tend not to pay close attention to it.

What does the evidence tell us? The overwhelming weight of experimental data suggests that, all other things being equal, the more frightened a person is by a communication, the more likely he or she is to take preventive action. In one of many experiments on fear and persuasion, Howard Leventhal and his associates[65] tried to induce people to stop smoking cigarettes and to get chest X-rays. In the low-fear condition, some participants were simply given a recommendation to stop smoking and get X-rayed. In the moderate-fear condition, others were shown a film depicting a young man whose X-rays revealed he had lung cancer. And in the high-fear condition, people saw the same film but also another, more gory film of a lung-cancer operation. Those who were most frightened were also most eager to stop smoking and most likely to get X-rays.

Is this true for everyone? It is not. There is a reason why common sense suggests that fear blocks us from acting: It does—for certain people, under certain conditions. What "certain people," for example? Leventhal and his colleagues discovered that people who had a high opinion of themselves were most likely to be motivated to take immediate action when they were frightened. People with a low opinion of themselves, however, were least likely to take immediate action—but (here is the interesting part) if there was a delay and they knew they could take action *later*, they behaved much like the participants with high self-esteem. People with negative self-images may have difficulty coping with threats, which explains why a high-fear communication overwhelms them and makes them feel like crawling into bed and pulling the covers up over their heads. They can deal more easily with low or moderate fear at the moment. But if given time—that is, if it's not essential that they act immediately—they will be more likely to act if the message truly scares the hell out of them.

Subsequent research by Leventhal and his coworkers supports this analysis. In one study, participants watched films of serious automobile accidents. Some watched the films on a large screen up close, which made the images really alarming; others watched them from far away on a much smaller screen. Among the participants with high or moderate self-esteem, those who saw the films on the large screen were much more likely to take subsequent protective action than were those who saw the films on the small screen. The reverse pattern applied to people with low self-esteem: They were more likely to act when they saw the films on a small screen; those who saw the films on a large screen couldn't cope and tuned out, saying they had difficulty even thinking of themselves as victims of auto accidents. Yet even people with high self-esteem will behave like people with low self-esteem if they are overwhelmed with fear and feel there is nothing they can do to prevent or manage a threatening situation. In that case, most of them will get into that bed and search for the blanket.

How, then, would you motivate people with low self-esteem if you wanted them to give up smoking or drive more safely? If you construct a message containing specific, optimistic instructions, it might make them more likely to believe they could confront their fears and cope with the danger. Indeed, Leventhal and his associates found that fear-arousing messages containing specific instructions about how, when, and where to take action are much more effective than generalized alarms with no recommendations for dealing with them.

For example, a campaign conducted on a college campus urging students to get tetanus shots was divided into two conditions: (1) instructions only—where and when they were available, along with the location of the student health service and a suggestion that each student set aside a convenient time to stop by; and (2) instructions plus a high-fear appeal, describing the awful things that can happen to you if you don't get a protective tetanus shot. The instructions on their own increased the students' favorable *attitudes* toward tetanus shots and increased their stated intentions to get one. But instructions weren't enough to get them to do it. Fear was the necessary shot in the arm, so to speak. Of the students who were frightened about what might happen to them if they didn't have a tetanus shot *and* who were instructed about how and where to get one, 28 percent got the tetanus shots; but of those who received no specific instructions or a high-fear appeal, only 3 percent did. Similarly, Leventhal found that scaring smokers about the dangers of nicotine increased their *intention* to stop smoking. But unless that message was accompanied by recommendations about how to quit, it didn't change the smokers' behavior. Conversely, giving them specific things they could do when they had the urge to smoke, but without scaring them about health risks, was relatively ineffective. The combination of fear arousal and specific instructions produced the best results; four months later, the students in this condition were smoking less.

And yet, there are some situations in which fear-arousing appeals—even when coupled with specific instructions—will not produce the desired effect. Sometimes fear appeals fail because they are not scary enough. Global warming, for example, is a serious threat that most scientists believe is a ticking time bomb. As temperatures rise, glaciers are melting and sea levels are rising, which means that many population centers will be under water in the coming years. Certain diseases, like malaria, will proliferate when the insects that carry them migrate to formerly cool places. Hurricanes will continue to become more frequent and intense, as will droughts and heat waves, killing people and imperiling the production of food. Yet despite these grim predictions, which were graphically depicted in the Oscar-winning movie *An Inconvenient Truth*, most Americans remain insufficiently frightened to demand action. A 2016 survey of American fears[66] found that people are more afraid of terrorism, identity theft, and biological warfare than they are of global warming. Why might this be?

Daniel Gilbert[67] suggests that part of the answer lies in the way our brains work. Our brains evolved to be frightened—and riled to action—by threats of clear and present dangers (like tigers, snakes, or enemies carrying weapons), not gradual ones that might happen later (like droughts, influenza, or more frequent hurricanes). We are also disposed to respond to human threats (like terrorism) that are intentional and thus arouse in us a sense of moral indignation. However, because climate change has the potential to inflict suffering and death on far more millions of people than terrorism does, ignoring or denying it is dangerously maladaptive for our species and our planet. Gilbert suggests that people would be far more likely to demand action on global warming if it were seen as a plot by terrorists instead of the unfortunate by-product of driving cars, burning coal, and cutting down forests. Perhaps more people would be inclined to take action if, like the stereotypical terrorist, global warming had a moustache and was intentionally coming after us like a predator.

Matthew McGlone and his colleagues[68] tested this proposition, not by putting a moustache on global warming, but by putting one on another nonhuman threat: the swine flu virus that became a pandemic in 2009. In April of that year, in response to the rapidly spreading flu, the Centers for Disease Control and Prevention made a series of recommendations, including frequent hand washing, avoiding contact with infected individuals, and above all, getting vaccinated. In the experiment, after these recommendations had been made but before the vaccine became available, McGlone and his team created informational pamphlets that varied in the way they presented facts about the swine flu. For half the people in the experiment, the flu was depicted as something that people contract ("Thousands of people may die from swine flu this year"). For the other half, the language was changed to depict the flu as a predator ("Swine flu may kill thousands of people this year"). People who received the pamphlet that described the flu as an active killer were significantly more likely to see the swine flu as frightening, more likely to see themselves as susceptible to it, and more likely to schedule a flu shot. Thus fear-inducing appeals are especially effective if they resonate with our evolutionary programming to fear being attacked by a threat that feels immediate and intentional.

Moral Emotions Moral emotions are feelings that have a normative judgment—what you are doing is wrong, disgusting, or evil. Anger, for example, is both a feeling and a judgment: "I feel angry because of the evil thing you have done." Moral emotions can be highly persuasive rhetorical devices—they tend to inspire action and unite like-minded communities—and they tend to be contagious.[69] For example, on Twitter, tweets that contain words associated with moral emotions (such as *outrageous* or *disgusting* or *bad*) tend to be re-tweeted more often than non-moral emotion words.[70] Politicians often try to inspire moral outrage because it unites their followers and gets them to sign petitions, donate money, and get off their butts to vote against whatever is claimed to be the reason for their outrage.[71] Charities often try to persuade people to donate money to the less fortunate by making potential donors feel guilty, an emotion that increases their intentions to contribute money and help in face-to-face situations.[72]

We can also be persuasive by appealing to people's better angels—their pro-social motivation—through *moral elevation*, the emotion we feel when we witness virtue in others. Experiments[73] find that when people watch videos depicting real-life acts of kindness or moral beauty—such as a teacher who goes the extra mile for her students, or a poor child who gives money to a less fortunate child—they are many times more likely to say yes to a request for help or money from another person. (This explains something I described in Chapter 1, when Joshua gave all his money to a panhandler after seeing a "morally elevating" movie, *Schindler's List*.)

In a similar vein, Adam Grant has studied the effects of different kinds of incentives for getting people to work hard.[74] In one of his studies, he examined the productivity of volunteers making cold calls to raise money for student scholarships. Grant discovered a lovely technique that persuaded his volunteer callers to nearly triple the donations they got. All he had to do was arrange a five-minute meeting between the volunteers and a past recipient of one of the fellowships they were soliciting for. Being able to connect their efforts to a human being—who expressed the moral emotion of gratitude—energized their fundraising efforts.

Statistics Versus a Personal Example Generally speaking, people use others' experiences and opinions to make decisions about what is a good course of action. That is why, as a general rule, we trust large groups of people more than a single person and are more inclined to follow the crowd than a single nonconformist. But this reasonable logic often goes out the window when we are faced with a compelling story or example. If Yelp has 300 positive reviews praising El Taco Loco, but only two negative ones, it's statistically likely that you'll enjoy the restaurant too. But let's say that you overhear someone at a party talking about a terrible experience they just had there ("I had to ask three times for a clean fork, and the chips were stale"). Will you say, "Well, okay, that's one of the two unhappy customers out of the 300 ecstatic ones"? Perhaps, but that one personal story is likely to overwhelm the preponderance of positive Yelp reviews. And the more vivid those personal stories are, the more persuasive they are.[75]

A real-life demonstration comes from the area of energy conservation. Several years ago, my students and I[76] set out to persuade homeowners to make the improvements necessary to have an energy-efficient house. We worked with home auditors from local utility companies and taught them to use vivid examples when recommending home improvements. Most auditors, when left to their own devices, would merely point to cracks around doors and recommend that the homeowner install weather-stripping. Instead, we trained them to tell homeowners that if all the cracks around all the doors were added up, they would equal a hole the size of a basketball in their living room wall. "And if you had a hole that size in your wall, wouldn't you want to patch it up? That's what weather-stripping does." Auditors trained to use such lively language increased their effectiveness fourfold. Whereas previously only 15 percent of the homeowners had the recommended work done, after the auditors began to use more vivid language, 61 percent of the homeowners did.

Because most people are more deeply influenced by one personal example than by an abundance of statistical data, your friend's Taco Loco story or the thought of a basketball-sized hole in your living room will probably be extraordinarily powerful. This is undoubtedly one reason that testimonials ("I lost 40 pounds on Jenny Craig!") are so effective, even when they are accompanied by statistical disclaimers ("These results may not apply to everyone"). It is also the reason that professional lobbyists are trained in how to persuade members of Congress to vote for some bill: Don't present a lot of statistics, they are warned; just tell an emotional story about one individual.

Appeals to Identity A persuader can get us to do things if those things resonate with our self-identity. One of the most charming examples comes from a highly successful ad campaign that the state of Texas developed to get its citizens to stop littering. (The campaign was targeted especially to 18- to 35-year-old males, who were the most likely to toss bottles and other junk out of their car windows.) Rather than put up signs saying "Don't litter," the Texas Department of Transportation crafted a slogan that tapped into the pride and sense of frontier don't-tread-on-me toughness that Texans are known for: *Don't Mess With Texas.* The phrase was prominently displayed on highways, television, radio, and print ads—and it worked. Litter on Texas highways dropped roughly 72 percent between 1986 and 1990.[77]

Invoking a person's identity can thus have subtle but powerful effects. Christopher Bryan and his colleagues[78] have shown that people are much more likely to vote if you change the phrasing of a pre-election survey question from one about action ("How important is it for you *to vote* in the upcoming election?") to one about fulfilling an identity that people approve of ("How important is it for you *to be a voter* in the upcoming election?"). Similarly, children helped more when they were asked "Who wants to be a helper?" rather than "Who wants to help?" Such labels can reduce bad behavior as well. And as we saw in Chapter 3, people cheat less when prompted with the warning "Don't be a cheater" instead of being asked not to cheat. By getting people to think of an action—good or bad—in terms of their larger identity, they see the action as something central to who they are rather than as an occasional action. Such is the power of identity.[79]

One-Sided Versus Two-Sided Arguments Suppose you are about to make a speech attempting to persuade your audience that capital punishment is necessary. Would you persuade more people if you just stated your view and ignored the arguments against capital punishment, or would you be more persuasive if you discussed the opposing arguments and attempted to refute them?

Before trying to answer this question, let's look at what is involved. If a communicator mentions the opposition's arguments, it might indicate that he or she is an objective, fair-minded person; this could enhance the speaker's trustworthiness and thus increase his or her effectiveness. But if a communicator so much as mentions the arguments on the other side of the issue, it might suggest to the audience that the issue is controversial; this could confuse them, make them vacillate, and would ultimately reduce the persuasiveness of the communication. And, in fact, there is no simple relation between one-sided arguments and their effectiveness. If audience members are well-informed about the topic, the less likely they are to be persuaded by a one-sided argument and the more likely they are to be persuaded by an argument that brings out the important opposing arguments and then proceeds to refute them. This makes sense: A well-informed person is more likely to know some of the counterarguments. When the communicator avoids mentioning them, the knowledgeable members of the audience are likely to conclude that the communicator is either being unfair or is unable to refute them. In contrast, an uninformed person knows little or nothing about opposing arguments, so they are likely to be persuaded by the side they hear; if they hear the counterargument, they may get confused about which position to agree with.

Another factor is the initial position of the audience. If the audience is already predisposed to believe the communicator's argument, a one-sided presentation has a stronger impact on their opinion than a two-sided presentation. If, however, the audience is leaning in the opposite direction, then a two-sided refutation is more persuasive.[80] Most politicians are well aware of this phenomenon, which is why they tend to present vastly different kinds of speeches, depending upon the audience. When talking to the party faithful, they almost invariably deliver a hell-raising set of arguments favoring their own party platform and candidacy. If they do mention the opposition, it is in a derisive, mocking tone. But when they are appearing on television or speaking to an audience of mixed loyalties, they tend to take a more diplomatic position, giving the opposing view a reasonably accurate airing before proceeding to demolish it.

The Size of the Discrepancy Between Communicator and Audience   Suppose you are talking to people who strongly disagree with your point of view. Will you be more effective if you present your position in its most extreme form or if you modulate your position by presenting it in such a way that it does not seem terribly different from your audience's position?

Let's say you believe that people should exercise vigorously every day to stay healthy; any physical activity would be helpful, but at least an hour's worth would be preferable. Your audience consists of college professors who seem to believe that turning the pages of a book is sufficient exercise for the average person. Would you be more likely to change their opinion by arguing that they should begin a rigorous daily program of running, weight training, and yoga or by suggesting a briefer, less-taxing regimen? What is the most effective level of discrepancy between the opinion of the audience and the recommendation of the communicator? This is a vital issue for any propagandist or educator.

At first the answer seemed obvious: The greater the discrepancy, the greater their opinion change should be. This line of reasoning would suggest that the communicator should argue for the daily program of rigorous exercise; the greater the discrepancy with the listeners' behavior, the more they should change their opinion. Indeed, several investigators have found that this linear relation holds true. Philip Zimbardo[81] recruited college women for an experiment, asking each one to bring a close friend with her to the laboratory. Each pair of friends was presented with a case study of a teenager who had committed a crime, and then each of the participants was asked, separately and in private, to indicate her recommendations on the matter. Each participant was led to believe her close friend disagreed with her—either by a small margin or by an extremely large margin. Zimbardo found that the greater the apparent discrepancy, the more the participants changed their opinions toward what they supposed were the opinions of their friends.

However, some experiments failed to support this result. James Whittaker[82] found a curvilinear relation between discrepancy and opinion change. By *curvilinear*, I mean that, as a small discrepancy increased somewhat, so did the degree of opinion change; but as the discrepancy continued to increase, opinion change began to slacken; and finally, as the discrepancy became large, the amount of opinion change became very small. When the discrepancy was very large, almost no opinion change was observed.

Intrigued by this finding, Carl Hovland, O. J. Harvey, and Muzafer Sherif[83] argued that if a particular communication differs too much from your own position—if it is, in effect, outside of your *latitude of acceptance*—you will not be much influenced by it. In their experiment, the communication was based on a red-hot issue, one the participants felt strongly about: whether their state should remain "dry" or "go wet"—that is, whether or not to change the law prohibiting the distribution and sale of alcoholic beverages. The voters in that state were divided on this issue, and the participants were a representative sample: Some felt strongly that the state should remain dry, others felt strongly that it should go wet, and the rest took a moderate position. The participants were divided into groups of people reflecting all three positions and then presented with arguments supporting one of the three opinions: a "wet" message, which argued for the unlimited and unrestricted sale of liquor; a "dry" message, which argued for complete prohibition; and a moderately "wet" message, which argued to allow some drinking but with certain controls and restrictions. Thus, each group consisted of participants who found the communication close to their own position, found it moderately discrepant from their own position, and found it extremely discrepant from their own position. The most opinion change occurred when there was a *moderate* discrepancy between the message and the opinion of individual members.

For a scientist, this is an exciting state of affairs. When a substantial number of research findings points in one direction and a substantial number points in a different direction, it doesn't necessarily mean someone has to be wrong; rather, it suggests there is a significant factor that hasn't been accounted for—and this is indeed exciting, for it gives the scientist an opportunity to play detective. That's why I want to dwell on this issue—not only for its substantive value, but also because it provides an opportunity to demonstrate the adventurous aspect of social psychology as a science.

There are two ways of proceeding with this game of detective. We can begin by assembling all the experiments that show one result and all those that show the other result and then (imaginary magnifying glass in hand) painstakingly scrutinizing them, looking for the one factor common to the experiments in group A and lacking in group B. Next we can try to determine, conceptually, why this factor should make a difference. Or we can begin by speculating about what factor or factors might make a difference; then we can glance through the existing literature, with this conceptual lantern in hand, to see if those in group A differ from those in group B on this dimension.

As a scientist, my personal preference is for the second mode. Accordingly, with my students Judith Turner and Merrill Carlsmith, I began to speculate about what factors might make a difference. We began by accepting the notion that the greater the discrepancy, the greater the discomfort for the members of the audience. But, we reasoned, this does not necessarily mean the members of an audience will change their opinion.

Consider this situation from the audience's point of view. As we saw in discussing cognitive dissonance (Chapter 3), when someone comes along who disagrees with us, it makes us feel uncomfortable because it suggests our opinions or actions may be wrong or based on misinformation—or maybe, God forbid, that we're incompetent or foolish. The greater the gap between what the other person says and what we believe, the greater our dissonance. How can individuals reduce this dissonance? There are at least three ways: (1) they can change their opinion; (2) they can seek support for their original opinion by finding other people who share their views, in spite of what the communicator says; or (3) they can disparage the communicator—convince themselves the person is incompetent, immoral, or a blithering nitwit—and thereby invalidate his or her opinion. Technically, there's a fourth way—they can induce the *communicator* to change his or her opinion—but that's not possible if the message is delivered by someone who is not approachable (on television, online, or at a lecture).

Under what circumstances would an individual find it easy or difficult to choose option 3 and denigrate the communicator? It would be difficult to do that with a liked and respected personal friend; it would also be difficult to dismiss someone who is a highly trustworthy expert on the issue under discussion. But if the communicator's credibility were questionable, we predicted that denigrating or dismissing that person would be the route that most people would take—*especially* if his or her opinion were extremely different from the listener's. The more discrepant the communicator's position is from that of the audience, the more the audience might begin to question his or her wisdom, intelligence, and sanity. And the more they question his or her wisdom, intelligence, and sanity, the less likely they are to be influenced.

Let's return to our example involving physical exercise: Imagine a 73-year-old man who had just won the Boston Marathon. If he told me that a good way to stay in condition and live a long, healthy life was to exercise vigorously for at least two hours every day, I would believe him. Boy, would I believe him! He would get much more exercise out of me than if he suggested I should exercise for only 10 minutes a day. But suppose a less credible person, such as a high-school track coach, suggested I exercise 10 minutes a day. This time his suggestion would be within my own latitude of acceptance, and he might influence my opinion and behavior. But if he advised me to embark on a program of vigorous exercise requiring two hours every day, I would be inclined to write him off as a quack or a health nut—and I could comfortably continue being lazy. Thus, I would agree with Hovland, Harvey, and Sherif: People will consider an extremely discrepant communication to be outside their latitude of acceptance—but only if the communicator is not highly credible.

Armed with these speculations, Turner, Carlsmith, and I scrutinized the existing experiments on this issue, paying special attention to the ways in which the communicator was described. Lo and behold, we discovered that each of the experiments showing a direct linear relation between discrepancy and opinion change happened to describe the source of the communication as more credible than did those whose results showed a curvilinear relation. This confirmed our speculations about the role of credibility.

But we didn't stop there: We constructed an experiment in which we systematically investigated the size of the discrepancy and the credibility of the communicator within one research design.[84] In this experiment, college women were asked to read several stanzas from obscure modern poetry and rank them in terms of how good they were. Then each woman was asked to read a criticism of modern poetry that specifically mentioned a stanza she had rated as poor. For some participants, the essayist described this particular stanza in glowing terms; this created a large discrepancy between the opinion of the communicator and the opinion voiced by the students. For other participants, the essayist was only mildly favorable in the way he described the stanza; this set up a moderate discrepancy between the essayist and the students. In a third condition, the essayist was mildly scornful in his treatment of the stanza, which placed the recipients of this communication in a mild-discrepancy situation. Finally, for half of the women in the experiment, the writer of the essay was identified as the renowned poet T. S. Eliot; for the other half, the writer was identified as a college student.

Now all of the women ranked the stanzas once again. When they thought Eliot had written the essay, he had the most influence on their assessment when his evaluation of the stanza was *most* discrepant from theirs. When they thought a fellow student of medium credibility was the essayist, his views produced little opinion change when it was slightly discrepant from the opinion of the students, more change when it was moderately discrepant, and only a little opinion change when it was extremely discrepant.

What, then, can we conclude about the interaction between a communicator's credibility and the audience's beliefs? When communicators have high credibility, the more likely it is that an audience will be persuaded by their arguments if there is a *great* discrepancy between the communicator's view and that of the audience. But when communicators have low credibility, the only way they will get an audience to go along is if their view is only *moderately* different from that of the audience.

Characteristics of the Audience

People differ; some are more difficult to persuade. In addition, as we have seen, the kind of communication that appeals to one person may not appeal to another. I have already noted that the amount of knowledge, ability, and motivation that audience members possess, as well as their prior opinions, will play major roles in determining whether a two-sided communication will be more effective than a one-sided communication.

Personality and Politics What effect does an individual's personality have on his or her openness to being persuaded? One personality trait that is most consistently related to persuasibility is self-esteem. Individuals who feel inadequate are more easily influenced by a persuasive communication than individuals who think highly of themselves.[85] This seems reasonable enough; after all, if people don't like themselves, then it follows that they don't place a high premium on their own ideas and have less confidence in their convictions. Consequently, if their ideas are challenged, they may be willing to give them up. If Emily, who has high self-esteem, listens to a communication at variance with her own opinion, she must make up her mind whether she stands a better chance of being right if she changes her opinion or stands pat. She may experience even more conflict if she finds herself in disagreement with a highly credible communicator. But if she has low self-esteem, she would feel little or no conflict. Because she doesn't think much of herself, she probably believes she stands a better chance of being right if she goes along with the communicator.

Anyone who is awake nowadays knows that Republicans and Democrats seem to disagree on most issues — and neither side seems able to be persuaded by the other. Why? After analyzing the data from 44 years of studies and more than 22,000 people in the United States and Europe, John Jost and his associates[86] have concluded that these disagreements are not simply philosophic disputes about how, say, to end poverty or fix schools; they reflect different ways of thinking, different levels of tolerance for uncertainty, and core personality traits, which is why conservatives and liberals are usually not persuaded by the same kinds of arguments.

As a result of such evidence, some evolutionary psychologists maintain that ideological belief systems may have evolved in human societies to be organized along a left–right dimension, consisting of two core sets of attitudes: (1) whether a person advocates social change or supports the system as it is, and (2) whether a person thinks inequality is a result of human policies and can be overcome or is inevitable and should be accepted as part of the natural order.[87] Evolutionary psychologists point out that both sets of attitudes would have had adaptive benefits over the millennia: Conservatism would have promoted stability, tradition, order, and the benefits of hierarchy, whereas liberalism would have promoted rebelliousness, change, flexibility, and the benefits of equality.[88] Conservatives prefer the familiar; liberals prefer the unusual. Every society, to survive, would have done best with both kinds of citizens, but you can see why liberals and conservatives argue so emotionally over issues such as income inequality and gay marriage. They are not only arguing about the specific issue, but also about underlying assumptions and values that emerge from their personality traits.

It is important to stress that these are general tendencies. Most people enjoy stability and change in their lives, perhaps in different proportion at different ages; many people will change their minds in response to new situations and experiences, as was the case in the acceptance of gay marriage; and until relatively recently in American society, the majority of members of both political parties were willing to compromise and seek common ground in passing legislation. Still, such differences in basic orientation help explain the frustrating fact that liberals and conservatives so rarely succeed in hearing one another, let alone in changing one another's minds.

The Mood and Mindset of the Audience Another factor that affects how audiences will react to a communicator's message is their frame of mind. Robert Cialdini, who has studied persuasion both in the laboratory and by working with sales and persuasion experts, argues that how you *prepare* people for a persuasive message is a critical factor in whether persuasion works: "By guiding preliminary attention strategically, it's possible for a communicator to move recipients into agreement with a message before they experience it."[89] For example, in one study, when researchers approached individuals and asked for help with a marketing survey, only 29 percent agreed to participate. But when the researchers approached individuals and preceded that request with a simple, "Do you consider yourself a helpful person?", 77.3 percent later volunteered. Why? When asked before the request if they were helpful, nearly everyone answered yes. Then, when the request was made, most agreed to participate in order to be consistent with the recently activated identity of themselves as helpful people. Because people like to see themselves as helpful, it makes it difficult—dissonance arousing—to answer yes and then refuse to help. (You will recognize this as an example of the hypocrisy paradigm, described in Chapter 3.)

Listeners are also more receptive to a persuasive communication if they are well fed, relaxed, happy, and feeling good about themselves. People who have been allowed to eat food they enjoy while reading a persuasive message are more influenced by what they read than are people in a control (noneating) group,[90] and being in a good mood can make people more vulnerable to persuasion by making them less critical.[91] Geoffrey Cohen, Joshua Aronson, and Claude Steele[92] found that people who had been given some self-affirming feedback (learning they are well liked on campus) were significantly more receptive to persuasive arguments attacking their beliefs.

Conversely, members of an audience can be made to be less receptive and less persuadable. One way is simply to warn them about what's coming.[93] When I was a young man, TV hosts would pause in the proceedings and say, "And now, a message from our sponsor." Even then, I thought that announcement would render the sponsor's message less persuasive than it would have been if the show had glided into it without prologue. The forewarning seems to say, "Watch out, I'm going to try to persuade you," and people tend to respond by marshaling defenses against the message. This phenomenon was demonstrated in an experiment by Jonathan Freedman and David Sears.[94] Teenagers were told they would be hearing a talk entitled "Why Teenagers Should Not Be Allowed to Drive." Ten minutes later, the speaker presented them with a prepared talk. In a control condition, he gave the same talk without the 10-minute forewarning. The teenagers in the control condition were more thoroughly convinced by what he said than were those who had been forewarned.

Resisting Propaganda and Persuasion

Let's end this chapter as we began, thinking about all the techniques and technologies now in play to persuade us to buy something, believe some claim, or do something to improve our lives. Fortunately, although all of us can be influenced by methods we are usually unaware of—notably, the familiar drumbeat of repetition, the evocation of fear, or appeals to aspects of our identities that matter most to us—we human beings are not sponges, passively absorbing whatever is poured into us. We want to maintain our sense of control and protect our sense of freedom.

According to Jack Brehm's theory of **reactance**,[95] when our sense of freedom is threatened, we attempt to restore it. Have you ever been warned sternly not to do something—"Don't touch this hot plate! Don't go out with that person! Don't smoke grass!"—and then promptly did it anyway? That's reactance. When people think that someone's message is too blatant or coercive, thereby intruding on their freedom of choice, they likely activate their defenses to resist it. For example, if I wander into a store just to browse and an aggressive salesperson tells me I *must* try this aftershave or *must* look at their line of trendy new shirts, my first reaction is to reassert my independence by leaving the store.

Studies have demonstrated reactance across a wide range of activities. In one, in an attempt to get people to stop writing graffiti on restroom walls, researchers placed one of two signs in the bathrooms:[96] "Do not write on these walls under any circumstances" or "Please don't write on these walls." The researchers returned two weeks later and observed how much graffiti had been written in the interval. As predicted, significantly more people wrote graffiti when the "Do not write ..." sign instructed them not to, than with the "Please don't write ..." sign. Likewise, smokers who receive stern warnings telling them not to smoke typically respond by lighting up in protest.[97]

Or suppose that, as you walk down the street, you are politely asked to sign a petition. You don't know much about the issue, and as it is being explained to you, another person approaches and vigorously advises you not to sign. Reactance theory predicts that, to counteract this pressure and reassert a freedom of choice, you would be more likely to sign. This scenario was actually staged by Madeline Heilman,[98] who found that, under most circumstances, the more intense the attempts to *prevent* people from signing the petition, the more likely they were to sign.

Of course, as we have seen in Chapter 4, people can be (and are) influenced to comply with implicit social pressures, as in the Asch experiment. But when those pressures are so blatant that they threaten people's feeling of freedom, they not only resist them, but they tend to react in the opposite direction. In fact, all other things being equal, when faced with information that runs counter to important beliefs, people have a tendency, whenever feasible, to invent counterarguments on the spot. In this way, they are able to prevent their opinions from being unduly influenced and protect their sense of autonomy.

On a personal level, therefore, reactance leads us to counteract orders or instructions telling us how we *must* behave. But there is a better, more mindful way to resist persuasion. We have already seen that a two-sided, pro and con presentation is more effective for convincing most audiences than a one-sided presentation. Expanding on this phenomenon, William McGuire and his associates developed what they called the **inoculation effect**:[99] When people receive a brief communication that they are then able to refute, they tend to be "immunized" against a subsequent full-blown presentation of the same argument, in much the same way that a small amount of a weakened virus immunizes people against a full-blown attack by that virus. By taking "small doses" of arguments against their position (mild attacks), people become immune to later, more powerful arguments against their original opinions. In contrast, if people have not thought much about the issue—that is, if they formed their attitudes via the peripheral route, such as through emotions, familiarity, or peers—they are particularly susceptible to a full-blown attack on their position. They will have had no practice in defending their views. That's why one experiment found that inoculating people with the facts about 9/11 increased their resistance to subsequent conspiracy theory propaganda about that tragedy.[100]

Inoculation increases our resistance to later persuasion because we become motivated to defend our beliefs, and we gain some practice in defending them by being forced to examine why we hold them.

Of course, sometimes being open to criticism and a reasoned argument by the opposition might lead to a better alternative: changing our minds! The larger point, in my view, is crucial to the very purpose of education: If we want to lessen the impact of simplistic propaganda, there is no substitute for free inquiry into ideas of all kinds. The person who is easiest to brainwash is the person whose beliefs are based on slogans that have never been seriously challenged.

For me, the upshot of this research is that having our ideas challenged can have great benefits—either by convincing us that some of our cherished beliefs might be wrong, or by forcing us to think about the reasons for our beliefs and understand those reasons on a deeper level than we had ever done before. That is why I have been saddened to read the stories of protests on college campuses over speakers considered "racist" or "sexist" or any other "ist." These speakers might well be prejudiced, but they might also be people who simply disagree with their protesters in some ways but not all. How would anyone know until they hear them speak freely? As the research on persuasion in this chapter shows, forbidding people to speak accomplishes nothing; it doesn't teach the protesters how to marshal persuasive arguments for their position, it doesn't persuade the person whose opinions differ, and it doesn't help resolve cultural misunderstandings and miscommunication.

My work as a social psychologist and professor persuades *me* that it is vital—especially on college campuses—to invite speakers who disagree with the prevalent beliefs and attitudes of the student body, even if many students find those arguments offensive. Shouting and silencing do not persuade anyone of anything. Lisa Feldman Barrett, a psychologist who studies the neuroscience of emotion, tells a story that I think beautifully captures the difference between *distasteful* speech and *abusive* speech:

> Entertaining someone else's distasteful perspective can be educational. Early in my career, I taught a course that covered the eugenics movement, which advocated the selective breeding of humans. Eugenics, in its time, became a scientific justification for racism. To help my students understand this ugly part of scientific history, I assigned them to debate its pros and cons. The students refused. No one was willing to argue, even as part of a classroom exercise, that certain races were genetically superior to others. So I enlisted an African American faculty member in my

department to argue in favor of eugenics while I argued against; halfway through the debate, we switched sides. We were modeling for the students a fundamental principle of a university education, as well as civil society: When you're forced to engage a position you strongly disagree with, you learn something about the other perspective as well as your own. The process feels unpleasant, but it's a good kind of stress ... and you reap the longer-term benefits of learning.[101]

In contrast, provocateurs, propagandists, and hatemongers—such as advocates for the Ku Klux Klan and other white supremacist groups—are engaging in *abusive* speech. They are not remotely interested in educating anyone or debating their ideas, so there is no reason to invite them to speak at an educational institution. But they should not be lumped in the same category as serious scholars with whom we happen to disagree, such as the political scientist Charles Murray, who has long argued that genetic factors help account for racial disparities in I.Q. scores. That argument offends many people, but it is an empirical hypothesis that can be debated and his data examined. And that process, in turn, can lead—and has led—to further experimental investigation to determine why Murray got the results he did and whether other explanations might account for them. In science, we don't get to say, "I don't like your findings because they go against my values!" and leave the room, slamming the door behind us. We are obligated to use *evidence* to make a case for why we think they are wrong. In Chapter 7 you will see how Murray's arguments have been disputed by social psychologists such as Claude Steele and Joshua Aronson and by geneticists such as Richard Lewontin.

John Stuart Mill was right on target when, in his famous 1859 essay "On Liberty," he asserted that we must allow for the expression of ideas we dislike because they may contain some grain of truth that can question and perhaps even correct the prevailing conventional wisdom or, at the very least, provide us with the motivation to reexamine the wisdom of the beliefs to which we had always adhered. Or, as Supreme Court Justice Louis Brandeis put it, when we confront ideas based on "fallacies and falsehoods," we must remember that "the remedy to be applied is more speech, not enforced silence." Education is sometimes disquieting—which is as it should be.

Saul Steinberg, *Untitled drawing*, ink on paper.
Originally published in *The New Yorker*, January 18, 1964.
© The Saul Steinberg Foundation / Artists Rights Society (ARS), New York

6

Human Aggression

Many years ago, at the height of the disastrous war our country was waging in Southeast Asia, I was watching the news on television. The anchorman (the inimitable Walter Cronkite) was reporting an incident in which U.S. planes dropped napalm on a village in South Vietnam, believed to be a Vietcong stronghold. My son Hal, who was about 10 years old at the time, asked brightly, "Hey, Dad, what's napalm?"

"Oh," I answered casually, "as I understand it, it's a chemical that burns people; it also sticks, so that if it gets on your skin, you can't remove it." And I continued to watch the news.

A few minutes later, I happened to glance at Hal and saw tears streaming down his face. Struck by his pain and grief, I grew dismayed as I began to wonder what had happened to me. Had I become so brutalized that I could answer my son's question so matter-of-factly—as if he had asked me how a baseball is made or how a leaf functions? Had I become so accustomed to human brutality that I could be casual in its presence?

In a sense, it is not surprising. The people of my generation have lived through an era of unspeakable horrors: the Holocaust in Europe, the dropping of atomic bombs on Hiroshima and Nagasaki, the Korean War, and the wars in Southeast Asia and the Middle East, to name a few. In the ensuing years, we have also borne witness to endless civil wars in Central America; the slaughter of more than one million civilians in the killing fields of Cambodia; "ethnic cleansing" in Bosnia; the bloodbaths in Rwanda, Sudan, and Algeria; the suicide attacks of September 11 on our own soil, and American retaliations in Afghanistan and Iraq; and on and on and on. As horrifying as these events are, mass killings are certainly not peculiar to our era. A friend once showed me a very thin book—only 10 or 15 pages long—that purported to be a capsule history of the world, a chronological list of the important events in recorded history. Can you guess how it read? Of course, one war after another, interrupted every now and then by a few nonviolent events, such as the birth of Jesus and the invention of the printing press. What kind of species are we if the most important events in the brief history of humankind are situations in which people kill one another en masse?

Moreover, we Americans display a chilling acceptance of violence that at times seems utterly absurd and mindless. When U.S. warplanes bombed Libya in retaliation for an upsurge in that country's acts of terrorism, a whopping 71 percent of our citizens approved of this military action, even though only 31 percent believed the raid would be effective in curbing future terrorism.[1] What else can we conclude but that a substantial number of Americans find acts of pure vengeance an acceptable part of U.S. foreign policy? To be sure, the majority of citizens in most countries support the wars their governments launch. But Americans lead the developed nations of the earth in tolerating the astonishing fact that a mass shooting—defined as at least four victims—occurs *daily* in this country, and more than 100,000 people die from gun violence every year (that includes murders, assaults, suicides, accidents, and deaths by police intervention).[2]

I define **aggression** as an intentional action aimed at doing harm or causing physical or psychological pain. The action might be physical or verbal. Whether it succeeds in its goal or not, it is still aggression. Thus, if an angry friend throws a beer bottle at your head and you duck, so that the bottle misses its mark, it is still an aggressive act. The important thing is your friend's intention. But if a drunk driver unintentionally runs you down while you're attempting to cross the street, it is not an act of aggression, even though the harm you suffered is far greater than that caused by the beer bottle that missed.

By this definition, we humans have proven ourselves to be a particularly aggressive species. No other animals so consistently and wantonly hit, torture, and kill members of their own kind.

For centuries, philosophers have debated why this is: Is aggression an inborn phenomenon, or must it be learned? Thomas Hobbes, in his classic work *Leviathan* (first published in 1651), took the view that we human beings, in our natural state, are brutes and that only by enforcing the law and order of society can we curb what to Hobbes was a natural instinct toward aggression. In contrast, Jean-Jacques Rousseau's concept of the noble savage (a theory he developed in 1762) suggested that we human beings, in our natural state, are gentle creatures and that it is a restrictive society that forces us to become hostile and aggressive. Hobbes's more pessimistic view was elaborated in the twentieth century by Sigmund Freud,[3] who theorized that human beings are born with an instinctual drive toward life, which he called *eros*, and an instinctual drive toward death, *thanatos*, leading to aggressive actions. About the death instinct, Freud wrote, "It is at work in every living being and is striving to bring it to ruin and to reduce life to its original condition of inanimate matter."

This age-old dispute about human nature prompts me to raise the following questions that I will attempt to answer in this chapter: Is aggression inborn—is it part of our very nature as human beings? Can aggression be modified? Are women as aggressive as men, though presumably in different ways? What are the social and situational factors that increase or decrease aggression? Today, psychological scientists across many disciplines understand that "aggression" is both biological *and* learned, part of our evolutionary heritage—and so are the countervailing forces that promote altruism and cooperation. Let's look at some of the many factors that influence—or discourage—the expression of aggression.

Aggression in Nonhuman Animals

To gain insight into the extent to which aggression may be innate, some scientists have turned to experiments with nonhuman species. Consider the common belief that cats will "instinctively" stalk and kill rats. More than half a century ago, biologist Zing Yang Kuo[4] attempted to demonstrate that this notion was a myth, by doing a simple little experiment: He raised a kitten in the same cage with a rat. Not only did the cat refrain from attacking the rat, but the two became close companions. Moreover, when given the opportunity, the cat refused either to chase or to kill other rats; thus the benign behavior was not confined to this particular buddy but generalized to rats the cat had never met. It's not science, but some of the most popular videos and photos online are those of cross-species "friendships," such as someone's dog and cat nestled in each other's paws.

Although charming, Kuo's experiment (and all those cute photos) do not mean that aggressive behavior is learned or that it isn't innate; it merely demonstrates that aggressive instincts can be curbed by early experience. What if an animal grows up without any contact with others of its species? Will it or won't it show aggressive tendencies when threatened? Rats raised in isolation (i.e., without any experience in fighting other rats) will attack a fellow rat introduced into the cage; moreover, the isolated rats use the same pattern of threat and attack that experienced rats use.[5] So even though aggressive behavior can be modified by early experience, apparently in some species it needn't be learned.

What can we humans learn about our own biological heritage by observing the behavior of animals with whom we are most alike genetically? Our closest genetic relatives, with whom we share 98 percent of our DNA, are the chimpanzee and the bonobo. Nevertheless, these primates could not be more unlike each other. The chimpanzee is extremely aggressive. Although chimps do not engage in full-scale war as humans do, male chimps will hunt and kill other chimps, sometimes torturing them and tearing them apart; females too can be very aggressive, cunning, and mean.[6] But the bonobo, our other close genetic relative, has been described by primatologists as more compassionate, empathic, and peaceful than chimps. Whereas the chimpanzee will act aggressively with little provocation, the bonobo is one of the least aggressive species on the planet. In fact, bonobos have been called the "make love not war" ape, because whenever a potentially dangerous conflict looms, bonobos have sex, which defuses tension. (They will have sex after a conflict, too, to make up.) When bonobos arrive at a feeding ground, they first have communal sex and then proceed to eat peacefully. In contrast, when chimps arrive at a feeding ground, they fight over the food. Also, unlike the chimps, bonobos form female-dominated societies, keeping males in line and displaying remarkable sensitivity to others in their group.[7]

So are human beings more like chimps or more like bonobos? Those who argue that aggressiveness is built into us point to the chimps; those who argue that we are cooperative point to the bonobos. Although we humans don't share the bonobos' sexual solutions to problems, we are more adept than chimps at cooperating in a way that prevents violent resolution to disputes.[8] Evolution has given us both a propensity to attack when we feel threatened or in competition for resources, and also strong inhibitory mechanisms that enable us to suppress aggression when it is in our best interests to do so.

Culture and Aggression

Human societies have not been equally warlike.[9] In close-knit cultures that depend on cooperation for the group's survival, anger and aggression are considered dangerous and disruptive, and an offender will be ostracized or punished. Many human groups, like the Lepchas of Sikkim, the Pygmy peoples of Central Africa, and the Arapesh of New Guinea, live in cooperative friendliness, both within their own group and in their relations with others; acts of aggression are rare.[10] At the other end of the human continuum are groups such as Nigeria's Boko Haram, who train their very youngest children to murder and die in suicide attacks.

Most social psychologists, therefore, believe that aggression is an optional strategy: We humans are born with the *capacity* for aggressive behavior, but how, whether, when, and where we express it is learned and depends on our circumstances and culture. You may be really angry if a police officer stops you for speeding, but it is likely that you will control your temper—and your behavior. Three major lines of evidence support the view that the expression of aggression depends on the external conditions that foster or suppress it: studies of how cultures change over time, studies across cultures, and laboratory experiments.

Consider the Iroquois of North America. The Iroquois lived in peace for hundreds of years as a hunting nation, but in the seventeenth century, growing trade with the newly arrived Europeans brought the Iroquois into direct competition with the neighboring Hurons over furs (to trade for manufactured goods). A series of wars developed—and the Iroquois became ferocious and successful warriors, not because they were inherently "aggressive," but because a social change increased competition.[11] It works in the other direction, too. Many societies that were once warlike—such as the Scandinavians or Portuguese—have become the most peaceful on the planet.

"Violence as entertainment" now takes place on movie screens, in video games, and at sports events, and not in gladiator arenas where actual people were once torn apart to the cheers of audiences. Steven Pinker[12] has argued that over the centuries, human violence has been declining, thanks in part to the rise of nation states that take care of decisions about war, justice, and retribution, and to the nearly universal condemnation and outlawing of slavery, gruesome punishments, and child abuse. Except for people living in war zones like Syria, Afghanistan, or Iraq, or in failed states like Somalia, human beings today are statistically less likely to encounter violence than we were in the past.

Cultures of Honor The malleability of violent tendencies is further reflected in striking regional differences in aggressive behavior and in the kinds of events that trigger it. Richard Nisbett[13] has shown that homicide rates for white Southern males are substantially higher than those for white Northern males, especially in rural areas. But this is true only for certain kinds of homicides—those provoked by perceived insults and by a perceived need to protect property—and only in certain areas—those that had originally been based on herding economies rather than agriculture.

Why would this be so? People who depend economically on agriculture tend to develop cooperative strategies for survival. But people who depend on their herds are extremely vulnerable; their livelihoods can be lost in an instant by the theft of their animals. To reduce the likelihood of theft, Nisbett theorized, herders learn to be hyperalert to any threatening act (real or perceived) and respond to it immediately with force. This would explain why cattle rustling and horse thievery were capital crimes in the Old West and why Mediterranean and Middle Eastern herding cultures even today place a high value on male aggressiveness. And indeed, when Nisbett looked at agricultural practices *within* the South, he found that homicide rates were more than twice as high in the hills and dry plains areas (where herding occurs) as in farming regions.

The emphasis on aggressiveness and vigilance in herding communities fosters, in turn, a *culture of honor* in which even small disputes put a man's reputation for toughness on the line, requiring him to respond aggressively to restore his status.[14] After all, if you are a farmer in Massachusetts, chances are no one is going to steal your entire apple crop; therefore, it's not as necessary to establish the reputation of being a person who will stand up and fight to protect his property. But if you are a cattle rancher, it is important to establish a tough reputation that makes anyone think twice before touching your property. Although the herding economy has become much less important in the South and West, the legacy of its culture of honor remains. These regions have rates of honor-related homicides (such as murder to avenge a perceived insult to one's family) that are five times higher than in other regions of the country.

Dov Cohen and Richard Nisbett[15] conducted a series of experiments at the University of Michigan, showing that norms characteristic of the culture of honor show up in the cognitions, emotions, behaviors, and physiological reactions of contemporary Southern white male students, young men whose families have not herded cattle for many generations. In one of their experiments, each participant was directed down a hallway where a male confederate "accidentally" bumped into him while passing by and insulted him by muttering a common vulgarity. Compared with Northern white males (who tended to shrug off the insult), Southerners were more likely to react aggressively. Their blood cortisol and testosterone spiked, they reported feeling their masculinity challenged, and ultimately, they were more likely to retaliate aggressively against the confederate whom they felt had "insulted" them.

Research on cultures of honor has found its effects in many varied domains. In one field experiment, Cohen and Nisbett[16] sent job application letters to companies across the United States, allegedly from people who had killed someone in an honor-related dispute. Companies located in the South and West were far more likely to respond in a receptive and understanding manner than those located in the North. High-school students in culture-of-honor states are far more likely than students from other states to bring a weapon to school and to use that weapon, and these states have more than twice as many school shootings per capita as do other states.[17] Men in cultures of honor around the world tend to distrust government and believe they are the ones who have the obligation to retaliate to a provocation, personally and sometimes violently. Cultures of honor also have higher rates of domestic violence. Both sexes in such cultures believe it is appropriate for a man to physically assault a woman if he believes she is threatening his honor and reputation by being unfaithful or by leaving him.[18]

As these findings show, we can see that although a physiological component of aggression is present in human beings and other primates, aggression is not a reflexive "instinct." Cultural influences "get under our skin," literally, to shape our responses to situational and social events, and thereby determine whether we will respond aggressively. That means that if certain situational and social conditions can predictably increase aggressive behavior, other conditions can reduce them.

Gender and Aggression

The research on cultures of honor suggests that male aggression ("Don't mess with me") is encouraged when it fulfills a central part of the male role and identity. When "being a man" is defined by competitiveness and strength, men are constantly trying to "prove" their masculinity and status in displays of aggression.[19] Conversely, when men live in cultures that lack internal and external threats to their survival—and admittedly, not many cultures are so blessed—they are not raised to be aggressive, sex differences are minimized, and cooperation is encouraged.[20]

Nevertheless, the number one predictor of violence is gender. As adults, men are more likely than women to get into spontaneous, unprovoked acts of picking a fight with a stranger, join in a mob bent on destruction and looting, and commit violent crimes such as assault, rape, and murder.[21] Starting in childhood, boys are consistently more likely than girls to engage in "rough and tumble play," along with nonplayful pushing, shoving, and hitting. And in cross-cultural study by Dane Archer and Patricia McDaniel,[22] teenagers from 11 countries read stories involving interpersonal conflict and then were asked to compose their own endings. In every country, young men showed a greater tendency to end the story with violence.

It is commonly believed that the hormone that fuels male aggression is testosterone, which both sexes have, although in higher proportion in males. Laboratory animals whose testosterone is removed (who are castrated) become less aggressive, and those injected with testosterone become more aggressive. James Dabbs and his colleagues[23] found that naturally occurring testosterone levels are significantly higher among prisoners convicted of violent crimes than among those convicted of nonviolent crimes, and among college students, men in fraternities who were considered cruder, more rambunctious, and less socially responsible by others were found to have the highest average testosterone levels.[24] Testosterone affects many of the behaviors we stereotypically associate with young males: aggressiveness, competition, and risk-taking. However, the reverse is also true: Aggressive or competitive behavior increases the release of testosterone, presumably to prepare the animal to behave aggressively.[25]

But all of these findings are correlational, not explanatory. And as we just saw, Northern young men have the same testosterone that Southern young men have, but they are not as roused to respond aggressively to perceived insults. The biologist and zoologist Robert Sapolsky, in his book *Behave: The Biology of Humans at Our Best and Worst*, summarized the matter this way: By looking at the correlational studies, we would conclude that "testosterone causes aggression. Time to see how wrong that is."[26] Why? Even when testosterone is completely eliminated in males, aggression continues to occur; moreover, "the more experience a male had being aggressive prior to castration, the more aggression continues afterward." Furthermore, Sapolsky adds, if testosterone is a strong predictor of violence, we would expect that differences in testosterone levels should predict which animals within a species—birds, fish, mammals, primates—will behave aggressively. They do not.

Physical Aggression If women aren't very likely to get into fistfights, start riots, or shoot someone to defend their family's reputation, does that mean that they are inherently less aggressive than men? Gender differences are obvious in the larger social world; in the private world of families and relationships, gender differences aren't always so clear.

Most cases of extreme violence in the family are perpetrated by men. For example, 8 in 10 murderers who kill a family member are male. And when men beat up their victims, they usually inflict more serious injury than women abusers do.[27] However, when it comes to forms of physical aggression that are less violent than murder and brutal beatings, there is often great overlap between males and females—and contrary to gender stereotypes, in many relationships both sides are equally aggressive. For example, in a study of nearly 500 first-year American college women who reported their experiences of violence with their boyfriends, most reported that the abuse was reciprocal.[28] A review of more than 200 studies of community samples found no significant gender differences in the percentage of men and women who were physically aggressive with their partners,[29] and they behaved that way for the same reasons: jealousy, anger, revenge, and self-defense.[30]

In some studies that compared young boys and girls in levels of physical aggression, most of the boys and girls were actually alike in being unaggressive; the sex difference was due primarily to a small number of extremely aggressive boys.[31] Among adults, the sex difference in the willingness to inflict physical harm often vanishes when both sexes feel provoked and entitled to retaliate. One meta-analysis of 64 separate experiments found that although men are more aggressive than women under ordinary circumstances, the gender difference shrinks when men and women are insulted and when women are given the same chance to retaliate aggressively—especially when others are unaware of their gender.[32]

Just as male aggression is influenced by culture, so is female aggression. The rate of the physical abuse of women, through beatings, stabbings, and hitting, is highest in cultures that regard such abuse as a male prerogative and a legitimate means of asserting power and control over women, as we see in countries where girls can be murdered just for wanting to attend school.[33] Yet in one international study, women from Australia and New Zealand showed greater evidence of aggressiveness than men from Sweden and Korea.[34] In a cultural community that admires physical aggression, both sexes may rely on violent tactics. Female teenage members of Mexican American gangs in Los Angeles carry any kind of weapon they can get hold of, from bats to guns, and told a researcher that they had joined not only for social support but for revenge.[35] A study of all known female suicide bombers throughout the world since 1981 (including Afghanistan, Israel, Iraq, India, Lebanon, Pakistan, Russia, Somalia, Sri Lanka, and Turkey) found that "the main motives and circumstances that drive female suicide bombers are quite similar to those that drive men": loyalty to their country or religion, anger at being occupied by a foreign military, and revenge for loved ones killed by the enemy.[36]

Relational Aggression Recall that I defined aggression as the intention to harm another person, and "harm" does not always mean through physical confrontation. Females are more prone than men to engage in a more social form of aggression, which Nikki Crick and her associates call **relational aggression**,[37] or hurting others by sabotaging their reputations and relationships. Shunning, spreading false rumors and malicious gossip, backbiting, and "slut shaming" are prime examples, and the consequences can be devastating.[38] The average gender difference in relational aggression starts early: In one study of three- to five-year-old children playing in groups of three, the kids were instructed to use a crayon to color in a picture on a white sheet of paper. Three crayons were provided, but only one was a color (orange) and the other two were white. Naturally, the children all wanted the orange crayon. The boys used physical aggression to get it, hitting or pushing the child who had the orange crayon. The girls used relational aggression, spreading rumors about the child with the orange crayon or ignoring her to make her cry.[39]

One especially harmful form of relational aggression is online bullying. With the advent of the internet, bullies are no longer limited to the school environment; victims can be bullied and harassed around the clock, seven days a week. The internet has given the relational bully a megaphone; a person's reputation can be attacked widely with the click of a mouse, undetected by teachers and parents.[40] Cyberbullying may be a one-time impulsive act or a planned campaign of harassment. Phoebe Prince, a 15-year-old Irish girl living in Massachusetts, was targeted by a group known as the Mean Girls in a dispute over her brief relationship with a popular boy at her school. Four girls and two boys began a relentless campaign against her of verbal assault (including calling her "Irish slut" and "whore" on Facebook and other social media) and threats of bodily harm. After four months of being slandered and harassed, Prince hanged herself at home.

According to a review prepared for the government on Child Safety and Online Technologies, the greatest source of danger that teenagers face on the internet does not come from pornography (which many teens themselves, usually boys, seek out) or even from predatory adults, let alone from sexting. The report found that the most frequent threats that minors face, both online and offline, are forms of relational aggression by their peers.[41]

Catharsis – Does It Work?

Let's turn now to the widespread belief that some kinds of aggressive acts can serve a useful and perhaps a necessary function: They "let off steam." That belief stems from the psychoanalytic concept of **catharsis**, or the release of energy. Sigmund Freud believed that aggressive energy must come out somehow, lest it continue to build up and produce illness. His theory rested on the analogy of water pressure building up in a container: Unless aggression is allowed to drain off, it will produce an explosion. According to Freud, society performs an essential function in regulating the "death instinct" and in helping people to sublimate it—that is, to turn the destructive energy into acceptable or useful activities.[42] The most acceptable forms of sublimation were generally thought to be art and sports. The psychiatrist William Menninger[43] asserted that "competitive games provide an unusually satisfactory outlet for the instinctive aggressive drive."

The belief in the emotional and physical benefits of catharsis has become part of our cultural mythology. In the movie *Analyze This*, a psychiatrist (played by Billy Crystal) is forced into a therapeutic relationship with a Mafia boss and murderer played by Robert De Niro. The De Niro character is suffering from hypertension, allegedly brought on by excessive anger and anxiety. During one of their therapy sessions, the Billy Crystal character says, "You know what I do when I'm angry? I hit a pillow. Try that." For a mobster, of course, "hit" means "kill." So De Niro promptly whips out his gun, and fires several bullets into a pillow. Billy Crystal gulps, forces a smile, and says, "Feel better?"

"Yeah, I do!" says De Niro.

Charming? Yes. Accurate? Nope. Abundant evidence indicates that the Billy Crystal solution simply does not work. In one experiment, Brad Bushman[44] made his participants angry by having his accomplice (a fellow student) insult them. Immediately afterward, the participants were assigned to one of three experimental conditions: In one condition, they were allowed to spend a few minutes slugging away at a punching bag, while being encouraged to think about the student who had made them angry. In a second condition, the students hitting the punching bag were encouraged to think of this activity as physical exercise. In the third condition, the participants simply were allowed to sit still for a few minutes without punching anything. At the end of the experiment, which students felt the least angry? Those participants who simply sat still without punching anything.

Bushman next gave the participants a chance to aggress against the person who had insulted them by blasting him with a loud, unpleasant noise. The students who had hit the punching bag while thinking about their "enemy" were the most aggressive, blasting him the loudest and the longest. Those who had just sat still after the insult were the least aggressive. Bushman's laboratory experiment is supported by a field study of high-school football players. Arthur Patterson[45] measured the general hostility of these football players, rating them before, during, and after the football season. If the intense physical activity and aggressive behavior that are part of playing football reduce the tension caused by pent-up aggression, we would expect the players to exhibit a decline in hostility over the course of the season. Instead, there was a significant *increase* in hostility among the players as the football season wore on.

What happens when acts of aggression are targeted directly against the person who provoked us? Does this satiate our need to aggress and therefore reduce our tendency to hurt that person further? Again, systematic research demonstrates that, as in the punching-bag experiment, exactly the opposite occurs. In an experiment by Russell Geen and his associates[46] each participant was paired with another student, who (as you might imagine by this time!) was a confederate of the experimenters. First, the confederate angered the participant. During this phase of the experiment, which involved the exchanging of opinions on various issues, the participant was given electric shocks when his partner disagreed with his opinion. Next, during a study of "the effects of punishment on learning," the participant acted as a teacher while the confederate served as learner. On the first learning task, some of the participants were required to shock the confederate each time he made a mistake; other participants merely recorded his errors. (As you might also imagine by this time, they weren't real shocks.) On the next task, all the participants were given the opportunity to deliver shocks to the confederate. What happened? Contrary to the catharsis hypothesis, people who had previously shocked the confederate delivered more frequent and more intense shocks the second time around.

The same kind of behavior has also been observed systematically in naturally occurring events in the real world, where verbal acts of aggression served to facilitate further attacks. In one "natural experiment," a number of technicians working for a company were laid off, and thus understandably angry at their employers. Several were then provided with a chance to verbalize their hostility against their ex-bosses. Later, all of the technicians were asked to describe their bosses. Those who previously had been allowed to vent their feelings were *much* nastier in their subsequent descriptions than those who had not.[47]

The message is clear: Physical activity—like punching a punching bag or playing an aggressive sport—neither dissipates anger nor reduces subsequent aggression against the person who provoked it. In fact, the data lead us in precisely the opposite direction: The more that people ventilate anger by behaving aggressively, the angrier they remain and the more aggressive they become. Venting anger—directly or indirectly, verbally or physically—does not reduce hostility; it increases it. Interestingly, similar experiments[48] find that people who *believe* in catharsis are more likely to aggress as a way of trying to feel better ("Yelling at you and kicking the sofa help me get it out of my system"), but it just makes them angrier and more likely to yell and kick. Apparently, the more you believe that aggression will make you feel better, the more aggressively you will act out, and the less peaceful it will make you.

Retaliation, Overkill, and Escalation Why does expressing anger aggressively lead to greater hostility? Once we express negative feelings toward another person—once we label our ex-boss a heartless jerk—it becomes that much easier to follow up with consistent statements and actions, particularly if we have retaliated in public. Moreover, retaliation is typically more severe than the initial insult or attack; we tend to engage in overkill, which sets the stage for dissonance reduction.

An experiment by Michael Kahn[49] showed how overkill operates, to our detriment. In Kahn's experiment, a medical technician, while taking physiological indicators from college students, made derogatory remarks about these students. In one condition, the students were allowed to vent their hostility by expressing their feelings about the technician to his employer—an action that they knew would get the technician into serious trouble, probably costing him his job. In another condition, they were not provided with the opportunity to express any aggression against him. Those given the opportunity to get the technician in trouble subsequently disliked him more and expressed greater hostility toward him than did those not given the opportunity to vent.

Overkill maximizes dissonance. The greater the discrepancy between what the perpetrator did to you and your retaliation, the greater the dissonance. The greater the dissonance, the greater your need to denigrate him and justify your treatment of him.[50] Recall the incident I described in Chapter 3, of four students who were shot and killed by the Ohio National Guard during an anti-war protest. Whatever those students might have been doing (shouting obscenities, teasing, taunting), it hardly merited being shot and killed. Yet after they were killed, the Guards and local townspeople described them in extremely hostile terms. If I have shot a student who was merely dissenting — or if I am a person who believes in law and order and support my local police — then I will try to convince myself they *really* deserved it, and I will hate the dissenting students even more than I did before they were shot.

This method of reducing dissonance in the face of an injustice or crime is universal. How do you think members of anti-American terrorist groups and their sympathizers felt about Americans *after* the slaughter of September 11? Do you think they felt sorrow and compassion for the thousands of innocent victims, rescue workers, and their families? Do you think they decided that Americans had suffered enough? In most situations, committing or condoning violence does not reduce the tendency toward violence. Committing acts of violence increases our negative feelings about the victims. Ultimately, this is why violence almost always breeds more violence.

But what would happen if we could somehow arrange it so that retaliation is not allowed to run roughshod over the instigator of aggression? That is, what if the degree of retaliation is reasonably controlled so that it is not significantly more intense than the action that precipitated it? In such a circumstance, I would predict that there would be little or no dissonance. "Sam has insulted me; I've paid him back exactly in kind; we are even." Experiments confirm that when the retaliation matches the provocation, people do not denigrate or belittle the provocateur.[51]

There is a major point here that must be emphasized: Most situations in the real world are far messier than this; retaliation almost always exceeds the original offense. Experimental research tells us why: The pain we receive always feels more intense than the pain we inflict. The old joke of "The other guy's broken leg is trivial; our broken fingernail is serious," turns out to be an accurate description of our neurological wiring. A team of English neurologists[52] paired people in a tit-for-tat experiment. Each pair was hooked up to a mechanism that exerted pressure on their index fingers, and each participant was instructed to apply the same force on their partner's finger that they had just felt. The researchers found that the participants were unable to retaliate exactly in kind, although they tried very hard to do so. Every time one partner felt the pressure, he "retaliated" with considerably greater force, thinking he was responding with the same force as he had received. In this way, the game that began with an exchange of soft touches quickly escalated into severe and painful pressure. The researchers concluded that the escalation of pain is "a natural by-product of neural processing." It helps explain why two boys who start out exchanging punches on the arm as a game soon find themselves in a furious fistfight, and why conflicts between nations frequently escalate. Each side justifies what they do as merely evening the score.

Causes of Aggression

Just as pain escalates retaliation of more pain, one major cause of violence—in addition to obvious causes like intergroup hatred, revenge, or war—is violence itself. When a person commits an act of aggression, especially with a force that exceeds what the victim may have done to elicit it, this sets up cognitive and motivational forces aimed at justifying that aggression, which open the door to more of it. Let us look at some of the other major causes of aggression.

Alcohol   One drug that many people throughout the world happily ingest is alcohol. Alcohol tends to lower our inhibitions, making drinkers friendlier and more gregarious but also loosening the restrictions on committing aggressive acts, including sexual assault.[53] Fistfights frequently break out in bars and nightclubs, and family violence is often associated with the abuse of alcohol, though it is also the case that some spouses drink in order to have an excuse to verbally or physically abuse one another.[54] In addition, controlled laboratory experiments demonstrate that when people drink enough alcohol to make them legally drunk, they tend to respond more violently to provocations than those who have ingested little or no alcohol.[55]

This does not mean that alcohol automatically increases aggression; people who have been drinking are not necessarily driven to go around picking fights. Rather, alcohol serves as a disinhibitor: It reduces social inhibitions, making us less cautious and more impulsive. But it does more than that: Alcohol also tends to disrupt the way we usually process information.[56] Intoxicated people often focus upon and respond to the earliest and most obvious aspects of a social situation and tend to miss the subtleties. That means, in practical terms, that if you are sober and someone accidentally steps on your toe, chances are you would know the person didn't do it on purpose. But if you were drunk, you might miss the subtle cues and respond as if he stomped on your foot with full intent. Accordingly (especially if you are a male), you might retaliate with an insult, shove, or punch. This is precisely the kind of ambiguous situation that males might interpret as provocative if they are not thinking clearly—and alcohol impairs clear thinking. Alcohol is one of the primary reasons for the pervasive miscommunications between women and men in claims of sexual assault, because alcohol significantly impairs the cognitive interpretation of the other person's behavior, sexual negotiations, and memory. As Deborah Davis and Elizabeth Loftus have found, men who are drunk are less likely to interpret nonconsent messages accurately, and women who are drunk convey less emphatic signs of refusal.[57]

There is another way in which alcohol facilitates aggression, however, and this is through what has been called the "think-drink" effect: When people *expect* alcohol to have certain effects on them, it often does. Indeed, when people expect that alcohol will "release" their aggressive impulses, they often do become more aggressive—even when they are drinking something nonalcoholic. In a study of 116 men ages 18 to 45, experimenters gave one-third of the men a nonalcoholic drink, one-third a drink targeting a modest blood alcohol level, and one-third a stronger drink targeting a high blood alcohol level. Within each of these three groups, the researchers manipulated the drinkers' expectancies of how much alcohol they were getting. They then measured the men's behavior toward a research confederate who had insulted them. Remarkably, the actual quantity of alcohol that the men drank was related less to their aggressive behavior than their *expectations* were. The more alcohol the men believed they were drinking, the more aggressively they behaved toward the confederate.[58]

Of course, alcohol does have potent physiological effects on cognition and behavior. But those effects interact with what people have learned about alcohol, such as whether it provides an excuse to behave aggressively or sexually and how they expect to feel after imbibing.

Pain, Discomfort, and Hunger If an animal experiences pain and cannot flee the scene, it will almost invariably attack; this is true of rats, mice, hamsters, foxes, monkeys, crayfish, snakes, raccoons, alligators, and a host of other animals.[59] They will attack members of their own species, members of different species, or anything else in sight, including stuffed dolls and tennis balls. Do you think this is true of human beings, as well? A moment's reflection might help you guess that it may well be. Most of us become irritable when we have been subjected to a sharp, unexpected pain (e.g., when we hit our thumb with a hammer) and hence are prone to lash out at the nearest available target. In a series of experiments, Leonard Berkowitz[60] showed that students who underwent the pain of having their hand immersed in excruciatingly cold water showed a sharp increase in committing aggressive acts against other students.

It follows that other forms of bodily discomfort, such as heat, humidity, air pollution, and offensive odors, increase anger and thereby lower the threshold for aggressive behavior.[61] One potent form of discomfort is hunger, which is accompanied by low blood glucose. Brad Bushman and his colleagues recruited 107 married couples for a study.[62] He began by assessing the quality of their relationships and taught them how to measure their blood sugar. Then he sent each volunteer home with a voodoo doll and 51 pins, telling them that the doll represented their spouse. Every night they were to stab the doll with pins that reflected how angry they were with their spouse that day—the more pins, the angrier. After three weeks, Bushman and his team assessed the damage done to each doll. Spouses who had the lowest blood sugar levels had stuck more than twice as many pins in the voodoo dolls, compared with people with the highest levels.

Did those angry feelings translate into aggressive behavior? In the next experiment, the researchers had the couples play a computer game in which the winner got to blast his or her spouse with a mixture of awful noises that most people hate, like fingernails scratching on chalkboards, dentist drills, and sirens. Once again, the lower a person's blood sugar, the more likely he or she was to blast a spouse. As Bushman put it, the husbands hurt their wives because they were feeling the toxic combination of anger and hunger—they were "hangry."

Heat and Global Warming Given the fact that our planet is heating up, what might that change foretell in terms of aggression?

In 1967, when the country was divided over the war in Vietnam and racial injustice, national leaders worried that riots and other forms of civic unrest would occur with greater frequency in the heat of summer than in the fall, winter, or spring. And in fact, during what came to be called "the long, hot summer of 1967," 159 race riots erupted across the nation. Was heat a contributing factor? As it happens, yes. In a systematic analysis of disturbances occurring in 79 cities between 1967 and 1971, Merrill Carlsmith and Craig Anderson[63] found that riots were far more likely to occur during hot days than during cold days. In subsequent studies, Anderson and his colleagues[64] have shown that, the hotter it is on a given day, the greater the likelihood that people will commit violent crimes. Moreover, heat did not increase the incidence of burglary and other property crimes, thus strengthening the linkage between heat and aggression (not simply general criminality).

But, as you know by now, we have to be cautious about interpreting events that take place in natural settings. The scientist in you might be tempted to ask whether increases in aggression are due to the temperature itself or merely to the fact that more people are apt to be outside (getting in one another's way!) on hot days than on cool or rainy days. So how might we determine that it's the heat itself that caused the aggression and not merely the greater opportunity for contact? We can bring the phenomenon into the laboratory, which turns out to be remarkably easy to do. In one such experiment, William Griffitt and Roberta Veitch[65] simply administered a test to students, some of whom took it in a room with normal temperature and some of whom took it in a room where the temperature was allowed to soar to 90°F. The students in the hot room not only reported feeling more aggressive but also expressed more hostility to a stranger whom they were asked to describe and rate. Additional evidence from the natural world helps bolster our belief that heat is the culprit: In major league baseball games, significantly more batters are hit by pitched balls when the temperature is above 90° than when it is below 90°.[66] And in the desert city of Phoenix, Arizona, drivers without air-conditioned cars are more likely to honk their horns in traffic jams than are drivers with air-conditioned cars.[67]

If heat increases hostility, global warming should have an effect on aggression as well. An analysis of 60 studies from archaeology, psychology, and other disciplines—with data going back (incredibly) to 10,000 BCE and covering all world regions—found that warmer temperatures substantially increase the risk of many types of conflict, from domestic violence, murder, and rape to riots and civil wars.[68]

Rejection, Exclusion, and Taunting As I noted in Chapter 2, social pain registers in our brains in much the same way as physical pain, and it, too, produces aggression. In 1999, at Columbine High School in Littleton, Colorado, two students (Eric Harris and Dylan Klebold), armed to the teeth and very angry, went on a rampage, killing a teacher and 14 students (including themselves). This was the most dramatic and most devastating of 11 such incidents that took place in schools in less than three years, and which occur with regularity, in part because they are covered by the media and thus inspire copycats.[69]

What drove the Columbine killers over the edge? Although it was later learned that Harris was most likely a psychopath, there is more to the story. After an intensive study of the situation, I am convinced that rampage killings are just the pathological tip of an enormous iceberg: the poisonous social atmosphere prevalent at many high schools in this country—an atmosphere fraught with exclusion, rejection, taunting, and humiliation.[70] In high school, there is an iron-clad hierarchy of cliques with athletes, class officers, cheerleaders, and "cool kids" at the top. At the bottom are kids who those at the top refer to as nerds, goths, geeks, loners, homos—kids who are too fat, too thin, too short, too tall, wear the wrong clothes, or whatever. The teenagers near the top of the hierarchy are constantly rejecting, taunting, and ridiculing those below them. Mark Leary and his associates[71] conducted a systematic analysis of over 15 school shootings that occurred during a five-year period and found that acute or chronic rejection—ostracism, bullying, or romantic rejection—was present in all but two of the incidents. The other factors were a fascination with guns, explosives, and Satanism, as well as psychological problems like depression and poor impulse control.

Research by Jean Twenge, Roy Baumeister, and others[72] demonstrates that being rejected has a plethora of negative effects, not the least of which is a dramatic increase in aggressiveness. In one experiment, college students met in a group and became acquainted. They were then asked to indicate which of their fellow students they would want to collaborate with in the future. A random sample of the participants received information that nobody wanted to work with them. When subsequently provided with an opportunity to aggress, the "rejects" expressed far more intense hostility (against those who rejected them, as well as against neutral individuals) than those who had not been excluded. In another experiment, people rejected during a game of cyber-ball were more likely to blast their rejecter with loud noise than those who had been included; and excluded participants were especially aggressive if they had measured low in impulse control.

Rampage shooters often make their sense of rejection abundantly clear. In a video that Harris and Klebold recorded just prior to their murder spree, they specifically railed against the in-group who had rejected and humiliated them. This was confirmed by a student in the Columbine in-group, who, when interviewed a few weeks after the tragedy, justified his own exclusionary behavior by saying this:

> Most kids didn't want them there. They were into witchcraft. They were into voodoo. Sure we teased them. But what do you expect with kids who come to school with weird hairdos and horns on their hats? If you want to get rid of someone, usually you tease 'em. So the whole school would call them homos.[73]

Likewise, before Elliot Rodger killed six people and wounded 23 others in Santa Barbara, he wrote a "manifesto" describing his many complaints. He was bullied in the 10th grade, he wrote, and added:

> I was completely and utterly alone. No one knew me or extended a hand to help me. I was an innocent, scared little boy trapped in a jungle full of malicious predators, and I was shown no mercy. Some boys randomly pushed me against the lockers as they walked past me in the hall. One boy who was tall and had blonde hair called me a 'loser,' right in front of his girlfriends ... I developed extreme feelings of envy, hatred, and anger towards anyone who has a sex life. I saw them as the enemy. I felt condemned to live a life of lonely celibacy while other boys were allowed to experience the pleasures of sex, all because girls didn't want me. I felt inferior and undesirable. This time, however, I couldn't just stand by and accept such an injustice anymore.

Of course, not all students who are rejected and taunted go on a murderous rampage. The behavior of shooters like these is pathological in the extreme, but certainly not unfathomable. My best guess is that there are hundreds of thousands of students undergoing similarly stressful experiences. They may suffer in silence, but they do suffer. In the weeks following the Columbine massacre, internet chat rooms were flooded with postings from unhappy teenagers. Although they did not condone the behavior of the shooters, the overwhelming majority said they understood it, expressing their own hurt and anger about having been rejected and taunted. They posted remarks that can best be summarized as, "Of course, I would never shoot anybody, but I sure have had fantasies about doing it!"

That kind of statement should make us sit up and take notice. Is there anything we can do to change the social atmosphere in our schools? Yes. I will discuss some tried-and-true interventions near the end of this chapter, as well as in the following chapter.

Frustration, Deprivation, and Aggression   Of all the unpleasant conditions that provoke aggression—anger, pain, excessive heat, hunger, and rejection—the major instigator of aggression is frustration. Imagine the following situation: You must drive across town for an important job interview. On your way to the parking lot, you realize you are a bit late for your appointment, so you break into a fast trot. When you find your car, you notice, to your dismay, that you have a flat tire. "Okay, I'll be twenty minutes late; that's not too bad," you say as you take the jack and lug wrench out of the trunk. After much tugging and hauling, you remove the old tire, put on the spare tire, tighten the lugs—and lo and behold, the spare tire also is flat! Seething with frustration, you trudge back to your dorm and enter your room. Your roommate sees you standing there, résumé in hand, sweaty, dirty, and rumpled. Immediately sizing up the situation, he asks humorously, "How did the interview go?" Should he be prepared to duck?

If an individual is thwarted on the way to a goal, the resulting frustration will increase the probability of an aggressive response. A demonstration of this **frustration–aggression** relationship comes from a classic experiment by Roger Barker, Tamara Dembo, and Kurt Lewin.[74] These psychologists frustrated young children by showing them a roomful of appealing toys, which were then kept out of reach. The children stood outside a wire screen, looking at the toys, hoping to play with them—even expecting to play with them—but were unable to reach them. After a painfully long wait, the children were finally allowed to play with the toys. In this experiment, a separate group of children was allowed to play with the toys directly without first being frustrated. This second group of children played joyfully with the toys. But the frustrated group, when finally given access to the toys, was extremely destructive. Many of them smashed the toys, threw them against the wall, and stepped on them. Talk about frustration leading to aggression!

Several factors can accentuate angry responses to frustration. Suppose you were about to bite into a Big Mac and somebody snatched it away. This would be more likely to frustrate you—and lead to an aggressive response—than if someone had stopped you if you were merely on your way to McDonald's to buy a Big Mac. An analogue of this situation was demonstrated in a field study by Mary Harris.[75] She had students cut in front of people waiting in line for tickets, outside of restaurants, or in a supermarket checkout line; sometimes they cut in front of the second person in line, other times in front of the twelfth person. The people standing behind the intruder became much more aggressive when the student cut into the second place in line. Frustration tends to be high when a goal is just within reach and in view when you are blocked from it.

When the interruption is unexpected or when it seems illegitimate, the frustration is increased still further, as an experiment by James Kulik and Roger Brown[76] demonstrated. Participants were told they could earn money by telephoning for donations to charity and obtaining pledges. Some of the callers were led to expect a high rate of contributions, being informed that previous calls had been successful almost two-thirds of the time; others were led to expect far less success. When the potential donor refused to contribute, as all of them did (since the participants were calling confederates of the experimenters), the callers with the high expectations spoke more harshly and hung up the telephone with more force. The experimenters also varied the reasons the confederates gave for refusing to contribute, sometimes making them sound legitimate ("I can't afford to contribute") and sometimes having them sound arbitrary and illegitimate ("Charities are a waste of time and a rip-off"). The people who heard refusals that seemed unjustified became more aggressive.

The frustrating experience of *perceived* unfairness also can provoke aggression, an effect so fundamental it has been demonstrated with monkeys. Sarah Brosnan and Frans de Waal[77] rewarded capuchin monkeys with cucumber slices in exchange for a token. Monkeys love cucumbers, so this was a happy transaction.

But if a nearby monkey received a grape for his token (monkeys like grapes more than cucumbers), the first monkey would get angry—the cucumber, in light of the grape transaction, was now an insulting offer. Some offended monkeys threw the cucumber at the experimenter in rage!

In sum, frustration is most pronounced when the goal is within reach, when expectations are high, when the rule of fairness has been violated, and when the goal is blocked without a compelling reason. These factors help draw the important distinction between frustration and deprivation. Children who don't have toys (and monkeys who don't have grapes) do not necessarily become angry or aggressive. Rather, as the toy experiment indicates, it was those children who had every reason to *expect* to play with the toys who felt frustrated when that expectancy was thwarted; this thwarted hope was what caused the children to behave destructively.

Experiments like these and sociological studies at a national level have led to the discovery that frustration is often not the result of simple deprivation; it is the result of **relative deprivation**, the deprivation we feel when we see others enjoying a better situation or when we are deprived of something relative to our expectations. If you ever fly coach, you probably know what I'm talking about. After waiting in line at security, and then waiting for other passengers to board at the gate, you now must pass through the first-class cabin to get to your seat. As you are beginning to doubt that you'll find overhead space for your carry-on bag, let alone space for your legs in ever-smaller seats, you are treated to the sight of first-class passengers relaxing in relative splendor, enjoying champagne and roasted nuts, and being waited on by a flight attendant who seems genuinely happy to have them on board. How do you feel?

According to studies of "air rage," the hostile and abusive behavior demonstrated by airline passengers, you're not feeling so good; you'd be much happier if there were no first-class section on the plane. Katherine DeCelles and Michael Norton[78] collected a complete set of all onboard air rage incidents over several years from a large international airline and found that the presence of a first-class cabin produced four times as many aggressive incidents among passengers in economy, especially when economy passengers had to board from the front and walk through the first-class cabin. When airline service is one class for everyone, there is no "relative" deprivation; it's absolute. Somehow, I doubt that airlines will take advantage of this important finding; where huge corporations are involved, short-term profit almost always trumps customer satisfaction.

Relative deprivation explains a persistent mystery about most social revolutions: They usually are not started by people whose faces are in the mud. They are most frequently started by people who have recently lifted their faces out of the mud, looked around, and noticed that other people are doing better than they are and that the system is treating them unfairly. Countries with the widest gaps in income have higher rates of homicide and other indicators of aggression, if citizens believe that income inequality is unfair.[79] In the 1960s, the most intense riots by African Americans did not take place in the geographical areas of greatest poverty; they took place in Los Angeles (Watts) and Detroit, where things were not nearly as bad for blacks, economically and socially, as they were in many other sections of the country. But they were bad relative to black people's perceptions, in those communities, of what white people had. As Alexis de Tocqueville wrote more than 150 years ago, "Evils which are patiently endured when they seem inevitable, become intolerable once the idea of escape from them is suggested."[80]

As long as people live with hopes that are unsatisfied, they will feel frustrations that can result in aggression. Aggression can be reduced by satisfying their hope—or by trying to extinguish it. Hopeless people are apathetic people. Ugandans, when they were living under the tyrannical, repressive, and wantonly violent dictatorship of Idi Amin, dared not dream of improving conditions or rebelling against Amin's rule. In the former Soviet Union, serious rebellion took place only after 1991, when the government had loosened the chains controlling the population. In South Africa, blacks did not revolt against apartheid as long as they were prevented from hoping for anything better. Clearly, eliminating people's hopes for better, fairer lives is an undesirable means of reducing aggression. The saving grace of our nation is that—theoretically, at least—this is a land of promise. We teach our children, explicitly and implicitly, to hope, to expect, and to work to improve their lives. But unless this hope stands a reasonable chance of being fulfilled, turmoil will be inevitable and peace elusive. Demagogues who cynically raise a population's hopes, without first having explored the means of fulfilling them, are sowing the seeds of revolution.

Social Learning and Aggression

I turn now to some findings from **social cognitive learning theory**, which holds that people learn how to behave—including aggressively or helpfully—through cognitive processes such as their beliefs and perceptions of events and through observation and imitation of others.

I noted that pain, hunger, heat, and frustration often provoke aggression, but social cognitive learning theory reminds us that in between the provocation and the reaction lies the human brain: our ability to take the intentions of others into account. Consider the following situations: (1) a considerate person accidentally steps on your toe; (2) a thoughtless person, whom you know doesn't care about you, steps on your toe. Let us assume the amount of pressure and pain is exactly the same in both cases (and that you haven't been drinking!). My guess is that the latter situation would evoke an aggressive response, but the former would produce little or no aggression.

To demonstrate the effect of intervening perceptions on behavior, Shabaz Mallick and Boyd McCandless[81] frustrated third-grade children by arranging things so that another child's clumsiness prevented them from achieving a goal that would have resulted in a cash prize. Some of these children were subsequently provided with a reasonable explanation for the behavior of the child who fouled them up; they were told he had been "sleepy and upset." The children in this condition directed much less aggression against the thwarting child than did children who were not given this explanation. Moreover, later research[82] using adults indicates that we are less apt to retaliate against someone who has provoked our anger when we hear a good excuse for their actions *before* they occur rather than after the fact. And if we know someone's history, we are less likely to blame them and be angered by their missteps.[83]

But just as these explanations can reduce aggression in a person who is frustrated, the presence of aggressive stimuli can increase aggression. Leonard Berkowitz and his colleagues have shown that, if an individual is angered or frustrated, the mere mention of a word or name associated with the provocation will increase that person's level of aggression. In one experiment,[84] participants were paired with another student (an accomplice of the experimenter) who was introduced either as a "college boxer" or as a "speech major." This accomplice angered the participants by shocking them; then half of them viewed a violent prizefighting scene from a movie while the others watched an exciting but nonaggressive film clip. When subsequently given the chance to shock the confederate, those who had seen the violent movie segment administered more and longer shocks. Moreover, those paired with the "boxer" delivered more shocks to that target than those paired with the "speech major." The very word *boxer* served as an aggressive stimulus.

As with words, so it is with objects. The mere presence of an object associated with aggression—a gun, rifle, or other weapon—can serve as a cue for an aggressive response. In a classic experiment of this **weapons effect**,[85] college students were insulted (and thus angered) in a room in which a rifle was left lying around (ostensibly from a previous experiment) and others in a room in which a neutral object (a badminton racket) was substituted for the rifle. The students were then given the opportunity to administer electric shocks to a fellow student. Those who had been made angry in the presence of the rifle, the *aggressive stimulus*, administered more electric shocks than did those made angry in the presence of the badminton racket.[86]

Experiments find that people drive more aggressively if randomly assigned to a condition where a gun (rather than a tennis racket) is on the passenger seat,[87] evidence that contradicts the slogan often seen on bumper stickers: "Guns don't kill people, people do." As Berkowitz put it, "The finger pulls the trigger, but the trigger may also be pulling the finger." Perhaps the rates of violence in America are so high because we are the most heavily armed society in the world, with more guns than citizens.[88] This means that we have not only the means for killing, but also a constant stream of cues provoking aggressive thoughts. Those cues associated with aggression unconsciously add fuel to the fire.

One aspect of social learning that tends to inhibit aggression is the tendency most people have to take responsibility for their actions. But what happens if this sense of responsibility is weakened? Philip Zimbardo[89] has demonstrated that persons who are anonymous, and therefore unidentifiable, tend to act more aggressively than persons who are not anonymous. In Zimbardo's experiment, female students were required to shock another student as part of a "study of empathy." Some students were made anonymous; they were seated in a dimly lit room, dressed in loose-fitting robes and large hoods, and never referred to by name. Others were easily identifiable; their room was brightly lit, they wore no robes or hoods, and each woman wore a name tag. As expected, those students who were anonymous administered longer and more severe shocks. Anonymity induces **deindividuation**, a state of lessened self-awareness, reduced concern about what other people think of them, and weakened restraints against prohibited forms of behavior. When we are made self-aware, we tend to uphold our own values (e.g., "Thou shalt not harm"); when we are anonymous and not self-aware, we tend to act more on impulse. This is why, for example, people eat less popcorn when they are standing in front of a mirror than when they are sitting in a darkened theatre.[90]

Because it was part of a controlled laboratory experiment, the kind of aggression displayed by the women in Zimbardo's research pales in comparison with the wild, impulsive acts of violence typically associated with mobs and vigilante justice, but deindividuation applies there, too. Brian Mullen[91] analyzed newspaper reports of 60 lynchings perpetrated between 1899 and 1946, and he found a strong relationship between mob size and violence: the larger the mob, the more heinous the atrocities committed. When people are part of a crowd, they are "faceless," less self-aware, and less mindful of prohibitions against destructive actions. They are therefore less likely to take responsibility for their behavior. In Harper Lee's *To Kill a Mockingbird*, a mob of white men assemble to lynch Tom Robinson, a black man who has been falsely accused of rape. Scout, the eight-year-old daughter of Robinson's attorney Atticus Finch, recognizes one of the men and calls him out by name. In so doing, she *individualizes* him, making him accountable for his own actions. The mob gradually disbands and goes home.

You don't have to be in a mob or gang to be deindividuated, though; you have only to sit at your computer. On the internet, no one needs to know who you are, and the result is all too apparent in the often vicious commentaries that people post. To counter the aggression facilitated by online deindividuation, many websites today are requiring that people sign in through Facebook or by name. Deindividuation, however, does not always and inevitably make people more aggressive; it increases their conformity to the group's norms. Happy people dancing on a boardwalk during spring break can be deindividuated, too, and led to behave in ways they might not otherwise do if they were self-aware—like stripping to the bare essentials and dancing on tabletops.[92]

The other major component in social cognitive learning theory is the power of imitation. In a series of classic experiments, Albert Bandura and his colleagues[93] set up a basic procedure in which an adult knocked around a plastic, air-filled "Bobo" doll (the kind that bounces back after it has been knocked down), while little kids observed and later had the opportunity to play with the Bobo doll themselves. Sometimes the adult accompanied her physical aggression with verbal abuse. Not only did the children imitate the adult's aggression, sometimes hit for hit and kick for kick, they also behaved in other aggressive ways after having watched her. In short, the children did more than copy the adult; her behavior served as an inspiration for them to come up with their own forms of aggression. Why are these experiments considered so important? Who cares what happens to a Bobo doll, anyway? Stay tuned.

Violence and the Mass Media

Most American children are immersed in images of violence through television, movies, video games, pop and rap music, music videos, comics, and the internet. Immersed in it? They are marinated in it! They see an unending parade of murders, rapes, beatings, explosions, and bad guys committing brutal acts, as well as good guys doing brutal things to catch them. Violence in films has more than doubled since 1950, and gun violence in films rated PG-13 has more than tripled since 1985. In fact, PG-13 films now contain as much violence as films rated R.[94]

Many people—psychologists as well as the general public—are worried about all the mayhem that children and teenagers observe; they figure there must be significant consequences, starting with making guns seem cool and exciting. For them, it is as obvious as the Bobo doll study that children imitate the violence they see on TV and in the movies and are otherwise affected emotionally by it. If, as we saw in Chapter 4, prosocial role models and media stories can increase helpful behavior in the children (and adults) who observe them, surely the far more common antisocial, violent videos can increase antisocial, violent behavior.[95]

For just as many others, though, this is a nonissue. How powerful can media violence be, they ask, if during the same years that gun violence in PG-13 movies tripled, real-world gun violence and overall violent crime by young people decreased to record lows? Besides, they add, media violence consists of cartoon-like stories and images that "everyone knows" are not real.[96] Indeed, that was the reasoning behind the Supreme Court's 2011 decision that video games can be sold to minors no matter how violent the games are, including the popular *Mortal Kombat* and *Grand Theft Auto* series.

And so the debate rages on. How would you resolve it? Stories in the news would seem to provide a compelling answer. For example, several years ago, a man drove his truck through the window of a crowded cafeteria in Killeen, Texas; emerged from the cab; and began shooting people at random, killing 22. In his pocket, police found a ticket stub to *The Fisher King*, a film depicting a deranged man firing a shotgun into a crowded bar, killing several people. Or how about the two teenagers in Tennessee who took their guns and went out sniping at passing cars on a freeway, killing one driver, because they wanted to act out their favorite video game, *Grand Theft Auto*? On the other hand, there is the case of a man who, having seen a movie showing women dancing on screen, became convinced that all women were immoral and deserved to die. He then committed four brutal rape-murders before he was caught. Ironically, the film that set him off was *The Ten Commandments*.

Anecdotes like these, no matter how interesting they may be, are not sufficient to answer the question of the effects of media violence. It's too easy to cherry-pick your examples to make a case either way; you could select examples of kids who play *Grand Theft Auto* and then go off to do their homework and take piano lessons. Accordingly, researchers have conducted experimental and field studies to try to untangle this complicated question.

Studying Media Violence The beauty of the laboratory experiment is that it allows us to determine whether images in the media have any impact at all on the behavior of a random sample of people. Most of the early experimental evidence demonstrated that watching violence does increase the frequency of aggressive behavior, angry emotions, and hostile thoughts.[97] But not every study found this "Bobo doll effect" (we will see why, shortly). Today, many researchers believe that the strongest effects of media violence occur when children are actively playing violent video games. Games that directly reward violence—for example, by awarding points or moving the player to the next level after a "kill"—are especially likely to increase feelings of hostility, aggressive thoughts, and aggressive acts.[98] A meta-analysis of 98 studies, with nearly 37,000 participants, found that both violent video games and prosocial video games have direct effects on their players.[99]

The lab allows us to demonstrate that something of significance is happening, but experiments cannot begin to capture the effects on a person who plays video games for hours every day and lives on a steady diet of violence for years. To investigate that effect, we need to use longitudinal studies in which children are followed for a year or longer. The researcher has less control over the factors being studied, but it is a better way of determining the effects of what a child is really being exposed to. In addition, unlike most laboratory experiments that must use artificial measures of aggression (such as administering loud noises or fake electric shocks), longitudinal studies can measure actual behavior. The disadvantage of this method is that people's lives are full of many other factors that can enhance or mitigate the effects of media violence.

That is why the results of longitudinal research are complicated. To begin, these studies generally do find that the more violence children watch, the more aggressively they behave later as teenagers and young adults. For example, one study followed 430 elementary-age children in the third to fifth grades over the course of a school year. The investigators measured three types of aggression—verbal, relational, and physical—and exposure to violence in television, movies, and video games. They measured both aggressive and prosocial behaviors in the children twice during the year, interviewing the children's peers and teachers as well as observing the children directly. They found that the children's consumption of media violence early in the school year predicted higher rates of all three kinds of aggression and less prosocial behavior later in the year.[100]

But the greatest challenge involved in trying to interpret the data in most longitudinal or survey studies is teasing apart cause and effect. The usual assumption has been that watching violence makes children and adults more aggressive, but aggressive people are also drawn to watching violence. Moreover, another entirely independent factor may be causing both. Some children are born with a mental or emotional predisposition toward violence; learn it as toddlers from the way they are treated by abusive parents or siblings; or in other ways develop aggressiveness as a personality trait. For these children, the effects of the media pale in comparison to the far more powerful predictors of aggressive behavior, including being socially rejected by peers, being the victim of physical abuse, being in a peer group that endorses and encourages violence, and living in a community where aggression is a way of life.[101] The result manifests itself in the children's aggressive behavior *and* in their liking for watching violence or playing aggressive games.[102]

In an experiment investigating the interaction between temperament and exposure to violence, children watched either a film depicting a great deal of police violence or an exciting but nonviolent film about bike racing. They then played a game of floor hockey. Watching the violent film did increase the number of aggressive acts the children committed during the hockey game, but primarily by those who had previously been rated as highly aggressive by their teachers. These kids hit others with their sticks, threw elbows, and yelled aggressive things at their opponents to a much greater extent than did either the kids rated as nonaggressive who had also watched the violent film or the kids rated as aggressive who had watched the nonviolent film.[103] Likewise, a few longitudinal studies have shown that exposure to violence in media or video games has the strongest relationship in children who are already predisposed to violence.[104]

Unexpected Effects of Media Violence Recall that at the beginning of this chapter, I asked, "How had I become so casual about seeing images of brutality in Vietnam while my young son was moved to tears?" There is good evidence that over time, exposure to graphic depictions of violence numbs us. We become decreasingly distressed by seeing people hurt, a process known as **desensitization**. People can become desensitized by watching scenes of war on the evening news, playing *Grand Theft Auto* for hours a day, and sadly, by witnessing actual violence, say between parents. In one of the earliest experiments on this issue, researchers measured the physiological responses of young men while they were watching a fairly bloody boxing match.[105] Those who had watched a lot of television in their daily lives seemed relatively indifferent to the mayhem in the ring; they showed little physiological evidence of excitement, anxiety, or other arousal. They were unmoved by the violence. But those who watched relatively little TV showed major physiological arousal; the violence really agitated them. Today, that "bloody boxing match" from a 40-year-old experiment seems tame compared to *Game of Thrones* or *The Walking Dead*. The very fact that violence has had to increase in gruesomeness and intensity to get the same reaction from audiences that mild violence once did may be the perfect illustration of the numbing effects of a diet of violence.

Although psychic numbing may protect us from feeling upset, it may also have the unintended effect of increasing our indifference to real victims of violence and others who need help. In one experiment, Brad Bushman and Craig Anderson[106] had participants play either a violent or nonviolent video game for 20 minutes and then fill out a lengthy questionnaire. While doing so, the participant was allowed to overhear a violent incident erupt in the next room. A verbal argument escalated into a shoving match and then an all-out physical brawl, after which the participant could hear one of the men leave, while the other was left groaning in pain, complaining about a hurt ankle and not being able to get up. (All of this was, of course, staged by the experimenter.) Those who played the violent video game took five times longer to respond to the victim in the next room. Why? Follow-up data suggests they had interpreted the incident as significantly less "serious" than had the participants who played the nonviolent game. In contrast to the extreme violence on the video screen, the real violence in the next room felt less urgent. After all, it's hard to get worked up over a twisted ankle when you've just decapitated several armies of invading mutants! Bushman and Anderson also conducted a field study, finding that people who had just seen a violent movie took longer to come to the aid of a woman struggling to pick up her crutches than did people who had seen a nonviolent movie or people still waiting to see one of the two movies.

And if the person needing help is not "one of us," watch out. When you are playing a violent video game, you are likely to see yourself as the hero who is blasting those evil creatures out of existence. That's fun, as far as it goes, but some research suggests it can go further: Once players get in the habit of dehumanizing the "enemy," that habit can be carried over into how players come to regard real people. In two experiments in England, researchers found that young men and women who played a violent video game (*Lamers*) were later more likely to dehumanize immigrants to Britain, seeing them as somehow less human and deserving than native Britons, in contrast to the students who played a prosocial version of the game (*Lemmings*) or a neutral game (*Tetris*).[107]

According to educational psychologists Douglas and Ronald Gentile, video games have another unintended consequence. When you are playing a video game, you are typically performing the same or similar activity, but the context changes as you advance to a new level of difficulty or change to an altogether different game. This process enhances and solidifies whatever concept is being taught; it maximizes the transfer of the learning from one situation to another. That means that if you play a variety of violent video games, you are likely to have thoughts about violence and aggression in situations that are far removed from the game. Gentile and Gentile[108] conducted a study of elementary school children and teenagers and found that those who played many different violent games were more likely to develop, over time, what's known as a **hostile attribution bias**, the tendency to interpret the ambiguous behavior of others in a hostile manner—rather than give others the benefit of the doubt. And by their own admission, they were also getting into more fights with their peers.

Finally, another unintended consequence of heavy exposure to media violence is the magnification of danger. If I am watching all this murder and mayhem on the home screen, wouldn't it be logical for me to conclude that it isn't safe to leave the house, especially after dark? That is exactly what many viewers do conclude. A study conducted at the Annenberg Public Policy Center compared annual changes in the amount of violence portrayed on popular prime-time broadcast dramas from 1972 through 2010 with responses to Gallup poll questions about fear of crime. The researchers found that the American public's fear of crime is directly, statistically related to the amount of violence portrayed on prime-time TV. Even after factoring out changes in actual crime rates, people's perceptions of the crime rate fell and rose along with TV violence. The number of violent sequences per TV hour fell from a high of 6.5 in 1972 to 1.4 in 1996, and then increased to 3.7 in 2010. Each additional violent sequence per hour predicted an increase of 1 percentage point in the people who told Gallup they were afraid of walking alone at night in their neighborhood.[109] In the last chapter I noted how the local news operates on the principle of "If it bleeds, it leads." It seems that if it bleeds, it also misleads.

Taking all this research together, I conclude that frequent exposure to violent media, especially in the form of violent video games, does have an impact on many children and adolescents, although the impact is greatest on those who are already prone to violent behavior. Watching violence seems to have effects on vulnerable viewers for five reasons: (1) it increases physiological arousal ("I guess I'm really angry rather than stressed"); (2) it triggers a tendency to imitate the hostile or violent characters, weakening previously learned inhibitions ("If they can do it, so can I"); (3) it triggers underlying feelings of anger, fear, or frustration ("I'd better get him before he gets me!"); (4) it promotes psychological numbing and reduces empathy ("Ho hum, another beating—what else is on?"); and (5) it often models approved ways of behaving when we are frustrated, angry, or hurt ("Oh, so that's how you do it!").[110]

Obviously, most people do not become motivated to behave aggressively as a result of what they observe. As social-cognitive learning theory predicts, people's interpretation of what they are watching, their personality dispositions, and the social context all affect how they respond. Children and teens watch many different programs and movies and have many models to observe besides those they see in the media, including parents and peers. But the fact that some people are influenced by violent entertainments, with tragic results, cannot be denied.

The Elements of Aggression: The Case of Sexual Assault

We are now in a position to consider how many of the themes that have been raised in this chapter might apply to understanding one of the most troubling and persistent kinds of aggression: rape and other forms of sexual assault. Definitions of "rape" have changed over the decades; for example, the law used to exempt married men, who were legally allowed to have forcible sex with their wives. Today the Department of Justice has made the definition of rape inclusive: the penetration of any bodily orifice with any part of the body or with any object, without the consent of the victim. Sexual assault is the broader term, including various other acts, but lack of consent remains the key criterion. Notice that the definition does not specify gender—men can be sexually assaulted and raped also, although many are ashamed to admit it.

Some men commit rape out of a desire to dominate, humiliate, or punish their victims. This motive is apparent among soldiers who rape captive women during war and then often kill them and among men who rape other men, usually by anal penetration.[111] The latter form of rape often occurs in youth gangs, where the intention is to humiliate rival gang members, and in prison, where the motive, in addition to the obvious sexual one, is to conquer and degrade the victim.

When most people think of a "rapist," they imagine a violent stranger or a serial predator. Some rapists are exactly that. They are often unable to empathize with women, may feel hostility and contempt toward women, and feel entitled to have sexual relations with whatever woman they choose.[112] This may be why sexual violence is more likely to be committed by high-status men, including sports heroes (professional, college, and high school athletic stars), powerful politicians, and celebrities, who could easily find consenting partners. They equate feelings of power with sex, angrily accuse women of provoking them, and endorse rape myths, such as "Women want to be raped."

In fact, however, about 85 percent of all rapes or attempted rapes—being forced to engage in sexual acts against one's will—occur between people who know each other. Rape may occur as a result of *physical force*, having sex under actual or threatened violence, or through *incapacitation*, having sex with a victim who has been induced into a blackout with Rohypnol ("roofies"), who is drunk or otherwise drugged, or who has passed out.

Sexual Scripts and the Problem of Consent Everyone understands that a sexual predator who rapes a woman by overt force, threats of violence, or drugs used to render her unconscious has committed a serious crime. But what is going on with the much larger numbers of women assaulted when they are incapacitated as a result of their voluntary enjoyment of alcohol and other drugs? One answer may stem from the different **sexual scripts** that males and females learn as part of their gender roles in American society.[113] Sexual scripts vary according to one's culture, sexual orientation, ethnicity, age, and geographic region, and they change over time. These scripts shape what women and men learn is the "right" way to be sexual and popular, primarily from observations of role models, peers, and media images and messages. Who gets to ask whom out? How many dates before sex is expected? What kind of sex? Who initiates? Is any kind of sex before marriage permitted, discouraged, or forbidden?

One dominant script in America for young, straight women and men is that the female's role is to resist the male's sexual advances and that the male's role is to be persistent.[114] Unfortunately, this script may explain why many people argue so much over the meaning of the word *no*. The repeated message of antirape groups—"What part of 'no' don't you understand?"—seems obvious. Yet research finds repeatedly that "no" can be as hard for women to say as it is for men to hear; many men who are following traditional sexual scripts think that "no" means "maybe" or "in a little while." Some women, following scripts that say, "It's okay to want sex, but be careful about saying yes too soon or they'll call you a slut," agree with them. The resulting confusion may also explain why some college women feel they need to drink heavily as a prelude to sex. If they are inebriated, they haven't said "yes," and if they haven't explicitly said "yes," no one can accuse them of being a slut.

Further complicating matters is that most couples communicate sexual interest and intentions, including a wish *not* to have sex, indirectly—through hints, body language, eye contact, and other nonverbal behaviors. Deborah Davis and her colleagues[115] call this indirect communication a "dance of ambiguity," which protects both parties: His ego is protected in case she says no, and she can accept without having to explicitly admit it's what she wants or reject the offer without rejecting the suitor and possibly angering him.

One of Joshua's undergraduate students wrote an essay that eloquently described what happens when a woman's script (often based on romantic fantasies) clashes with a man's script (often fed by watching porn, which conveys inaccurate ideas about sexuality and what women "want"):

> Frank Sinatra was my imaginary boyfriend. His songs filled my head with romance and thoughts of being loved and treasured, as I imagined women in my parents' era were. In college, my first real boyfriend sent me a text with a link to a pornographic movie. The text said, "You really need to work on your blowjobs. Check out my favorite porn star. Watch her technique and learn." So I watched, and I saw the source of my boyfriend's beliefs about who I was, what I wanted, and what felt good to me, and presumably what he wanted sex and romance to be. It was devastating. Both my ideas and his ideas were lies—the Sinatra fantasy just as much as Pornhub. I talked to my friends. Not a single one has ever wanted a man to ejaculate on her face; yet nearly every scene in porn concludes this way. The man's pleasure is what it's all about, and men seem to enjoy seeing women on their knees rather than

on a pedestal. There is little foreplay, the conversation is degrading, and worst, women seem to enjoy rough treatment, often by more than one man at a time. My now ex-boyfriend learned virtually all his ideas about sex from porn. I wish I had known to talk about this when it occurred; there would have been so much less pain and disillusionment.

Her story is not about rape or assault, yet she had not known how to "talk about this" with a serious boyfriend. And if she couldn't talk about "this," how much more difficult would it be to say no clearly to pressure to engage in any other unwanted sexual acts?

Today, as college administrators and students struggle with the problems caused by the "dance of ambiguity"—when to accept the accounts of victimized women, when and how to punish perpetrators, and how to handle issues of sexual misconduct when both parties had been drinking heavily—I think that these findings from social-psychological research can lead us toward greater clarity and fairness. For example, as psychologists Deborah Davis and Elizabeth Loftus have written, in a "he said/she said" situation, *both sides can be right, and both sides can also be wrong.*[116] The scripted sexual dance, they say, can lead to "honest false testimony" by both sides: She really thinks he should have known to stop, and he really thinks she gave consent. Studies find that sometimes young women, following a script that says they should "be nice" and not offend or anger the initiator, try to convey "no" without saying no, in nonverbal ways such as by stepping a few inches back, not resisting but not agreeing, or pretending not to notice the man's advances. For their part, many men are motivated to overinterpret women's nonverbal actions as signs of sexual interest rather than friendly flirting, or just friendliness. They justify their persistence.

Other social psychological factors are at play in the problem of rape and sexual assault on college campuses. Cultural and social norms dictate whether men feel entitled to assault an unwilling woman or whether that would be considered despicable by their peers. Does a college, fraternity, or country endorse a "rape culture" that lets men off the hook, especially when the men are athletic heroes? How does a culture of binge drinking affect women's decisions about sex, and how might the "think-drink" affect apply? Perhaps the most important steps toward reducing date and acquaintance rape, therefore, are that (1) both sexes understand the rules and norms clearly, to decide if they want to abide by them or resist them; (2) both sexes make sure that they are following a script that is in the same play; (3) women learn to express their wishes in a direct way; and (4) men learn that an intoxicated woman cannot legally consent to sex and that having sex with someone who is incapacitated, even if she chose to get drunk, is immoral and illegal.

Toward the Reduction of Violence

If we believe that reducing our propensity toward aggression is a worthwhile goal, how should we proceed? It is tempting to search for easy solutions. A long time ago, no less an expert than a former president of the American Psychological Association suggested that we develop an anticruelty drug to be fed to people (especially national leaders) as a way of reducing violence on a universal scale.[117] The quest for such a solution is understandable and even somewhat touching, but it is extremely unlikely that a drug could be developed that would reduce cruelty without completely tranquilizing its users. Drugs cannot make distinctions between psychological processes. Gentle, peace-loving people who are also energetic, creative, courageous, and resourceful are produced by a combination of inherited capacities, experiences, and learned values. It is difficult to conceive of a drug that could target one aspect of that combination and not another. Moreover, medical control of human behavior has the quality of an Orwellian nightmare. Whom could we trust to administer such drugs? If an "anticruelty drug" isn't the answer, let's speculate about some possibilities based upon what we've learned so far.

Punishment To the average citizen, an obvious way of reducing aggression is to punish it. If one man robs, batters, or kills another, just put him in prison. Surely, living in the harsh, restrictive environment of a prison would deter that person, once released, from committing crimes—or would it? Determining the specific consequences of imprisonment is difficult, however; in most instances, it is impossible to isolate the effects of being incarcerated because too many other factors are involved.[118] Does being in prison knock the aggressiveness out of most convicts, making them less likely to reoffend when they are out, or does going back to a world that supports their law-breaking behavior have a greater impact?

Although these possibilities are hard to test, evidence from a natural experiment suggests that prisons themselves fail to deter crime among the inmates who are released. A Supreme Court decision made the experiment possible, isolating the effects of imprisonment on recidivism. In 1963, after the *Gideon* v. *Wainwright* ruling that people could not be convicted of a felony without being provided with a lawyer, a number of the inmates of Florida prisons were released early—way before they had served their full sentence. The only systematic difference between these prisoners and those remaining in prison was that the released prisoners had not previously been represented by counsel. Thus, researchers could compare two groups of convicts who were nearly identical; some had been prematurely released, and others had been punished and "rehabilitated" to the full extent of their sentences. A startling difference emerged between the two groups: The prisoners who served their complete term were *twice as likely to return to prison* as those who were released early.[119]

Does this mean that imprisonment fails to reduce crime? Not necessarily. This study does offer persuasive evidence that lengthy prison terms do not deter the future criminal behavior of released inmates, but it does not completely rule out the possibility that the mere prospect of harsh punishment might curb the criminal tendencies of those who have never been convicted. It is certainly possible that the threat of punishment deters many would-be criminals from ever breaking the law in the first place.

Although this is possible, I consider it unlikely. For one thing, the likely punishment is far down the road, and for another, states that have the harshest punishment—the death penalty for murder—have higher murder rates than states without the death penalty.[120] What I *do* know is that, although severe punishment, if administered promptly, frequently results in compliance, it rarely produces internalization. If a young girl slaps her parents, siblings, or peers, we can spank her, scream at her, remove her privileges, or make her feel guilty. The assumption here is that this punishment will "teach her a lesson," that she will "think twice" before she misbehaves again, and that the more severe the punishment, the better. But punishment, which can be effective temporarily, tends to have the opposite effect in the long run.[121] Not all children who are spanked or beaten will become violent, but what parents do is a powerful lesson in social learning, teaching their children: "Oh, so *that's* what I should do when I'm mad at someone: yell at them or hit them."

If people are to establish long-term nonaggressive behavior patterns, they must, as children, internalize a set of values that opposes aggressive responses. In two separate experiments discussed more fully in Chapter 3, Merrill Carlsmith and I, and subsequently Jonathan Freedman,[122] demonstrated that, with young children, threats of mild punishment are far more effective than threats of severe punishment. Although these experiments dealt only with toy preference in children, they strongly suggest that threats of mild (rather than severe) punishment would curb aggression in the same way.

As we suggested in Chapter 3, here's how it works: Suppose a mother threatens to punish her young son to induce him to refrain, momentarily, from aggressing against his little sister. If she is successful, her son will experience dissonance. The cognition "I like to wallop my little sister" is dissonant with the cognition "I am refraining from walloping my little sister." If he were severely threatened, he would have an abundantly good reason for refraining; he would be able to reduce dissonance by saying, "The reason I'm not hitting my sister is that I'd get the daylights beaten out of me if I did—but I sure would like to."

However, suppose his mother threatens to use a punishment that is mild rather than severe, a punishment just barely strong enough to get the child to stop his aggression. In this instance, when he asks himself why he's not hitting his infinitely hittable little sister at the moment, he can't use the threat as a way of reducing dissonance. That is, he can't easily convince himself that he would be walloped if he hit his sister because it's not true—yet he must justify the fact that he's not hitting her. In other words, his external justification (the severity of the threat) is minimal; therefore, he must add his own to justify his restraint. He might, for example, convince himself that he no longer enjoys hitting his little sister and, besides, it's wrong to hit people who are smaller than you. This would not only explain, justify, and make sensible his momentarily peaceful restraint, but more important, it would decrease the probability of his hitting his little sister in the future. In short, he would have internalized a counteraggressive value. He would have convinced *himself* that, for him, hitting someone is neither desirable nor fun.

This general notion has been applied with success in the real world of the schoolyard. Dan Olweus,[123] working in the Norwegian school system, was able to curtail the frequency of bullying by as much as 50 percent by training teachers and administrators to be vigilant to the problem and to take swift but *moderate* punitive action. Taken as a whole, this research indicates that children who have not yet formed their values are more apt to develop a distaste for aggression if the punishment for aggressive actions is both timely and moderate.

Punishing Aggressive Models Might it be possible to reduce aggression by showing children aggressive models who come to a bad end? The theory here is that as long as the violence that children see is punished, they will, in effect, be vicariously punished for their own aggression and accordingly will become less aggressive—and less inclined to mimic what they observe. Unfortunately, the evidence doesn't support this widespread belief. Experimental studies present a more precise—and complex—picture. Typically, in these experiments, children watch a film of an aggressive person who subsequently is either rewarded or punished for acting aggressively. Later, the children are given an opportunity to behave aggressively under circumstances similar to the ones shown in the film. The consistent finding is that children who watch a film in which the aggressive person is *punished* do act less aggressively than the children who watch a film of the person being *rewarded*. And they are less aggressive than children who watch an aggressive film character who is neither rewarded nor punished.[124] On the other hand—and this point is crucial—seeing a model being punished for aggression did not decrease the general level of aggression below that of a group of children who were not exposed to an aggressive model. In other words, the major thrust of the research seems to indicate that (1) seeing an aggressor rewarded will increase the child's aggressive behavior, and (2) seeing an aggressor punished will *neither* increase nor decrease the child's aggressive behavior. It is just as effective not to expose the child to aggressive models at all.

Rewarding Alternatives to Aggression Another possibility that has been investigated is to ignore a child when he or she behaves aggressively and to reward the child for behaving unaggressively. This strategy is based in part on the evidence that young children (and adults, as well) frequently behave aggressively as a way of attracting attention. For them, being punished is preferable to being ignored. Paradoxically, then, punishing aggressive behavior may be interpreted as a reward—"Hey! Mommy pays attention to me every time I slug my little sister. I think I'll do it again."

Paul Brown and Rogers Elliot[125] tested this idea in an experiment conducted at a nursery school. The nursery-school teachers were instructed to ignore all aggressive acts on the part of the kids, but also to be very attentive to the children, especially when they were doing things incompatible with aggression, such as playing in a friendly manner, sharing toys, and cooperating with others. After a few weeks, there was a noticeable decline in aggressive behavior. In a more elaborate experiment, Joel Davitz[126] demonstrated that frustration need not necessarily result in aggression; rather, it can lead to constructive behavior if such behavior has been made appealing by prior training. In this study, children were allowed to play in groups of four. Some of these groups were rewarded for constructive behavior, while others were rewarded for aggressive or competitive behavior. Then Davitz deliberately frustrated the kids by building up the expectation that they would see entertaining movies and be allowed to have fun. Indeed, he went so far as to begin to show a movie and hand out candy bars to be eaten later. But then he created the "frustration" part of the experiment by abruptly terminating the movie at the point of highest interest and taking away the candy bars. The children were then allowed to play freely. As you have learned, this is a setup for the expected occurrence of aggressive behavior. But the children who had been trained to behave constructively played in a far more constructive way and far less aggressive way than those in the other group.

This research is encouraging, but I find it necessary to state my firm belief that it would be naïve to expect many children in our society to spontaneously choose constructive rather than aggressive solutions to conflicts and frustrating circumstances. American society presents us with all kinds of evidence that violent solutions to conflict and frustration are valued. Explicitly or implicitly, whether in the guise of the avenging action hero or the suave secret agent who blows people away in exotic and entertaining displays, these movie heroes demonstrate to young kids what society values and rewards. Needless to say, our exposure to violent solutions to problems is not confined to films and video games; these events dominate the nightly news, as well. Accordingly, it should come as no surprise that children learn that adults often solve their conflicts by resorting to violence, and many don't even learn that alternative solutions are feasible or appropriate. If we would prefer our children to grow up favoring nonviolent strategies, it might be a good idea to offer them specific training in these techniques, as well as encouragement to use them. As we will see shortly, there is no reason why such training cannot be provided both in the home and in school.

Providing Nonaggressive Models An important curb to aggression is the clear indication that it is inappropriate. And the most effective indicator is social—that is, the presence of other people in the same circumstances who choose conciliation over retaliation. In a study by Robert Baron and Richard Kepner,[127] participants were insulted by the experimenters' confederate and then observed that individual receiving electric shocks at the hands of a third person. The third person delivered either intense shocks or very mild shocks. (A control group did not observe a model administering shocks.) Everyone was then given the opportunity to shock their tormentor. Those who had witnessed a person delivering intense shocks to him delivered more intense shocks than those in the control condition; those who had witnessed a person delivering mild shocks delivered milder shocks than those in the control condition. Does this paradigm seem familiar? The expression of aggressive behavior, like the expression of any other behavior, can be viewed as an act of conformity, which means that in an ambiguous situation, people look to other people for a definition of what is appropriate.

In Chapter 4, I described the conditions under which you might belch at the dinner table of a Freedonian dignitary. Here I am suggesting that, if you and your friends are frustrated or made angry, and all around you people in your group are throwing snowballs at your tormentors, it will increase the probability that you will throw snowballs; if they are merely talking angrily, it will increase the probability that you will talk angrily; and alas, if they are swinging baseball bats at the heads of their tormentors, it will increase the probability that you will pick up a bat and start swinging along with them.

Building Empathy Picture the following scene: There is a long line of cars stopped at a traffic light at a busy intersection. The light turns green. The lead driver hesitates for 15 seconds. What happens? Of course, an eruption of horn-honking—not simply a little toot designed to supply the lead driver with the information that the light has changed, but there is prolonged and persistent blasting from frustrated drivers behind the lead car, venting their annoyance. Indeed, an experiment found that, in this situation, approximately 90 percent of the drivers of the second car honked their horns in an aggressive manner. As part of the same experiment, a pedestrian crossed the street between the first and second cars *while the light was still red for the drivers* and was out of the intersection by the time the light turned green. Still, almost 90 percent of the second-car drivers tooted their horns the second the light changed—never mind that the first driver might have wanted to make sure the pedestrian had safely crossed. But what happened when the pedestrian was on crutches? Apparently, seeing a person on crutches evoked an empathic response; the feeling of empathy overwhelmed the desire to be aggressive, and the percentage of people honking their horns decreased dramatically.[128]

Empathy is crucial to human life; it is the antidote to dehumanization. If, as we have seen, most individuals dehumanize their victims to justify committing an act of aggression against them, then, by building empathy among people, aggressive acts will become more difficult to commit. Indeed, Norma and Seymour Feshbach[129] have demonstrated a negative correlation between empathy and aggression in children: The more the level of empathy, the less the likelihood of behaving aggressively. Norma Feshbach,[130] who has pioneered the teaching of empathy in elementary schools, designed a 30-hour empathy-training program for children. The kids had to think hard about questions, such as "What would the world look like to you if you were as small as a cat?" and "What birthday present would make each member of your family happiest?" Thinking about the answers expands children's ability to put themselves in another's situation. The children also listened to stories and then retold them from the point of view of each of the different characters in each story. The children played the role of each of the characters, and their performances were videotaped. The children then watched the tapes and talked about how people look and sound when they express different feelings. At the end of the program, the children not only had learned to be more empathic but also had higher self-esteem, were more generous, and were less aggressive than were students who had not participated in the program.

Georgina Hammock and Deborah Richardson[131] demonstrated similar benefits of empathy in studies of college students who were placed in a situation in which they were instructed to deliver electric shocks to a fellow student. Those who had learned to feel concern for the feelings of others delivered less severe shocks than those who were less empathic. Kenichi Obuchi and his colleagues,[132] working with Japanese students, found the same thing. Obuchi instructed students to deliver electric shocks to another student as part of a learning experiment. In one condition, prior to receiving the shocks, the victims first disclosed something personal about themselves—thus opening the door to the formation of empathy. In the control condition, the victims were not afforded an opportunity for self-disclosure. Students in the disclosure condition administered much milder shocks than those in the nondisclosure condition.

Teaching Altruism and Mindfulness A powerful antidote to aggression is *altruism*—doing something for others, even at the cost of our own immediate comfort or pleasure. Altruism makes us feel good. It relieves the unpleasant emotions we feel when we see others suffer, and giving to others is repeatedly found to elevate our mood more reliably than giving to ourselves. For example, it turns out that in terms of happiness and well-being, *how* people spend their money is at least as important as how much they earn. Using three different research methods, Lara Aknin and her colleagues[133] investigated this question. One measure was a nationally representative survey; the second was a longitudinal field study of how people spent unexpected, "windfall" income. In both studies, people who spent money on others were happier than those who spent it on themselves. But of course the results could work in either direction: Does altruism cause happiness, or do happy people behave more altruistically? So the researchers did an experiment in which participants were randomly assigned either to spend money on themselves or on others. This time they pinned down the causal sequence: Behaving altruistically produces greater feelings of happiness.

As we saw in discussing social cognitive learning theory, *how we think about events*—how we perceive, interpret, and explain something that might normally annoy, frustrate, or anger us—is a crucial intermediate step in determining how we respond.

That is the reason for the final antidote to aggressiveness I want to mention: *mindfulness* and forms of *meditation,* which teach people to focus attention on the present moment. In practicing mindfulness and meditation, people reduce reflexive, aggressive responses to a perceived provocation or insult, giving a person time to reflect and decide how to respond more calmly and constructively. People who are being mindful would disagree with statements like, "It seems I am 'running on automatic' without much awareness of what I'm doing," and the goal is precisely to enable them to become aware. In experiments, even a brief session of mindfulness training reduces "mind-wandering," unfocused thoughts that impede the ability to pay close attention to the task at hand. While occasional day-dreaming is fine and pleasant, *habitual* mind-wandering predicts worse mood, greater stress, lower self-esteem, and less concern for the welfare of others.[134] Its benefits are therefore physical (lower levels of stress hormones), emotional (reduced feelings of hostility), and behavioral (reduced aggressiveness).[135]

Meditation has similar benefits. Meditators are instructed to pay attention to sensations in the present moment, rather than being caught up with memories or images pertaining to the past or future—memories and images that typically produce anger or anxiety. One of numerous randomized controlled trials found that a meditation program for young adults reduced their blood pressure and feelings of psychological distress and helped them cope more constructively.[136] By calming the mind and body, meditation reduces a person's impulse, when provoked, to retaliate aggressively.[137]

Final Thoughts on the Nature of Human Nature

At the start of this chapter, I noted how philosophers and scientists have debated whether human beings are "naturally" aggressive or "naturally" kind. Following the brilliant discoveries of Charles Darwin and the rise of evolutionary approaches to understanding behavior, the pendulum swung to the "naturally aggressive" side. The reasoning was that aggression—between individuals and between groups—is useful and necessary for survival, because dominating and hurting others is an efficient way for people to secure resources and sexual partners. The zoologist Konrad Lorenz[138] argued that aggression is "an essential part of the life-preserving organization of instincts."

But other scientists were skeptical. The anthropologist Ashley Montagu[139] maintained that an oversimplification and a misinterpretation of evolutionary theory had provided the average person with the mistaken idea that conflict is common because it is necessary, a law of nature. Montagu saw this view as a convenient excuse that wealthy industrialists could use to justify their exploitation of workers: Life is a struggle, after all, so it is natural for the strongest and most aggressive to survive. The danger, Montagu said, is that this kind of reasoning can become self-fulfilling and can lead us to ignore or downplay the obvious survival value of nonaggressive and noncompetitive behavior.

More than 100 years ago, the Russian scientist and social reformer Peter Kropotkin[140]—a prince who had been born into an aristocratic family—concluded that cooperation and mutual aid have great survival value for most forms of life. We had to learn to cooperate to live in groups, he wrote, and like many social animals, we evolved prosocial tendencies alongside our aggressive ones. Kropotkin's ideas were largely ignored, perhaps because they did not fit the temper of the times or the needs of those who were profiting from the Industrial Revolution. But he was proved right. The cooperative abilities of social insects, such as termites, ants, and bees, have been well documented,[141] and as we saw in Chapter 2, today we know that cooperation is as much embedded in our biology as aggression is.

Yet the belief that aggression is adaptive and beneficial remains embedded in our very language and approaches to solving problems—and blinds us to cooperative alternatives. People assume that the same mechanism that drives human beings to kill drives others to "conquer" outer space, "sink their teeth" into a difficult mathematical equation, "attack" a logical problem, start a "war" on drugs, "fight a battle" with disease, or "master" the universe. But this reasoning is based on an exaggerated definition of aggression. To equate high achievement and advancement with hostility and aggression is to confuse the issue. A problem or skill can be mastered without harming other people or even without attempting to conquer them. And metaphors that turn the effort to find cures for terrible diseases and solutions to entrenched social problems into "wars" end up defining the problem the wrong way, and thereby limit our ability to solve it.

This is a difficult distinction for us to grasp because we Americans have been trained to equate success with victory, to equate doing well with beating someone. As a culture, we thrive on competition; we reward winners and are disdainful of losers. For two centuries, our educational system has been based on competitiveness. With few exceptions, most schools do not teach our kids to love learning; we teach them to strive for high grades and great scores on the SAT.[142] When sportswriter Grantland Rice said, "It's not whether you win or lose, it's how you play the game," he certainly was not describing the dominant theme in American life; he was expressing a hope that we might somehow rid ourselves of our morbid preoccupation with winning at all costs and focus instead on playing with dignity, competence, and generosity of spirit. From the Little League ballplayer who bursts into tears after his team is defeated to the college students in the football stadium chanting "We're number one!"; from former President Lyndon Johnson, whose judgment during the Vietnam war was almost certainly distorted by his desire "not to be the first American president to lose a war," to the third-grader who envies and despises her classmate for a superior performance on an arithmetic test, we manifest a staggering cultural obsession with victory. Vince Lombardi, the legendary coach of the Green Bay Packers, summed it up when he said, "Winning isn't everything, it's the *only* thing." This philosophy implies that the goal of victory justifies whatever means we use to win, even if it's only a football game—which, after all, was first conceived as a recreational activity.

To be sure, competition and aggression are adaptive—for *some* groups, under *some* conditions. But as I look about and see a world full of international, interracial, and intertribal hatred and distrust, of senseless slaughter, of terrorism, of daily mass shootings, of enough nuclear warheads floating around to destroy the world's population many times over, I feel justified in questioning the current survival value of this behavior. Anthropologist Loren Eiseley[143] paid tribute to our ancient ancestors but warned against imitating them when he wrote, "The need is now for a gentler, a more tolerant people than those who won for us against the ice, the tiger, and the bear."

The good news is that, despite the fact that modern weaponry has enabled humans to be far more destructive, modern society appears to have made us less psychologically prone than our ancestors to act on our violent tendencies. Modernity has enabled us to cooperate and trade with people well beyond our family, tribe, and country; we buy their products, eat their cuisines, read their literature. These social and cultural exchanges have allowed us to see into the lives of strangers in a way that humanizes them, thus making it harder to harm them. Perhaps we can find other ways of summoning, and following, what Abraham Lincoln called "the better angels of our nature."

Saul Steinberg, *Untitled drawing*, ink on paper.
Published in Steinberg, *The Art of Living*, 1949.
© The Saul Steinberg Foundation / Artists Rights Society (ARS), New York

7

Prejudice

When I was a young professor, I heard Thurgood Marshall being interviewed on the radio, and he told a story that had a powerful effect on me. When Marshall was a young lawyer working for the National Association for the Advancement of Colored People (NAACP), he was sent to a small town in the South to defend a black man who was accused of a serious crime. When he arrived, he was shocked and dismayed to learn that the defendant was already dead—lynched by an angry white mob. With a heavy heart, Marshall returned to the railroad station to wait for a train back to New York. While waiting, he realized he was hungry and noticed a small food stand on the platform. Walking toward the stand, he debated whether to go right up to the front and order a sandwich (as was his legal right) or to go around to the back of the stand (as was the common practice for African Americans in the South at that time). But before he reached the stand, he was approached by a large, heavyset white man who looked at him suspiciously. Marshall took him to be a lawman of some sort because he walked with an air of authority and had a bulge in his pants pocket that could only have been made by a handgun.

"Hey, boy," the man shouted at Marshall. "What are you doing here?" "I'm just waiting for a train," Marshall replied.

The man scowled, took a few steps closer, glared at him menacingly, and said, "I didn't hear you. What did you say, boy?"

Marshall realized that his initial reply had not been sufficiently obsequious.

He said, "I beg your pardon, sir, but I'm waiting for a train."

There was a long silence, during which the man slowly looked Marshall up and down, and then said, "And you'd better catch that train, boy—and soon, because in this town, the sun has never set on a live nigger."

As Marshall later recalled, at that point his debate about how to get the sandwich proved academic. He decided not to get a sandwich at all but to catch the very next train out—no matter where it was headed. Besides, somehow he didn't feel hungry anymore.[1]

Thurgood Marshall went on to become chief counsel for the NAACP; in 1954, he argued the case of *Brown* v. *Board of Education* before the U.S. Supreme Court. His victory there put an end to legalized racial segregation in public schools. Subsequently, Marshall was appointed to the Supreme Court, where he served with distinction until his retirement in 1991. I am not sure what became of the man with the bulge in his pocket.

What Is Prejudice?

Prejudice is one of the most common and most troubling fixtures of the human experience, yet it is poorly understood. Many white people believe that stories like Marshall's represent a bygone era, that modern society has evolved to the point that it is "post-racial," colorblind, and fair. After all, we elected a black president; Oprah, Beyoncé, and LeBron are so successful that we know them by their first names; it is now virtually forbidden to use the "n-word." Therefore, when surveyed, many people say that we needn't worry about policies to protect vulnerable minorities from prejudice and discrimination anymore; indeed, if anything we've become *too* sensitive, too "politically correct."[2] This became more than merely an academic debate in 2013. That year, the discrimination-is-over argument was key when the Supreme Court struck down vital protections in the voting rights act of 1964, which had made it illegal for states to prevent African Americans from voting.[3]

Undoubtedly we have much progress to celebrate: Barack Obama's election was unimaginable in Thurgood Marshall's time, when people of color and women were confined to subservient roles and interracial marriages were forbidden by law, when gay men and lesbians were considered "perverted" or mentally ill and could be jailed in some states, and when lynching was still used in Southern states to terrorize black people. Surveys conducted during the 1960s found that whites actively wanted to maximize their distance from African Americans—nearly 80 percent said they would move out of their neighborhood if a black family moved in. Today 84 percent of whites are comfortable with interracial marriage, and the numbers of interracial couples are steadily rising.[4]

Still, despite this progress, no social psychologist believes that human beings can be post-racial or simply shed their biases like overcoats. Prejudice, as we shall see, is fundamental to the human condition. In a very real sense, we are built for it. Because prejudice exists in all cultures, it is reasonable to conclude that it helped our hunter-gatherer ancestors survive by making them wary of strangers. Treating strangers as potential attackers is a better way to survive in a dangerous world than treating them as friends. Thus, although many of our prejudiced attitudes and behaviors have changed as social norms have changed, and as intergroup relations have generally improved and antidiscrimination policies have taken hold, we are no less naturally inclined to prejudice than we were in the 1960s—or the 1860s, or the 1360s, etc.

After Obama's election, the number of hate groups proliferated threefold, suggesting a backlash against growing African American political power. Online, hundreds of thousands of self-identified white nationalists proudly express their contempt for Muslims, gays, blacks, Mexicans, Jews, and liberals.[5] Here and abroad, terrorists have murdered thousands of innocent victims, pledging their allegiance to the Islamic State, and engendering widespread fear and suspicion of Muslims as a group.[6] In 2015, a 21-year-old white supremacist posted a hate manifesto with photos of himself with the Confederate flag, before gunning down nine African American worshipers at a prayer meeting in South Carolina. As President Obama told an interviewer after the shooting, "It's not just a matter of it not being polite to say 'nigger' in public. That's not the measure of whether racism still exists or not. It's not just a matter of overt

discrimination. Societies don't, overnight, completely erase everything that happened 200 to 300 years prior."[7]

Indeed, recent American history is a potent reminder that racism, sexism, and many other *isms* don't just go away. And so long
as we have prejudices, there will be politicians willing to exploit
them—and by the example they set, influence others to feel justified
in their hatreds. Donald Trump's campaign and presidency have been
marked by a number of overtly hostile slurs against women, Muslims,
Hispanics, and people with disabilities. He explained his remarks
thus: "I don't, frankly, have time for total political correctness. And
to be honest with you, this country doesn't have time either."[8] The
country apparently was listening. Here's just a sample of American
prejudices that made the news in the months following the election:

- In February 2017, Dyne Suh, a UCLA law student, reserved
  a cabin on Airbnb for a much-needed vacation with friends.
  Driving to the cabin during a severe snowstorm, she received
  a last-minute text from the owner of the cabin, cancelling her
  reservation. When Suh complained and texted screen shots of
  the rental agreement, her host replied, "I wouldn't rent to u if you
  were the last person on earth. One word says it all: Asian." When
  Suh threatened to report the discrimination to Airbnb, the host
  replied, "Go ahead ... It's why we have Trump."[9]

- The noose, a symbol of bigotry and hatred directed at African
  Americans, proliferated in 2017. Following the abolition of slavery, nooses were used to lynch thousands of black people, and the
  practice did not subside until the late 1960s. Their reappearance
  sends a terrifying message to African Americans: *We hate you and
  want you dead.* After the election, nooses were found hanging
  in many public places, including in a Museum on the National
  Mall; in a gallery at the National Museum of African American
  History and Culture; at an elementary school; at a middle school;
  outside a black fraternity house; and on the campus of American
  University the day before the first black woman was set to assume
  the presidency of its Student Government Association.[10]

- In Portland, Oregon, in May 2017, on the first day of Ramadan
  (the holiest month for Muslims), Jeremy Joseph Christian spotted
  two women sitting together on a commuter train, one of whom was
  wearing a hijab, and began angrily shouting anti-Muslim slurs at
  them. When two men intervened and tried to calm him, he stabbed
  them to death, wounded a third, and jumped off the train.[11]

- In July 2017, the president, on his own, declared a ban on all transgender individuals serving in the military in any capacity, reversing the Pentagon's 2016 policy that had lifted a long-standing ban against the estimated 16,000 transgender men and women serving openly.

- In August 2017, in Charlottesville, Virginia, a rally was organized by neo-Nazis, the Ku Klux Klan, the alt-right, and other white supremacists. Carrying banners with swastikas and confederate symbols, the "unite the right" marchers vowed to "take the country back" from all the racial and ethnic groups they despise. One neo-Nazi rammed his car into a crowd of counter-demonstrators, killing one woman and injuring 19 other people.

Like aggression, prejudice is endemic to human nature; it ebbs and flows with changes in social conditions; it cycles with the times. Its outward expression can be discouraged by cultural norms and antidiscrimination laws—or encouraged by the public bigotry of others—but it never disappears completely. The better we understand its nature, the better our chances of minimizing our very human prejudicial tendencies. What is prejudice? How does it come about? What are its effects on people? What can we do to reduce it? Social psychology has produced some useful answers.

Let me begin with a definition. Social psychologists have defined **prejudice** in a variety of ways, but I will define it as a negative attitude toward all members of a distinguishable group, based solely on their membership in the group. Prejudice is complex; like any attitude, it is partly *cognitive*, partly *emotional*, and partly *behavioral*. Thus, when we say an individual is prejudiced against gay people, we mean he or she has preconceived beliefs about them, feels negatively about them, and is disposed to behave toward them with bias or hostility. Like any attitude, prejudice influences and is influenced by our behavior.

The Cognitive Component of Prejudice: Stereotypes

Some prejudices are largely cognitive, rooted in misinformation; they can usually be changed relatively easily. Let's say you have a prejudice against visiting Iceland because, well, it's so *icy* and cold. But if I tell you it is actually a beautiful island covered in green rolling hills and it got its name because the Norwegian explorers who landed there didn't want their pursuers to follow them, your prejudice will probably evaporate. Unfortunately, most prejudices are not so easily changed.

Just as we mentally organize the physical world into categories, we group people according to characteristics that matter. The grouping of objects or people by key characteristics is called *categorization*, a process fundamental to cognition. Babies begin creating categories almost as soon as they are born.[12] Newborns show no preference for faces of one race or another, but if they live in a setting that is "mono-racial," by three months of age they will show a preference for faces of their own race.[13] Yet if they repeatedly encounter faces of two or more races, they do not develop a preference. Thus, we are not hardwired to categorize people by race per se, but instead appear more generally predisposed to be attracted to people who are like us and wary of people who are different. The fundamental category for social animals is *us or them*. By an early age we can categorize by gender, age, and race, which we easily determine visually. Later, we *learn* to use ethnicity, sexual orientation, religion, political ideology, and other less visual but meaningful categories to decide who is an *us* and who is a *them*. Categorization does not automatically generate prejudice, but it can be the first step.

Once we divide the world into categories, we often apply labels to them that sum up the essence of the group—a stereotype. A **stereotype** reflects the belief that a particular attribute is characteristic of the group as a whole, regardless of the actual variation among the group's members. Walter Lippmann, the distinguished journalist who was the first to use the term, described the difference between reality—the "world out there"—and the "little pictures in our heads."[14] To stereotype is to allow those little pictures to dominate our thinking, generating expectations and shaping the narratives we construct about people and their behavior. Consider the images brought to mind by the terms high-school cheerleader, computer expert, black musician, or terrorist—pretty easy, right? We all walk around with images of various types of people in our heads. Within a given culture, these images are shared through social interaction and the media. I would be surprised, therefore, if your image of the computer tech was very different from mine: most likely a guy, most likely nerdy, most likely introverted. I would be surprised if the computer tech you imagined was Latina or that the black musician you brought to mind was conducting a symphony orchestra or the terrorist was a white teenager from South Carolina.

If we think about it, we know that there are male cheerleaders, Latina computer programmers, black classical musicians, and homegrown white terrorists. Yet we don't often think about it; we are cognitive misers who rapidly categorize other people according to what we regard as normative or typical. Because the world is too complicated for us to have a highly differentiated attitude about everything and everyone, we develop elegant, accurate narratives about our *own* group and all of the variations we see in people who belong to it, while relying on simple, sketchy ideas about other groups. Carefully controlled experiments confirm this energy-saving function of stereotypes. In one, Galen Bodenhausen[15] asked a group of "morning people," who do their best thinking early in the day, to evaluate a case of potential cheating on an exam. Participants were more likely to say the cheater was guilty if he was identified as an athlete—but primarily if they were tested at night, when they were not mentally fresh. Night people showed the opposite effect, resorting to the athletes-are-bad-students stereotype more in the morning.

Contrary to conventional wisdom, stereotypes are often accurate, and as such can be an adaptive, shorthand way of dealing with complexity.[16] Indeed, as Lee Jussim and his colleagues have shown,[17] the accuracy of stereotypes turns out to be among the strongest and most reliable findings in social psychology, despite the frequent assumption that they always lead us astray. And this makes sense; if stereotyping consistently led us to error, why would it have survived as a central feature of cognitive functioning? Many stereotypes capture reality well enough to be helpful and adaptive, to keep us out of trouble. For example, by far most of the violence in the world is perpetrated by young men. So if you happen to be walking alone in a dark alley late at night and hear footsteps behind you, it's perfectly reasonable to be more frightened if the footsteps belong to a young man rather than an old man or a woman. Likewise, certain groups tend to do better than others in school, and if we use ethnic stereotypes to predict which groups do better on average, we'll generally predict correctly.

Nonetheless, such predictions, although accurate, may be woefully incomplete because they say nothing about the underlying *reasons* for the observed differences. If your ethnic stereotypes lead you to predict that Asian students are likely to do better than Latino students on the math section of the SAT, you'd likely be right. As a group, Asian students do tend to score higher than Latinos (and blacks and whites) on math tests. But if your stereotype leads you to believe that these scores reflect immutable, genetic differences in intelligence or math skills, you would be mistaken.[18]

Moreover, stereotypes can lead us astray when we apply them to an individual group member, and this can be unfair and potentially harmful—even if the stereotype is positive. Asian Americans are often considered a "model minority," a culture of people who are hardworking, ambitious, intelligent, and excellent in math. But what happens when a particular Asian student dislikes math or needs some help in passing the course?[19] One of Joshua's students confessed that as a Chinese male who hates math, he has suffered numerous episodes of shame, embarrassment, and feeling "extra stupid," thanks to other people's expectations of his "natural" math superiority. Teachers frequently assumed he was bored or lazy; classmates, during tests in math or science, would try to sit close to copy his answers—much to their eventual chagrin. Another Chinese student said, "People look at me as though I don't have difficulty in school, like I'm some kind of robot without feelings or problems. Like I don't feel pain. It's incredibly lonely." Thus, even generally benign or flattering stereotypes can sometimes be misleading because no stereotype is characteristic of every group member.

Experiments show that once we have clear and specific information about a given individual, we readily abandon stereotypes as guides to what that individual is like.[20] Once we learn that our Chinese friend hates math and isn't good at it, we don't need the good-at-math stereotype when thinking about him. Human beings are motivated, after all, to understand people, and information specific to an individual is often more valuable than a stereotype for navigating our interactions with a "category." In cases where we know little about a person, a stereotype about their group can influence our judgments and assessments of their character or behavior, and to the extent that the stereotype is inaccurate for a particular group member, that will cause misunderstandings and trouble for both parties.

That is why, despite the general accuracy and utility of stereotypes, social psychologists have focused more attention on the dark side of stereotyping, cases where stereotypes distort reality, justify discrimination, generate conflict, or inflame prejudices, as when one ethnic group considers another to be "lazy" or "violent." Further, by lumping all "Anglos" or "Asians" or "Hispanics" or "black people" together in one category, people often accidentally make another set of mistakes. There are 20 Spanish-speaking countries, each with its own culture, identity, and points of pride, but people in America who come from Spain, Puerto Rico, Peru, Cuba, or the Dominican Republic are typically assumed to be Mexican. Thus, in the eyes of others, seemingly benign or even positive stereotypes can rob us of our individuality, culture, and humanity.

Laboratory experiments show how embedded stereotyping can be. In one experiment, Jeff Stone and his colleagues[21] had college students listen to a 20-minute audiotape of a college basketball game. They were asked to focus on one of the players, given the name "Mark Flick," and were allowed to look at a folder containing information about him, including a photograph. Half of the participants saw a photo of an African American male; the others saw a photo of a white male. After listening to the game, the students rated Flick's performance. Their ratings reflected the prevailing stereotypes: Students who believed Flick was African American rated him as having more natural athletic ability and as having played a better game than did those who thought he was white. Those who thought he was white rated him as having greater hustle and greater basketball smarts.

Stereotypes affect us even if the stereotype we are relying on is about our own group. Birt Duncan[22] showed people a film of a black man and a white man in an argument. At one point in the film, one of the men shoves the other. Duncan found that people interpreted the shove differently depending on who did the shoving. If the black man shoved the white man, they were more likely to see it as aggression; if the white man shoved the black man, they were more likely to interpret the shove as playful. This bias—seeing the same gesture as more violent when it comes from a black man—showed up even when the people interpreting the film were themselves black.

Stereotypes, Sexism, and Gender Everyone holds stereotypes of women and men—some positive, some negative. Women are assumed to be more empathic and talkative, men to be more competent and aggressive.[23] But gender stereotypes, like all stereotypes, exaggerate differences *between* two groups and tend to overlook differences in personality traits and abilities *within* each group.[24] Are women really "more empathic" than men? Which women? Empathic toward whom? Women don't feel more empathic toward their perceived enemies than men do, and men can feel just as empathic toward an injured child. When women's and men's actual behavior is observed systematically under a variety of conditions, the sexes do not differ in their ability to both feel and express empathy for others.[25] Or consider the pop-psych stereotype that women are "more talkative" than men. James Pennebaker and his colleagues wired up a sample of men and women with voice recorders that tracked their conversations while they went about their daily lives. Both sexes used about 16,000 words per day on average. Obviously, some people do talk more than others, but there is no overall gender difference; the girls-talk-more stereotype is simply false.[26]

Even positive stereotypes of women can be demeaning—and have negative consequences. In research involving 15,000 men and women in 19 nations, Peter Glick and Susan Fiske[27] have found that, around the world, sexism takes two basic forms, which they call **hostile sexism** and **benevolent sexism**. Hostile sexists hold negative stereotypes of women: Women are inferior to men because they are inherently less intelligent, less competent, less brave, less capable of math and science, and so on. Benevolent sexists hold positive stereotypes of women: Women are kinder than men, more empathic, more nurturing. However, both forms of sexism assume that women are the weaker sex: Benevolent sexists tend to idealize women, seeing them in romantic terms, admiring them as cooks and mothers, and wanting to protect them. Romantic? Perhaps, but also patronizing. Glick and Fiske found that both forms of sexism can legitimize discrimination against women, relegating them to traditional stereotyped roles—after all, they need "protection"—and justifying male dominance in work and politics.[28]

Stereotypes of women can have surprising, even insidious consequences. In the years between 1950 and 2012, about twice as many people died in hurricanes named after women than in hurricanes named after men. Why might this be? According to Kiju Jung and his associates,[29] people appear to be less frightened of hurricanes with female names than those with male names, and so take fewer safety precautions than they should. This hypothesis was interesting, but the study's conclusions were fatally flawed for two main reasons: (1) The study included hurricanes from a time period (1950–1978) in which only female names were used; and (2) the gender difference in hurricane deaths was based on only a small number of very deadly storms. So the real world data were suggestive but hardly conclusive—as you know by this time, that's why we do experiments. To test their theory experimentally, the researchers had participants predict the intensity of 10 hurricanes, half with female names and half with male names. Raters thought the male hurricanes were more intense than the female hurricanes. They regarded Hurricane Alexander as being more threatening than Hurricane Alexandra, and they said they'd be more likely to evacuate their homes if an impending hurricane was named Christopher than they did when the identically described hurricane was called Christina.

The Emotional Component of Prejudice: Gut Feelings and Hatreds

In his classic book *The Nature of Prejudice,* Gordon Allport offered the following conversation to describe a fundamental problem with prejudice:

> *Mr. X:* The trouble with the Jews is that they only take care of their own group.
>
> *Mr. Y:* But the record of the Community Chest campaign shows that they gave more generously, in proportion to their numbers, to the general charities of the community, than did non-Jews.
>
> *Mr. X:* That shows they are always trying to buy favor and intrude into Christian affairs. They think of nothing but money; that is why there are so many Jewish bankers.
>
> *Mr. Y:* But a recent study shows that the percentage of Jews in the banking business is negligible, far smaller than the percentage of non-Jews.
>
> *Mr. X:* That's just it; they don't go in for respectable business; they are only in the movie business or run night clubs.[30]

In effect, the prejudiced Mr. X is saying, "Don't trouble me with facts; my mind is made up." He makes no attempt to dispute the data presented by Mr. Y. He either distorts the facts to make them support his hatred of Jews or he ignores them, and turns to a new line of attack. A deeply prejudiced person is virtually immune to information at variance with his or her cherished stereotypes. Famed jurist Oliver Wendell Holmes Jr. once compared the mind of a bigot to the pupil of an eye: "The more light you pour on it, the more it contracts."[31]

Why is this so? The second component of prejudice is emotional, rooted in gut feelings that resist rational argument. As Allport put it, "Defeated intellectually, prejudice lingers emotionally." This is the reason that trying to talk people out of their prejudices tends to be futile; such beliefs are rarely grounded in logic, so they will seldom yield to it. In fact, the emotional roots of prejudice often result in stereotypes and attributions that are mutually contradictory. For example, in Nazi Germany and Argentina, Jews were persecuted for being communists, whereas in the communist Soviet Union, they were considered greedy, anti-communist capitalists. Their persecutors hated them for being too secular but also for being too mystical, for being weak and ineffectual *and* (somehow) for being powerful enough to dominate the world.[32] The gut feelings of prejudice drive the boat; logical reasons follow in its wake to rationalize them. In other words, people didn't decide to hate and attack Jews because they were communists; they called Jews communists because they hated them. Stereotypes can thus be seen as having two distinct purposes: They provide energy-saving informational shortcuts and after-the-fact rationalizations for prejudiced feelings.[33]

Social neuroscientists investigate which parts of the brain might be involved in forming stereotypes, holding prejudiced beliefs, and feeling disgust, anger, or anxiety about an ethnic or stigmatized group.[34] In a series of studies led by Elizabeth Phelps and her colleagues,[35] African Americans and whites were shown pictures of black people and white people while their brains were scanned. They found elevated activity in the amygdala (the brain structure associated with fear and other negative emotions) when they saw pictures of the outgroup member, but little response when people saw pictures of members of their own group. These differences arouse a sense of concern or danger, which our conscious minds will then work to evaluate or rationalize. However, studies like these do not mean these participants were "prejudiced" toward members of the other group or that the amygdala is a "prejudice" center of the brain. In a similar experiment, when participants were registering the faces as individuals or as part of a simple visual test rather than as members of the category *blacks*, their amygdalas showed no increased activation. The brain may be designed to register differences, it appears, but any negative associations with those differences depend on context and learning.[36]

All of us have some degree of prejudice, whether it is against an ethnic, national, or racial group, against people with different sexual orientations from ours, against specific areas of the country as places to live, or even against certain kinds of food. In this culture, most of us don't eat insects and probably find the idea rather disgusting. Suppose Mr. Y were to tell you that caterpillars or earwigs were a great source of protein and, when perfectly prepared, extremely tasty. Would you rush home and fry up a batch? Doubtful. Like Mr. X, your gut response to eating insects would probably motivate you to find some other reason for your prejudice, such as the fact that insects are ugly. After all, in our culture, we eat only aesthetically beautiful creatures — like lobsters!

The Behavioral Component of Prejudice: Discrimination

Prejudice often leads to **discrimination**, unfair treatment of members of a stigmatized group. Although most forms of explicit discrimination in schools and the workplace are now illegal in America, prejudice can nonetheless express itself behaviorally in subtle but significant ways. All kinds of people have been the targets of discrimination: short men, old people, disabled people, and fat people. Despite the fact that nearly 40 percent of the American population qualifies as obese,[37] heavy people are often targets of jokes, harassment, and humiliation; they are less likely than slender people to be hired and promoted; and they are less likely to receive appropriate medical treatment from their physicians. Weight discrimination is said to be one of the few remaining "acceptable" prejudices, probably because obesity is considered, usually mistakenly, to be under a person's control.[38]

Even when discrimination against a group becomes illegal, it may continue in other forms. In 2015, the Supreme Court issued a decision allowing same sex marriage, which represented a remarkable advance in the LGBTQ movement's quest for full acceptance. Nonetheless, gay men, lesbians, and trans people are still victimized by prejudice and discrimination. In a survey conducted in 2016, gay and lesbian high school students were about three times as likely as heterosexual students to report being raped or otherwise victimized while on a date; more than a third reported having been bullied at school; 40 percent had seriously considered suicide; and 29 percent had attempted it in the year the survey was taken.[39]

Racial and Ethnic Discrimination Since the earliest days of the United States, racial discrimination has plagued the nation. As I said, though the situation has greatly improved in many ways, discrimination persists, often in nonobvious ways. In schools, black children are suspended at nearly three times the rate of white children, even in preschool—but not because they are behaving more aggressively or disruptively.[40] The acts that get black students suspended tend to be substantially less severe and more vague than those of white students. For example, whereas both black and white students are more likely to be disciplined for concrete offenses like smoking, leaving school without permission, using obscene language, and vandalizing property, black students are more likely to get in trouble for such subjective offenses as being disrespectful, making excessive noise, having a threatening attitude, and loitering.[41] Teachers often call upon their negative stereotypes of black children to decide that their students' ambiguous behavior is worse than it is. In one experiment, the researchers showed teachers a video of four young students at play: a black boy and girl and a white boy and girl. They were told to look for potentially problematic behavior, which actually did not occur in the film; the children played without incident throughout the video. Eye-tracking technology, which indicated precisely where the teachers' attention was focused, revealed that all of the teachers—both white and black—spent considerably more time watching the black children, especially the boy.[42]

Race discrimination is unfortunately rampant in law enforcement. African Americans are much more likely than whites to be arrested, convicted, and incarcerated for the same crime. Thus, possession of crack cocaine, which is more available in African American communities, carries more severe penalties than the possession of powder cocaine, which is more available in white communities—though both are the same chemical.[43] White people abuse drugs with far greater frequency than their minority counterparts, but are arrested, prosecuted, and punished far less frequently.[44] Of the roughly 1.4 million American men in prison, 40 percent are black and

30 percent are Hispanic; indeed, in her book *The New Jim Crow: Mass Incarceration in the Age of Colorblindness*, law professor Michelle Alexander reports that more black men are behind bars or under the watch of the criminal justice system today than were enslaved in 1850.[45] Research studies of police records[46] find that black and Latino suspects are stopped, roughed up, handcuffed, and arrested nearly four times more often than white suspects for the same "suspicious" behavior. In research led by Philip Goff, undergraduate students and police officers evaluated young black, white, or Latino crime suspects and were asked to estimate their age and culpability for their actions. Black boys were perceived to be significantly older and less innocent than white boys and were rated as more deserving of police force. Another of Joshua's African American students, a straight-A student who had attended a charter school in New York City, described his relationship with the police: "If it's warm and I'm just wearing my school uniform, they pretty much leave me alone. But if it gets cold out and I put on my hoodie, all of a sudden I'm a gangster and they're all over me, looking for drugs and guns."

Field experiments show how race matters in hiring. When applying for a job, applicants with black names like DeShawn or Queenisha are less likely to get called for an interview by employers than applicants with names like Emily or Greg, even if they submit identical resumes.[47] Sociologist Devah Pager[48] sent pairs of well-groomed, well-spoken college graduates with identical resumes to visit more than 350 employers advertising entry-level job openings in the Milwaukee area. Half of the applicants were white and half were black. They were taught to behave politely with all of the employers. Within each group, half indicated on their job application that they had served 18 months in prison for cocaine possession. Who would be called back for an interview? Whites with a clean record were called three times as often as black applicants with a clean record. Among the ex-convicts, the employers contacted the whites twice as often as the black applicants. Indeed, employers showed a preference for white convicts over black applicants with a clean record!

Gender Discrimination As with race, many people believe gender discrimination has ceased to be a barrier for women in the United States. After all, as is the case in most developed countries, girls now perform better than boys in most subjects in school and are more likely to attend and graduate from college.[49] Nonetheless, they continue to be discriminated against, on the prejudiced belief that they are less competent than men. When science professors at leading universities were asked to evaluate resumes of students applying for a position managing a science laboratory, male and female professors alike thought the male applicant was superior to the female—more capable, more worthy of being hired, and more deserving of a higher starting salary and career mentoring. Yet the resumes showed identical skills and accomplishments; the only difference was a randomly assigned male or female name.

In 1963 Congress passed the Equal Pay Act, requiring that men and women in the same work place be given equal pay for equal work. Yet the gender gap in pay persists. In 2014, the typical American woman earned about 77 cents for every dollar earned by the typical American man. The pay gap is even greater for African American and Latina women, with African American women earning 64 cents and Latina women earning 56 cents for every dollar earned by a white man.[50] Even after factoring in the kind of work people do, or qualifications such as education and experience, the pay gap remains.[51]

One way to evaluate the effect of bias in hiring practices is to see what happens when people can apply or audition for a job without revealing their race or gender. In 1970, women made up only 5 percent of the musicians in our best orchestras. Symphony orchestras were boys' clubs run by male directors and committees. Anyone attending the symphony in those days would have the grounds for believing that more men played in orchestras because men were better musicians. When symphony orchestras began conducting auditions with the use of a screen—so that the conductor was blind to the identity of the auditioning musicians—the number of women hired by major symphony orchestras shot up. Today, in large part because of blind auditions, most symphony orchestras are evenly divided between male and female musicians.[52]

Identifying Unconscious Prejudices

In the past, people felt more comfortable wearing their prejudices on their sleeves, and in the 1960s and 1970s social psychologists could simply ask people how they felt about members of various groups—and they told you, all too frankly, how much they disliked "those people."

With the rise of civil rights movements, it became increasingly taboo for people to express overt prejudice, in word or deed; they could lose their jobs as well as their friends. Although many people now feel that they have permission to be "politically incorrect" about their prejudices (certainly on the internet), social scientists believe that a significant number of people continue to be prejudiced but are concealing it—even from themselves.

Measuring Implicit Biases A method that allegedly detects prejudices that people don't know they have has garnered worldwide attention. The **Implicit Association Test (IAT)**, developed by Mahzarin Banaji and Anthony Greenwald, measures the speed of people's positive and negative associations to a target group.[53] Here's how it works: You sit at a console and are shown a series of faces you must sort as quickly as you can, pressing a left key for a black face, say, and a right key for a white face. Now you have to do the same for a series of positive or negative words: Press the left key for positive words (such as triumph, joy, honest) and the right key for negative words (such as devil, maggot, failure). Once you've mastered these sorting tasks, the faces and words are combined. Now, as quickly as possible, you must press the left key when you see a black face or a positive word and the right key when you see a white face or a negative word. You are given a rapid set of combinations: *black + triumph, black + poison, white + peace, white + hatred,* etc. The pairings get harder as you go along.

Repeatedly, studies find that people respond more quickly when white faces are paired with positive words and when black faces are paired with negative words. That speed difference is said to be a measure of their *implicit attitudes* toward African Americans because it's harder for their unconscious minds to link African Americans with positive words. Versions of the IAT have been administered using many target groups, including people who are young or old, male or female, Asian or white, disabled or not, gay or straight, fat or thin. More than 15 million people of all ages and walks of life, all over the world, have taken the test online, in school, or in their workplaces, and most learn that they hold implicit prejudices.[54]

Banaji and Greenwald[55] report that people are often surprised and alarmed to be told they have prejudices they are unaware of. Banaji herself, a woman of color who was born and raised in India, says that she "failed" the racial IAT, revealing antiblack associations that she consciously repudiates. One gay activist they describe was stunned to learn that "her own mind contained stronger gay = bad associations than gay = good associations." Young people have faster reaction times to *old + bad* than to *old + good*, but the great majority of old people do also. And writer Malcolm Gladwell, who is biracial, likewise was shocked by his responses on the IAT. The researchers quoted from his interview with Oprah Winfrey: "The person in my life [his mother] who I love more than almost anyone else is black, and here I was taking a test, which said, frankly, I wasn't too crazy about black people, you know?"

Not so fast, Malcolm! The IAT could mean you are prejudiced, but it might not. Psychological scientists have debated the ambiguities surrounding interpretations of the test. If Gladwell's response to *black + good* is a few milliseconds slower than to *black + bad*, that could mean that he holds an unconscious (implicit) bias. But it could also mean that the IAT is not always measuring what it says it is measuring.[56] Some researchers think it simply captures a cultural association or stereotype, in the same way that people would be quicker to pair *bread + butter* than *bread + avocado*. Thus, old people may really be as biased against other old people as young people are, but it could also be that old and young are aware of the same cultural stereotypes and associations about the elderly, or any other groups.[57]

One way to judge the IAT's validity is to see if a high score predicts actual behavior toward old people, fat people, African Americans, or any other group. The study's originators maintain that the higher a person's IAT score, the more likely he or she is to discriminate against the target in some way; for example, one study found that whites who reveal racial bias on the IAT tend to find black people less trustworthy[58] and another found that whites with high scores don't communicate as warmly with blacks in professional settings as they would with whites.[59] Overall, however, the evidence linking IAT scores with overt behavior is weak. That means that if any given individual were to take the IAT and get a high score, it doesn't necessarily mean that person is prejudiced. It doesn't even mean the individual would get the same score a few weeks later.[60]

Moreover, when Adam Hahn and his colleagues[61] directly asked people to predict their responses toward five different groups on the IAT, they found that people were "surprisingly accurate," regardless of whether they were told that implicit attitudes are "true" prejudices or culturally learned associations. The researchers concluded that the "findings cast doubt on the belief that attitudes or evaluations measured by the IAT necessarily reflect unconscious attitudes."

Implicit Bias and Behavior Although it is unclear whether the IAT is really measuring unconscious prejudices, I am convinced that Banaji and Greenwald are trying to get at something important. We do know that many people who genuinely regard themselves as being unprejudiced will, under certain conditions, behave in a prejudiced way.[62] When such individuals interact with people for whom they have implicit negative feelings, they may be uncomfortable, expressing that discomfort in subtle ways that the recipient feels but can't quite identify.

One condition under which people are more likely to reveal their prejudices (or other biases) is mental fatigue: when they are tired, drunk, distracted, frightened, angered, or doing anything that depletes or distracts their cognitive resources. Under such circumstances, people tend to fall back on their stereotypes, even if they are highly motivated to get things right.

For example, people are more likely to reveal their biases when they are angry. In one experiment,[63] white students were told they would be inflicting electric shock on another student, the "learner," whom they were told was either white or African American, as part of an apparent study of biofeedback. The students initially gave a lower intensity of shock to black learners than to white ones, reflecting a desire, perhaps, to demonstrate to the experimenter (and perhaps to convince themselves) that they were not prejudiced. The students then overheard the learner making derogatory comments about them, which naturally made them angry. Now, given another opportunity to inflict electric shock, the students who were working with a black learner administered higher levels of shock than did students who worked with a white learner. The same pattern appears in studies of how English-speaking Canadians behave toward French-speaking Canadians, straights toward gays, non-Jewish students toward Jews, and men toward women.[64]

Christian Crandall and Amy Eshleman[65] suggest that precisely because suppressing prejudices takes effort, people may be particularly attracted to information that justifies their negative feeling and allows them to express it. A valid justification for disliking a group enables us to express prejudice without feeling like bigots—thus avoiding the cognitive dissonance that would be created by "I'm a fair, just, unprejudiced person" and "But I really dislike those people." David Frey and Samuel Gaertner[66] demonstrated this conflict by studying the conditions under which whites would be likely to offer help to a black person in need. In their study, they found that white participants were just as willing to help a black student as a white student, but only when the person needing help had demonstrated sufficient effort. When white students were led to believe that the student had not worked hard enough at the task, they were more likely to refuse a black student's request for help than a white student's. They felt justified in withholding help when the person asking confirmed their stereotype of being lazy, and therefore undeserving.

Another key factor in justifying our biases is whether we believe an individual has *control* over his or her situation. I suggested earlier that anti-fat prejudice was the last "acceptable" form of prejudice, because most people believe that fat people can control their weight. (Today scientists know that while people have control over losing relatively small amounts of weight, obesity is entirely different and not a matter of "will power.") Another way of saying acceptable is "easily rationalized." The more easily we can rationalize our prejudice, the more likely we are to hold onto and act upon it. I can feel better about discriminating against you if I'm convinced your disagreeable traits are your own fault. An experiment by Eden King and her associates[67] tested this logic. A young woman was sent into department stores to interact with salespeople. Half the time she was made to look obese, by wearing a "fat suit" under her clothing; half the time she was of average weight. On some of these visits, she was drinking a diet soda; on others, she was drinking a milkshake. When she was fat but seemed motivated to lose weight by drinking the diet soda, the salespeople treated her just as nicely as when she was thin. But when she was drinking the milkshake, her obesity seemed to be a matter of choice. Although salespeople did not treat her with blatant hostility, they smiled at her less frequently, made less eye contact with her, and spoke with her in a more abrupt and less friendly manner.

Causes of Prejudice

What factors give rise to prejudice? What encourages and sustains it? We have seen repeatedly in this book that, as tribal animals, we are inclined to see the world in us–them terms. In Chapter 2, I discussed us–them thinking at length, showing how easy it is to create an "us" over trivial matters in the laboratory ("Are you in 'Group X' or 'Group W'?") and at sports events ("Our team is the best!"), as well as over major group differences of religion, nationality, and other deeper aspects of our social identities. Once a person differentiates between *us* and *them*, the stage is set for stereotyping, prejudice, discrimination, and the rationalizing that follows. That group-protective mechanism and the resulting **ingroup bias** is a biological survival mechanism inducing us to favor our own kin and tribe, and to be wary of outsiders. Because of geographical barriers, it is almost certain that our ancient ancestors never saw strangers of another race, which is why we did not evolve to be "racist" but to be "other-ist."

Regardless of any evolved predispositions, however, social psychologists know that the specific content of prejudice must be learned, through the institutions that set norms of attitudes and behavior, through imitating and conforming to the attitudes and behavior of others, and through the ways in which we construct our own psychological reality.

In this section, I will look at four basic social-psychological causes of prejudice: (1) economic and political competition or conflict, (2) displaced aggression, (3) maintenance of status or self-image, and (4) conformity to existing social norms. These causes are not mutually exclusive — indeed, they may all operate at once — but it would be helpful to determine the importance of each one, because any action we are apt to recommend in an attempt to reduce prejudice will depend on what we believe to be the major cause. One of the reasons I was first drawn to social psychology is that it is a field that studies change and progress. If I believed that prejudice is largely a result of ingrained personality traits, I might throw my hands up in despair and conclude that, in the absence of deep psychotherapy, the majority of prejudiced people will always be prejudiced. This would lead me to scoff at attempts to reduce prejudice by reducing competitiveness or by attempting to counteract the pressures of conformity. Let us take a close look at each of the four causes.

Economic and Political Competition   Prejudice often results from economic and political forces. According to this view, given that resources are limited, the dominant group might attempt to exploit a minority group to gain some material advantage. Prejudiced attitudes tend to increase when groups are in conflict over mutually exclusive goals. This is true whether the goals are economic, political, or ideological. Thus, in the last hundred years, white Americans have manifested hatred toward Jewish, Japanese, German, Irish, Iranian, Mexican, and many other fellow citizens, all as a function of who was accused of stealing our jobs at a particular time. In one of his classic early studies of prejudice in a small industrial town, John Dollard[68] documented the fact that, although there was initially no discernible prejudice against Germans who had recently arrived there, it increased as jobs became scarce: "Scornful and derogatory opinions were expressed about these Germans, and the native whites had a satisfying sense of superiority toward them ... The chief element in the permission to be aggressive against the Germans was rivalry for jobs and status in the local wooden ware plants."

Or consider how attitudes toward Chinese immigrants in the United States fluctuated wildly throughout the nineteenth century, spurred largely by changes in economic competition. When the Chinese were attempting to mine gold in California, competing with the white men who had arrived in droves to get rich fast, they were described as "depraved and vicious ... gross gluttons ... bloodthirsty and inhuman."[69] However, just a decade later, when they were willing to accept dangerous and arduous work building the transcontinental railroad—work that white Americans were unwilling to undertake—they were generally regarded as sober, industrious, and law-abiding. Indeed, Charles Crocker, one of the Western railroad tycoons, wrote, "They are equal to the best white men ... They are very trusty, very intelligent, and they live up to their contracts." After the completion of the railroad, however, jobs became scarcer; when the Civil War ended, there was an influx of former soldiers into an already tight job market. This was immediately followed by a sharp increase in negative attitudes toward the Chinese. The stereotype changed again to criminal, conniving, crafty, and stupid.

These data suggest that competition and conflict breed prejudice. In a survey conducted in the 1970s, most anti-black prejudice was found in groups that were just one rung above black people socioeconomically. And this tendency was most pronounced in situations in which whites and blacks were in close competition for jobs.[70] Today, negative feelings toward Mexicans—and others wrongly thought to be competing for white Americans' jobs—are on the rise.

However, there is some ambiguity in interpreting the data because, in some instances, the variable of competition is intertwined with other factors, such as education level, family background, literacy levels, and job skills. To determine whether competition *itself* causes prejudice, an experiment is needed. Such an experiment was conducted by Muzafer Sherif and his colleagues[71] in the natural environment of a Boy Scout camp called Robbers Cave. Healthy, well-adjusted 12-year-old boys were randomly assigned to one of two groups, the Eagles or the Rattlers. Within each group, the youngsters were taught to cooperate through activities that made the members of each group highly interdependent: building a diving board for the swimming facility, preparing group meals, building a rope bridge, and so on.

After a strong feeling of cohesiveness developed within each of the two groups, the stage was set for an us-versus-them conflict. The researchers arranged a series of competitions—games of football, baseball, and tug-of-war—and awarded prizes to the winning team. This set-up produced hostility and ill will between teams during the games. In addition, the investigators devised rather diabolical situations for putting the groups into conflict. In one, the investigators arranged a camp party so that the Eagles were allowed to arrive a good deal earlier than the Rattlers. The refreshments consisted of two vastly different kinds of food: About half the food was fresh and appetizing, just what boys would enjoy; the other half was squashed, ugly, and unappetizing. Perhaps because of the general competitiveness that already existed, the early arrivers confiscated most of the appealing refreshments, leaving the less appetizing food for their adversaries. When the Rattlers finally arrived and saw how they had been taken advantage of, they were annoyed—so annoyed that they began to call the Eagles rather uncomplimentary names. Because the Eagles believed they deserved what they got (first come, first served), they resented this treatment and responded in kind. Name calling escalated into food throwing, and within a short time a full-scale riot was in progress.

Following this incident, Sherif and his team eliminated the competitive games and allowed the boys to get together. Once hostility had been aroused, however, simply stopping competition was not enough to eliminate it. Indeed, the bad feelings continued to escalate, even when the two groups were merely sitting around watching movies. Eventually, the investigators succeeded in reducing the conflict between the Eagles and the Rattlers, and I will tell you how they did it later in this chapter.

Displaced Aggression: The Scapegoat Theory In the preceding chapter, I made the point that aggression is caused, in part, by frustration and other aversive states like pain or boredom. In that chapter, we saw that there is a strong tendency for frustrated individuals to lash out at the cause of their frustration. Frequently, however, the cause of a person's frustration is either too big or too vague for direct retaliation. For example, if a 6-year-old boy is humiliated by his teacher, how can he fight back? The teacher has too much power. But this frustration may increase the probability of his aggressing against a less powerful bystander—even if the bystander had nothing to do with his humiliation. By the same token, if there is mass unemployment, who is the frustrated, unemployed worker going to strike out against, the economic system? The system is much too big and much too impersonal. Accordingly, the unemployed worker might try to find a person or group to blame.

The ancient Hebrews had a solution. During the days of atonement, a priest placed his hands on the head of a goat while reciting the sins of the people, symbolically transferring sin and evil from the people to the goat. The goat was then allowed to escape into the wilderness, thus cleansing the community of sin. The animal was called a *scapegoat*. In modern times, the term **scapegoating** describes the process of blaming innocent—and powerless—others for our troubles. Has globalization outsourced your job? Has inflation drained your bank account? You can't beat up on the president or the economic system, but you can find a scapegoat. Throughout history, victims were not allowed to escape into the wilderness but subjected to cruel treatment or death. In Nazi Germany, the scapegoats were Jews; in nineteenth-century California, they were Chinese immigrants; in the rural South, they were African Americans.

Laboratory experiments[72] suggest that individuals, especially when they are feeling frustrated, will displace aggression onto groups that are disliked, that are visible, and that are relatively powerless. Although mistreatment of outgroups can arise on its own as a product of displaced aggression, the form it takes depends on the social context, what is allowed or approved by the ingroup. For example, the lynching of African Americans and pogroms (organized massacres) against Jews occurred only when the dominant culture or subculture approved of these violent actions and even called for them.[73] Norms are crucial. People can hold many prejudices but keep them in check when the social rules emphasize civility and kindness. Conversely, an inflammatory politician or preacher may incite followers to break those rules and encourage the ugly, flagrant expression of any and all prejudices. That is what demagogues do, political leaders who seek power by exploiting people's prejudices, fears, and resentment, channeling these feelings onto scapegoats—minority groups, outside "enemies"—that are blamed for all problems. In 1949, two social psychologists analyzed a large number of speeches given by demagogues throughout history.[74] They found a striking regularity in their messages:

- You've been cheated. Your place in the society is insecure through no fault of your own.

- There is a widespread conspiracy; this system is rigged against us.

- Good people like us are always dupes.

- Our enemies are low animals: reptiles, insects, subhuman.

- We can't trust foreigners; they're taking all our jobs.

- We can't trust our own government either; it's corrupt. Civil liberties are "silly liberties."

- We are heading for disaster. Doom is just around the corner. Sincere, simple, good people like you need a leader. Behold, I am he! I'll change the whole rotten mess!

- Everybody is against me—the press, the Jews, the stinking bureaucrats are trying to shut me up. Enemies plot against my life, but God will protect me. I'll lead you.

This was written in 1949! You may have heard an echo of these statements in recent elections around the world. Demagogues emerge during conditions of anxiety and uncertainty, appealing especially to those who feel they are falling behind or have lost status in the social order.[75] Uneducated white males, for example, have lost opportunities as the economy has become more knowledge-driven, and automation and globalization have reduced the number of available factory jobs. To such individuals, the demagogue's narrative that the system has been rigged against them—that their failure is not their own fault but the fault of foreigners and immigrants who threaten their prosperity and security—is psychologically comforting.

The Maintenance of Self-Image and Status A powerful determinant of prejudice is embedded in our need to justify our behavior and sense of self. We have already seen that if we have done something cruel to a person or a group of people, most of us will try to blame that person or vilify that group to justify our cruelty. If we can convince ourselves that a group is unworthy, subhuman, stupid, or immoral, we feel free to enslave members of that group, deprive them of a decent education, or aggress against them, without questioning our own sense of morality. We can then continue to feel like good Christians or Jews or Muslims because we have not hurt a decent fellow human being but someone "subhuman." If we're skillful enough, we can even convince ourselves that the barbaric slaying of old men, women, and children is a religious virtue. That is what Christian crusaders did hundreds of years ago when they butchered European Jews on their way to the Holy Land, where they then butchered thousands of Muslims, all in the name of the Prince of Peace; it is what ISIS does today, butchering Christians, Jews, and fellow Muslims indiscriminately in the name of Allah, "the most Merciful." Again, this form of self-justification serves to intensify subsequent brutality. It preserves the self-image but also leads to increased hostility against the target person or group.

Conversely, if our status is low on the socioeconomic hierarchy, the presence of a downtrodden minority group allows us to feel superior to *somebody*. Several studies have shown that a good predictor of prejudice is whether a person's social status is low or declining. For example, Jennifer Crocker and her colleagues[76] found that college women who belonged to low-status sororities expressed more prejudice and disparagement of other sororities than did members of higher-status sororities. Similarly, when researchers have investigated the prejudice of whites against blacks[77] or of Gentiles against Jews,[78] they found that those whose social status is low or declining are more prejudiced than those whose social status is high or rising. Steven Fein and Stephen Spencer[79] found that threats to self-esteem tend to increase prejudice. In their experiment, anti-Semitic students became especially biased in their evaluation of a woman they thought was Jewish if they received a low score on a supposed test of intelligence. In a very real sense, then, looking down on outgroups can boost our self-esteem.

Prejudice Through Conformity

For some people, prejudice may be rooted in childhood conflicts, observation of role models, experiences, or assorted personality traits (some of which we discussed in Chapter 5). But many people simply learn it from others, following the prevailing norms of their community. A famous example comes from a study of coal miners in a small mining town in West Virginia, during the era of legal segregation in the South.[80] The black miners and the white miners developed a pattern of living that consisted of complete integration while they were underground and complete segregation while they were above ground. How can we account for this inconsistency? Personality traits can't explain it and neither can economic competition. If you truly hate someone, you want to keep away from him; why associate with him belowground and not aboveground? Thomas Pettigrew concluded that the answer is conformity. In this case, the white miners were conforming to the prejudiced norm that existed in their community once they were aboveground; but belowground, working together, they came to respect one another as equals and conformed to an *unprejudiced* norm.

A great deal of prejudiced behavior is driven by conformity to social norms. How can we be certain that conformity is responsible? One way is to see what happens to people's prejudice when they move to a different area of the country. If conformity is a factor in prejudice, we would expect individuals to become more prejudiced when they move to areas where the norm is more prejudicial, and to become less prejudiced when they move to places characterized by a less prejudicial norm. And that is what happens. In one study, Jeanne Watson[81] found that individuals who had recently moved to a large city and had come into direct contact with anti-Semitic people became more anti-Semitic themselves. In another study conducted during the 1950s, Pettigrew found that as Southerners entered the army and came into contact with a less discriminatory set of social norms, they became less prejudiced against blacks.

The pressure to conform to the prejudices of your peers and coworkers can be overt, as in the Asch experiment (see Chapter 4), but it might also be due to the unavailability of accurate evidence and a preponderance of misleading information. For example, Christopher Marlowe's play *The Jew of Malta* and William Shakespeare's *The Merchant of Venice* both depict the Jew as a conniving, money-hungry coward. We might be tempted to conclude that Marlowe and Shakespeare had had some unfortunate experiences with unsavory Jews, which resulted in these bitter and unflattering portraits—except for one thing: The Jews had been expelled from England some 300 years before these works were written. Thus, it would seem that Marlowe and Shakespeare were conforming to the stereotype of Jews that most British people held at the time.

Even casual exposure to prejudice can affect our attitudes and behavior: Merely overhearing someone use a racial or ethnic epithet can increase people's conformity to negative opinions about the disparaged group. Shari Kirkland and her colleagues[82] asked people to read a transcript of a criminal trial in which a white defendant was represented by a black attorney whose picture was attached to the transcript. While reading, participants overheard a brief exchange between two experimental confederates. Some heard the first confederate describe the black lawyer with an ugly racial slur, while others heard the confederate use a derisive comment unrelated to the lawyer's race. In both conditions, the second confederate expressed agreement with the first confederate's derogatory opinion of the black lawyer. With this conformity dynamic in place, the experimenters then asked each participant to evaluate the attorney and the defendant. The people who overheard the racial slur rated the black lawyer more negatively than those who overheard the derisive comment. Conformity to prejudiced norms even extended to the poor defendant, who received particularly harsh verdicts from those who heard the racial slur against the black attorney.

Finally, prejudice can also be fostered through the law and custom of a society's institutions. A society that promotes segregation is supporting the notion that one group is inferior to another. In the days of apartheid in South Africa, one investigator[83] interviewed white South Africans in an attempt to find reasons for their race prejudice. He found that the typical white South African was convinced that the great majority of crimes were committed by black people—an erroneous belief. How did such a misconception develop? The interviewees reported that they saw many black convicts working in public places; they never saw any white convicts. Didn't this prove that blacks were convicted of more crimes than whites? No. In fact, the rules forbade white convicts from working in public places!

That is how a society creates prejudiced beliefs, as people conform to the accepted practices of their major institutions. In our own
recent history, laws and customs that forced black people to ride
in the back of the bus; that kept women out of clubs, universities,
and careers; and prevented Jews from staying at exclusive hotels
all perpetuated prejudices through conformity. If the rules require
us to treat "those people" that way, after all, we'll go along. My
country, my club, my profession, and this elegant hotel must have a
reason — mustn't they?

Stereotypes and Attributions

Stereotyping is a special form of attribution. As we saw in Chapter 2,
we are the explaining species; we are forever making attributions to
explain our own and other people's behavior. In ambiguous situations,
people tend to construct narratives consistent with their prejudices. If
Mr. Bigot sees a well-dressed, white Anglo-Saxon man sitting on
a park bench sunning himself at 3:00 p.m. on a Wednesday, he
thinks nothing of it. If he sees a well-dressed black man doing
the same thing, he is apt to leap to the conclusion that the man is
unemployed — and Mr. Bigot is likely to become infuriated because
he assumes his own hard-earned money is being taxed to pay that
shiftless, good-for-nothing enough in welfare subsidies to keep him
in fancy clothes. If Mr. Bigot passes Mr. Anglo's house and notices
that a trash can is overturned and garbage is strewn about, he is apt
to conclude that a stray dog has been searching for food. If he passes
Mr. Latino's house and notices the same thing, he is inclined to
become annoyed and think, "Those people live like pigs." Not only
does prejudice influence his attributions and conclusions, his erroneous conclusions justify and intensify his negative feelings. Thus,
the entire attribution process can spiral.

Thus far in this chapter I have been considering prejudices from
the standpoint of the person who holds them. What is the effect of
being subjected to prejudice — and to attributions that you just don't
have what it takes to make it? For example, if people hold a prejudice against women, believing, say, that women are by nature less
competent and able than men, how will they interpret evidence of a
woman's doing well on a difficult task? Janet Swim and Lawrence
Sanna analyzed more than 50 experiments and found remarkably

consistent gender effects: If a man was successful on a given task, observers tended to attribute his success to natural ability; if a woman was successful on that same task, observers tended to attribute her success to hard work (meaning, it wasn't "natural" for her). If a man failed on a given task, observers tended to attribute his failure either to bad luck or lower effort; if a woman failed, observers felt the task was too hard for her ability level—she didn't "have what it takes."

Now, how do those attributions about reasons for success or failure affect how others come to see themselves? Janis Jacobs and Jacquelynne Eccles[84] explored the influence of mothers' gender stereotypic beliefs on the way these women perceived the abilities of their 11- and 12-year-old sons and daughters and what impact their beliefs might have on the children's perceptions of their own abilities. Those mothers who held the strongest stereotypic gender beliefs also believed that their own daughters had relatively low math ability and that their sons had relatively high math ability. Those who did not hold stereotypic beliefs did not see their daughters as being "naturally" less able in math than their sons. These beliefs, in turn, had an impact on their children: The daughters of women with strong gender stereotypes came to believe that they weren't good at math. The daughters of women who did not hold gender stereotypes showed no such self-defeating belief.

Attributional Ambiguity Interpreting other people's behavior is often fraught with uncertainty. Does that person like me or do they want something? Prejudice complicates this problem, because our social identities create more potential reasons for a given actor's behavior. Let's say you are African American and your professor is white. You may wonder why you received a poor grade on your last paper. Did your teacher dislike your writing, or is she prejudiced against black students? What if you got a terrific grade on your last paper? Did your teacher really think it was terrific, or is she bending over backward to show she's not prejudiced? This extra layer of complexity is called **attributional ambiguity**, and it creates the difficulty that members of minority groups may have in interpreting the feedback they receive about their work.

It's a real problem, especially when the teacher or employer fails to give honest feedback precisely to avoid being seen as racist or otherwise prejudiced. Kent Harber[85] had white college students read and evaluate poorly written essays supposedly written by other students enrolled in a writing workshop. Half of the evaluators were led to believe that the essay writer was black; the other evaluators thought that the writer was white. You might expect that the supposed black writers would receive unduly harsh feedback, but that is not what happened. Instead, the evaluators went out of their way to say positive things about the content of the black writers' essays. Now, their willingness to appear unprejudiced is a good thing, but their unwillingness to be honest is not such a good thing. How is any student, of any ethnicity or race, supposed to improve and learn without honest feedback?

Marlene Turner and Anthony Pratkanis showed how attributional ambiguity can arise from unfortunate side effects of affirmative action programs. Affirmative action programs have been generally beneficial, inasmuch as they have created employment opportunities for talented women (and other minorities) who had been previously overlooked when applying for high-level jobs. Unfortunately, some of these programs unintentionally stigmatize talented women by creating the illusion that they were selected primarily because of their gender rather than their talent. What effect does this have on the women involved? In a well-controlled experiment,[86] Turner and Pratkanis led some women to believe that they had been selected for a job because the company needed to hire more women, while others were given a difficult test and then told they were selected for that job on the basis of their high performance. Those women who were told they were selected because of their gender (not their merit) later denigrated their own abilities—and worse, stopped trying as hard to succeed on a difficult task as did women who believed they had been selected on the basis of merit.

Self-Fulfilling Prophecies Our stereotypes about other people not only influence our own behavior toward them; they cause us to act in such a way as to elicit from those others the very characteristics and behaviors we expect. This is the *self-fulfilling prophecy* I described in Chapter 2. Here's how it works: Imagine that you and I had never met, but my prejudice about your group leads me to suspect you will be hostile, cold, or aloof. When we finally meet, I might keep my distance and do not try to engage you in a lively conversation. Even if you are usually warm and outgoing, my behavior would not afford you the opportunity to show me how nice you really are. In response to my aloofness, you would probably keep your distance from me, and my expectation that you're a cold and unfriendly person would be confirmed by your natural response to the way I treated you, perhaps confirming my prejudicial expectations. "See," I might say to myself, when you meet my hostile or cold attitude with hostility or coldness, "I was right all along about those people."

When we hold beliefs about others, the self-fulfilling prophecy ensures that we create a social reality in line with our expectations. If we believe that women are "more emotional" than men, for example, we will tend to notice and recall instances that confirm the stereotype and not count the times we see men roaring in anger or emoting jubilantly at a football game—or the times that female CEOs, politicians, and flight attendants keep their emotions to themselves.

Stereotype Threat One unexpected outcome of self-fulfilling prophecies is that people who are targets of negative stereotypes can, ironically, end up confirming them by trying to disconfirm them. Consider the average gap in academic performance between African American and white college students. Although there are many possible historical and societal explanations for this discrepancy, Claude Steele and Joshua Aronson[87] have argued that these explanations cannot account for the fact that the gap is as great for students who are highly prepared academically (as measured by earlier grades and test scores) as it is for those who are relatively unprepared. Something seems to be happening that keeps bright, motivated, and well-prepared black students from performing as well as white students with the same level of ability.

In researching this problem, Steele and Aronson reasoned that a major contributing factor might involve apprehensiveness among black students about confirming the existing negative stereotype of "intellectual inferiority" that black people have been subjected to since the days of slavery. Steele and Aronson call this apprehension **stereotype threat**, and they hypothesized that worrying about confirming the stereotype might interfere with the ability to perform well on tests. In one experiment,[88] they administered a difficult verbal test (the Graduate Record Examination) individually to black and to white college students. Half of the students were led to believe that the investigator was interested in measuring their intellectual ability; the other half were led to believe that the investigator was merely testing the test, and that the investigators were not interested in evaluating them.

The results were dramatic: White students performed equally well regardless of whether or not they believed the test was being used to measure their intelligence. Black students, however, were affected by the way the test was described. The evaluative nature of the situation activated stereotypes in their minds and made them anxious, and they performed about half as well as the black students who believed the test was not being used to evaluate them. Such is the power of stereotypes; when people think their behavior may confirm a negative reputation about themselves or their group, the resulting anxiety can interfere with their performance.

Stereotype threat afflicts other groups too, such as women working on math problems, Latinos working on tests of verbal ability, and elderly people taking tests of memory, because the stereotypes portray women as inferior to men at math, Latinos as inferior to Anglos in verbal ability, and elderly people as having trouble remembering.[89] Indeed, any group stereotyped as inferior to some other group can experience stereotype threat to a meaningful degree, even if by all objective standards that group excels in the relevant domain. Joshua Aronson and his associates[90] gave white male engineering majors, all of whom had near-perfect scores on their math SATs, a difficult math test and told them that the test would measure their math ability. But half of these gifted engineers were confronted with a stereotype threat: The experimenter informed them that he was trying to understand why Asians appear to have superior math ability. This group performed significantly worse on the test than their peers who were not thinking about Asian math "superiority." The situation imposed upon the white engineering majors—an unflattering comparison with a supposedly superior group—is commonplace for blacks and Latinos, who contend daily with such comparisons in any integrated academic setting. That such obviously bright and accomplished engineering students can falter on a test when faced with stereotype threat should make us think twice before casually assuming that the lower performance of blacks and Latinos indicates a lack of ability.

There is good news in this research. After all, if merely thinking about a negative stereotype inhibits a person's performance, then some kind of alternative mindset that counters the stereotype should be able to boost performance. Matthew McGlone and Joshua Aronson[91] subtly reminded young men and women who were about to take a difficult test of spatial ability that they were students at a highly selective university. This reminder was enough to completely eliminate the male–female gap they had observed in the control condition, in which the test-takers were merely reminded of the fact that they were "residents of the northeast." The "I'm a good student at a prestigious school" mindset effectively countered the "women aren't good at math" stereotype. Likewise, exposing black test-takers to images or thoughts of successful African American role models—such as the great intellectual W.E.B. Dubois and the celebrated astrophysicist Neil deGrasse Tyson—or having a black professional administering the test can ease their performance anxiety.[92] Similarly, reminding minority students that their abilities are improvable rather than fixed or that anxiety on standardized tests is perfectly normal among members of stereotyped groups helps reduce test anxiety, improve test scores,[93] and boost grades.[94]

Stereotype threat appears to operate much like other threats to the self-concept in that they can be buffered by focusing on valued aspects of the self. Thus, in one study, when women under stereotype threat (taking a test they were told indicated "math intelligence") first affirmed a value of importance to them, they scored as well as men and as women in the no-threat control condition.[95] Self-affirmation makes people feel more confident and good about themselves. Geoffrey Cohen and his colleagues[96] took these findings into schools and found that minority students improved their grades after being given a few writing assignments in which they explained why certain values were so important to them. Buffering the self-concept, focusing on what makes you feel good and special and worthwhile, can counteract the negative effects of stereotypes on performance and learning.

Blaming the Victim It is not always easy for people who have never experienced prejudice to understand fully what it is like to be a target of it. For relatively secure members of the dominant majority, empathy does not come easily. They may sympathize and wish that it weren't so, but frequently a hint of self-righteousness may nevertheless creep into their attitudes, producing a tendency to lay the blame on the victim. This may take the form of the "well-deserved reputation." It goes something like this: "If the Jews have been victimized throughout their history, they *must* have been doing *something* wrong" or "If that woman got raped, she must have been doing *something* provocative" or "If those people [African Americans, Latinos, Native Americans, gay people] don't *want* to get into trouble, why don't they just do something about it [stay out of the headlines, keep their mouths shut, not go where they're not wanted]." Such a suggestion constitutes a demand that the outgroup conform to standards more stringent than those the majority sets for itself.

Paradoxically, this tendency to blame victims for their victimization, attributing their predicaments to their own personalities and flaws, is often motivated by a desire to see the world as fair and just. As Melvin Lerner and his colleagues[97] have shown, people tend to attribute personal responsibility for any inequitable outcome that is otherwise difficult to explain. For example, if two people work equally hard on the same task and, by a flip of a coin, one receives a sizable reward and the other receives nothing, most observers will rate the unlucky person as having worked less hard. Similarly, negative attitudes toward the poor and unemployed—including blaming them for their own plight—are more prevalent among individuals who believe most strongly that the world is a just place.[98]

The astute reader may have noticed that this is a milder form of our tendency to disparage a person we ourselves have victimized. In Chapters 3 and 6, we saw that, when one person hurts another, the aggressor tends to blame the target, turn the victim into a nonperson, and hurt that other person again. Now we see that, if one person notices that another is the recipient of hate messages and other expressions of prejudice, he or she somehow feels the victim must have done something to deserve it. Apparently, we find it frightening to think about living in a world where people, through no fault of their own, can be deprived of what they deserve or need, be it equal pay for equal work or the basic necessities of life—or life itself: If 6 million Jews are exterminated for no apparent reason other than their being Jewish, it is comforting to believe they must have done something to warrant such treatment. It gives us a sense that we can control our own destiny.

Reducing Prejudice Through Contact and Familiarity

In 1954, the U.S. Supreme Court declared that separate but equal schools were, by definition, unequal. In the words of Chief Justice Earl Warren, when black children are separated from white children on the basis of race alone, it "generates a feeling of inferiority as to their status in the community that may affect their hearts and minds in a way unlikely ever to be undone." Without our quite realizing it, this decision launched our nation into one of the most exciting large-scale social experiments ever conducted.

In the aftermath of this historic decision, many well-meaning people, including politicians and school administrators, were opposed to integrating the schools on "humanitarian" grounds. They predicted a disaster if blacks and whites were forced to mingle in schools. Laws cannot force people to get along with each other, they said, echoing the sentiments of the distinguished sociologist William Graham Sumner, who half a century earlier had stated, "Stateways don't change folkways." Sumner meant that you cannot legislate morality or tolerance. Many people urged that desegregation be delayed until attitudes changed. Once you can get bigoted white adults to feel less prejudiced toward blacks, they believed, *then* they would be far more likely to allow their children to attend integrated schools.

Early efforts to change the hearts and minds of the American public were based on the idea that you combat misinformation with information. If prejudiced people believe that black people are shiftless and lazy, then all you have to do is show them a movie depicting blacks as industrious, decent people. If most white South Africans believe that blacks commit virtually all the crimes, show them all the white convicts and they'll change their beliefs. If only it were that simple. Whether prejudice is largely a function of economic conflict, conformity to social norms, a need to maintain status, or displaced aggression—when it reflects a deep emotional hostility—it is not easily changed by an information campaign. A movie cannot undo a way of thinking and a way of behaving that has persisted throughout the history of this country.

Moreover, as the reader of this book knows by now, where important issues are involved, information campaigns usually fail because people are not inclined to sit still and take in information that is dissonant with their beliefs and attitudes. Paul Lazarsfeld[99] described a series of radio broadcasts in the early 1940s designed to reduce prejudice by presenting information about various ethnic groups in a warm, sympathetic manner. One program was devoted to a description of Polish Americans, another to Italian Americans, and so forth. Who was listening? The major part of the audience for the program about Polish Americans consisted of Polish Americans. And guess who made up most of the audience for the program on

Italian Americans? Right. Moreover, as we have seen, if people are compelled to listen to information uncongenial to their deep-seated attitudes, they will reject it, distort it, or ignore it—in much the same way Mr. X maintained his negative attitude against Jews despite Mr. Y's disconfirming information. (The same process is at work—more loudly amplified—in today's "filter bubbles" on social media.) To be sure, sometimes, instead of revising their stereotypes in light of the new evidence, people reduce dissonance by creating a subcategory—such as "competent female" or "African Americans I admire"—allowing them to preserve the stereotype while seeing the person in front of them as a rare exception, perhaps even "the exception that proves the rule."

For most people, therefore, prejudice is too deeply rooted in their own belief systems, is too consistent with their day-to-day behavior, and receives too much support and encouragement from the people around them to be overturned by a book, film, or podcast.[100] Well, then, what works?

The Contact Hypothesis The 1954 Supreme Court decision may have alarmed many laypeople, but it generated excitement and optimism among social psychologists, who had long known that changes in behavior can affect changes in attitudes. They predicted that once black children and white children could be brought into direct contact, prejudiced children and their parents would encounter real human beings rather than stereotypes, eventually leading to greater mutual understanding and friendship. This view came to be called the *contact hypothesis*.

There was good reason for optimism because not only did it make sense theoretically, but empirical evidence also supported the power of contact between two groups. As early as 1951, Morton Deutsch and Mary Ellen Collins[101] examined the attitudes of white Americans toward African Americans in two public housing projects that differed in their degree of racial integration. In one, black and white families had been randomly assigned to separate buildings in the same project. In the other, black and white families lived in the same building. After several months, white residents in the integrated housing reported a greater positive change in their attitudes toward their black neighbors than residents of the segregated housing did, even though the former had not initially chosen to live in an integrated building.

The contact hypothesis has been supported by many studies in the laboratory and in the real world: young people's attitudes toward the elderly, healthy people's attitudes toward the mentally ill, nondisabled children's attitudes toward the disabled, and straight people's prejudices toward gay men and lesbians.[102] Indeed, today's multiethnic college campuses are a living laboratory of the contact hypothesis. White students who have roommates, friends, and relationships across racial and ethnic lines tend to become less prejudiced and find commonalities.[103] Cross-group friendships benefit minorities and reduce their prejudices too. Jim Sidanius and his colleagues[104] found that minority students who join ethnic student organizations tend to develop, over time, a stronger ethnic identity and pride, as we might expect—but they also tend to develop an increased sense of ethnic victimization. Just like white students who live in white fraternities and sororities, they come to feel that they have less in common with other ethnic groups. But when Rodolfo Mendoza-Denton and Elizabeth Page-Gould[105] conducted a longitudinal study of black and Latino students at a predominantly white university, they found that friendships with white students increased their feelings of belonging and reduced their feelings of dissatisfaction with the school. This was especially true for students who had previously been feeling insecure and sensitive about being rejected as members of a minority.

Although contact between ethnic groups in college can obviously be beneficial to both parties, the desegregation of public schools in the aftermath of the Supreme Court decision did not work as smoothly as social psychologists had expected. On the contrary, it usually created tension and turmoil in the classroom and even *increased* prejudice between racial groups. And if you had taken an aerial photograph of the schoolyards of most desegregated schools, you would have found almost no integration: White kids tended to cluster with white kids, black kids tended to cluster with black kids, and Hispanic kids tended to cluster with Hispanic kids. Obviously, in this instance, mere contact did not work as anticipated.

What went wrong? Why did desegregated housing work better than desegregated public schools? To answer these questions, we need to take a closer look at the conditions under which contact is effective, or ineffective.[106] When people's prejudices are largely based on unfamiliarity with another group, contact is a good way to reduce their discomfort of not knowing how to behave or what to say. But for contact to reduce prejudice and foster friendships, it must take place in a situation in which blacks and whites have *equal status*. Throughout history, many whites have had a great deal of contact with blacks, but typically in situations in which the latter held menial roles as porters, dishwashers, washroom attendants, and domestic workers. This kind of contact can perpetuate stereotyping by whites and add fuel to their prejudices, while increasing the resentment and anger of black people. In much of American history equal-status contact has been rare, both because of educational and occupational inequities in our society and because of residential segregation.

Now picture what happened when American schools were desegregated. The contact between white and minority-group children (especially if it did not begin until high school) was usually not equal status. In all sections of the country, most schools in predominantly minority neighborhoods had poorer facilities, equipment, and instruction than schools in predominantly white neighborhoods. A tenth-grade boy from a poor black or Latino family, after being subjected to a second-rate education, is suddenly dropped into a learning situation in a predominantly white, middle-class school taught by white, middle-class teachers, where he finds he must compete with white, middle-class students who have been reared to hold white, middle-class values. In effect, he is thrust into a highly competitive situation for which he is unprepared, a situation in which the rules are not his rules and payoffs are made for abilities he has not yet developed. He is competing in a situation that, psychologically, is far removed from his home turf. These factors tend to diminish his self-esteem — the very factor that influenced the Supreme Court decision in the first place. In his analysis of the research on desegregation, Walter Stephan[107] found no studies indicating significant increases in self-esteem among black children, while 25 percent of the studies he researched showed a significant drop in their self-esteem following desegregation. In addition, white prejudice was not substantially reduced; Stephan found that it increased in almost as many cases as it decreased. Understandably, minority-group students would attempt to raise their self-esteem by sticking together, lashing out at whites, asserting their individuality, and rejecting "white" values of education.

Contact, then, is obviously the first step, but it's not enough. What's the next step? Let's take a closer look.

Reducing Prejudice Through Cooperation and Interdependence

The issue is not simply getting youngsters of various races and ethnic backgrounds into the same school; it's what happens after they get there that is crucial. The tension that frequently accompanies school desegregation might remind you of the behavior of the young boys in the summer camp experiment by Muzafer Sherif and his colleagues. Recall that hostility was produced between two groups by placing them in situations of conflict and competition. Once the hostility was established, it could no longer be reduced simply by removing the conflicts and the competition. As a matter of fact, once distrust was firmly established, bringing the groups together in noncompetitive situations served to *increase* the hostility and distrust. The Eagles and the Rattlers had trouble with one another even when they were simply sitting together watching a movie.

How did Sherif eventually succeed in reducing the hostility? By placing the two groups of boys in situations in which they had to cooperate to accomplish their goal.[108] One time, the investigators set up an emergency situation by damaging the water-supply system. The only way the system could be repaired was if all the boys cooperated immediately. On another occasion, the camp truck broke down while the boys were on a camping trip. To get the truck going again, they had to pull it up a rather steep hill—a task they could accomplish only by all of them pulling together, regardless of whether they were Eagles or Rattlers. Eventually, the boys' hostility toward their former enemies subsided and they made friends across groups, began to get along better, and began to cooperate spontaneously.

The key factor seems to be **interdependence** in reaching mutual goals: a situation in which individuals need one another to succeed. Several researchers have demonstrated the benefits of interdependence in well-controlled laboratory experiments. Morton Deutsch,[109] for example, showed that problem-solving groups are both friendlier and more attentive when a cooperative atmosphere is introduced than when a competitive atmosphere prevails. Similarly, research by Patricia Keenan and Peter Carnevale[110] has shown that cooperation within groups can also foster cooperation between groups. That is, cooperative relations that are established in one group often carry over when that group is later called upon to interact with a different group. In their study, groups that engaged in a cooperative task were more cooperative in a subsequent negotiation with another group than groups that had initially worked in a competitive fashion.

Inventing the Jigsaw Classroom Unfortunately, cooperation and interdependence are not characteristic of the process that exists in most American classrooms, even at the elementary level. On the contrary, intense competition reigns in most classrooms in this country. I got a chance to observe this up close when I was asked to intervene during a major crisis in the Austin, Texas, public schools. The year was 1971. Desegregation had just taken place and had precipitated some ugly incidents. Because Austin had been residentially segregated, youngsters of various ethnic and racial groups encountered one another for the first time, bringing their suspicions and stereotypes with them. The contact made matters worse; taunting frequently escalated into fistfights. The situation was both ugly and dangerous, shattering our illusions that desegregation would automatically reduce prejudice.

When the school superintendent asked for help, my graduate students and I entered the system, not to smooth over the unpleasantness but rather to see if there was anything we might do to help desegregation achieve some of the positive goals envisioned for it. The first thing we did was to systematically observe the dynamics taking place in various classrooms. By far, the most common process we observed was typified by this scenario in a sixth-grade class: The teacher stands in front of the room, asks a question, and waits for the students to indicate that they know the answer. Most frequently, 6 to 10 youngsters strain in their seats and raise their hands, some waving them vigorously in an attempt to attract the teacher's attention. Several other students sit quietly with their eyes averted, as if trying to make themselves invisible.

When the teacher calls on one of the students, there are looks of disappointment, dismay, and unhappiness on the faces of those students who were eagerly raising their hands but were not called on. If the student comes up with the right answer, the teacher smiles and nods approvingly, providing a great reward for that student. At that moment, however, an audible groan can be heard coming from the youngsters who were striving to be called on but were ignored. They are upset because they missed an opportunity to show the teacher how smart they are.

Through this process, students learn several things in addition to the material being covered. First, they learn there is only one expert in the classroom: the teacher. They learn that the payoff comes from pleasing the teacher by actively displaying how smart they are; there is no payoff for consulting with their peers. Indeed, many learn that their peers are their enemies, to be defeated. Moreover, most teachers frown on collaboration during class time; they see it as disruptive.

In this highly competitive dynamic, if you are a student who knows the correct answer and the teacher calls on one of your peers, chances are you will hope that he or she will come up with the wrong answer, so you will have a chance to show the teacher how smart you are. Those who fail when called on, or those who do not even raise their hands to compete, tend to resent those who succeed. The successful students, for their part, often hold the unsuccessful students in contempt; they consider them to be stupid and uninteresting. This process discourages friendliness and understanding and tends to create enmity, even among students of the same racial group. When this competitive classroom dynamic is added to a situation already strained by interracial distrust, it sets the stage for the kind of turmoil we encountered in Austin.

Although, at that time, competitiveness in the classroom was nearly universal, as social psychologists we realized that it didn't have to be that way. Based, in part, on the experiment by Muzafer Sherif at Robbers Cave, we reasoned that a cooperative process might be precisely what was needed in this situation. But how to do it? Actually, it wasn't that difficult. Within a few days, my grad students and I succeeded in developing a simple cooperative method designed specifically for the classroom. As it turned out, our method was virtually foolproof. We designed it so that, in order to learn the material and do well on the upcoming exam, students had to work *with* each other and cooperate. Trying to win became dysfunctional. We called our method **the jigsaw classroom** because it works like a jigsaw puzzle.[111]

An example will clarify: In a fifth-grade classroom, the children were studying biographies of famous Americans. The upcoming lesson happened to be a biography of Joseph Pulitzer, the famous journalist. First, we divided the students into groups of six, making certain that each group was as diverse (in terms of race and gender) as possible. We then constructed a biography of Pulitzer, consisting of six paragraphs. Paragraph one was about Pulitzer's ancestors and how they came to this country; paragraph two was about Pulitzer as a little boy and how he grew up; paragraph three was about Pulitzer as a young man, his education, and his early employment; paragraph four was about his middle age and how he founded his first newspaper; and so forth. Each major aspect of Joseph Pulitzer's life was contained in a separate paragraph. We copied our biography of Joseph Pulitzer, cut each copy of the biography into six one-paragraph sections, and gave every child in each of the six-person learning groups one paragraph about Pulitzer's life. Thus, each learning group had within it the entire biography of Joseph Pulitzer, but each student had no more than one-sixth of the story. To get the whole picture, each student needed to listen carefully to the other students in the group as they recited.

The teacher informed the students that they had a certain amount of time to communicate their knowledge to one another. She also informed them that they would be tested on their knowledge at the end of that time frame.

Within a few days, the students learned that none of them could do well without the aid of each person in the group. They learned to respect the fact that each member (regardless of race, gender, or ethnicity) had a unique and essential contribution to make to their own understanding and subsequent test performance. Now, instead of only one expert (the teacher), each student was an expert on his or her own segment. Instead of taunting each other, they began encouraging each other, because it was in each student's own best interest to make sure that their classmates were able to communicate their material in the best possible way.

It took a few days for this new method to sink in; cooperative behavior doesn't happen all at once. The students in our experimental group had grown accustomed to competing during all of their years in school. For the first few days, most of them tried to compete against each other—even though competitiveness was dysfunctional. Here's an actual example, typical of the way the children stumbled toward the learning of the cooperative process: In one of our groups there was a Mexican American boy, whom I will call Carlos. Carlos's task was to report on Joseph Pulitzer's young manhood. He knew the material, but he was nervous and having a hard time. During the previous few weeks, some of the Anglo students had taunted him about his accent, and he was afraid they would do so again.

He stammered, hesitated, and fidgeted. Sure enough, the other kids in the circle were unhelpful. Being well versed in the rough-and-tumble tactics of the competitive classroom, they knew what to do when a kid stumbled, especially a kid whom they believed to be stupid: They ridiculed him. A child I'll call Mary said, "Aw, you don't know it; you're dumb; you're stupid. You don't know what you're doing." In our initial experiment, the groups were being loosely monitored by a research assistant who was floating from group to group. When this incident occurred, our assistant made one brief intervention: "Okay, Mary, you can talk to Carlos that way if you want to. It might even be fun for you. But it's not going to help you learn about Joseph Pulitzer's young adulthood. By the way, the exam will take place in less than an hour." Notice how the reinforcement contingencies had shifted. No longer did Mary gain much from needling Carlos; she now stood to lose a great deal.

After a few similar experiences, it dawned on the students in Carlos's group that the *only* way they could learn about the segment Carlos was trying to teach them was by paying attention to what Carlos had to say. Gradually, they began to develop into good listeners. Some even became pretty good interviewers. Instead of ignoring or ridiculing Carlos when he was having a little trouble communicating what he knew, they began asking gentle, probing questions—the kinds that made it easier for Carlos to answer. Carlos responded to this treatment by becoming more relaxed; with increased relaxation came an improvement in his ability to communicate. After a couple of weeks, the other children realized that Carlos was a lot smarter than they had thought he was. Because they were paying attention, they saw qualities in him they had never seen before. They began to like him. For his part, Carlos began to enjoy school more and began to see the Anglo students in his group not as tormentors but as helpful friends. Moreover, as he began to feel increasingly comfortable in class and gained more confidence in himself, his academic performance improved. The vicious cycle had been reversed; the elements that had been sending him into a downward spiral were changed—the spiral now began to move upward. Within a few weeks, the entire atmosphere in that classroom had changed.

We then randomly assigned several classrooms to the jigsaw condition and compared them with classrooms using the traditional competitive method. We could not have been more pleased by the results: Children in jigsaw classrooms performed better on objective exams, liked each other better, and developed a greater liking for school and greater self-esteem than children in traditional classrooms. Absenteeism dropped. Friendships among children in the jigsaw classroom crossed ethnic and racial barriers, resulting in a sharp decrease in prejudice and stereotyping. We replicated the same experiment in dozens of classrooms in several cities, always getting similar results.[112]

Over the years, research has shown that the jigsaw method's effectiveness is not limited to either Americans or to young children. The jigsaw method has been used with great success in Europe, Africa, the Middle East, and Australia—with students at all levels, from elementary schools to universities.[113] Researchers have also applied the jigsaw method to other prejudices that people hold, such as toward people with physical and emotional disabilities. In one such experiment,[114] college students interacted with a fellow student who had been portrayed as a former mental patient. The interactions were part of a structured learning situation, with some of the students interacting with the "former mental patient" in a jigsaw group, while others interacted with him in a more traditional learning climate. Those in the jigsaw group quickly let go of their stereotypical expectations; they liked him better and enjoyed interacting with him more than did those who encountered him in the more traditional learning situation. Moreover, those who went through the jigsaw session with the "former mental patient" subsequently described mental patients, in general, far more positively.

Why the Jigsaw Method Works Why does the jigsaw method produce such positive results? One reason for the success of this technique is that the process of participating in a cooperative group breaks down ingroup versus outgroup perceptions and allows the individual to develop the cognitive category of "oneness"—we're in this together.[115] One reason for its effectiveness is that this cooperative strategy places people in a favor-doing situation. That is, each individual in a group, by sharing his or her knowledge with the other members, is doing them a favor. As cognitive dissonance theory would predict, and as shown in an experiment by Mike Leippe and Donna Eisenstadt,[116] people who act in a way that benefits others subsequently feel more favorable toward them: "If I'm helping them, it must be because they deserve it."

A different but complementary mechanism was illustrated in an experiment by Samuel Gaertner and his colleagues,[117] demonstrating that cooperation lowers barriers between groups by changing the cognitive categories people use. In other words, cooperation changes our tendency to categorize the outgroup from "those people" to "us people." But how does this change from "those people" to "us people" actually come about? I believe that the mediating process is empathy, the ability to experience what your group member is experiencing. In the competitive classroom, the primary goal is simply to show the teacher how smart you are, so you don't have to pay much attention to the other students. But the jigsaw situation is different. To participate effectively in the jigsaw classroom, each student needs to pay close attention to whichever member of the group is reciting. In the process, the participants learn that great results can accrue if they approach each classmate in a way that is tailored to fit his or her special needs. For example, Alice may learn that Carlos is a bit shy and needs to be prodded gently, while Phyllis is so talkative that she might need to be reined in occasionally. Peter can be joked with, while Serena responds only to serious suggestions.

If this analysis is sound, then it should follow that working in jigsaw groups would lead to the sharpening of a youngster's general empathic ability. To test this notion, Diane Bridgeman[118] conducted a clever experiment with 10-year-old children, half of whom had spent two months participating in jigsaw classes and the others in traditional classrooms. In her experiment, Bridgeman showed the children a series of cartoons aimed at testing a child's ability to empathize, to put themselves in the shoes of the cartoon characters. In one cartoon, the first panel shows a little boy looking sad as he waves good-bye to his father at the airport. In the next panel, a letter carrier delivers a package to the boy. In the third panel, the boy opens the package, finds a toy airplane inside, and bursts into tears. Bridgeman asked the children why they thought the little boy burst into tears at the sight of the airplane. Nearly all of the children could answer correctly: because the toy airplane reminded him of how much he missed his father. Then Bridgeman asked the crucial question: "What did the letter carrier think when he saw the boy open the package and start to cry?"

Most children of this age make a consistent error; they assume that everyone knows what they know. Thus, the youngsters from the traditional classrooms thought that the letter carrier would know the boy was sad because the gift reminded him of his father leaving. But the children who had participated in the jigsaw classroom responded differently. Because of their experience with the jigsaw method, they had developed the ability to take the perspective of the letter carrier and to put themselves in his shoes. Therefore, they realized that he would be confused by seeing the boy cry over receiving a nice present, because he hadn't witnessed the farewell scene at the airport.

At first glance, this might not seem important. After all, who cares whether kids have the ability to figure out what is in the mind of a cartoon character? In point of fact, we should all care—a great deal. Recall our discussion of the Columbine tragedy in the preceding chapter. In that chapter we suggested how important empathy is in curbing aggression. The extent to which youngsters can develop the ability to see the world from the perspective of another human being has profound implications for all of their relationships. When we develop the ability to understand what another person is going through, it increases the probability that our heart will open to that person. Once our heart opens to another person, it becomes virtually impossible to feel prejudice against that person, to bully that person, to taunt that person, to humiliate that person. My guess is that, if the jigsaw strategy had been used in Columbine High School (or in the elementary and middle schools that feed into Columbine), the tragedy could have been avoided.[119]

My grad students and I developed the jigsaw technique in 1971, and since then, others have developed similar cooperative methods.[120] The implications of this work have only become clearer over the years. If you want to reduce prejudice, put people on a team with a common purpose. Even unconsciously held "implicit attitudes" can be modified by teamwork and empathy. Jay Van Bavel and William Cunningham[121] put some participants in a mixed-race group (six blacks and six whites) and others in a same-race group and had them take an IAT-like test of implicit associations. White members of a control group who were simply looking at unaffiliated faces revealed the familiar IAT effect, a racial bias of white is greater than black. But participants assigned to a mixed-race team had more positive automatic evaluations of black ingroup members than white outgroup members, a preference that was driven by ingroup bias ("They're on my team!") more than outgroup denigration. And a series of five experiments by Andrew Todd and his colleagues[122] showed that having participants engage in *perspective taking*—actively contemplating others' experiences, otherwise known as empathy—strongly reduced automatic expressions of racial bias.

Together, the striking results described in this chapter have been repeated in thousands of classrooms in all regions of the country. John McConahay,[123] a leading expert on race relations, has called cooperative learning the single most effective practice for improving race relations in desegregated schools. Unfortunately, although most teachers learn about jigsaw and other forms of cooperative education, these methods are used less frequently than you would expect. Educational systems, like all bureaucracies, tend to resist change, and the standard, competitive classroom structure continues to be the norm.

The Challenge of Diversity

Diversity in a nation, city, neighborhood, or school can be an exciting thing—or a source of turmoil. Desegregation has given us the opportunity to benefit from that diversity. But to maximize those benefits, it is vital for us to learn to relate to one another across racial and ethnic lines in as harmonious a way as possible. It goes without saying that we have a long way to go before achieving anything resembling full harmony in this country.

The challenges presented to an ethnically diverse nation have been graphically depicted by the Pulitzer Prize–winning reporter David Shipler,[124] who traveled the length and breadth of the United States, interviewing a wide variety of people about their racial feelings and attitudes. His rather bleak conclusion is summed up in the title of his book, *A Country of Strangers*. Shipler observed that most Americans do not have close relationships with people of other races, religions, and ethnic groups; therefore, a great deal of suspicion and misunderstanding prevail. Reading Shipler's book reminded me of a Texas school principal who complained to me that desegregation was causing problems in his school: "Look, professor, the government can force black kids and white kids to go to the same school," he said, "but no one can force them to enjoy hanging out with each other." (I don't think he had read William Graham Sumner, but he was making the same point.)

As if to underscore his point, that same day, during lunchtime, as I wandered around the schoolyard, what I saw was not an integrated school—far from it. Instead there were several clusters of self-segregated groups: black youngsters clustered together in one group; Latino youngsters clustered together in another group; white youngsters clustered together in still another group. It is not surprising to find that people of the same race and ethnicity might prefer one another's company. And, by itself, there is certainly nothing wrong with that—unless such preferences become rigidified into exclusionary behavior. A few months after initiating the jigsaw technique at that same school, I was walking through the schoolyard and was struck by the realization that virtually all of these clusters of students were fully integrated. No one was "forcing" the youngsters to like one another; they were actually choosing to relate to one another, across racial and ethnic boundaries. The jigsaw experience was visibly easing some of the earlier distrust and suspicion.

Shipler is undoubtedly right that we are "a country of strangers," and perhaps we always have been. But those tens of thousands of children who have experienced learning cooperatively give us hope for the future—a hope that they will eventually grow into adults who have learned to enjoy and benefit from diversity, who have learned to like and respect one another, and who understand that "they" are part of "us."

Great humanitarians have repeatedly sought to teach this message. Nelson Mandela spent 27 years in prison for his activism in the cause of ending apartheid in South Africa. And when it ended, and he was elected South Africa's first black president, he did not seek revenge or bloody retaliation; he formed a working relationship with the white former president, F.W. de Klerk, to usher South Africa into a full multiracial democracy. (Both men shared a Nobel Peace Prize for their remarkable collaboration.) "No one is born hating another person because of the color of his skin or his background or his religion," Mandela wrote. "People must learn to hate, and if they can learn to hate, they can be taught to love. For love comes more naturally to the human heart than its opposite."

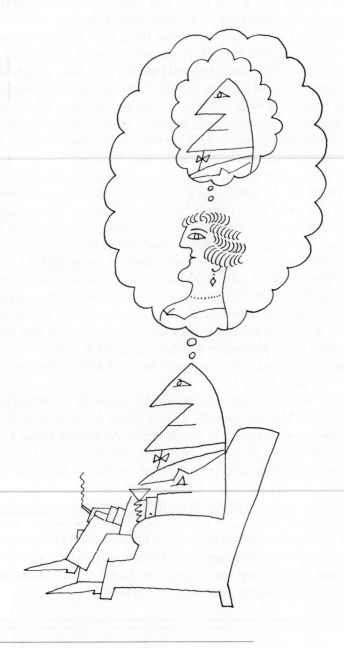

Saul Steinberg, *Untitled drawing*, ink on paper.
Originally published in *The New Yorker*, June 30, 1962.
© The Saul Steinberg Foundation / Artists Rights Society (ARS), New York

8

Liking, Loving, and Connecting

The 1946 Broadway musical "Annie Get Your Gun" was based on the real-life story of the legendary sharpshooter Annie Oakley, who, in 1875, at the age of 15, defeated the 26-year-old sharpshooter and reigning star of the Buffalo Bill Wild West Show, Frank Butler. In the musical, Annie falls instantly in love with her handsome competitor but is persuaded that her superior shooting skills would threaten his ego. She realizes that she must choose between sharp-shooting success and love. After singing "You Can't Get a Man with a Gun," Annie intentionally loses a second shooting match with Frank, who, masculine pride restored, falls in love with Annie immediately; they live happily ever after as Wild West Show stars.

The play was a smash hit and inspired a Hollywood movie and a TV series, but it took liberties with some key facts. The real Annie and Frank indeed lived happily ever after, but Frank never envied Annie's skills; he delighted in them and happily gave up his own stardom to support her in the role of business manager and on-stage assistant. The couple toured the United States and Europe, where Annie dazzled audiences with her rifle: extinguishing lit candles, hitting small coins tossed high in the air, and in a hair-raising test of Annie's aim and Frank's trust, shooting a lit cigarette dangling from his lips. Frank and Annie remained happily married for 50 years, until her death from anemia. Frank was apparently so hard hit when Annie died that he lost the will to live, stopped eating, and died 18 days after her funeral.[1]

Why didn't the musical tell the real love story? The fictionalized version of the musical reflected gender stereotypes prevalent at the time (and for decades after), where the woman was expected to make herself pretty, be sweet, and above all else, avoid outshining men with less talent or intelligence. The false Annie of the musical did all of those things to attract Frank. Their story has a lot to say about what follows in this chapter—about attraction, friendship, loving, and human connection. What attracts people to one another? What fuels liking, passion, and the more mysterious thing we call love? Why do some couples like Annie and Frank stay together till death, while others flame out quickly, or, like half of all marriages, end in divorce after about eight years?

The question of "who likes whom" is an ancient one. The first amateur social psychologist, who lived in a cave, undoubtedly wondered what he could do to make the fellow in a neighboring cave like him more or dislike him less—or, at least, to make him refrain from clubbing him on the head. Perhaps he brought over some saber-toothed tiger meat as a gift, hoping that would do the trick. Maybe he tried a new way of showing his teeth—not in a snarling, threatening grimace but in a softer, more submissive way—a way that eventually evolved into that gesture we call smiling.[2]

After meeting basic survival needs, our most potent motive is to have meaningful connections with others.[3] In addition to keeping us happy, good relationships literally keep us alive. Consider the remarkable Harvard study, which has been following two groups of men in the Boston area (one of well-off men who attended Harvard; the second of working-class men) for 75 years, from adolescence to old age. (There were only men because the study began before women were permitted to attend Harvard.) The goal of the study was to identify the factors (including experiences, resources, and conditions of life) that predict health, psychological well-being, and happiness in later life. The conclusion? According to the study's current director Robert Waldinger, "the clearest message that we get from this 75-year study is this: Good relationships keep us happier and healthier. Period."[4] The happiest men in the Harvard study were not those with the most impressive accomplishments, the most money, or the happiest childhoods; they were the ones who had prioritized their relationships with others. These were the men who were most likely to reach—and enjoy—their eighties and nineties.

Many studies confirm the health benefits of relationships that provide support, companionship, and love during both stressful and happy times.[5] Loneliness, in contrast, does not produce more stressful events, but it is a risk factor for stressors turning into disease. Lonely people have been found to have less efficient sleep patterns and higher blood pressure, and, when wounded, they heal more slowly than people who are not lonely.[6] It's important, however, not to interpret these data to mean that people must marry or be in a committed romantic relationship in order to reap the long-term benefits of relationships. Living single is perfectly healthy. It is *feeling* alone and *being isolated* that cause the problems.[7] People can be surrounded by others and feel lonely; they can live alone and have a rich social life. In the 1950s, most people believed that adults who preferred remaining single were "immoral" or "neurotic," but today that stigma is gone; half of American adults choose to live alone, more than twice as many as did in 1950. Indeed, the single life has its own social and physical advantages: People who live alone are more likely than those who are married or cohabiting to eat out with a friend, exercise, go to art and music classes, enjoy lectures, and do volunteer work.[8] You don't have to be in a committed relationship, in other words, to be connected.[9] As that lonely widower Frank Butler might have said, but George Valliant, past director of the Harvard health study, *actually* did say of the research, "Connection is the whole shooting match."[10]

Liking: What Attracts Us to Others — and Gets Them to Like Us?

When I ask people why they like some of their acquaintances better than others, I get a wide variety of responses. The most typical are that they like other people whose beliefs and interests are similar to their own; who have skills or abilities that are useful to us; who have pleasant or admirable qualities, such as beauty, charm, wit, loyalty, honesty, and kindness; and who like them in return.

These reasons make good sense. They are also consistent with the advice given by Dale Carnegie[11] in his book with the manipulative title *How to Win Friends and Influence People.* This recipe book for interpersonal relations seems to have been exactly what people were looking for. First published in 1937, it is still in print and proved to be one of the greatest best sellers of all time. That's not surprising. People want to belong and feel important; we want to be liked. Polls taken of high school students across the decades[12] indicate that their most important concern is the way others react to them—and their overwhelming desire is for people to like them more. Such concerns may be greatest during adolescence, when the peer group assumes enormous importance, but the desire to be liked is certainly not limited to American adolescents. The search for a single formula to attract others is universal. After all, Dale Carnegie's book was translated into 35 languages and is still read around the globe.

Carnegie's advice was simple: If you want people to like you, be pleasant, pretend you like them, feign an interest in things they're interested in, shower them with praise, be agreeable, don't criticize—and be sure to use their name as often as possible because "the average person is more interested in their own name than in all the other names in the world put together." In other words, Carnegie was convinced that most of us are like the fictional Frank Butler; if you want to win our love or influence us, then do whatever you can to make us feel good and avoid doing things that make us feel bad, like defeating us in a sharpshooting contest.

Is it true? Are these tactics effective? To a limited extent they are, at least in the early stages of becoming acquainted. Laboratory experiments indicate that we like people with pleasant characteristics more than those with unpleasant characteristics;[13] we like people who agree with us more than people who disagree with us; we like people who like us more than people who dislike us; we like people who cooperate with us more than people who compete with us; we like people who praise us more than people who criticize us. These aspects of attraction can be gathered under one sweeping generalization: We like people whose behavior provides us with maximum reward at minimum cost.[14]

Generally speaking, we know we like people who make us feel good in some way, but beyond these rather obvious reasons for liking others, what draws people to one another? John Thibaut and Harold Kelley[15] long ago argued that we calculate a person's value as a friend or romantic partner partly by comparing what they bring to us with what we might get from other potential friends or romantic partners. Attraction, in short, is partly determined by our *comparison level for alternatives*. Max is a nice guy but Roger is even cuter, has more education, and lives closer to me. If I think I'm attractive enough to win Roger's affection or friendship, Max may start looking less attractive.

But relationships aren't always so straightforward and don't always lend themselves to a cost–benefit calculation. People want to feel good, but they have other motives as well, and long-term friendships and romantic relationships involve more than just making one another feel happy for the moment. Thus, we need more than a plain reward theory of attraction to understand the complex and sometimes confusing nature of attraction, friendship, and love.

I turn now to five consistent factors that have a profound influence on our choice of friends and lovers: We tend to like people who live in close *proximity* to us; who we think are *similar* to us; who *like us*; and who are *physically attractive*. And to these I will add a relatively recent phenomenon created by our high-tech world, one that profoundly affects whom we like, whom we choose, and whether we stay: It's called *the paradox of choice*.

Proximity The likelihood that you will find someone attractive and get to know them starts with how close they live to you. What could be more obvious? Asked to name the people that they liked the best, college students who had been randomly assigned to dorm rooms named their next-door neighbors about half the time.[16] It's hard to make friends with people you do not meet, and it is easy to maintain friendships with people close by, so this makes sense: rewards of friendship at little cost. But proximity increases attractiveness for reasons other than ease and availability. Proximity simply makes it likelier that we will have repeated exposure, and, all other things being equal, people become more likable and attractive as they become more familiar. Much like a song we hear over and over again, people grow on us over time. Moreover, as I noted in Chapter 3, people become more attractive to us when we expect to interact with them in the future; when we know we will be stuck with someone for a while, dissonance helps us see their good qualities and ignore or deemphasize their flaws.[17]

Proximity has always been a huge factor in marriage. James Brossard[18] analyzed the marriage records in Philadelphia in the 1930s and found that most marriages involved people who lived close by: One in three marriages were between people who lived within five blocks of each other, one in six lived on the same block, and one in eight were from the same apartment building. Only about one in five marriages involved partners from different cities! When comedian Aziz Ansari and sociologist Eric Klinenberg[19] ran focus groups in retirement homes in New York City, they were struck by the consistency of where these elderly people had met their life partners. "People were marrying people in the same neighborhood, on the same street, and even in the same building," Ansari writes. "It seemed a little bizarre. I said, 'Guys, you live in New York City. Did you ever think, 'Oh, maybe there's some people outside my building?' Why limit yourself? They just shrugged and said that wasn't what was done."[20]

Today as then, the incontrovertible fact is that the people who are geographically nearest to you are most likely to become dearest to you as well. It makes a shambles of the romantic myth that there is one and only one person (perhaps in Yazoo City or Bulgaria!) waiting out there for you to come along. From ancient times to the present, people have been most likely to love and live with those who are in a nearby cave or a nearby home, or who study nearby or work in the same store, office, or factory. Even in this internet age of dating apps, proximity is still the first step toward finding love: You and your "one and only" would have to have picked the same dating site at the same time *and* one of you would have to come across the other one lazy afternoon (or "some enchanted evening") with enough time and motivation to send out a charming text. *Then* the other would have to read it *and* remember to reply amidst a sea of other texts sent by other potential suitors. Your true love in Yazoo City may be more accessible now, but he or she is only one of millions in a teeming digital crowd, which means you are going to find your beloved in Yazoo City only if you live there. Everyone else will choose someone closer to home.

Similarity Lynne goes to a party and is introduced to Suzanne. While they chat for only a few moments, it turns out that they agree completely in their feelings about George Bush, George Clooney, George Eliot, and King George III of England. Each goes back to her dorm and tells her roommate that she just met a wonderful, intelligent woman. Lynne and Suzanne would find themselves among the literally hundreds of experiments that have shown that the more similar a person seems to you in attitudes, opinions, and interests, the more you like the person. Opposites may attract, but they don't stick.

Why does perceived similarity make people attractive? There are at least two major reasons. First, it is obvious to most of us that people who share our attitudes and opinions on major issues are uncommonly intelligent and thoughtful, and it is always rewarding and interesting to hang out with intelligent and thoughtful people. Of course they are—they agree with us! Second, they provide us with social validation for our beliefs; that is, they satisfy our desire to feel right.

Moreover, we humans are so certain of the relationship between attitude similarity and liking that if we happen to like someone for some irrelevant reason—we both share an interest in birdwatching, say—we will assume that we share attitudes about politics, religion, and movies, too. Thus, causality works in both directions: We like people whose attitudes are similar to ours, and if we like someone, we attribute attitudes to him or her that are similar to ours.[21] If we *perceive* similarity with another person, that's enough to boost attraction.[22] This principle applies to all kinds of relationships and has proven to be an effective marketing method. Telemarketers are often trained to make pitches that identify and point out a similarity ("Hey, I'm a student, too!"), because we are more likely to buy things from people we like—and who we think are like us.[23]

Hunter Gelbach and his associates[24] even harnessed the similarity and liking effect to improve relationships between students and teachers. Teachers and students in a large high school filled out surveys on a broad range of topics, including their preferences for what they like do in their free time. With the responses in hand, the researchers randomly assigned teachers and students to be made aware of five of these similarities. Half of the students learned that their teacher was similar to them those ways, and their teachers were given the same information. This small intervention—learning that you have interests in common, even with that mysterious person of your teacher or your student—increased mutual feelings of liking and respect. This improvement in relationships was particularly elevated among the minority students, suggesting that realizing our commonalities in activities, values, and skills can overcome the primary perceived dissimilarity of race and ethnicity.

Personal Attributes: Competence When individuals are asked in public opinion polls, or on dating sites, to describe the personality traits and other attributes of people they like, they cheerfully list qualities such as sincere, competent, and intelligent. But in studies of this sort, it is difficult to establish the direction of causality: Do we like people who have pleasant attributes, or once we like them, do we convince ourselves that they have pleasant attributes? Chances are that causality flows in both directions. To find out which causes what, it is necessary to examine this relation under more controlled conditions than exist on questionnaires. Here I will examine two of the most important personal attributes: competence and physical attractiveness.

It would seem obvious that the more competent someone is, the more we will like that person. By "competence," I mean a cluster of qualities: smartness, the ability to get things done, wise decisions, etc. We stand a better chance of doing well at our life tasks if we surround ourselves with people who know what they're doing and have a lot to teach us. But the research evidence is paradoxical: In problem-solving groups, the participants who are considered the most competent and have the best ideas tend not to be the ones who are best liked.[25] Why? One possibility is that, although we like to be around competent people, those who are *too* competent make us uncomfortable. They may seem unapproachable, distant, superhuman—and make us look bad (and feel worse) by comparison. If this were true, we might like people more if they reveal some evidence of fallibility. For example, if your friend is a brilliant mathematician, superb athlete, and gourmet cook, you might like him or her better if, every once in a while, they screwed up.

I was spurred to create an experimental investigation of that hypothesis in 1961, when President John F. Kennedy made a terrible decision to invade Cuba at the Bay of Pigs in an attempt to overthrow Fidel Castro. The invasion was such a phenomenal blunder that it was immediately dubbed, and is still commonly known as, "the Bay of Pigs fiasco." But instead of JFK's popularity plummeting, it spiked—people liked him more, not less. I wondered why. One possibility is that Kennedy may have been "too perfect." In that year, Kennedy was at the height of his attractiveness. He was a character of almost storybook proportions—indeed, his presidency was referred to as Camelot. He was young, handsome, bright, witty, charming, and athletic. He was a voracious reader, the author of a best-selling book, and a war hero who suffered chronic physical pain without complaining. He was married to a talented and beautiful woman who spoke several foreign languages, had two cute-as-a-button kids (one boy, one girl), and was part of a wealthy, prominent, close-knit family. In other words, he was enviably perfect. Could it be that some evidence of fallibility, like being responsible for a major tactical miscalculation, could have served to make him more human in the public eye and, hence, more likable?

As you know all too well by now, the real world is no place to test such a hypothesis. In the real world, too many things are happening simultaneously, any one of which could have increased Kennedy's popularity. For example, after the fiasco occurred, he did not try to make excuses or to pass the buck; he accepted full responsibility. This action alone could also have done much to make him more attractive in the eyes of the populace.

Curious about that jump in JFK's popularity, I tested this question experimentally with my colleagues Ben Willerman and Joanne Floyd.[26] We told our participants, male college students, that we wanted them to evaluate candidates who were trying out for a quiz show in which students represent their college in a *Jeopardy*-like test of knowledge. Their job was to evaluate the candidates on the impressions they made and how likable they seemed. They then listened to a recording of an interview between a young man (the stimulus person) and an interviewer who asked a set of difficult questions. We had four versions of this recorded interview. On one, the candidate showed a high degree of competence—indeed, he seemed to be virtually perfect, answering 92 percent of the questions correctly—and when asked about his activities in high school, he modestly admitted he had been an honor student, the editor of the yearbook, and a member of the track team. On a second tape, the candidate came across as a person of average ability: He answered only 30 percent of the questions correctly, and during the interview he admitted he had received average grades in high school, had been a proofreader on the yearbook staff, and had tried out for the track team but had failed to make it. On the other two recordings, both the "superior" candidate and the "mediocre" candidate committed an embarrassing blunder, clumsily spilling a cup of coffee all over himself. (We created this "pratfall" version by recording sounds of commotion and clatter, the scraping of a chair, and the anguished voice of the candidate expressing alarm that he had spilled coffee all over his new clothes.)

The results confirmed what we called the **pratfall effect**: The superior person who committed a blunder was rated most attractive;

the average person who committed the same blunder was rated least attractive. The perfect person (no blunder) was second in attractiveness, and the mediocre person (no blunder) finished third. Clearly, there was nothing inherently attractive about spilling a cup of coffee. Although it did serve to add an endearing dimension to the perfect person, making him more attractive, the same action made the mediocre person appear that much more mediocre and, hence, even less attractive. This experiment gave us evidence to support our contention that, although a high degree of competence does make us more attractive, some evidence of fallibility increases our attractiveness still further.

This general phenomenon has been extended to longer-term relationships as well. Abraham Tesser[27] found that we derive great satisfaction and self-esteem out of having highly competent friends and relatives. Being close to competent people is rewarding; we can learn from them, bask in their reflected glory, enjoy their success.[28] Yet if they are more competent than we are *in areas that matter to us*, and therefore make us feel incompetent and inadequate by comparison, their attractiveness will be diminished in our eyes. Tesser's research suggests that siblings, close friends, and romantic partners might have an easier time staying close if they establish different domains of excellence. By giving up his career as a sharpshooter for a career of managing Annie Oakley, the real Frank Butler took a smart step toward ensuring a lifetime of intimacy. No longer her competitor, he could bask in the reflected glory of her competence without being diminished by it.

Personal Attributes: Physical Attractiveness Imagine you've just had a date. It is near the end of the evening, and you are deciding whether you want to go out with this person again. Which of your date's characteristics will weigh most heavily: warmth, sensitivity, intelligence, compassion? How about good looks? You guessed it!

Most people don't want this to be true. We'd prefer to believe that beauty is only skin deep and, therefore, a trivial determinant of liking. Also, it seems so unfair; why should something like physical attractiveness, which is largely beyond a person's control, matter so much? Although many people believe that attractiveness matters more to men than to women, an analysis of more than 29,000 people found that attractiveness matters equally to both sexes.[29] And in study after study of their actual behavior, college students, as well as the population at large, are overwhelmingly influenced by another person's looks.[30] Many years ago, Elaine Walster and her associates[31] randomly matched incoming students at the University of Minnesota for a blind date. The students previously had been given a battery of personality tests. Which of their many characteristics determined whether they liked each other: intelligence, masculinity, femininity, dominance, submission, dependence, independence, sensitivity, sincerity? The *one* determinant of whether a couple liked each other and repeated their date was their physical attractiveness. The very success of Tinder and other dating apps that have dispensed with "personality profiles" and "your ideal mate's qualities" shows how quickly and completely we can dismiss another human being on the basis of a snapshot alone.

But as the similarity effect might suggest, people tend to pair off at the same levels of attractiveness. In the study by Walster and colleagues, if a handsome man was paired with a beautiful woman, they were most likely to desire to see each other again. Gregory White,[32] studying relatively long-term relationships among young couples at UCLA, found that physical attractiveness mattered, but it was the *similarity* of the attractiveness of the partners that was crucial in determining whether they stayed together. Many months after the couples started dating, those who were well matched in physical attractiveness had remained more deeply involved with each other than those who were mismatched. Even Beauty's Beast eventually reveals his handsome self.

Beauty also influences a wide range of attributions that we make about others. Karen Dion and her colleagues[33] showed college students photos of three college-age people: one who was attractive, one who had average looks, and one who was unattractive. The participants rated each of the people depicted on 27 different personality traits and predicted their future happiness. By far, the physically attractive people were assigned the most desirable traits and given the greatest prognosis for happiness. This was true whether men were rating men or women, and whether women were rating men or women.

Some evolutionary psychologists think that certain aspects of what people consider "beautiful" are hardwired, reflecting a preference for mates who look healthy and free of disease.[34] But this is a subject of considerable controversy, because the round face and plump body that are gorgeous in Tonga may be considered unattractive in Tallahassee, and the features considered sexy within one racial or ethnic group may be unfamiliar and hence unattractive to members of other groups. Nonetheless, the Western association between *beautiful* and *good* starts with childhood experiences and cultural associations: Walt Disney movies and popular cartoons teach children that white heroines like Snow White, Cinderella, Sleeping Beauty, and the Little Mermaid—along with more recent ethnic heroines like Tiana, Pocahontas, Aurora, Mulan, Jasmine, and Moana, and the princes who charm and win them—all have regular features, small noses, big eyes, shapely lips, blemish-free complexions, and slim, athletic bodies. They all look like Barbie and Ken dolls. And how are the wicked stepmothers, stepsisters, giants, trolls, and evil queens depicted?

And then there is advertising, the continuous barrage of propaganda aimed at selling the idea that beauty in a bottle will make us desirable, socially successful, and thus happy and whole. Exposure to these images *does* have an impact, particularly on adolescents. In one experiment, female high school students watched 15 commercials extolling the virtues of beauty preparations.[35] A control group of teenagers watched 15 commercials unrelated to beauty products. Later, all of the young women were asked to rank the relative importance of 10 attributes, including sex appeal, intelligence, a pretty face, and industriousness. The young women who had been shown the beauty ads were more likely than the control group to consider beauty-oriented attributes as being more important than other qualities.

Sadly, the beauty bias means that unattractive children pay a price for their looks. Karen Dion[36] asked women to evaluate reports of classroom disturbances, apparently written by a teacher. Attached to each report was a photo of the child who was said to have caused the trouble. In some photos, the child was attractive, in others not so attractive. The women tended to place more blame on the less attractive children and to infer that this incident was typical of their everyday behavior. When the child was pictured as good looking, however, they tended to excuse the disruptive behavior. As one of the women put it, "She plays well with everyone, but like anyone else, a bad day can occur. Her cruelty ... need not be taken seriously." When an unattractive girl was pictured as the culprit in exactly the same situation, described in exactly the same way, a typical respondent said, "I think the child would be quite bratty and would probably be a problem to teachers. She would probably try to pick a fight with other children her own age ... All in all, she would be a real problem." Thus, it seems that we tend to give attractive children the benefit of the doubt; their misbehaviors are forgivable aberrations, caused by the situation. We don't let less attractive children off the hook so easily; their misdeeds are attributed to stable, negative personality dispositions. Similar effects have been found at all ages and in contexts such as business, where attractive workers are often paid better and promoted more often.[37]

Beauty imparts power, but there is a downside to good looks: People can be harder on beautiful people who are critical of them. In an experiment I did with Harold Sigall,[38] a woman was made to appear either physically attractive or unattractive—with unflattering clothes and an ugly wig—and then interview several college men. Afterward, she gave each student her own clinical evaluation of him. Half of the students received highly favorable evaluations and half received unfavorable evaluations. When the evaluator was unattractive, the men didn't seem to care much whether they received a good evaluation or a poor one from her; in both situations, they liked her a fair amount. When she was beautiful, however, they liked her a lot when she gave them a favorable evaluation, but when she had criticized them, they disliked her more than in any of the other conditions.

Taking all of this research into consideration, we must face the fact that beauty is more than skin deep. We like beautiful people more, we treat them more favorably, and we think they are warmer, sexier, and more exciting than homely people. Moreover, in ambiguous situations where it's not certain who is to blame for an unfortunate event, we tend to give them the benefit of the doubt. This "pro-beauty bias" begins at a very young age, and, unfortunately, over time it can generate a self-fulfilling prophecy, as Mark Snyder, Elizabeth Decker Tanke, and Ellen Berscheid showed in a classic experiment.[39] Put yourself in the place of a typical male undergraduate in their study: You have volunteered to participate in an investigation of "how people become acquainted with each other," and you have been paired with a female student who is located in another room, ostensibly because the two of you are assigned to the "no nonverbal communication" condition of the study. Though you haven't seen your partner, you have been given a packet of information that contains her photo. When you proceed to have a conversation with her over an intercom, do you think the physical attractiveness of the woman in the photo will influence your impressions of her?

As you might suspect, the photo did not depict the participant's actual partner. For half of them, it pictured a very attractive woman; for the others, it pictured a relatively unattractive woman. The men who thought they were talking with a beautiful woman rated her as more poised, humorous, and socially adept than did those who thought they were talking with a less attractive woman. So far, just what we would expect. But what was startling was that when independent observers listened to a tape recording of only the woman's half of the conversation (without looking at a photo), they were far more impressed by the woman whose male partner thought she was physically attractive. That means that when the male partner thought he was talking to a beautiful woman, he spoke to her in a way that brought out her best qualities. When the independent observers listened to her conversation, they rated her as being more attractive, more confident, more animated, and warmer than the woman whose partner thought her to be less beautiful. This study illuminates a dramatic and touching example of the self-fulfilling prophecy: Whether or not a person is physically beautiful, treating them *as if they are attractive* brings out those desirable qualities.

I want to emphasize that this discussion of "beauty" has focused on visual beauty. Our perceptual mechanisms exercise a terribly conservative influence on our feelings and behavior—and the way we determine who is generally attractive. But there are other kinds of beauty. In the 1960s and 1970s, when sensitivity-training groups were at the height of their popularity, many people volunteered to engage in nonvisual sensory experiences. In one group that I led, 50 people were told to close their eyes and wander around the room, becoming acquainted with each other solely through the sense of touch and by talking to one another. After participating in this exercise, group members typically reported that their prior stereotypes had been shattered. You can't think of other people as being "homely" if you can't see them, and you can't therefore assume they have the traits that "homely" people allegedly do. When participants subsequently opened their eyes, they were frequently astonished to learn that, for example, the funny-looking guy with the big nose and pimples standing in front of them was the very same person who, five minutes ago (when their eyes were closed) had impressed them as an incredibly warm, gentle, sensitive human being. It was an experience that many of the participants never forgot.

In so many of our judgments, our hearts follow our eyes. But our eyes can also follow our hearts, over time. Many of us have known the experience of finding a person more beautiful as our liking for them increases, not simply averaging their looks and other qualities into an overall evaluation, but rather, seeing them as being beautiful because our feelings for them have intensified.[40] The reverse happens too: People we think of as handsome or gorgeous become less beautiful as we get to know and dislike their annoying personalities or obnoxious beliefs. What is beautiful is good—but what is good becomes beautiful.[41] Social neuroscientist Jon Freeman[42] points out that we bring a tremendous amount of "psychological baggage" to our perception of faces. If we evaluate potential mates mainly with our eyes, as we do on Tinder, we're apt to miss out on some potentially wonderful people, whose beauty requires more than a quick glance to appreciate. That was surely true for Frank Butler; Annie Oakley was no beauty, but it wasn't her looks that won his heart for life.

Being Liked One of the strongest determinants of whether we will like someone is the belief that someone likes us. How does this work? Imagine that you and I are having a brief, rather uneventful conversation at a party after a mutual friend introduced us. A few days later, you run into our friend on campus, and she informs you that, following the party, I had some very complimentary things to say about you. How do you suppose you might act the next time you and I happened to meet? My hunch is that your knowledge that I liked you would probably lead you to like me and to act in ways that let me know that you liked me, too. You'd probably smile more, disclose more about yourself, and generally behave in a warmer, more interested, more likable manner than if you hadn't already learned that I liked you. And what effect do you think your actions would have on me? Faced with your warm and likable behavior, my fondness for you would undoubtedly grow, and I, in turn, would convey my liking for you in ways that made me even more likable to you.

But consider this: What if our mutual friend hadn't been telling the truth? What if she had figured that you and I really would like each other a great deal once we got to know each other and, to get the ball rolling, had told you that I liked you, even though I had not said a word? What are the chances that her well-intentioned plan would work? Well, if you and I were like the participants in an experiment by Rebecca Curtis and Kim Miller,[43] her scheme would have worked like a charm! These researchers led some people to believe that another person liked them and led others to believe that that same person disliked them. In a subsequent interaction, those individuals who thought they were liked behaved in more likable ways: They disclosed more about themselves, disagreed less, and generally behaved in a warmer, more pleasant manner toward the other person than did those individuals who thought they were disliked. Moreover, the people who believed they were liked were, in fact, subsequently liked by the other person, while those who believed they were disliked were disliked by the other person. Another self-fulfilling prophecy in action. Our beliefs, whether right or wrong, play a potent role in shaping reality.

And so, being liked makes the heart grow fonder. Furthermore, the greater our insecurity and self-doubt, the fonder we will grow of the person who likes us. In a fascinating experiment by Elaine Walster (Hatfield),[44] female college students, while waiting to receive the results of personality tests, were approached by a smooth, good-looking young man who was an accomplice of the experimenter. He struck up a conversation with each student, indicated he liked her, and proceeded to make a date. At this point, the experimenter entered and led each student into an office to inform her of her test results. Half of the students received highly positive descriptions designed to raise their self-esteem temporarily. The others received somewhat negative descriptions designed to lower their self-esteem temporarily. Finally, the students were asked to rate how much they liked an assorted list of people—a teacher, a friend, "and since we have one space left, why don't you rate that fellow you were waiting with?" The students who had received unfavorable feedback liked their male admirer more than did those who received favorable feedback. In short, we like to be liked—and the more insecure we feel, the more we like someone who likes us.

One implication of this experiment is that people who are secure about themselves are less "needy"; that is, they are less likely to accept overtures from just anyone who comes along. Just as a starving person will accept almost any kind of food and a well-fed person can afford to turn down an offer of a soggy cheese sandwich, an insecure person will accept almost anyone who expresses interest, while a secure person will be more selective. Moreover, a person who feels insecure may even seek out a less attractive person to diminish the possibility of being rejected. This idea was tested in an experiment by Sara Kiesler and Roberta Baral,[45] who led male college students to believe they had done either very well or very poorly on a test of intellectual achievement. They then took a break, and the experimenter joined the student for a cup of coffee. As they entered the coffee shop, the experimenter "recognized" a female student seated alone at a table, joined her, and introduced the male participant. Of course, the female student was a confederate, intentionally planted there. Half of the time, the confederate was made up to look attractive; the other half of the time, she was made to look quite plain. The investigators observed the degree of romantic interest displayed by the male participants: whether they asked to see her again, offered to pay for her coffee, asked for her phone number, or tried to get her to stay longer. Those who felt secure about themselves (i.e., who had been led to believe they had performed well on the test) showed more romantic interest toward the "attractive" woman; those induced to feel insecure showed more romantic interest toward the "unattractive" woman.

While insecurity certainly increases our desire to connect with whomever we expect will have us, in the context of dating we tend to be more romantically attracted to those who seem to like us *exclusively*—just me, not all those other thousands waiting for a swipe right. Those who seem to like everyone appear to be less discerning with their affections and therefore aren't nearly as desirable as those who are more choosy. This phenomenon was investigated in an experiment by Paul Eastwick and Eli Finkel,[46] in which a group of young men and women took part in a speed-dating session involving multiple quick dates. Afterward, they were asked to evaluate each date for desirability, attractiveness, chemistry, whether they'd agree to another date, and, most interesting, perceived selectivity, how many other people they expected their date to have said yes to. People who reported more interest for all dates across the board were also perceived by their dates as highly likely to say yes to all potential second dates. But their dating partners regarded these eager, easily pleased participants as being less desirable and having less chemistry for them personally. When participants thought their partner wished to date only them the second time, they more readily reciprocated. This research may explain that heady feeling people have when a flirtation is going well and it feels like there's no one else in the room but you and that special person. It is an exciting, uplifting, and esteem-building sensation, far more so than watching that "special person" come on to every other person in the room before finally getting to you.

The Paradox of Choice So now you have found Mr. or Ms. Right: someone who lives right near you; who shares many of your values and beliefs; who likes you, and only you, *a lot*; and who is great looking. Now what? Do you say, "I've found my life partner! Grab this chance while you can!" or do you say, "Hmm, wait—is this really the best person for me? Maybe someone better is just down the block"?

The modern world has expanded our range of choices in every realm of life. Once there was one brand and style of blue jeans—Levis—that either fit your body well or did not. Now there are countless brands, each with several options, like boot cut, straight leg, slim fit, relaxed fit, high waist, low waist, or ripped. Where once you could choose among a few kinds of cereal, now you have an entire aisle of them, with over 400 different choices. As Barry Schwartz[47] points out, people believe that having more options is always preferable to having few, so they always *say* they want more choices when you ask them. But having too many choices, Schwartz has found, can create a paradox: It's obviously nice to be able to choose among various alternatives, but it's not so nice when all those choices impede us from making any decision at all. If we look long enough, we think, we can always find a perfect pair of jeans, cereal, school, job ... or partner. Our expectations for perfection have risen as our options have multiplied, which means we are often left wondering if we might have done better if we had looked longer. Schwartz argues that, as a result, we become pickier, less happy with our eventual choices, and exhausted by having to weigh and evaluate so many options in the quest for perfection that we know is out there if only we look long enough. Sometimes we are simply paralyzed by the number of options and do nothing at all.

In one of the first demonstrations of the paradox of choice, Sheena Iyengar and her associates[48] went into a supermarket and set up a table with free samples of jams. At regular intervals, they switched from offering a selection of 24 jams to a selection of six. The array of 24 choices was impressively alluring: 60 percent of the passersby stopped, compared with only 20 percent who came to the table when it had only six jams. Regardless of the number of jams on the table, the typical shopper who stopped tasted two samples. After tasting them, shoppers were given one coupon good for $1 off one jar. The question was, who would buy jam? Although more choices drew more shoppers to the table, only 3 percent of those with the wide array of choices ended up buying any of the jars. Fully 30 percent of those with the narrow array of choices left the store with a jar of jam.

Like our grandparents, Annie Oakley did not have the luxury of much choice in jeans, jams, or romantic prospects. She was like a shopper in the six-jam condition of the choice experiment; a hand-ful of options would present themselves, and if you found someone attractive, you moved forward and made the best of it. You might have compared them with a few people you had met ("Frank is way more exciting than that boring sheep farmer down the road!"—and he undoubtedly was), but you did not compare them with all the other possible mates in a sea of options. Today, meeting people is easier because technology can connect us immediately with more potential mates who live near us than our grandparents could have met in a lifetime. But, as with jam, the endless choices can generate paralysis.

Yesterday's search for a romantic partner led us to ask, "Am I happy with this person?" Today's apps leave us looking at our current choice and ask, "Could I do better?" Aziz Ansari tells the story of "Derek," a fairly boring guy, "not immediately magnetic or charming":

> At our focus group on online dating in Manhattan, Derek got on OkCupid and let us watch as he went through his options … The first woman he clicked on was very beautiful, with a witty profile page, a good job, and lots of shared interests, including a love of sports. After looking the page over for a minute or so, Derek said, "Well, she looks O.K. I'm just gonna keep looking for a while." I asked what was wrong, and he replied, "She likes the Red Sox." I was completely shocked. I couldn't believe how quickly he had moved on. Imagine the Derek of 20 years ago, finding out that this beautiful, charming woman was a real possibility for a date. If she were at a bar and smiled at him, Derek of 1993 would have melted. He wouldn't have walked up and said, "Oh, wait, you like the Red Sox?! No thank you!" before putting his hand in her face and turning away. But Derek of 2013 simply clicked an X on a

web-browser tab and deleted her without thinking twice. Watching him comb through those profiles, it became clear that online,
every bozo could now be a stud.[49]

As Barry Schwartz succinctly concludes, "This is a recipe for
misery." In study after study, Schwartz and others find that the kind
of mindset produced by an abundance of choice leads people to be
less happy with the choices they finally make, even if by objective
standards their choices match what they say they want and need
from a relationship or career.[50]

The inevitable human process of social comparison makes the
paradox of choice even worse, because it often seems that everybody
else has found their dream partner and you haven't. Ansari tells of
going to a friend's wedding and listening to the couple say "the most
remarkable, loving things about each other. Things like 'You are a
prism that takes the light of life and turns it into a rainbow' and
'You are a lotion that moisturizes my heart. Without you, my soul
has eczema.' After the wedding, I found out about four different
couples that had broken up, supposedly because they didn't feel like
they had the love that was expressed in those vows. Did they call it
off too early? I, too, felt scared hearing that stuff. Did I have what
those people had?"[51] And there is the paradox of choice in action:
Unlimited choice leaves us comparing our current choice to a fantasy. And nobody can compete with a fantasy.

The Effects of Praise and Favors

Dale Carnegie advised his readers that a good way to win friends
is to "dole out praise lavishly." This seems like good old-fashioned
common sense, but does it always work? Common sense also suggests that there are situations in which criticism might be more
useful than praise. Suppose you are a brand-new hire at a tech
company and presenting a proposal to your team. One coworker is
nodding and smiling, enraptured by your words, and afterward he
tells you that you are a genius and your ideas are the most brilliant
he's ever heard. It feels good to hear that, of course. In contrast,
another colleague has been shaking her head and scowling during
your presentation, and afterward she tells you that there are several
aspects of your proposal that don't make sense. That evening, while
ruminating on what they said, you realize that the remarks made by

the second person, which you didn't enjoy, did contain some valid points and forced you to rethink a few of your assumptions and improve your proposal. Which of these two people will you like better? It's hard to know, because although praise is clearly rewarding, disagreement that leads to improvement carries other rewards.

Some research shows that a negative evaluation generally increases the admiration we feel for the evaluator, so long as he or she is not evaluating us! In one experiment, Teresa Amabile[52] asked college students to read excerpts from two scholarly reviews of novels. Both reviews were similar in style and quality of writing, but one was extremely favorable and the other extremely unfavorable. Students considered the negative reviewer to be considerably more intelligent, competent, and expert than the positive reviewer—but less likable.

Sometimes the human motive for accuracy and shared understanding wins out over the desire to be liked, appreciated, and showered with praise. We certainly want love and admiration, but just as important, we also want to be known and understood.[53]

If our close friends and romantic partners hew closely to the Dale Carnegie playbook, it may come at a cost of our ability to trust them to be honest with us. If their praise is dissonant with whom we think we are, we may figure they don't really know us—or we may grow suspicious that they are trying to manipulate us.

Perceptions of the reason for praise, therefore, influence how we will respond to the person praising us. Jason Lawrence and his associates[54] had black female college students take a difficult test. Half of the time, the white woman who evaluated the test simply wrote the number correct on the test (12/14); but for the other half, she added the words, "Great job!" Although the praise made the students feel good about their performance, they appeared wary of the evaluator who doled out the praise, rating her as significantly less polite than her counterpart who merely recorded the score. Adding "great job" suggested to them that their evaluator was surprised by their high performance, perhaps reflecting racial bias. The praise functioned as a reward in one sense, but it also seemed to undermine the test-takers' trust in their evaluator.

As you can see, people like to be praised and tend to like the person who is complimenting them, but they also dislike being deceived or condescended to. If the praise is too lavish ("That's the best essay I've ever read in my entire life!"), if it suggests surprise ("Great job—I had no idea you were smart!"), or if it seems that the praiser is being ingratiating for an ulterior motive, then praise can backfire. In an experiment by Edward Jones,[55] participants liked the evaluators who praised them more than those who were negative, but there was a sharp drop in their liking for the evaluators whose praise came with a possible ulterior motive. Thus the old adage "flattery will get you nowhere" is wrong. As Jones put it, "flattery will get you *somewhere*" — but not everywhere.

Favors, like praise, can be considered rewards, and we tend to like people who do us favors — but, as with praise, not if we think those favors come with strings attached. Such strings constitute a threat to the freedom of the receiver.[56] People do not necessarily like gifts if they feel obligated to give something back; and they do not like to receive favors from individuals who are in a position to benefit from them. If you were a teacher, you might enjoy receiving gifts from your students if you felt they did so out of respect or affection or fun; but you will probably feel uncomfortable if a borderline student presented you with an expensive gift just before you were about to grade his or her term paper.

For a starving rat or a starving person, a bowl of dry cereal is a reward, and it is a reward during the day or during the night, in winter or in summer, if offered by a man or by a woman. For a drowning person, a rescue launch is a reward under all circumstances. Such rewards are *trans-situational*. But in most domains of our lives, whether or not praise and favors function as rewards depends on the *specific situation*; sometimes, praisers or favor-doers become less attractive than they would have been had they kept their mouths shut or their hands in their pockets. That's why Dale Carnegie's advice is not always sound. If you want someone to like you, doing them a favor as a technique of ingratiation may not succeed. Instead, you might try to get the other person to do *you* a favor. Recall that, in Chapter 3, I described a phenomenon called the justification of cruelty. If individuals harm another person, they will often attempt to justify their behavior by blaming or denigrating the victim. But the justification process should also work with kind acts. If you do someone a favor, you will try to justify this action by convincing yourself that the recipient of your favor is an attractive, likable, deserving person. In effect, you will say to yourself, "Why in the world did I go to all of this effort (or spend all of this money, or take all that time helping him move) for William? Because Will is a wonderful person — that's why!"

This notion is not new. In 1869, one of the world's greatest novelists, Leo Tolstoy, wrote in his novel *War and Peace*, "We do not love people so much for the good they have done us, as for the good we have done them." A century before Tolstoy's observation, Benjamin Franklin[57] used this strategy as a political ploy, with apparent success. Disturbed by the political opposition and animosity of a member of the Pennsylvania state legislature, Franklin set out to win him over.

> I did not ... aim at gaining his favour by paying any servile respect to him but, after some time, took this other method. Having heard that he had in his library a certain very scarce and curious book I wrote a note to him expressing my desire of perusing that book and requesting he would do me the favour of lending it to me for a few days. He sent it immediately and I returned it in about a week with another note expressing strongly my sense of the favour. When we next met in the House he spoke to me (which he had never done before), and with great civility; and he ever after manifested a readiness to serve me on all occasions, so that we became great friends and our friendship continued to his death. This is another instance of the truth of an old maxim I had learned, which says, "He that has once done you a kindness will be more ready to do you another than he whom you yourself have obliged."

Benjamin Franklin was obviously pleased with the success of his maneuver, but scientists would not be totally convinced, because it is not clear whether his success was because of his get-them-to-do-you a favor strategy or to any one of the many charming aspects of his personality. To know the reason, a well-controlled experiment is necessary. Some 230 years after Franklin borrowed the book, Jon Jecker and David Landy[58] conducted just such an experiment. Students completed a task that enabled them to win a substantial sum of money. After the experiment was over, some participants were approached by the experimenter, who explained that he was using his own funds for the experiment and was running short, which would mean he might be forced to stop the experiment. He asked, "As a special favor to me, would you mind returning the money you won?" Another group of participants was approached by the departmental secretary, who asked them if they would return the money as a special favor to the psychology department's research fund, which was running low. The remaining participants were not asked to return their winnings. Finally, all of the participants filled out a questionnaire, which included an opportunity to state their feelings about the experimenter. Those who had been cajoled into doing a special favor for him liked him best; having done him a favor, they were motivated to see him as a decent, deserving fellow, worthy of their sacrifice.

The Gain-Loss Theory of Attraction

Imagine that you've met your OKCupid contact at a bar and you like each other. You are having an animated conversation. After a while, you excuse yourself to go to the restroom, and when you return, you overhear this person talking about you on the phone. So, naturally, you pause to listen. If you hear yourself described as bright, witty, charming, and hot, my guess is that your liking for this new person will increase. If you hear yourself described as dull, boring, and unsexy, my guess is that your liking will deflate. Hardly surprising, since you've always known that the more good things we hear about ourselves, the better we like the speaker (unless that speaker is trying to con us), and the more bad things we hear about ourselves, the more we dislike the person who says them. Everybody knows that—but it happens to be untrue.

Some years ago, I developed a theory of interpersonal attraction, called the **gain-loss theory**, which makes a different prediction.[59] My theory suggests that *increases* in positive, rewarding behavior from another person have more impact on us than does constantly rewarding behavior from that person. We will like someone whose liking for us increases over time more than good old Fred or Molly, who have always liked us. This will be true even if good old Fred or Molly actually provide more rewards, favors, and praise than the new person does. Similarly, we will dislike someone whose esteem for us *decreases* over time more than Frank or Moira, who have always disliked us. The theory predicts that you will like someone most in a *gain situation* (where the person begins by disliking you and gradually comes to like you more), and you will like the person least in a *loss situation* (where the person begins by liking you and gradually begins to dislike you).

To test my theory, I needed an experimental analogue of the bar. It would be crucial that the participant be absolutely certain that the person evaluating her is totally unaware of being overheard.

(If the participant suspected the evaluator of intentional flattery, the experiment would be toast.) In collaboration with Darwyn Linder,[60] I came up with a believable situation in which, in a relatively brief period, the participant interacts with a preprogrammed confederate, eavesdrops while the confederate evaluates him or her to a third party, engages in another conversation with the confederate, eavesdrops again, converses again, eavesdrops again, and so on, through several pairs of trials. To provide a sensible cover story that would prevent people from becoming suspicious would seem impossible, but we did, with imagination and dogged persistence.

We had four experimental conditions: (1) positive—the successive evaluations of each woman made by the confederate were all highly positive; (2) negative—the successive evaluations were all highly negative; (3) gain—the first few evaluations were negative, but they gradually became more positive, reaching a level equal to the level of the positive evaluations in the positive condition; and (4) loss—the first few evaluations were positive, but they gradually became negative, leveling off at a point equal to the negative evaluations in the negative condition.

The results confirmed our predictions: The women in the gain condition reported in the postexperimental interview that they liked the confederate significantly better than those in the positive condition; the women in the loss condition disliked the confederate more than those in the negative condition. In sum, a single gain has more impact on liking than a set of events that are all positive, and a single loss has more impact than a set of events that are all negative. The philosopher Baruch de Spinoza[61] may have had something like this process in mind when, about 300 years ago, he observed:

> Hatred which is completely vanquished by love passes into love, and love is thereupon greater than if hatred had not preceded it. For he who begins to love a thing which he was wont to hate or regard with pain, from the very fact of loving, feels pleasure. To this pleasure involved in love is added the pleasure arising from aid given to the endeavor to remove the pain involved in hatred.

Two conditions are necessary for the gain-loss effect to be operative. First, it is not just any sequence of positive or negative statements that constitutes a gain or loss; there must be an integrated sequence implying a true change of heart.[62] If you tell me that you think I'm stupid and insincere, and later you tell me that you think

I'm generous and athletic, this does not constitute a gain according to my definition. But if you tell me that you think I'm stupid and insincere but later say that you've changed your mind—that you now believe me to be smart and sincere—this is a true gain because it indicates a reversal, a replacement of a negative attitude with its opposite. Second, the change of heart must be gradual. If, out of the blue, you suddenly tell me that your opinion of me has just changed 180°, I'm likely to react with confusion and suspicion, especially if I see no reason for you to have changed your mind about me. "You thought I was pretty stupid the first three times we met, but now you think I'm brilliant? What exactly do you want from me?" A gradual change makes sense and reassures me, increasing my liking for you.[63]

I would never have imagined that gain-loss theory would end up being used as a seduction technique, but it has. A few years ago, journalist Neil Strauss infiltrated the world of pick-up artists, men who are successful in seducing attractive women despite lacking most of the hallmarks of romantic attraction: confidence, looks, wealth, status, charm, or, in Strauss's case, hair. In his book *The Game*, he detailed the tricks that induce women to overlook these deficits and say yes to men they aren't immediately attracted to. One tactic in particular—negging—caught my eye, because it depends on the gain-loss phenomenon. To *neg* someone means to begin the contact with a mild insult, often in the form of a compliment. (For example, "Wow, those shoes must be comfortable, given how ugly they are.") Theoretically, negging has two effects. First, it distinguishes the speaker from all the other suitors who approach the woman with compliments; this makes him seem interesting. Second, it deals a blow to the woman's self-esteem, which can make her want the insulter's approval, which in turn motivates her to try to get it by spending more time with him. She then feels a warm gratification when she is able to change his apparently low opinion of her into a higher one. It's a devious trick and, according to Strauss, good for starting a conversation with a woman or even getting her to go home with the guy. But is it the basis for a good relationship? I don't think so. Indeed, at the end of Strauss's book, he falls in love with a woman, in part because she responded to none of his tactics.

Precisely. I would argue that relationships that depend on tricks rather than authenticity are bound to fail, a point that Strauss articulated in discussing his aptly named follow-up to *The Game*, which he called *The Truth*: "*The Game* was about being in this power relationship—okay, you're safe because you're in control, you're not being vulnerable." You may feel safe, he adds, but "There's no way you can have intimacy from that."[64]

Communal and Exchange Relationships

Relationships differ in all kinds of ways, ranging in closeness from the Facebook "friend" you've never met in person to a lifelong friend you've known since kindergarten to an intimate life partner; and our behavior in all of these relationships differs accordingly. Suppose you are sharing an apartment with a casual friend we'll call Jackie. Jackie almost never washes the dishes, empties the trash, or straightens up the living room. If you want a clean and orderly house, you usually need to do these things yourself. My guess is that, after a while, you might become upset and feel ripped off. Ah, but suppose Jackie is a very special friend. Would you still feel ripped off? Perhaps, but perhaps not. It depends on what we mean by "very special." And what if Jackie were your life partner?

Margaret Clark and Judson Mills[65] made an important distinction between two fundamentally different types of relationships, *exchange relationships* and *communal relationships*. In **exchange relationships**, the people involved are concerned about reciprocity and making sure that some sort of equity is achieved, that there is fairness in the distribution of the rewards and costs to each of the partners. In this trade-like kind of relationship, if there is a major imbalance, both people become unhappy; the person getting less than they contribute feels angry or depressed, and the person getting more than they contribute usually feels guilty.[66] In contrast, a **communal relationship** is one in which neither of the partners is keeping score. Rather, a person will be inclined to give in response to the other's need and will readily receive the same kind of care when he or she is feeling needy.

Although the partners in a communal relationship are not totally unconcerned about achieving equity in general—it *is* important that both parties feel the relationship is fair, balanced, and reciprocal[67]—they are relaxed about it and have faith that, over the long haul, things will even out. These issues are difficult to study scientifically. Nevertheless, Clark and Mills, along with

David Corcoran,[68] have done some clever experiments that succeeded in capturing the essence of this distinction. In one experiment, each participant was paired with either a very close friend or a stranger. The partner was then taken to another room to work on a complex task. Half of the participants were told that, if their partner needed help, they would signal by flicking a switch that changed the pattern of lights in the participant's room. The other half were told that the signal meant only that their partner was doing well, didn't need any help, and would soon complete the task for a reward that they would both share. The experimenters then observed how frequently the participants looked at the lights to see if their partner was signaling them. If the partner was a stranger (exchange relationship), they spent far more time looking at the lights when they were told that it meant they might be getting a reward; if the partner was a close friend (communal relationship), they spent far more time looking at the lights when they thought it meant their partner might need help. In short, even in this sterile scientific setting, the investigators were able to show that people in communal relationships are eager to respond to the needs of their partners.

The closer and more intimate the relationship—between good friends as well as partners—the more communal it becomes. Clark and Mills suggested that prenuptial agreements, in which people about to be married specify precisely what they expect from their partner in case the relationship fails—and, increasingly, what they expect their partner to do while the relationship exists—are more likely to undermine than enhance the intensity of their feelings for each other. Even in nonromantic friendships, an explicit focus on equity can have a depressing effect on feelings. A friend of mine once met a new acquaintance for dinner, had a wonderful time, and thought to himself that this was the beginning of a beautiful friendship. "When the bill came I began to reach for my wallet, planning to pick up the entire check, thinking, 'We're good friends now, he'll pick up the check next time we meet,'" my friend told me. "But then he starts going over the bill, calculating down to the penny what each of us owed, noting that I had ordered a more expensive drink and that I ate more sushi than he did, and so I owed more than half. It completely ruined the feelings I had for him.'" Someone who counts every little thing they give and every little thing they get back is telling the other person that they want an exchange relationship rather than a communal one.

Love: What Is It and How Does It Happen?

Given all of the factors we have considered in what draws people together, let's turn now to that complex and delicious experience we call love. Given that liking and loving share some of the same major antecedents, does this mean that love is simply a more intense version of liking? Isn't there something special about love?

Just about all love researchers draw a distinction between two basic types of romantic love: passionate and companionate.[69] **Passionate love** is characterized by strong emotions, exhilaration, unquenchable sexual desire, and intense preoccupation with the beloved. Many describe passionate love as literally an altered state of consciousness, like that produced by marijuana or alcohol.[70] The couple is, in fact, on a drug high: The brain is flooded with dopamine, the same neurotransmitter that gets released with cocaine, producing euphoria, restlessness, sleeplessness, and loss of appetite. "Falling in love" provides a rush that is physiologically not much different from eating chocolate and winning the lottery; indeed, when gamblers win or people are imbibing their favorite chocolate, their brains show increased activity in dopamine-rich areas.[71]

Like all drugs, though, the high of passionate love wears off after about a year to 18 months. If the relationship is solid, **companionate love** arises to take its place—a milder, more stable experience marked by feelings of mutual trust, dependability, and warmth. Compared with the typically short-lived intensity of romantic passion, companionate love generally lasts longer and deepens over time. Companionate lovers feel free to talk to each other about anything and feel deeply understood by one another. Thus, if passionate love is like cocaine, then companionate is more like a glass of fine wine—something delicious and pleasurable, but with fewer heart palpitations and less mania.

Although being in a state of romantic love is certainly exciting, you probably don't want to be making decisions with long-range, far-reaching consequences while you're under its influence! Indeed, in his book *The Happiness Hypothesis*, Jonathan Haidt[72] identifies two danger points in every romantic relationship. One is at the peak of the passionate-love phase, when partners in a state of wild excitement dive in headfirst. High on passionate love, wanting to be together every second, they move in together or get married way too quickly. Sometimes these couples are able to transition from the passionate stage to the companionate one. But if, at this crucial moment, they believe that the only real love is the kind defined by obsession, sexual passion, and hot emotion, they may decide they are out of love when the initial phase of attraction fades, as it eventually must—and they will be repeatedly disappointed. Philosopher Robert Solomon[73] argued that, "We conceive of [love] falsely ... We expect an explosion at the beginning powerful enough to fuel love through all of its ups and downs instead of viewing love as a process over which we have control, a process that tends to increase with time rather than wane."

The second danger point, therefore, occurs when passionate love starts wearing off. As couples come down off that initial high, they start noticing the beloved partner's flaws, which somehow they had managed to ignore. They stop sending sexts or passionate texts and just send reminders to feed the cat. Haidt argues that when a couple hits this stage, they should be patient. With luck, if they allow themselves to invest more in the other person, they may find themselves with a truly wonderful life companion. But I think it takes more than luck, and I don't think that companionate love requires a sacrifice of passion. What factors permit a smooth transition from the initial, intense romantic discovery to a passionate, satisfying, and intimate lifelong affair?

To answer that question, let's avoid the self-help books and ads for pheromones and love potions and consider findings from three nonobvious areas of research: the influence of our implicit theories of love; the effects of our ability or inability to become securely attached; and what we can do to compensate for the loss of the initial phase of intense desire.

Implicit Theories of Love When I was a teenager, my friends and I clung to the romantic notion that there was one, and only one, true love with whom we were meant to spend our lives in passionate bliss. (And as I noted earlier, we did not have a way to meet thousands of people on dating apps.) This belief was nourished by the popular songs of the day. So I knew that "some enchanted evening," I would "see a stranger, across a crowded room," and "once I had found her, [I would] never let her go." I could then dance with her, hold her close, and croon in her ear, "I was meant for you, you were meant for me; I'm content, the angels must have sent you, and they meant you just for me."

My friends and I were not unusual in holding that "soul mate" theory of love, the belief that one day the perfect person would come along, the ideal life companion. A lot of young people had that belief then and many have it now. That was our *implicit theory* of love and relationships, and it governed our behavior and how our romances played out. Other couples (and cultures) have different implicit theories: Some think of love as something that deepens over time, that you have to "work out" problems, and that relationships are more about growth and effort than about having a perfect match from the start. This is certainly the assumption behind arranged marriages, where couples assume that love is what develops long after the wedding.[74] As Ansari describes his Indian parents' arranged marriage:

> [My dad] told his parents he was ready to get married, so his family arranged meetings with three neighboring families. The first girl, he said, was "a little too tall," and the second girl was "a little too short." Then he met my mom. He quickly deduced that she was the appropriate height (finally!), and they talked for about 30 minutes. They decided it would work. A week later, they were married.
>
> And they still are, 35 years later. Happily so — and probably more so than most people I know who had nonarranged marriages.

Extensive research finds that Ansari's parents are not unusual;[75] they, like most other couples in arranged marriages, turn out to be as happy as couples who start out in a delirium of romantic passion, with stars in their eyes and lust everywhere else.

It turns out that our implicit theories of love can enhance or hurt our relationships. Spike W.S. Lee and Norbert Schwarz[76] compared soul-mate people who frame love as unity ("We were made for each other," "She's my other half") and work-it-out people who frame love as a journey ("Look how far we've come," "We've been through all these things together"). These two ways of thinking about relationships, they found, affect how partners manage the potentially damaging effect of conflicts. After all, if two people were really made in heaven for each other, if they are "one soul," why should they have any conflicts? And if they do have a conflict, that must mean they aren't one soul after all. In one experiment, Lee and Schwarz had people in long-term relationships complete a knowledge quiz that included expressions related to either unity or journey, then recall either conflicts or celebrations with their romantic partner, and finally evaluate their relationship. As predicted, recalling conflicts led those holding a unity frame of mind to feel less satisfied with their relationship—but for people who saw themselves on a journey together, conflicts did not affect their level of satisfaction.

A longitudinal study by C. Raymond Knee[77] found that the link between satisfaction and length of time together was stronger for those who believe in romantic destiny, but it was also associated with avoidance strategies in coping with stressors. "Destiny" relationships are happiest on smooth seas, but when a storm rises up, their love boat founders. These couples find it difficult to remain satisfied in the relationship when, as inevitably happens, their partner no longer meets their ideal standards. In contrast, couples who hold an implicit theory about love as growth put more effort into coping strategies. Over time, they remain more satisfied, even when they report that their partner no longer meets their original ideal. They *expect* their partner to evolve and change over time, and they have a better sense of the temporary nature of relationship slumps. For "let's work it out" couples, conflicts have no connection to their assessment of the relationship's quality; on the contrary, they are motivated to discuss problems with their partner and repair any fraying seams in their connection.

Secure Attachment Once you find someone to love, do you feel happy and secure, or do you begin worrying immediately that the beloved will abandon you at Starbuck's? According to Phillip Shaver, Cindy Hazan, and Mario Mikulincer,[78] adults can be secure, anxious, or avoidant in their attachments. *Securely attached* lovers are rarely jealous or worried about being rejected. They are more compassionate and helpful than insecurely attached people and are quicker to understand and forgive their partners if the partner does something thoughtless or annoying. *Anxious* lovers are always agitated about their relationships; they want to be close but worry that their partners will leave them. Other people often describe them as "clingy," which may be why they are more likely than secure lovers to complain that they suffer from unrequited love. *Avoidant* people distrust and often avoid intimate attachments altogether. If they are in a relationship, they tend to be distant, signaling the partner to keep away, precisely when intimacy would help them the most, such as after an injury, setback, or failure at work.[79]

According to the attachment theory of love, people's characteristic attachment styles derive in part from how their parents cared for them.[80] In their earliest years, children form internal "working models" of relationships: Can I trust others? Am I worthy of being loved? Will my parents leave me? If a child's parents are cold and rejecting and provide little or no emotional and physical comfort, the child learns to expect other relationships to be the same. In contrast, if children form secure, trusting attachments with their parents, they become more trusting of others, expecting to form other secure attachments with friends and lovers in adulthood.[81] However, a child's own temperament and genetic predispositions could also help account for the consistency of attachment styles from childhood to adulthood, as well as for the working models of relationships that are formed during childhood.[82] A child who is temperamentally fearful or difficult may reject even the kindest parent's efforts to console. That child may therefore come to feel anxious or ambivalent in his or her adult relationships.

The Minnesota Longitudinal Study of Risk and Adaptation[83] has followed a large sample of children from birth to adulthood, to see how early attachment styles can create cascading effects on adult relationships. Children who are treated poorly and lack secure attachments may end up on a pathway that makes committed relationships difficult. As children, they have trouble regulating negative emotions; as teenagers, they have trouble dealing with and recovering from conflict with their peers; as adults, they tend to "protect" themselves by becoming the less-committed partner in their relationships. In doing so, they create—as by now you can predict—their own self-fulfilling prophecy: I'm insecure, so I doubt you really love me, so I don't notice how many kind and supportive things you do for me, and since you aren't doing kind and supportive things for me, I must be right that you don't love me.[84] Insecurely attached individuals are skeptical of genuine compliments and tend to lash out in response to minor transgressions. Over time, their partners often become weary of offering repeated reassurances that aren't heard. Through these self-fulfilling dynamics, fear of rejection elevates the chances of actually being rejected, which in turn reinforces the view that the person isn't worthy of love.

All is not bleak for insecurely attached adults, however. If they are lucky enough to get into a relationship with a securely attached partner, their vulnerabilities in maintaining a stable partnership can be overcome.[85] Eli Finkel, a psychologist who has been studying close relationships for many years, tells this story about his own avoidant attachment style:

> Although Alison certainly didn't ask for a husband with avoidant tendencies, she's had to adapt. She's securely attached, so her natural impulse when someone she loves is hurting is to approach and nurture. Over the years, she's learned to do the opposite with me—to give me space and let me heal myself. These days, if I double over in pain because I've slammed my fingers in a door or am unusually quiet following a setback at work, she keeps her distance. In our early years together, my fierce independence under duress hurt her, but she's slowly learned that it has nothing to do with her. One metric of how much she understands and loves me is her willingness to let me recover on my own in those situations. Her ability to do so has also made me less avoidant over time. Her willingness to give me space when I need it has made me less defensive about protecting my independence.[86]

Finkel went on to do research with Ximena Arriaga and others,[87] in which they found that the ability to trust the partner—"to have faith that he or she will treat us, when we're vulnerable, in a way that's sensitive to our needs"—predicts a reduction in avoidant tendencies over time. Finkel's example, supported by research, shows that it is a great idea for insecure individuals to find a partner with a history of secure attachments, but, as we will see, that is not the only remedy for them.

The Porcupine's Dilemma Compared with the ups and downs of a passionate love affair, the steadier, predictable rhythm of a companionate relationship offers its own special rewards. The benefits of a thriving, long-term relationship include emotional security and the priceless comfort of being accepted by someone who knows your shortcomings, as well as your strengths.

In addition to these enormous benefits, however, there is a potential dark side to being in a long-term, close relationship.[88] The fundamental irony is aptly expressed in the words of the classic ballad "You Always Hurt the One You Love." Why might this be so? Recall from our earlier discussion of gain-loss theory the rather surprising fact that we find it more rewarding when someone's initially negative feelings toward us gradually become positive than if that person's feelings for us were entirely positive all along.

Conversely, we tend to find it more noxious when a person who once evaluated us positively slowly comes to view us in a negative light than if he or she expressed uniformly negative feelings toward us from the beginning.

This process suggests that once we have grown certain of the rewarding behavior of our long-term partner, that person may become less effective as a source of reward than a stranger. We know that gains are important, but a long-term lover or spouse is probably behaving near ceiling level and, therefore, cannot provide us with much of a gain. But a loved one has great potential to hurt us, by withdrawing support, appreciation, and other rewards. The closer the relationship and the greater the past history of invariant esteem and reward, the more devastating is their withdrawal. In effect, then, the long-term lover has more power to inflict loss than to provide additional gain, thereby hurting the one he or she loves.

Consider the Dotings, a couple married for 20 years. As they dress to go out to dinner with friends, he compliments her on her appearance: "Hey, you look great." She hears his words, which are nice but don't exactly fill her with delight. She already knows her husband thinks she's attractive; chances are she will not turn cartwheels at hearing it for the thousandth time. On the other hand, if the doting husband (who in the past was always full of compliments) told his wife that he was starting to find her unattractive, she would feel seriously hurt because his comment represents a loss in his positive feelings about her. So he stops complimenting her, and she starts feeling ignored. Fortunately, other people in the world might offer her compliments that make her feel good about herself—and who thereby increase her positive feelings about them. O.J. Harvey[89] found that people react more positively to compliments from strangers than to compliments from friends, and why not? Approval from a stranger is a gain and, according to gain-loss theory, makes us feel better.

These results suggest a rather bleak picture of the human condition; we seem to be forever seeking favor in the eyes of strangers while being hurt or let down by familiarity with our most intimate friends and lovers. The solution, as the Roman politician Cicero suggested far back as 46 BCE, is to turn those losses and hurt feelings into exciting gains and new understandings. How?

The first thing a couple has to do is resolve the *porcupine's dilemma*: the desire to achieve deep intimacy while remaining invulnerable to hurt. The term comes from the philosopher Arthur Schopenhauer's famous parable:

> On a cold winter day, a group of porcupines huddled together closely to save themselves by their mutual warmth from freezing. But soon they felt the mutual quills and drew apart. Whenever the need for warmth brought them closer together again, this second evil was repeated, so that they were tossed back and forth between these two kinds of suffering until they discovered a moderate distance that proved tolerable ... To be sure, this only permits imperfect satisfaction of the need for mutual warmth, but it also keeps one from feeling the prick of the quills.[90]

Psychologists have investigated the ways that people try to achieve a solution that satisfies the need for intimacy and also the need for security.[91] We want to feel that our partner truly and deeply understands and accepts us—and know this without fearing we will be rejected or abandoned if they "really" did understand our deepest, meanest flaws and mistakes. People who are insecurely attached will have a special difficulty finding that balance. So will spouses who have low self-esteem and who are highly sensitive to rejection, and thus feel they are unworthy of love. Sandra Murray and John Holmes[92] have found that because such individuals fear rejection, they tend to place self-protection over self-revelation; they put up their quills, and thus lose the warmth of connection they would dearly love to have.

Living with another person requires innumerable sacrifices and compromises, from what movie to see to how you'll raise your children. When an event arises that could cause discord, our perceptions of our partner's regard for us influence how we respond: back away and protect our self-interest or admit vulnerability and pursue connection? Couples must choose between taking a riskier but more honest path that deepens the bond with their partner—and provides many new emotional *gains*—or taking a path that protects them from further harm—but increases the likelihood of further *losses*. In relationships, as with many things in life, more risk equals more potential reward.[93]

Although Mr. Doting has great power to hurt his wife by criticizing her, because of the importance of their relationship, she is apt to listen closely and be responsive to such criticism and will be inclined to make some changes to regain his interest. The reverse is also true: If Ms. Doting were to suddenly change her high opinion of Mr. Doting, he would be likely to pay close attention and eventually take action to regain her approval. A relationship becomes truly creative and continues to grow when both partners resolve conflicts not by papering them over, as couples with a soul-mate theory of love tend to do, but by striving to grow and change in creative ways. In this process, **authenticity**—the freedom to share your true feelings and beliefs (even negative ones) with your partner—is the key to avoiding a descent into deadening stagnation. It reduces the likelihood of a relationship ending up on a bleak plateau, like the one the Dotings are headed for. When people suppress their annoyances and keep their negative feelings and true opinions to themselves, they often end up on a fragile plateau that appears stable and positive but that can be devastated by a sudden shift in sentiment.

Couples in an authentic relationship don't reach that flat plateau. Rather, there is a continuous zigzagging of sentiment around a point of relatively high mutual regard. In a relationship of this sort, the partners are reasonably close to the gain condition of the gain-loss experiment. An exchange of intimate aspects of *oneself*, both positive and negative, is required. In general, we like a person better after we have disclosed something important about ourselves—even if it is unsavory—and when they honor us by revealing something intimate and negative about themselves.[94]

An essential factor in maintaining love is the belief that our partners understand and support us; they trust us, care about us, feel secure with us, know what's important to us, will actively help us meet our needs, and, most centrally, know who we are at our core. That is what allows us not only to love the other, but also to feel loved in return, in a way that connects us to our partners even when they're not with us. This bedrock feeling of being understood predicts feelings of well-being, security, and adjustment better than practical behavioral indicators, such as who is doing what around the house.[95]

People who support each other in times of need and stress are more likely to have a healthy relationship than people who don't. But how about when things go right? It turns out that a strong predictor of happiness in a close relationship is not only the ability of each partner to be there for the other in times of trouble, but also in times of success. Shelley Gable and her associates[96] found that people who received positive responses from their romantic partners when they were describing a recent triumph ("What fantastic news! I knew you could do it! Let's go celebrate immediately!") were happier with their relationship several months later than those who received less enthusiastic responses ("Nice job, honey. What's for dinner?"). And this makes sense. In many relationships a partner's triumph can bring mixed emotions; the joy can be tinged with envy. Gable's research suggests that couples are happiest when whatever envy there might be is far overshadowed by the joy.

To summarize, the data indicate that, as a relationship moves toward greater intimacy, what becomes increasingly important for continued passion, commitment, and growth is authenticity: our ability to give up trying to make a good impression and begin to reveal things about ourselves and about the relationship that are honest, even if unpleasant. Authenticity implies a willingness to communicate a wide range of feelings to our friends and loved ones, under appropriate circumstances, and in ways that reflect our caring.

Intimacy, Authenticity, and Communication

Although honest communication with loved ones has beneficial effects, the process is not as easy as it might sound. As I said, honest communication entails sharing negative feelings and unappetizing aspects of ourselves that increase our vulnerability. And it entails telling the other person truthfully that you are unhappy or angry about something—something in your relationship, in their behavior, or to do with an ongoing problem. Marriage partners who use an intimate, nonaggressive, yet direct method of conflict resolution report higher levels of marital satisfaction.[97] Easier said than done, though.

John Gottman has been studying married couples for many years, following them over time to see whether he would be able to predict which marriages would last and which would crumble. As it turned out, he could.[98] In particular, he identified four destructive, but entirely too common, forms of communication that are strong indicators that a marriage will fail.

1. Hostile criticism, in which each blames the other in angry "you always" or "you never" terms. "You are always late! And you never listen to me!" "No I'm not! And I do too!" The partner will feel under attack and respond defensively; neither side feels heard or validated.

2. Defensiveness, in which the recipient of a criticism replies with a counter-complaint instead of trying to hear the other person's real concern. "Late? Late? You're the one who is obsessive about getting places two days early!"

3. Contempt, the most devastating sign, in which one partner mocks the other with ugly names, sneers in disgust, or uses belittling and demeaning language and nonverbal gestures. Clinical psychologist Julie Gottman worked with an angry couple in therapy. When she asked, "How did the two of you meet?" the wife said, her voice dripping with contempt, "At school, where I mistakenly thought he was smart."[99]

4. Stonewalling, in which the listener simply withdraws, refusing to talk or even stay in the same room.

In the discussion that follows, I want to propose an alternative to this fruitless and usually endless style of arguing. Imagine, if you will, the following scenario: Phil and Alice are washing the dishes. They have had several friends over for dinner, the friends have left, and Phil and Alice are cleaning up. During the evening, Alice was her usual charming, witty, vivacious self. But Phil, who is usually delighted by her charm, is feeling hurt and a little angry. It seems that, during a political discussion, Alice had disagreed with his position and sided with Tom. Moreover, she seemed to express a great deal of warmth toward Tom in the course of the evening. In fact, her behavior was flirtatious.

Phil is thinking, "I love her so much. I wish she wouldn't do things like that. Maybe she's losing interest in me. God, if she ever left me, I don't know what I'd do. Is she really attracted to Tom?" But Phil is reluctant to share his vulnerability, so he says, "You sure were throwing yourself at Tom tonight. Everybody noticed it. You really made a fool of yourself."

Alice loves Phil. She felt that she had said some very bright things that evening—especially during the political discussion—and felt that Phil didn't acknowledge her intellectual contribution. "He thinks I'm just an uninteresting housewife. He is probably bored with me." The following conversation ensues:

Alice: I don't know what you're talking about. You're just mad because I happened to disagree with you about the president's tax proposal. Tom saw it my way. I think I was right.

Phil: He saw it your way! Are you kidding? What else could he do? You were practically sitting in his lap. The other guests were embarrassed.

Alice (teasing): Why, Phil, I do believe you're jealous!

Phil: I'm not jealous! I really don't give a damn. If you want to act like a slut, that's your business.

Alice (angrily): Boy, are you old-fashioned. You're talking like some Victorian, for God's sake! You're always doing that!

Phil (coldly): That just shows how little you know about me. I'm more of a feminist than you are. The women I work with think I'm great.

Alice (sarcastically): Yeah, I'm sure all the women at your office really are hot for you.

Phil: Now, what's *that* supposed to mean?

Alice falls into a stony silence. Phil makes several attempts to get a response from her, fails, and then storms out of the room, slamming the door. What is going on? Here are two people who love each other. How did they get into such a vicious, wounding argument?

One of the major characteristics that separate humans from other organisms is our ability to communicate complex information. Our language gives us truly awesome powers of conversation, yet misunderstandings are frequent, even in relationships that are close and caring. Though hypothetical, the argument I wrote between Phil and Alice is not unrealistic; rather, it is typical of hundreds of such conversations I have heard as a consultant trying to help couples straighten out their garbled, indirect, and misleading ways of talking to each other.

Phil and Alice each had a major concern, but neither was able or willing to state it in a straightforward way. For Alice, the major concern was her intellectual competence. She was afraid Phil thought she was dumb or boring; her *implicit* complaint in this argument was that Phil didn't acknowledge the cogency of her statements during the political discussion, and he seemed to be implying that the only reason Tom paid attention to her was sexual attraction. As a result, Phil's comments hurt her, threatened her self-esteem, and made her angry. She didn't express the hurt, however. Alice expressed the anger, but not by revealing it; rather, she took the offensive and attacked Phil by implying that he is stodgy and uninteresting.

Phil's major concern stemmed from a different feeling of insecurity. Although he enjoys Alice's vivacity, he is afraid of the possibility that, with increasing age, he is losing his own sexual attractiveness. Thus, he assumed that Alice's agreeing with Tom politically was akin to her siding with Tom against him — and he attached sexual connotations to it because of his own insecurities. When Alice called him "old-fashioned," he seemed mostly to hear the "old," and he quickly defended his masculinity and sex appeal, which Alice, driven by her own anger, promptly ridiculed.

This kind of argument is familiar among people living together. Both sides have feelings and concerns, but instead of discussing them openly — and identifying them correctly — the feelings are allowed to escalate into hostility, which only exacerbates the hurt and insecurity that initiated the discussion in the first place. It would be silly to proclaim that all anger, disagreement, hurt, and hostility between people who supposedly care about each other are functions of poor or inadequate communication. Often, people in close relationships have different needs, values, desires, and goals, about work, money, children, sex, household chores, which values to live by, and countless other issues. These natural differences produce stresses and tensions, which must either be lived with or resolved by compromise, yielding, or the dissolution of the relationship. But frequently the problem is miscommunication. How might Phil and Alice have communicated differently?

Pretend for the moment that you are Phil. And Alice, a person you love, approaches you and makes the following statement in a tone of voice that is nonblaming and nonjudgmental:

> Sweetheart, let me explain. I'm feeling insecure about my intelligence, or at least the way people view me on that, because I don't have all the degrees that you do. Since you are the most important person in my world, I would be so gratified if you would acknowledge something I say that you think is smart and worthwhile. When we disagree on a substantive issue and you speak harshly or dismiss my points or become impatient with me, I feel insecure and disrespected. Earlier this evening, during our political discussion, I would have felt so good if you had complimented me on some of my ideas and willingness to speak up.

Imagine, now, that you are Alice, and Phil had opened the after-dinner discussion in the following way.

> Look, honey, this is difficult for me to talk about, but I'd like to try. I don't know what it is with me lately, but I was feeling some jealousy tonight. This isn't easy to say, but here goes: You and Tom seemed kind of close—both intellectually and physically—and I was feeling hurt and lonely. You may not realize this, but I've been slowing down, feeling tired, developing a paunch. I need some reassurance. Do you still find me good looking? I would love it if you'd look at me the way you seemed to be looking at Tom this evening.

My guess is that most people would be receptive and responsive to that kind of **straight talk** from a loved one. By straight talk, I mean a person's clear statement of his or her feelings and concerns without accusing, blaming, judging, or ridiculing the other person. Straight talk is effective precisely because it enables the recipient to listen nondefensively.

Straight talk seems easy, and it is effective. Why don't people use it more often? Growing up in a competitive society, most of us have learned how to protect ourselves by making ourselves relatively invulnerable—those quills again. Thus, when we are hurt, we have learned not to show it. Rather, we have learned either to avoid the person who hurt us or to lash out at him or her with anger, judgment, or ridicule, which in turn, as Gottman observed, makes the other person defensive or produces a counterattack, and the argument escalates.

Moreover, when we are busy criticizing, we often fail to give the other person *the benefit of the doubt*. As we have seen, a person's judgments about another person can take the form of dispositional attributions (attributing the cause of that person's behavior to a flaw in their personalities) or to situational attributions (attributing the cause to something going on at work or in other outside circumstances). When you don't know why your best friend or life partner is behaving in a weird or unpleasant way or hasn't gotten back to you when they said they would, you have a choice: You can jump to a hostile, dispositional attribution ("She's being thoughtless again!" "He's a selfish pig!"), or you can wait to find out why they are behaving that way and give them the benefit of the doubt with a situational attribution ("She's under stress"; "I hope his mom isn't sick again"). Frank Fincham and Thomas Bradbury[100] studied

130 newly married couples over time and found that those couples who made dispositional attributions early in their marriages became increasingly unhappy with their spouses. In contrast, couples who engaged in straight talk and made situational attributions became increasingly happy with their marriages.

It is unwise to reveal your vulnerability to someone who is your sworn enemy and will use that knowledge against you. But it is almost certainly unwise to conceal your vulnerability from someone who is your loving friend and cares about you. If Alice and Phil had been aware of the other's insecurity, they each could have acted in ways that would have reassured the other. Because each of them had overlearned the societal lesson of "attack rather than reveal," they inadvertently placed themselves on a collision course.

Often, the problem is even more complicated than the one in this example. Alice and Phil know what their feelings are, and they got into serious conflict primarily because they had difficulty communicating them. But often, people are not fully aware of their own needs, wants, and feelings. Instead, they may have a vague feeling of discomfort or unhappiness that they can't easily pinpoint. Often they misattribute that vague feeling; at first, Phil blames Alice for her allegedly flirtatious behavior when he is really feeling insecure about his advancing middle age. Thus, if we are not in touch with our own feelings and cannot articulate them to ourselves, we cannot communicate them to anyone else. The key issue is sensitivity. Can we learn to be more sensitive to our own feelings? Can we learn to be sensitive to others so that, when people do make themselves vulnerable, we treat that vulnerability with care and respect?

The Importance of Immediate Feedback For communication to be effective in a close relationship, we are able to give and receive immediate feedback on how our words and behaviors are interpreted. This give us the information we need to gain insight into the impact of our actions and statements and to consider our options for meeting our own needs, as well as our partner's.

Suppose I do something that angers my best friend, who also happens to be my wife. If she doesn't express this anger, I may never become aware that what I did made her angry. Suppose she gives me immediate feedback; suppose she tells me how my action makes her feel. Now I have at least two options: I can continue to behave in the same way, and continue to make her angry, or I can stop behaving that way. The choice is mine. What I've done may be so important to me that I don't want to give it up. Conversely, my wife's feelings may be so important to me that I choose to stop doing the thing that angers her. In the absence of any knowledge of how my behavior makes her feel, I don't have a choice. Moreover, knowing exactly how she feels about a particular action may allow me to explore a different way of satisfying my needs as well as hers.

The value of immediate feedback is not limited to the recipient. Frequently, in providing feedback, people discover something about themselves. If Sharon believes, for example, that it's always destructive to express anger in any way, she may block out her awareness of this feeling. When she learns that it is legitimate for her to express that feeling, she has a chance to bring it out in the open, look at it, and become aware that her expression of anger has not caused the world to come to an end. Moreover, the direct expression of a feeling helps prevent its escalation that is harder to resolve. If my wife has learned to express her anger not by shouting or accusing but by stating her feelings and grievances directly, it keeps our discussion on the issue at hand. If she suppresses the anger but it leaks out in other ways—at different times and in different situations, or if she withdraws and seems sullen—I do not know where her hostility is coming from, and I become confused, hurt, or angry.

Feelings Versus Judgments People are often unaware of how to provide constructive feedback, instead doing it in a way that angers or upsets the recipient, thereby causing more problems than they solve. Let me offer an example of dysfunctional feedback and then show how people can learn to modify it (without diluting its content) to maximize communication and understanding. This example is an actual event that took place in a communication workshop I conducted for corporation executives.

In the course of the workshop, one of the members (Mike) looked squarely at another member (Dave) and said, "Dave, I've been listening to you and watching you for a day and a half, and I want to give you some feedback: I think you're a phony."

Now, that's quite an accusation. How can Dave respond? He has several options: He can (1) agree with Mike; (2) deny the accusation and say he's not a phony; (3) express anger by retaliating, telling Mike what he thinks is wrong with *him*; or (4) feel sorry for himself and go into a sulk. None of these responses is particularly productive.

But doesn't Mike have the right to express this judgment? After all, he's only being open and honest. Don't we value openness and authenticity?

This sounds like a dilemma. Effective communication requires openness, but openness can be hurtful to the recipient. The solution is to be open and, at the same time, to express yourself in a manner that causes a minimum of pain and maximizes the recipient's ability to understand your complaint. The key to effective communication rests on our willingness to express *feelings* rather than judgments. In this instance Mike was not expressing a feeling; he was interpreting Dave's behavior and judging it. The word feeling has several meanings. In this context I don't mean "hunch" or "hypothesis," as when we say "I feel I'm right." By feeling I mean, specifically, anger or joy, sadness or happiness, annoyance, fear, discomfort, warmth, hurt, envy, jealousy, excitement, and the like.

In the workshop, I began my intervention by asking Mike if he had any feelings about Dave. Mike thought for a moment and then said, "Well, I feel that Dave is a phony." Needless to say, this is not a feeling, as I just defined it; this is an opinion or a judgment expressed in the language of feelings. A judgment is nothing more or less than a feeling that is inadequately understood or inadequately expressed. Accordingly, I probed further by asking Mike what his feelings were. Mike still insisted that he felt Dave was a phony.

"And what does that do to you?" I asked.

"It annoys the hell out of me," answered Mike.

"What kinds of things has Dave done that annoyed you?" I asked.

"I'm annoyed by his phony way of charming people in the group," he replied.

On further probing, it turned out that what really annoyed Mike was Dave's apparent attractiveness to women. Eventually Mike owned up to his real feeling of envy; he wished he had Dave's easy charm and popularity.

Note that Mike had initially masked this feeling of envy; instead, he had discharged his feelings by expressing disdain, by saying Dave was a phony. He was protecting his ego. Because we live in a competitive society, Mike had learned over the years that, if he had admitted to feeling envious, it might make him look vulnerable and weak. By expressing disdain and anger, however, Mike was trying to portray himself as strong and assertive.

Although his behavior was successful as an ego-protecting device, it didn't contribute to Mike's understanding of his own feelings and of the events that caused them. It certainly didn't contribute to Mike's understanding of Dave or to Dave's understanding of Mike. As an ego-defensive measure, Mike's behavior was adaptive; as a form of communication, it was maladaptive. Although it made Mike vulnerable to admit the truth, that he envied Dave, that admission opened the door to better communication and mutual understanding.

It's easier for all of us to hear feedback that is expressed in terms of feelings—"I'm upset"—than feedback expressed as a judgment or accusation—"You are a thoughtless jerk!" When Mike told Dave he was a phony, Mike was telling Dave what kind of person he (Dave) is. Generally, people resent being told what kind of person they are—and for good reason, because such attributions are purely a matter of conjecture. Mike's dispositional attribution about Dave's behavior may reflect reality or, just as likely, it may not; it is merely Mike's theory about Dave. Only Dave knows for sure whether he's an insincere phony; Mike is only guessing. But Mike's statement that he is feeling envious or angry is not a guess or a theory; it is an absolute fact. Mike is not guessing about his own feelings—he knows them. Dave may or may not care about Mike's judgments, but if he wants to be Mike's friend, he might want to know Mike's feelings and what he (Dave) did to trigger them. And now Dave has a choice: He can modify his behavior or he can keep doing what he does, while recognizing that his behavior might evoke envy, hostility, and competitiveness from other men.

Mike and Dave were not lovers. They were merely two guys in a workshop, trying to improve their communication skills. When people learn to express their feelings without judging the other person as being wrong, insensitive, or uncaring, escalation rarely follows. Effective communication is useful for everyone, but especially crucial in maintaining our closest, most important connections, with family members, friends, and romantic partners.

Social scientists and historians who have studied the past and future of marriage have identified aspects of modern relationships that are better than ever before, and also aspects that are worse than ever before.[101] In the past, marriages were less about love and more about business arrangements, uniting families, combining resources, or producing children to run the farm. Today's marriages of love are surely better in many ways. Gender roles have become more egalitarian and flexible, and the division of family labor is much less stereotyped; the Annie Oakleys of the world need not give up their talents and ambitions for love, and the Frank Butlers of the world need not cling to notions of male dominance and assert their rights over those of their partner. But modern marriages, precisely because they are based on love and equality and not a business arrangement, are also often freighted with a heavy load of expectations and responsibilities: We expect a life partner to provide companionship, sex, passion, help with child-rearing and chores, income, adventure, freedom, and self-expression. I'm persuaded that those who can peel away the unrealistic expectations of modern love, while keeping their eyes on the enduring benefits of intimacy and connection, can achieve lasting love and a better marriage or relationship than at any other time in human history. Perhaps the Beatles said it best in their song "The End":

> And in the end
> the love you take
> is equal to the love
> you make.

Saul Steinberg, *Untitled drawing*, ink on paper.
Originally published in *The New Yorker*, September 10, 1960.
© The Saul Steinberg Foundation / Artists Rights Society (ARS), New York

Social Psychology as a Science

9

When I was in college, I first got interested in social psychology because it dealt with some of the most exciting aspects of being human: love, hate, prejudice, aggression, altruism, social influence, conformity, and the like. At that time, I didn't care a great deal about how this impressive body of knowledge came into existence. I simply wanted to know what was known. It wasn't until I entered graduate school that it suddenly dawned on me that I could be more than a consumer of this knowledge—I could become a producer, as well. And a whole new world opened up for me: the world of scientific social psychology. I learned how to ask significant questions and do the experiments to find the answers to those questions, contributing, in my own small way, to the body of knowledge that I had read about as a student. And I have been passionately involved in that activity ever since.

Reading this chapter is not going to make you into a scientist. My intention for you is a bit less ambitious but no less important. My aim is to help you improve your ability to think scientifically about things that are happening in your own social world. I have always found this a useful thing to be able to do, but occasionally it can be disillusioning as well. Several years ago, I picked up a copy of *The New Yorker*, in which I read an excellent, highly informative essay by James Kunen[1] about college-level educational programs in our prisons. Kunen wrote enthusiastically about their effectiveness. He then went on to decry the fact that a generally punitive congressional majority was eliminating these programs after characterizing them as wasteful and coddling criminals.

Kunen's essay contained a few vivid case histories of convicts who, while in prison, completed the college program and went on to lead productive lives after being released. The case histories were heartwarming. But, as a scientist, I wanted to know if there were any systematic data that I might use to evaluate the overall effectiveness of the program. Well, yes—Kunen reported one study by the New York State Department of Correctional Services, which found that four years after their release from prison, the recidivism rate of male inmates who had completed one or more years of higher education in prison was 20 percent lower than the average for all male inmates.

That sounds pretty impressive, right? Let's take a closer look. As scientists we need to ask one basic and vital question: Prior to participating in the program, were the prisoners who signed up for the program similar to those who didn't sign up? Might it be the case that the prisoners who signed up for the program and completed a year of it were different to begin with (say, in motivation, ability, intelligence, prior education, mental health, or what have you) from those who did not sign up? If they were different *at the outset* from the general run of prisoners, then it is likely (or, at least, possible) that they would have had a lower rate of recidivism even without having taken the course of study. If that were the case, then it wasn't the program that caused the lower recidivism.

While I was reading Kunen's article, the humanist in me wanted to get excited by the results of this study; it would be terrific to have convincing data proving that educating prisoners pays off. But, alas, the scientist in me took over and was skeptical. Thus, looking at the social world through the eyes of a scientist requires us to face our biases and preferences. But it also gives us the ability to separate the wheat from the chaff so that, as concerned citizens, we can demand that innovative programs be properly evaluated. In that way, we can determine, with some degree of clarity, which of thousands of possible programs are worthy of our time, effort, and money. And the truth is that, in most cases, it is not difficult to do the experiment properly—as you will see.

What Is the Scientific Method?

The scientific method—regardless of whether it is being applied in physics, chemistry, biology, or social psychology—is the best way we humans have of satisfying our hunger for knowledge and understanding. We use the scientific method in an attempt to uncover lawful relationships among things, whether the things are chemicals, planets, or the antecedents of human prejudice or love.

The first step in the scientific process is observation. In physics, a simple observation might go something like this: If there is a rubber ball in my granddaughter's wagon and she pulls the wagon forward, the ball seems to roll to the back of the wagon. (It doesn't actually roll backward; it only seems that way.) When she stops the wagon abruptly, the ball rushes to the front of the wagon. In social psychology, a simple observation might go something like this: When I am waiting on tables, if I happen to be in a good mood and smile a lot at my customers, my tips seem to be a bit larger than when I am in a foul mood and smile less frequently.

The next step is to make a guess as to why that happens; this guess is our taking a stab at uncovering the "lawful relationship" I mentioned. The third step is to frame that guess as a testable hypothesis. The final step is to design an experiment (or a series of experiments) that will either confirm or disconfirm the hypothesis. If a series of well-designed, well-executed experiments fails to confirm that hypothesis, we give it up. As my favorite physicist, Richard Feynman,[2] once put it, "It doesn't matter how beautiful the guess is or how smart the guesser is, or how famous the guesser is; if the experiment disagrees with the guess, then the guess is wrong. That's all there is to it." In my own opinion, this is both the essence of science and its beauty. There are no sacred truths in science.

Science and Art   In my opinion, there is plenty of room for art in our science. I believe that the two processes—art and science—are different but related. Pavel Semonov,[3] a distinguished Russian psychologist, did a pretty good job of defining the difference: As scientists, we look closely at our environment and try to organize the unknown in a sensible and meaningful way; as artists, we reorganize the known environment to create something entirely new. To this observation, I would add that the requirements of a good experiment frequently require skills from both of these domains. In a very real sense, as experimenters, we use artistry to enrich our science. I believe this to be particularly true of experiments in social psychology.

Why is this blending of art and science especially true of social psychology? In social psychology, we are not studying the behavior of chemicals in a beaker or of rubber balls in wagons; we are investigating the behavior of adults who have been living in a social world for their entire lives, with all the emotions, perceptions, beliefs, biases, and experiences they bring to that world. It goes without saying that, like the experimenters who are studying them, the people who serve as participants in our experiments have developed their own ideas and theories about what causes their feelings and behavior, as well as the feelings and behavior of the people around them. This is not the case when you are performing experiments with chemicals, with laboratory animals, or even with humans in nonsocial situations.

The fact that we are dealing with socially sophisticated human beings is part of what makes social psychology so fascinating as a topic of experimental investigation. At the same time, this situation also demands a great deal of art if the experimenter stands a chance of generating valid and reliable findings. In this chapter, I will try to communicate exactly how this happens.

From Speculation to Experimentation

In Chapter 8, I told the story of President John F. Kennedy, whose popularity increased immediately after he committed a stupendously costly blunder. After his tragic miscalculation known as the Bay of Pigs fiasco, a Gallup poll showed that people liked him better than they had prior to that incident. Like most people, I was dumbfounded by this event. How could we like a guy better after he screwed up so badly? As a scientist, I speculated about what could have caused that shift. My guess was that, because Kennedy previously had been perceived as a nearly perfect man—handsome, warm, charming, witty, competent—committing a blunder might have made him seem more human, thus allowing ordinary people to feel closer to him.

An interesting speculation, but was it true? How might we have tried to find out? Well, we might have simply asked people why they liked Kennedy more now than they did the prior week. That sounds simple enough. Unfortunately, it is not that easy, because social psychologists have learned that people are often unaware of why they act in certain ways or change their beliefs in one direction or another; so, in a complex situation, simply asking people to explain their behavior will usually not yield reliable results.[4] This is precisely why social psychologists perform experiments. But how could we conduct an experiment on John F. Kennedy's popularity? We couldn't. In a case like this, we would try to conduct an experiment on the underlying phenomenon, not on the specific example of it. And, indeed, it was really the underlying phenomenon — not the specific event — that interested me: Does committing a blunder increase the popularity of a nearly perfect person?

My colleagues and I[5] thus designed an experiment that allowed us to control for extraneous variables and test the effects of a blunder on attraction in a less complex situation, one in which we could control the exact nature of the blunder, as well as the kind of person who committed it. And in that simple situation we found, as predicted, that "nearly perfect" people become more attractive after they commit a blunder, while "rather ordinary" people become less attractive after committing the identical blunder. (I described the details of this experiment in Chapter 8.)

As you see, in striving for control, the experimenter must bring his or her ideas out of the helter-skelter of the real world and into the rather sterile confines of the laboratory. This typically entails concocting a situation bearing little resemblance to the real-world situation that originally generated the idea. In fact, a frequent criticism is that laboratory experiments are unrealistic, contrived imitations of human interaction that don't reflect the real world at all. How accurate is this criticism?

Perhaps the best way to answer this question is to examine one laboratory experiment in detail, considering its advantages and disadvantages, as well as an alternative, more realistic approach that might have been used to study the same issue. The initiation experiment I did in collaboration with Judson Mills[6] suits this purpose admirably, because it contains many of the advantages and disadvantages of the laboratory. You may recall that Mills and I hypothesized that people might come to like things more if they have suffered to get them. We then designed and conducted a laboratory experiment in which we showed that people who expended great effort (by undergoing a severe initiation) to gain membership in a group liked the group more than did people who became members with little or no effort. Here's how we constructed the experiment.

The Aronson-Mills Experiment Up Close   Sixty-three college women who initially volunteered to engage in several discussions on the psychology of sex participated in the study. Each student was tested individually. At the beginning, I explained that I was studying the "dynamics of the group-discussion process." I said the actual topic of the discussion did not matter to me, but because most people are interested in sex, I selected that topic to be certain of having plenty of participants. I also explained that I had encountered a major drawback in choosing sex as the topic: Many people were shy and found it difficult to discuss sex in a group setting. Because any impediment to the flow of the discussion could seriously invalidate the results, I needed to know if the women felt any hesitancy to enter a discussion about sex. When they heard this, each one said she would have no difficulty.

These elaborate instructions set the stage for the event to follow. Up to this point, the instructions had been the same for all participants. Now it was time to give each of the women in the various experimental conditions a different experience—an experience that we experimenters believed would make a difference.

We randomly assigned the participants in advance to one of three conditions: (1) one-third of them would go through a severe initiation, (2) one-third would go through a mild initiation, and (3) one-third would not go through any initiation at all. For the no-initiation condition, I simply told participants they could now join the discussion group. For the severe- and mild-initiation conditions, however, I told each participant that, because it was necessary to be positive she could discuss sex openly, I had developed a screening device—a test for embarrassment—that I then asked her to take. This test constituted the initiation. For the severe-initiation condition, the test was highly embarrassing. It required the woman to recite a list of 12 obscene words and two detailed descriptions of sexual activity taken from contemporary novels. (That may not sound like a "severe" initiation today, but trust me, when we did this study, now many years ago, saying these words out loud was excruciating.) The mild-initiation participants had to recite only a list of words related to sex that were not obscene.

The three conditions to which participants were assigned constituted the **independent variable** in this study. Every investigator's goal in designing and conducting an experiment is to determine if *what happens to participants* has an effect on how they respond. Our goal was to determine if severity of initiation—the independent variable—caused systematic differences in participants' behavior. Would participants who experienced a severe initiation act differently from those who experienced a mild initiation or no initiation at all?

But act differently in what way? After the initiation, each participant was allowed to eavesdrop on a discussion being conducted by members of the group she had just joined. To control the content of this material, we used a tape recording but told the women they were hearing a live discussion. In that way we made sure that all participants—regardless of whether they had gone through a severe initiation, a mild initiation, or no initiation—heard the same group discussion. The group discussion was as incredibly dull and boring as we could make it. The people on the tape spoke with long pauses, a great deal of hemming and hawing, interruptions, and incomplete sentences as they discussed, inarticulately, the secondary sex characteristics of lower animals: changes in plumage among birds, intricacies of the mating dance of certain spiders, etc.

At the end of the discussion, I returned with a set of rating scales and asked each woman to rate how interesting and worthwhile the discussion had been. This response is called the **dependent variable** because, quite literally, the response is assumed to be "dependent" on the particular experimental conditions the participant had been assigned to. The dependent variable is what the experimenter measures to assess the effects of the independent variable. In short, if the independent variable is the *cause*, then the dependent variable is the *effect*.

The results supported our hypothesis: Women who went through a mild initiation or no initiation at all saw the group discussion for what it was and rated it as being dull. But those who suffered embarrassment in order to be admitted to the group thought it was really exciting. Remember, all the students were rating exactly the same discussion.

Why Do an Experiment? Designing and conducting this experiment was a laborious process. Mills and I spent hundreds of hours planning it, creating a credible situation, writing a script for the tape recording of the group discussion (That was fun!), rehearsing the actors who played the roles of group members, constructing the initiation procedures and the measuring instruments, recruiting volunteers to serve as participants, pilot-testing the procedure, running the participants through the experiment, and explaining the true purpose of the experiment to each participant (the reason for the deception, what it all meant, and what we hoped to learn). What we found was that people who go through a severe initiation to join a group liked that group a great deal more than people who go through a mild initiation or no initiation at all.

Surely there must be a simpler way! There is. You may have noticed a resemblance between our experimental procedure and other initiations, such as those used by some college fraternities and other exclusive clubs or organizations. Why, then, didn't we take advantage of a real-life situation, which is not only easier to study but also far more dramatic and realistic? Let's look at the advantages. Real-life initiations would be more severe (i.e., they would have more impact on the members); we would not have had to go to such lengths to design a group setting that participants would find convincing; the social interactions would involve real people rather than mere voices on a tape recording; we would have eliminated the ethical problem created by the use of deception and the use of a difficult and unpleasant experience in the name of science; and, finally, it could all have been accomplished in a fraction of the time the experiment consumed.

Thus, when we take a superficial look at the advantages of a natural situation, it appears that Mills and I would have had a much simpler job if we had studied existing fraternities. Here is how we might have done it. We could have rated each fraternity's initiation procedures for their degree of severity and interviewed the members later. If the members who had undergone a severe initiation liked their fraternities more than the mild- or no-initiation fraternity members, the hypothesis would be supported. Or would it? Let's take a closer look at why people bother to do experiments.

When I asked my students to name the most important characteristic of a laboratory experiment, the great majority said "control." Experiments have the advantage of controlling the environment and the variables so that the effects of each variable can be precisely studied. By taking our hypothesis to the laboratory, Mills and I eliminated a lot of the extraneous variation that exists in the real world. The severe initiations were all equal in intensity; this condition would have been difficult to match if we had used several severe-initiation fraternities. Further, the group discussion was identical for all participants; in the real world, however, fraternity members would have been rating fraternities that were, in fact, different from one another. Assuming we had found a difference between the severe-initiation and mild-initiation fraternities in how much their new members liked being in them, how would we have known whether this was a function of the initiation rather than of differences in likeability that already existed in the fraternity members themselves? In the experiment, the only difference was the severity of the initiation, so we know that any difference was because of that procedure.

The Importance of Random Assignment

Control is a central aspect of the laboratory experiment, but it is not the major advantage. An even more critical advantage is that participants can be randomly assigned to the different experimental conditions. This means each participant has an equal chance to be in any condition in the study. Indeed, the random assignment of participants to conditions is the crucial difference between the experimental method and nonexperimental approaches. And the great advantage of the random assignment of people to conditions is this: Any variables not thoroughly controlled are, in theory, distributed randomly across the conditions. This means it is extremely unlikely that such variables would affect results in a systematic fashion.

An example might help to clarify this point: Suppose you are a scientist and you have the hypothesis that men who marry intelligent women become happier than men who marry not-so-intelligent women. How do you test this hypothesis? Let us say you proceed to find 1,000 men who are married to intelligent women and 1,000 men who are married to not-so-intelligent women, and you give them all a happiness questionnaire. Lo and behold, you find that the men married to intelligent women are happier than the men married to less intelligent women. Does this mean that being married to an intelligent woman makes a man happy? No. Perhaps happy men are sweeter, more good-humored, and easier to get along with, and, consequently, intelligent women seek out these men and marry them. So it may be that being happy causes men to marry intelligent women. The problem doesn't end there. It is also possible that there is some third factor that causes both happiness and being married to an intelligent woman. One such factor could be money; perhaps being rich helps make men happy and being rich is what attracts the intelligent women. So it is possible that neither causal sequence is true: Happiness does not cause men to marry intelligent women and intelligent women do not cause men to be happy.

The problem is even more complicated because we usually have no idea what these third factors might be. In the case of the happiness study, it could be wealth; it could also be that a mature personality causes men to be happy and also attracts intelligent women; it could be social grace, athletic ability, power, popularity, using the right toothpaste, being a cool dresser, or any of a thousand qualities the poor researcher does not know about and could not possibly account for. But if the researcher performs an experiment, he or she can randomly assign participants to various experimental conditions. Although this procedure does not eliminate differences because of any of these variables (money, social grace, athletic ability, or clothes), it neutralizes them by distributing these characteristics randomly across experimental conditions. If participants are randomly assigned, there will be approximately as many rich men in one experimental condition as in the others, as many socially adept men in one condition as in the others, and as many athletes in one condition as in the others. Thus, if we do find a difference between conditions, it is unlikely that this would be because of individual differences in any single characteristic because all of these characteristics had an equal (or nearly equal) distribution across all of the conditions.

Admittedly, the particular example of intelligent women and their happy husbands does not easily lend itself to the confines of the experimental laboratory. But let us fantasize about how we would do it if we could. Ideally, we would take 50 men and randomly assign 25 of them to marry intelligent women and 25 to marry less intelligent women. A few months later, we could come back and administer the happiness questionnaire. If the men assigned to the intelligent wives are happier than the men assigned to the less intelligent wives, we would know what caused their happiness—we did! In short, their happiness couldn't easily be attributed to social grace, handsomeness, money, or power; these were randomly distributed among the experimental conditions. It almost certainly was caused by their wives' characteristics.

This example is pure fantasy; even social psychologists must stop short of arranging marriages for scientific purposes! But this does not mean we cannot test meaningful, relevant events under controlled laboratory conditions. This book has been loaded with such examples. Let's look at one of them as a way of clarifying the advantages of the experimental method: the correlation between the amount of time children spend watching violence on television and their tendency to choose aggressive solutions to their problems. (See Chapter 6.)

Does this mean watching aggression on television causes young-sters to become aggressive? Not necessarily, but it might. It might also mean that aggressive children simply like to watch aggression, and they would be just as aggressive if they watched *Sesame Street* all day long. But then, as we saw, some experimenters came along and proved that watching violence increases violence.[7] How? The experimenters randomly assigned some children to a situation in which they watched a video of an episode of a violent TV series, an episode in which people beat, slug, bite, and kill each other for 25 minutes. As a control, the experimenters randomly assigned other children to a situation in which they watched an athletic event for the same length of time. The crucial point: Each child stood an equal chance of being selected to watch the violent video as the non-violent video; therefore, any differences in personality dispositions among the children were neutralized across the two experimental conditions. Thus, the finding that youngsters who watched the violent video became more aggressive afterward than those who watched the athletic event suggests quite strongly that watching violence can lead to violence.

You may recall that this was precisely the problem with the evalu-ation of the prison college program that I described at the beginning of this chapter: The prisoners who volunteered for the program were probably different in many ways from those who did not volunteer, so it was misleading to compare their recidivism rate with that of the nonvolunteers. Such a comparison would stack the deck, mak-ing the program appear more effective than it actually was. How do you solve that problem? One way would be to attract twice as many volunteers for the program as you can handle. Then you can randomly select half of the volunteers for the program and place the other half in the control condition. If the selection is truly random, comparing the recidivism rate of the two groups would give you meaningful data.

Let us return to the initiation experiment. If we conducted a sur-vey and found that members of severe-initiation fraternities like one another more than do members of mild-initiation fraternities, then we would have evidence that severity of initiation and liking for other members are positively correlated. This means that the more severe the initiation, the more a member will like his fraternity brothers. No matter how highly correlated the two variables are, however, we cannot conclude, from our survey data alone, that severe initiations cause liking for the group. All we can conclude from such a survey is that these two factors are associated with each other.

It is possible that the positive correlation between severe initiation and liking for other members of a fraternity exists not because severe initiations cause members to like their groups more, but for just the opposite reason. It could be that the high personal appeal of the group causes severe initiations. If group members see themselves as the cream of the crop, they may try to keep the situation that way by maintaining an elite group. And they might try to maintain an elite group by requiring a severe initiation to discourage less motivated people from joining. From our survey data alone, we cannot conclude that this explanation is false and that severe initiations really do lead to liking. The data give us no basis for making this choice, because they tell us nothing about cause and effect.

Moreover, as we have seen, a third variable could be causing *both* severe initiations and liking. Who would like to give and receive a severe initiation? Why, people with strong sadomasochistic tendencies, of course. Such people may like one another not because of the initiation but because "birds of a feather" (in this case pretty cruel birds) tend to like one another. Although this may sound like an outlandish explanation, it is certainly possible. What is more distressing for the researcher are the countless other explanations he or she can't even think of. The experimental method, based as it is on the technique of random assignment to experimental conditions, eliminates all of these in one fell swoop. Sadomasochists in this experiment have just as much chance of being assigned to the no-initiation condition as to the severe-initiation condition. In a real-world study, almost all of them would assign themselves to the severe-initiation condition, thus making the results uninterpretable.

The Challenge of Experimentation in Social Psychology

All is not sunny in the world of experimentation. There are some serious problems connected with doing experiments. Control is one of the major advantages of the experiment, yet it is impossible to exercise complete control over the environment of human participants. One of the reasons many psychologists work with rats rather than people is that researchers are able to control almost everything that happens to their participants from the time of their birth until the experiment ends: climate, diet, exercise, degree of exposure to playmates, absence of traumatic experiences, and so on. Social psychologists do not keep human participants in cages to control their experiences. Although this makes for a happier world for the participants, it also makes for a slightly sloppy science.

Control Versus Impact   Control is further limited by the fact that individuals differ from one another in countless subtle ways. Social psychologists try to make statements about what people do. By this we mean, of course, what most people do most of the time under a given set of conditions. To the extent that unmeasured individual differences are present in our results, our conclusions may not be precise for all people. Differences in attitudes, values, abilities, personality characteristics, and recent experiences can affect the way people respond in an experiment. Thus, even with our ability to control the experimental situation itself, the same situation may not affect each person in exactly the same way.

Furthermore, when we do succeed in controlling the experimental setting so that it is exactly the same for every person, we run the risk of making the situation so sterile that the participant is inclined not to take it seriously. The word sterile has at least two meanings: (1) germ-free and (2) ineffective or barren. The experimenter should strive to make the experimental situation as "germ-free" as possible, without making it barren or unlifelike for the participant. If participants do not find the events of an experiment interesting and absorbing, chances are their reactions will not be spontaneous, and our results, therefore, will have little meaning.

Thus, in addition to control, an experiment must have an *impact* on the participants. They must take the experiment seriously and become involved in it, lest it not affect their behavior in a meaningful way. The difficulty for social psychologists is that these two crucial factors, impact and control, often work in opposite ways: As one increases, the other tends to decrease. The dilemma facing experimenters is how to maximize the impact on the participants without sacrificing control over the situation. Resolving this dilemma requires considerable creativity and ingenuity in the design and construction of experimental situations. This leads us to the problem of realism.

Realism   Early in this chapter, I mentioned that a frequent criticism of laboratory experiments is that they are artificial and contrived imitations of the world—that they aren't "real." What do we mean by real? Several years ago, in writing about the experimental method, Merrill Carlsmith and I[8] tried to pinpoint the definition of real. We reasoned that an experiment can be realistic in two separate ways: First, if an experiment has an impact on the participants, forces them to take the matter seriously, and involves them in the procedures, we can say it has achieved *experimental realism*. Second, if the laboratory experiment is similar to the events that frequently happen to people in the outside world, we can say it has achieved *mundane realism*. Often, confusion between experimental realism and mundane realism is responsible for the criticism that experiments are artificial and worthless because they don't reflect the real world.

The difference between the two realisms can best be illustrated by an example of a study high in experimental realism but low in mundane realism. Recall the experiment by Stanley Milgram, discussed in Chapter 4, in which each participant was asked to deliver shocks of increasing intensity to another person who was supposedly wired to an electrical apparatus in an adjoining room. Now, honestly, how many times in everyday life are we asked to deliver electric shocks to people? The set-up was unrealistic, but only in the mundane sense. Did the procedure have experimental realism—that is, were the participants wrapped up in it, did they take it seriously, did it have an impact on them, was it part of their real world at that moment? Or were they merely playacting, not taking it seriously, going through the motions, ho-humming it? Milgram reports that his participants experienced a great deal of tension and discomfort. But I'll let Milgram describe, in his own words, what a typical participant looked like.

> I observed a mature and initially poised businessman enter the laboratory smiling and confident. Within 20 minutes he was reduced to a twitching, stuttering wreck, who was rapidly approaching a point of nervous collapse. He constantly pulled on his earlobe, and twisted his hands. At one point he pushed his fist onto his forehead and muttered: "Oh God, let's stop it." And yet he continued to respond to every word of the experimenter, and obeyed to the end.[9]

This hardly seems like the behavior of a person in an unrealistic situation. The things happening to Milgram's participants were real, even though they didn't happen to them in their everyday experience. Accordingly, it would seem safe to conclude that the results of this experiment are a reasonably accurate indication of the way people would react if a similar set of events did occur in the real world.

Deception The importance of experimental realism cannot be overemphasized. The best way to achieve this essential quality is to design a setting that will be absorbing and interesting to the participants. At the same time, it is frequently necessary to disguise the true purpose of the study. Why the need for disguise?

At the beginning of this book, I noted that just about everybody is an amateur social psychologist, in the sense that we all live in a social world and are constantly forming hypotheses about things that are happening to us. That is just as true for the individuals who serve as participants in our experiments. Because they are always trying to figure things out, if they knew what we were trying to get at, they might be apt to behave in a manner consistent with their own hypotheses—instead of behaving in a way that is natural and usual for them. For this reason, experimenters try to conceal the true nature of the experiment from the participants. Because we are almost always dealing with intelligent adults, this is not an easy task; but it is an absolute requirement in most experiments if we are to stand a chance of obtaining valid and reliable data.

This requirement puts the social psychologist in the position of a film director who is setting the stage for action but not telling the actor what the play is all about. Such settings are called cover stories and are designed to increase experimental realism by producing a situation in which the participant can act naturally, without being inhibited by knowing just which aspect of behavior is being studied. For example, in the Aronson-Mills initiation study, we told participants that they were taking a test for embarrassment to screen them for membership in a group that would be discussing the psychology of sex; this was the cover story. It was pure deception. In reality, we were subjecting them to an initiation to see what effect, if any, this would have on their liking for the group. If the participants had been aware of the true purpose of the study before their participation, the results would have been totally meaningless.

In fact, researchers who have studied this issue have shown that if participants know the true purpose of an experiment, they do not behave naturally but either try to perform in a way that puts themselves in a good light or try to "help out" the experimenter by behaving in a way that would make the experiment come out as the participants think it should. Both of these outcomes are disastrous for the experimenter. The experimenter can usually succeed in curbing the participant's desire to be helpful, but it is harder to curb the participant's desire to look good. Most people do not want to be thought of as obedient, weak, abnormal, conformist, unattractive, stupid, or crazy. Thus, if given a chance to figure out what the experimenter is looking for, most people will try to make themselves look good or what they think is "normal." For example, in an experiment designed specifically to examine this phenomenon,[10] when my colleagues and I told participants that a particular outcome indicated they possessed a good personality trait, they did what they could to produce that outcome far more often than when we told them it reflected a negative trait. Although this behavior is understandable, it does interfere with meaningful results. For this reason, experimenters find it necessary to deceive participants about the true nature of the experiment.

To illustrate, let's look again at Solomon Asch's[11] classic experiment on conformity. Recall that, in this study, a student was assigned the simple task of judging the relative size of a few lines. But a few other students, who were accomplices of the experimenter, purposely stated an incorrect judgment. In this situation, a sizable number of the participants yielded to the implicit group pressure and stated an incorrect judgment. The participants were deceived: They thought they were in an experiment on perception, but they were actually in a study of conformity. Was this deception necessary? I think so. Let's play it back without the deception: Imagine you enter this study and the experimenter says to you, "I am interested in studying whether or not you will conform in the face of group pressure," and then he tells you what is going to happen. My guess is that you wouldn't conform. My guess is that almost no one would conform, because conformity is considered a weak and unattractive act. What could the experimenter have concluded? That people tend to be nonconformists? Such a conclusion would be erroneous and misleading. Such an experiment would be meaningless.

In Milgram's experiments on obedience, around 65 percent of the average citizens were willing to administer intense shocks to another person in obedience to the experimenter's command. Yet, each year, when I describe the experimental situation to the students in my class and ask them if they would obey such a command, only

1 percent indicate that they would. Does this mean my students are nicer people than Milgram's participants? I don't think so. I think it means that people, if given half a chance, will try to look good. Thus, *unless* Milgram used deception, he would have come out with results that simply do not reflect the way people behave when they are led to believe they are in real situations. If we were to give people the opportunity to sit back, relax, and make a guess as to how they would behave in a certain situation, we would get a picture of how people would like to be rather than a picture of how people are.

Replication Problems

Scientific inquiry does not end when an experiment does. Rarely does a single experiment, even one that is perfectly constructed and yields beautiful, clear results, give us final answers. The next step in the process of science is *replication*, in which the original study is repeated by other investigators in other labs. Replication helps clarify the research, establishing the conditions under which it applies and those under which it doesn't apply, as well as for whom it is most applicable—e.g., does it work only for young adults, Americans, and college students or for older people, Europeans, and blue-collar workers as well? Replication also can determine whether the phenomenon is robust and lasting or something of a fluke. If scientists are unable to duplicate the original results, one of two things must be true: They didn't do the replications accurately or appropriately, or the original investigators' conclusions were limited or wrong.

Earlier in this chapter I said that doing a good experiment is a matter of both art and science. When I worked with my colleagues doing dissonance experiments, for instance, I spent a lot of time getting things just right, working, as I said, as much like a film director as a scientific investigator. The "science" part is easier to replicate than the "art" part. After all, I can eat a magnificent soufflé in a restaurant and be so impressed by the chef's creation that I immediately buy his cookbook on how to create the perfect soufflé. I can use his recipe to try to "replicate" that creation, but I guarantee that mine will look (and taste!) more like a brick than his light and fluffy concoction. Theories and procedures are like recipes. Sometimes a failed replication is a failure of the technique, a misreading of the recipe, not a failure of the hypothesis.

Sometimes a replication catches a mistake in the original experimenters' procedures, analysis of data, or even their unintentional biases. One well-done, indeed irresistible study conducted in the 1970s showed that newborn infants imitate the facial expressions of adults—for example, the experimenter would stick out his tongue, and the baby would do the same—suggesting that babies are born with the ability to imitate. But a much better-controlled experiment conducted recently has found that this skill at imitation is learned, beginning at about six months of age.[12]

Finally, sometimes a replication fails, but in so doing reveals a previously unknown, missing ingredient that was crucial to the original research but that was absent in the second. Consider a study in which minority students who wrote essays describing an important personal value later received higher grades than students in a control group who wrote essays about other people's values.[13] This was a dramatic finding, so there were many attempts to replicate, but only some of them worked. Does this mean that the original study was false? Not at all. It turns out that this intervention does not work in every school; it replicates only when it is used in schools where the minority students feel a great deal of prejudice against them.[14]

Nevertheless, a new problem across all the sciences has emerged, enabled by social media: A number of "hot" findings now get instant attention (often followed by a TED talk)—and then often cool off when other researchers try to replicate them. Here are a few examples of studies that went viral but failed to be supported by other experimenters: Reading a list of age-related words triggers images of "old people" and makes young people walk more slowly, washing your hands makes you feel less guilty, working in a room with a large poster of a man's eyes staring at you makes you more honest, sniffing the "cuddle hormone" oxytocin makes you more empathic, and holding a warm cup of coffee makes you feel more loved. One of the most popular was the alleged "power pose": Putting your hands on your hips and widening your stance would make people feel bolder and more confident and even increase their testosterone levels. Before long one of the study's researchers had written a best-selling book and given a TED talk that became one of the most viewed in TED history, "Your Body Language Shapes Who You Are." (Indeed, this idea became *so* popular that I would not be surprised if millions of people around the world are beginning their day standing in front of a full length mirror in the Wonder Woman power pose.) Unfortunately, most of the many replications of this research failed to produce significant results, especially regarding the testosterone claims and the persistence of the effect. Joseph Simmons and Uri Simonsohn[15] conducted a statistical analysis on 33 of the subsequently published studies, which used much larger samples than the originals, and concluded that "the existing evidence is too weak to ... advocate for people to engage in power posing to better their lives."

Today, unfortunately, there have been many pop social psychology "findings" that get public attention and then don't pass the test of replication.[16] But that does not mean that the basic *methods* of social-psychological experimentation are at fault—it means that science is moving along as it should, correcting its mistakes and advancing the findings that hold up. It also means, however, that the public should be wary of sensational, improbable, or simplistic findings and ask, "But have they been replicated?"

Ethical Problems

Using deception may be the best (and often the only) way to get useful information about the way people behave in complicated situations, but it does present the experimenter with three ethical problems:

1. It is simply unethical to lie to people. In today's world of "fake news" and the blatant lies of politicians, can social scientists justify adding to the pollution of deception that currently exists?

2. Deception frequently leads to an invasion of privacy. When participants do not know what the experimenter is really studying, they are in no position to give their informed consent. For example, in Asch's experiment, some students might not have agreed to participate had they known in advance that Asch was interested in examining their tendency toward conformity rather than their perceptual judgment.

3. Experimental procedures often entail some unpleasant experiences, such as pain, boredom, anxiety, or embarrassment.

Ethical problems arise even when deception is not used and when experimental procedures are not extreme. Sometimes even the most seemingly benign procedure can profoundly affect a few participants in ways that could not easily have been anticipated, even by the most sensitive and caring experimenters. Consider a series of experiments on "social dilemmas," conducted by Robyn Dawes, Jeanne McTavish, and Harriet Shaklee.[17] Typically, participants are faced with the decision to cooperate with a partner or to "defect."

If everyone cooperates, everyone benefits financially; but if one or more participants choose to defect, they receive a high payoff, and those who choose to cooperate are at a financial disadvantage. Responses are anonymous and remain so throughout the course of the study. The rules of the game are fully explained to all participants at the beginning of the experiment. And no deception is involved. This scenario seems innocuous enough.

But 24 hours after one experimental session, a man telephoned the experimenter. He had been the only defector in his group and had won $190. He wanted to return his winnings and have them divided among the other participants (who had cooperated and won only $1 each). He felt miserable about his greedy behavior, he said, and hadn't slept all night. After a similar experiment, a woman who had cooperated while others defected reported that she felt gullible and had learned that people were not as trustworthy as she had earlier believed. Despite careful planning by the investigators, therefore, these experiments had a powerful impact on participants that could not have been easily anticipated. My point is simple, but important: No code of ethics can anticipate all problems, especially those created when participants discover something unpleasant about themselves or others in the course of their participation.

Social psychologists who conduct experiments are deeply concerned about ethical issues, precisely because their work is constructed on an ethical dilemma. Let me explain. This dilemma is based on two conflicting values to which most social psychologists subscribe. On the one hand, they believe in the value of free scientific inquiry. On the other hand, they believe in the dignity of humans and their right to privacy. This dilemma is a real one and cannot be dismissed either by piously defending the importance of preserving human dignity or by glibly pledging allegiance to the cause of science. And social psychologists must face this problem squarely, not just once but every time they design and conduct an experiment—for there is no concrete and universal set of rules or guidelines capable of governing every experiment.

Obviously, some experimental techniques present more problems than others. In general, experiments that employ deception are cause for concern because the act of lying is, in itself, objectionable, even if the deception is at the service of uncovering the truth. And procedures that cause pain, embarrassment, guilt, or other intense feelings present obvious ethical problems.

A more subtle ethical problem results when participants confront some aspect of themselves that is not pleasant or positive, as some of the people in the experiments by Dawes, McTavish, and Shaklee did. And many of Solomon Asch's participants learned that they would conform in the face of group pressure; many participants in our own experiment (Aronson and Mettee[18]) learned that they were capable of cheating at a game of cards; most of Milgram's participants learned that they would obey an authority even if such obedience (apparently) involved harming another person.

It could be argued that such self-discovery is of therapeutic or educational benefit to participants; indeed, many participants themselves have made this point. But this does not, in itself, justify these procedures. After all, how could an experimenter know in advance that it would be therapeutic? Moreover, it would be arrogant of any scientist to decide that he or she has the right or the skill to provide people with a therapeutic experience without their prior permission to do so.

Given these problems, do the ends of social psychological research justify the means? This is a debatable point. Some argue that, no matter what the goals of this science are and no matter what the accomplishments, they are not worth it if people are deceived or put through some discomfort. On the opposite end of the spectrum, others insist that social psychologists are finding things out that may have profound benefits for humankind, and accordingly, almost any price is worth paying for the results.

My own position is somewhere in between. I believe the science of social psychology is valuable, and I also believe that the health and welfare of experimental participants should be protected at all times. When deciding whether a particular experimental procedure is ethical, I believe a cost–benefit analysis is appropriate. That is, we should consider how much good will derive from doing the experiment and how much harm will be done to the experimental participants. Put another way, the benefits to science and society are compared with the costs to the participants, and this ratio is entered into the decision calculus. Unfortunately, such a comparison is difficult to make because we can never be absolutely certain of either the benefit or the harm in advance of the experiment.

Consider the obedience experiment. On the face of it, it was a difficult procedure, all right—no doubt about it. But Milgram had no way of knowing exactly how difficult it was until he was deeply

into the experiment. In my opinion, it was also an extremely illu-
minating experiment, one that taught us a great deal about human
behavior. In the balance, I'm glad that Milgram went ahead with it.
However, I know that not everyone will agree with me. Immediately after its publication, the experiment was lambasted on ethical
grounds, both by the popular press and by serious scientists.

A few years after having published his results, Stanley Milgram
confided in me—sadly, and with a tinge of bitterness—that he
believed much of the criticism was fueled by the results he obtained
rather than by the actual procedure he employed. That, in and of
itself, evokes an interesting question: Would the criticisms of the
ethics of Milgram's procedure have been less vehement if none
of the participants had administered shocks beyond a moderate
level of intensity? More than a decade later, Leonard Bickman
and Matthew Zarantonello[19] discovered that Milgram's rumina-
tions were on target. They did a simple little experiment in which
they asked 100 people to read the procedure section of Milgram's
experiment. Those who were informed that a high proportion of
Milgram's participants had been fully obedient rated the procedure
as more harmful (and, therefore, less ethical) than those who were
informed that hardly anyone had been fully obedient.

On a more general note, I would suggest that the ethics of any
experiment would seem less problematic when the results tell us
something pleasant or flattering about human nature than when
they tell us something we'd rather not know. That certainly doesn't
mean that we should limit our research to the discovery of flattering
things! Milgram's obedience experiment is an excellent case in point.
I believe that, if a scientist is interested in studying the extent to
which a person will harm others in blind obedience to authority, there
is no way of doing it without producing some degree of discomfort.

In sum, a social psychologist's decision whether or not to do a
particular experiment depends on an assessment of its potential costs
and benefits. I've always advised my students to follow these five
guidelines:

1. Procedures that cause intense pain or intense discomfort should
   be avoided, if at all possible. Depending on the hypothesis being
   tested, some discomfort may be unavoidable.

2. Experimenters should provide their participants with the real
   option of quitting the experiment if their discomfort becomes
   too intense.

3. Experimenters should be alert to alternative procedures to deception. If some other viable procedure can be found, it should be used.

4. Experimenters should spend considerable time with each participant at the close of the experimental session, carefully explaining the details of the experiment, its true purpose, and the reasons for the deception or discomfort. During this **debriefing** session, they should go out of their way to protect the dignity of participants, to avoid making them feel stupid or gullible about having "fallen for" the deception. They should make certain that participants leave the scene in good spirits, feeling good about themselves and their role in the experiment. This can be accomplished by any earnest experimenter who is willing to put in the time and effort to repay each participant (with information and consideration) for the vital role that he or she has played in the scientific enterprise.

5. Finally, experimenters should not undertake an experiment that relies on deception or creating discomfort "just for the hell of it." Before entering the laboratory, experimenters should be certain their experiment is sound and worthwhile, that they are seeking the answer to an interesting question and doing so in a careful, well-organized manner.

Experimenters in social psychology try hard to be as sensitive as possible to the needs of their participants. Although many experiments involve procedures that cause some degree of discomfort, the vast majority of these procedures contain many safeguards for the protection of participants. Again, let us return to the obedience experiment simply because, from the perspective of the participants, it is among the most stressful procedures reported in this book. Milgram worked hard after the experiment to turn the overall experience into a useful and exciting one for his participants, and his efforts paid off. Several weeks after the experiment, 84 percent of the participants reported that they were glad to have taken part in the study; 15 percent reported neutral feelings; and only 1 percent stated that they were sorry they had participated. (We should view these findings with caution, however. The discussion of cognitive dissonance in Chapter 3 has taught us that people sometimes justify their behavior by changing their previously held attitudes.) More convincing evidence comes from a follow-up study: One year after the experimental program was completed, a university psychiatrist interviewed a random sample of the participants and found no evidence of injurious effects; rather, the typical response was that their participation was instructive and enriching.[20]

Our Debt to Participants I have been discussing the advantages of the experimental method and have shown how complex and challenging it is to design a laboratory experiment in social psychology. I have shared some of the excitement I feel in overcoming difficulties and discussed ways of ensuring the well-being, as well as the learning, of the participants in our experiments. The knowledge, information, and insights into human social behavior described in this book are based on the techniques and procedures discussed in this chapter. They are also based on the cooperation of tens of thousands of individuals who have allowed us to study their behavior in laboratories all over the world. We owe them a lot. Ultimately, our understanding of human beings in all their complexity rests on our ingenuity in developing techniques for studying behavior, which are well controlled and influential without violating the essential dignity of those individuals who contribute to our understanding by serving as experimental participants.

What If Our Discoveries Are Misused?

There is one additional ethical consideration: the moral responsibility of the scientist for what he or she discovers. Throughout this book, I have been dealing with some powerful antecedents of persuasion. This was particularly true in Chapter 3, where I discussed techniques of inducing self-persuasion, and in some of the subsequent chapters, where I discussed applications of these techniques. Self-persuasion is a powerful force because the persuaded never know what hit them. They come to believe that a particular thing is true, not because some demagogue or advertisement or Facebook friend convinced them it is true, but because they have convinced themselves. What's more, they frequently do not know why or how they came to believe it. This renders the phenomenon not only powerful but frightening as well. As long as I know why I came to believe X, I am relatively free to change my mind; but if all I know is that X is true—and that's all there is to it—I am far more likely to cling to that belief, even in the face of a barrage of disconfirming evidence.

The mechanisms I have described can be used to get people to floss their teeth, stop bullying smaller people, reduce pain, or love their neighbors. Many people might consider these good outcomes, but they are manipulative just the same. Moreover, the same mechanisms can also be used to get people to buy particular brands of toothpaste and perhaps to vote for particular political candidates. In this era of political spin doctors, propagandists, and hucksters, isn't it immoral to use powerful techniques of social influence?

As my readers must know by now, as a real person living in the real world, I have many values—and have made no effort to conceal them; they stick out all over the place. For example, if I had the power, I would use the most humane and effective methods at my disposal to end bigotry and cruelty. I am equally aware that, once these methods are developed, others might use them to achieve ends I might not agree with; every tool we humans invent can be used for good or ill, to build or destroy. This realization causes me great concern. I am also aware that others do not share my values.

At the same time, the phenomena I have been describing in this book are neither new nor solely the domain of social psychologists. After all, it was not a social psychologist who got Mr. Landry hooked on Marlboros or who invented lowballing; it was not a social psychologist who induced soldiers to justify the wanton killing of civilians; it was not a social psychologist who taught the Nazis how to use the "Big Lie" to manipulate the German citizenry. They did what they did on their own.

Social psychologists are attempting to understand these phenomena and scores of others that take place in the world every day, and have been since time immemorial, the better to help people understand how and why we do what we do. This goal does not free us from moral responsibility. Our research often yields easily applicable techniques of social influence, and some individuals may use these techniques for personal gain, control over others, and even, in the hands of a demagogue, to turn our society into an Orwellian nightmare. It is not my intention to preach about the responsibilities of social psychologists in general. I can only specify what I believe to be my own responsibilities: to educate the public about how social-psychological knowledge and techniques might be used for the greater good; to remain vigilant against the abuse of social-psychological knowledge and techniques; and to promote good research aimed at furthering our understanding of us social animals—how we think, how we behave, what makes us aggressive, and what makes us loving. Frankly, I can think of no endeavor more interesting or more important.

Glossary

aggression: intentional action aimed at doing harm or causing physical or psychological pain

altruism: any act that benefits another person but does not benefit the helper, often involves some personal cost to the helper

amygdala: the area in the core of the brain associated with aggressive behaviors

attitude: a special type of belief that includes emotional and evaluative components—in a sense, a stored good or bad evaluation of an object

attribution theory: a theory that describes the way in which people explain the causes of their own and other people's behavior

attributional ambiguity: a phenomenon whereby members of a stigmatized group have difficulty in interpreting feedback on their work or actions

authenticity: our ability to give up trying to make a good impression and begin to reveal honest things about ourselves

availability heuristic: a mental rule of thumb that refers to judgments that are based on how easy it is for us to bring specific examples to mind

benevolent sexism: an attitude toward women that appears to be favorable but is actually patronizing; holds stereotypically positive views of women but underneath assumes that women are the weaker and less competent sex

bias blind spot: the belief that we are more objective and less biased than most other people

blaming the victim: the tendency to blame victims for their victimization, attributing their predicaments to their own personalities, disabilities, or behavior

bystander effect: what occurs when another bystander or other bystanders tend(s) to inhibit helpful actions

catharsis: specifically, the release of energy; Freud believed that unless people were allowed to express aggressive behavior, the aggressive energy would be dammed up, the pressure would build up, and the energy thus produced would seek an outlet, resulting in violence or a symptom of mental illness

central route to persuasion: the route that involves weighing arguments and considering relevant facts and figures, thinking about issues in a systematic fashion, and coming to a decision

cognitive dissonance: a state of tension that occurs whenever an individual simultaneously holds two cognitions (ideas, attitudes, beliefs, opinions) that are psychologically inconsistent

cognitive misers: the idea that people look for ways to conserve cognitive energy; they do that by attempting to adopt strategies that simplify complex problems

communal relationship: relationships in which neither partner is keeping score, feeling that over the long haul some semblance of equity will take place

companionate love: a love that is a milder, more stable experience marked by feelings of mutual trust, dependability, and warmth

compliance: describes the behavior of a person motivated by the desire for reward or to avoid punishment

confirmation bias: a tendency to seek confirmation of initial impressions or beliefs

conformity: changes in a person's behavior or opinions as a result of real or imagined pressure from a person or a group of people

contrast effect: an object appears to be better or worse than it is, depending on the quality of the objects with which it is compared

credibility: if the source of a communication is both expert and trustworthy, that source is likely to have an impact on the beliefs of the audience

debriefing: the procedure whereby the purpose of the study and exactly what transpired is explained to participants at the end of an experiment

dehumanize: the process of seeing victims as nonhumans, which lowers inhibitions against aggressive actions, and also makes continued aggression easier and more likely

deindividuation: a state of reduced self-awareness, reduced concern over social evaluation, and weakened restraints against prohibited forms of behavior

dependent variable: a response assumed to be "dependent" on a particular experimental condition

desensitization: a process whereby we become decreasingly distressed when we see people hurt

diffusion of responsibility: a phenomenon where the awareness of other witnesses diffuses a bystander's feelings of responsibility to take action

discrimination: unfair treatment of members of a stigmatized group

dispositional view: the assumption that a person's behavior is the result of his or her personality (disposition) rather than of pressures existing in the situation

emotional contagion: the rapid transmission of emotions or behaviors through a crowd

empathy: the ability to understand or share the feelings of another

entrapment: the process by which people make a small decision, justify it, and over time find themselves increasingly committed to a belief or activity

eros: the instinct toward life, posited by Freud

exchange relationships: relationships in which the people involved want to make sure that some sort of equity is achieved and that rewards and costs to each of the partners is fairly distributed

experimental realism: when experimental procedures have an impact on the participants, force them to take the experiment seriously, and involve them in the procedures

external justification: a person's justification for his or her dissonant behavior that is situation-determined

foot-in-the-door technique: the process of using small favors to encourage people to accede to larger requests

frustration–aggression: when a person is thwarted on the way to a goal, the frustration will increase the probability of an aggressive response

fundamental attribution error: the tendency to overestimate the general importance of personality or dispositional factors relative to situational or environmental influences when describing or explaining the cause of social behavior

gain-loss theory: the theory that increases in positive, rewarding behavior from another person has more impact than constantly rewarding behavior, and that losses in positive behavior have more impact than constant negative behavior from another person

groupthink: a kind of thinking in which maintaining group agreement overrides a careful consideration of the facts in a realistic manner

halo effect: a bias in which a favorable or unfavorable general impression of a person affects our inferences and future expectations about that person

heuristics: mental shortcuts that provide general rules of thumb to guide problem-solving and decision-making

hindsight bias: our tendency (usually erroneous) to overestimate our powers of prediction once we know the outcome of a given event

hostile sexism: reflecting an active dislike of women; holding stereotypical views of a woman that suggest that women are inferior to men

hypocrisy: what occurs when people insulate themselves from dissonance by denial, producing a discrepancy between what they practice and what they preach

identification: a response to social influence brought about by an individual's desire to be like the influencer

Implicit Association Test (IAT):   measures the speed of people's positive and negative associations to a target group

independent variable: the variable an experimenter changes or varies to see if it has an effect on some other variable

ingroup: our group, the one with which we identify and feel we belong

ingroup bias: when we favor our own group over another

inoculation effect: the process of making people immune to attempts to change their attitudes, by initially exposing them to small doses of the arguments against their position

interdependence: a situation in which individuals need one another to succeed

internal justification: the reduction of dissonance by changing something about oneself (e.g., one's attitude or behavior) in the direction of one's statements

internalization: the most deeply rooted response to social influence; motivation to internalize a particular belief rooted in the desire to be right

jigsaw classroom: a cooperative classroom structure designed to reduce ethnic, race, and gender prejudice and raise the self-esteem and confidence of children by having them work in small, racially mixed, cooperative groups

justification of effort: when a person goes through a difficult or painful experience in order to attain some goal or object, thus making that goal or object more attractive

loss aversion: a phenomenon where, when given a choice, people are more likely to try to avoid loss than to try to achieve gains

lowballing: an unscrupulous strategy in which a customer agrees to purchase a product at a very low cost, after which the salesperson claims that price was an error and then raises the price, betting that the customer will agree to make the purchase at the inflated price, which he or she often does

mundane realism: how similar an experiment is to events that frequently happen to people in the outside world

opinion: that which a person believes to be factually true

outgroup: a group with which we do not identify; the members of which we tend to see as being all the same

passionate love: a love characterized by strong emotions, sexual desire, and intense preoccupation with the beloved

peripheral route to persuasion: the route in which a person responds to simple, often irrelevant cues that suggest the rightness or wrongness of an argument without giving it much thought

persuasion: a communication from one person that changes the opinions, attitudes, or behavior of another person

pluralistic ignorance: the collective belief in a false norm created by the ambiguous behavior of others

pratfall effect: a phenomenon in which, even though a person has a high degree of competence, some evidence of fallibility increases his or her attractiveness

prejudice: a hostile or negative attitude toward a distinguishable group, on the basis of generalizations derived from faulty or incomplete information; contains a cognitive, an emotional, and a behavioral component

primacy effect: the effect that occurs when information encountered first has more impact on our impressions or beliefs than subsequent information

priming: a procedure based on the notion that ideas that have been recently encountered or frequently activated are more likely to come to mind and thus will be used in interpreting social events

proximity: one of the major factors determining whether we like or love someone is their physical proximity; it is more likely that we will fall in love with someone who lives in or near our town, or attends our university, than with someone who lives far away

random assignment: the process in which all participants have an equal chance to be in any condition of an experiment; through random assignment, any variables not thoroughly controlled are, in theory, distributed randomly across the conditions

reactance: when our sense of freedom is threatened and we attempt to restore it

reference groups: groups that we belong to and identify with

relational aggression: a more social, nonphysical form of aggression aimed at hurting others, by sabotaging reputations and relationships with peers, exemplified by spreading false rumors and malicious gossip

relative deprivation: the feeling that occurs when people notice that other people have more or are doing better than they are, and that the system is treating them unfairly relative to what people around them have

romantic love: a combination of passion and intimacy

scapegoating: the process of blaming a relatively powerless innocent person for something that is not his or her fault

scripts: ways of behaving socially that we learn implicitly from the culture

self-concept: our perception of our own thoughts, beliefs, and personality traits; how we view ourselves

self-esteem: people's evaluations of their own worth—that is, the extent to which they view themselves as good, competent, and decent

self-fulfilling prophecy: the process that occurs when people (1) have an expectation about what another person is like, which then (2) influences how they act toward that person, and (3) causes that person to behave in a way that confirms those people's original expectations

self-justification: the tendency to justify one's actions in order to maintain one's self-esteem

sexual scripts: implicit rules that specify proper sexual behavior for a person in a given situation, varying with the person's gender, age, sexual orientation, ethnicity, and peer group

social cognition: the study of how people think about the social world and make decisions about socially relevant events

social cognitive learning theory: the theory that people learn how to behave through their cognitive processes, such as their perceptions of events and through observation and imitation of others

social comparison: the process by which we evaluate our abilities, achievements, attitudes, and other attributes by comparing ourselves to others

social influence: the influences that people have upon the beliefs, feelings, and behaviors of others

social learning: the process by which we learn social behavior by observing others

social psychology: the scientific study of the ways in which people's thoughts, feelings, and behaviors are influenced by the real or implied presence of other people

stereotype: to generalize characteristics, motives, or behavior to an entire group of people; the images in our head that shape our impressions of people or groups of people

stereotype threat: the apprehension experienced by members of a minority group that they might confirm an existing (negative) cultural stereotype; this apprehension has been shown to interfere with intellectual performance

straight talk: a clear statement of a person's feelings and concerns without accusing, blaming, judging, or ridiculing the other person

testosterone: a male sex hormone shown to influence aggression

thanatos: according to Freud, an instinctual drive toward death leading to aggressive actions

weapons effect: when the mere presence of an object associated with aggression—gun, rifle, or other weapon—serves as a cue for an aggressive response

Notes

Chapter 1 What Is Social Psychology?

1. Clark, K., & Clark, M. (1947). Racial identification and preference in Negro children. In T. M. Newcomb & E. L. Hartley (Eds.), *Readings in social psychology* (pp. 169–178). New York: Holt.

2. Voigt, R., Camp, N., Prabhakaran, V., Hamilton, W., Hetey, R., Griffiths, C., Jurgens, D., Jurafsky, D., & Eberhardt, J. (2017). Language from police body camera footage shows racial disparities in officer respect. *PNAS* 114:6521–6526.

3. Hawkins, S. A., & R. Hastie. (1990). Hindsight: Biased judgments of past events after the outcomes are known. *Psychological Bulletin* 107:311–327.

4. Kang, C. (2016). Fake news onslaught targets pizzeria as nest of child-trafficking. *New York Times*, November 21.

Chapter 2 Social Cognition

1. Panati, C. (1987). *Extraordinary origins of everyday things*. New York: Harper & Row.

2. Suskind, P. (2001). *Perfume: The story of a murder*. New York: Vintage.

3. Golden, C. (2003). *Images of the woman reader in Victorian British and American fiction*. Gainesville, FL: University Press of Florida

4. Nin, A. (1961). *Seduction of the minotaur*. Athens, OH: Swallow Press.

5. Bentham, J. (1876/1948). *A fragment on government and an introduction to the principles of morals and legislation*. Oxford: Blackwell. For a modern version of the felicific calculation, see Fishbein, M., & Ajzen, I. (1975). *Belief, attitude, intention, and behavior: An introduction to theory and research*. Reading, MA: Addison-Wesley.

6. Fiske, S. T., & Taylor, S. E. (1991). *Social cognition.* New York: McGraw-Hill; Kool, W., McGuire, J. T., Rosen, Z. B., & Botvinick, M. M. (2010). Decision making and the avoidance of cognitive demand. *Journal of Experimental Psychology, 139,* 665.

7. Mani, A., Mullainathan, S., Shafir, E., & Zhao, J. (2013). Poverty impedes cognitive function. *Science, 341,* 976–980.

8. Watson, J. B. (1930). *Behaviorism* (Revised edition). Chicago: University of Chicago Press.

9. Pinker, S. (2003). *The blank slate: The modern denial of human nature.* New York: Penguin.

10. Bloom, P. (2013). *Just babies: The origins of good and evil.* New York: Crown.

11. Barkow, J. H., Cosmides, L., & Tooby, J. (Eds.). (1995). *The adapted mind: Evolutionary psychology and the generation of culture.* New York: Oxford University Press; Zihlman, A. L., & Bolter, D. R. (2015). Body composition in Pan paniscus compared with Homo sapiens has implications for changes during human evolution. *Proceedings of the National Academy of Sciences, 112,* 7466–7471.

12. Dunbar, R. M. (1992) Neocortex size as a constraint on group size in primates. *Journal of Human Evolution, 22,* 469–493; Gonçalves, B., Perra, N., & Vespignani, A. (2011). Modeling users' activity on twitter networks: Validation of Dunbar's number. *PLoS One, 6,* e22656.

13. Gonçalves, B., Perra, N., & Vespignani, A. (2011). Modeling users' activity on twitter networks: Validation of Dunbar's number. *PLoS One, 6,* e22656.

14. Bickel, R., & Howley, C. (2000). The influence of scale on school performance. *Education Policy Analysis Archives, 8,* 22; McRobbie, J. (2001). *Are small schools better?* San Francisco: Wested.

15. Medina, J. (2008). *Brain rules.* Seattle, WA: Pear Press.

16. Kenrick, D. (2013). *Sex, murder, and the meaning of life.* New York: Basic Books.

17. Pronin, E., Lin, D. Y., & Ross, L. (2002). The bias blind spot: Perceptions of bias in self versus others. *Personality and Social Psychology Bulletin, 28,* 369–381; Banaji, M. R., & Greenwald, A. G. (2013). *Blindspot: Hidden biases of good people.* New York: Delacorte Press.

18. Bronowski, J. (1973). *The ascent of man.* Boston: Little, Brown.

19. Nickerson, R. S. (1998). Confirmation bias: A ubiquitous phenomenon in many guises. *Review of general psychology, 2,* 175; Snyder, M., & Swann, W. B. (1978). Hypothesis-testing processes in social interaction. *Journal of Personality and Social Psychology, 36,* 1202–1212.

20. Greenberg, J., Pyszczynski, T., & Solomon, S. (1982). The self-serving attributional bias: Beyond self-presentation. *Journal of Experimental Social Psychology, 18,* 56–67; Arkin, R. M., & Maruyama, G. M. (1979). Attribution,

affect, and college exam performance. *Journal of Educational Psychology, 71,* 85–93; Gilovich, T. (1983). Biased evaluation and persistence in gambling. *Journal of Personality and Social Psychology, 44,* 1110–1126; Ross, M., & Sicoly, F. (1979). Egocentric biases in availability and attribution. *Journal of Personality and Social Psychology, 37,* 322–336; Breckler, S. J., Pratkanis, A. R., & McCann, D. (1991). The representation of self in multidimensional cognitive space. *British Journal of Social Psychology, 30,* 97–112; Johnston, W. A. (1967). Individual performance and self-evaluation in a simulated team. *Organization Behavior and Human Performance, 2,* 309–328; Cunningham, J. D., Starr, P. A., & Kanouse, D. E. (1979). Self as actor, active observer, and passive observer: Implications for causal attribution. *Journal of Personality and Social Psychology, 37,* 1146–1152.

21. Gilovich, T., Medvec, V. H., & Savitsky, K. (2000). The spotlight effect in social judgment: An egocentric bias in estimates of the salience of one's own actions and appearance. *Journal of Personality and Social Psychology, 78,* 211–222.

22. Petty, R. E., & Brock, T. C. (1979). Effects of "Barnum" personality assessments on cognitive behavior. *Journal of Consulting and Clinical Psychology, 47,* 201–203.

23. Baumeister, R. F., Bratslavsky, E., Finkenauer, C., & Vohs, K. D. (2001). Bad is stronger than good. *Review of General Psychology, 5,* 323.

24. Luhmann, M., Hofmann, W., Eid, M., & Lucas, R. E. (2012). Subjective well-being and adaptation to life events: A meta-analysis. *Journal of Personality and Social Psychology, 102,* 592–615.

25. Baumeister, R. F., Bratslavsky, E., Finkenauer, C., & Vohs, K. D. (2001). Bad is stronger than good. *Review of General Psychology, 5,* 323.

26. Kahneman, D., & Tversky, A. (1992). Advances in prospect theory: Cumulative representation of uncertainty. *Journal of Risk and Uncertainty, 5,* 297–323.

27. Fryer Jr, R. G., Levitt, S. D., List, J., & Sadoff, S. (2012). *Enhancing the efficacy of teacher incentives through loss aversion: A field experiment* (No. w18237). National Bureau of Economic Research.

28. Gonzales, M. H., Aronson, E., & Costanzo, M. (1988). Increasing the effectiveness of energy auditors: A field experiment. *Journal of Applied Social Psychology, 18,* 1046–1066.

29. Two excellent treatments on the social psychology of happiness are: Haidt, J. (2006). *The happiness hypothesis: Finding modern truth in ancient wisdom.* New York: Basic Books; Lyubomirsky, S. (2008). *The how of happiness: A scientific approach to getting the life you want.* New York: Penguin.

30. Lyubomirsky, S., Dickerhoof, R., Boehm, J. K., & Sheldon, K. M. (2011). Becoming happier takes both a will and a proper way: An experimental longitudinal intervention to boost well-being. *Emotion, 11,* 391.

31. Kahneman, D. (2011). *Thinking, fast and slow.* New York: Macmillan.

32. Ophir, E., Nass, C., & Wagner, A. D. (2009). Cognitive control in media multitaskers. *Proceedings of the National Academy of Sciences, 106,* 15583–15587.

33. Haidt, J. (2012). *The righteous mind: Why good people are divided by politics and religion*. New York: Vintage.

34. Liu, J., Li, J., Feng, L., Li, L., Tian, J., & Lee, K. (2014). Seeing Jesus in toast: Neural and behavioral correlates of face pareidolia. *Cortex, 53,* 60–77.

35. Heider, F., & Simmel, M. (1944). An experimental study of apparent behavior. *American Journal of Psychology, 57,* 243–259.

36. Lieberman, M. D. (2013). *Social: Why our brains are wired to connect*. New York: Crown.

37. Hamilton, D. L., Katz, L. B., & Leirer, V. O. (1980). Cognitive representation of personality impressions: Organizational processes in first impression formation. *Journal of Personality and Social Psychology, 39,* 1050.

38. Eisenberger, N. I. (2012). Broken hearts and broken bones: A neural perspective on the similarities between social and physical pain. *Current Directions in Psychological Science, 21,* 42–47.

39. Eisenberger, N. I., Lieberman, M. D., & Williams, K. D. (2003). Does rejection hurt? An fMRI study of social exclusion. *Science, 302,* 290–292; Eisenberger, N. I., & Lieberman, M. D. (2004); Eisenberger, N. I., Lieberman, M. D., & Williams, K. D. (2003). Why rejection hurts: A common neural alarm system for physical and social pain. *Trends in Cognitive Sciences, 8,* 294–300.

40. Olson, K. (2015). *Wounded by school: Recapturing the joy in learning and standing up to old school culture*. New York: Teachers College Press.

41. Crisp, R. J., & Hewstone, M. (Eds.). (2007). *Multiple social categorization*. San Diego, CA: Elsevier Academic Press.

42. Tajfel, H. (1981). *Human groups and social categories*. Cambridge: Cambridge University Press.

43. Meissner, C. A., & Brigham, J. C. (2001). Thirty years of investigating the own-race bias in memory for faces: A meta-analytic review. *Psychology, Public Policy, and Law, 7,* 3–35.

44. Tajfel, H., Billig, M. G., Bundy, R. P., & Flament, C. (1971). Social categorization and intergroup behaviour. *European Journal of Social Psychology, 1,* 149–178.

45. Cohen, G. L. (2003). Party over policy: The dominating impact of group influence on political beliefs. *Journal of Personality and Social Psychology, 85,* 808.

46. Hastorf, A. H., & Cantril, H. (1954). They saw a game; a case study. *Journal of Abnormal and Social Psychology, 49,* 129.

47. Steven S., & Fernbach, P. (2017). *The knowledge illusion*. New York: Riverhead Books.

48. Yudkin, D., & Van Bavel, J. (2016). The roots of implicit bias. *New York Times*, December 9.

49. Yudkin, D. A., Rothmund, T., Twardawski, M., Thalla, N., & Van Bavel, J. J. (2016). Reflexive intergroup bias in third-party punishment. *Journal of Experimental Psychology: General, 145,* 1448–1459.

50. Fiske, S. T. (2009). *Social beings: Core motives in social psychology*. New York: John Wiley & Sons.

51. Baumeister, R. F., & Leary, M. R. (1995). The need to belong: Desire for interpersonal attachments as a fundamental human motivation. *Psychological Bulletin, 117,* 497.

52. Casella, J., Ridgeway, J., & Shourd, S. (2016). *Hell is a very small place: Voices from solitary confinement.* New York: The New Press.

53. Haney, C. (2003). Mental health issues in long-term solitary and "supermax" confinement. *NCCD News, 49,* 124–156.

54. Baumeister, R., & Tice, D. (2017). The social animal encounters social rejection: Cognitive, behavioral, emotional, and interpersonal effects of being excluded. In J. Aronson & E. Aronson (Eds.), *Readings about the social animal,* 12th edition. New York: Worth/Freeman.

55. Bastian, B., & Haslam, N. (2010). Excluded from humanity: The dehumanizing effects of social ostracism. *Journal of Experimental Social Psychology, 46,* 107–113; Wesselmann, E. D., Grzybowski, M. R., Steakley-Freeman, D. M., DeSouza, E. R., Nezlek, J. B., & Williams, K. D. (2016). Social exclusion in everyday life. In *Social Exclusion* (pp. 3–23). New York: Springer International Publishing; Pickett, C. L., & Gardner, W. L. (2005). The social monitoring system: Enhanced sensitivity to social cues and information as an adaptive response to social exclusion and belonging need. In K. D. Williams, J. P. Forgas, & W. von Hippel (Eds.), *The social outcast: Ostracism, social exclusion, rejection, and bullying* (pp. 213–226). New York: Psychology Press; Bernstein, M. J., Young, S. G., Brown, C. M., Sacco, D. F., & Claypool, H. M. (2008). Adaptive responses to social exclusion: Social rejection improves detection of real and fake smiles. *Psychological Science, 19,* 981–983.

56. Loersch, C., & Arbuckle, N. L. (2013). Unraveling the mystery of music: Music as an evolved group process. *Journal of Personality and Social Psychology, 105,* 777.

57. de Berker, A. O., Rutledge, R. B., Mathys, C., Marshall, L., Cross, G. F., Dolan, R. J., & Bestmann, S. (2016). Computations of uncertainty mediate acute stress responses in humans. *Nature Communications, 7,* 10996.

58. McEwen, B. S., & Gianaros, P. J. (2010). Central role of the brain in stress and adaptation: Links to socioeconomic status, health, and disease. *Annals of the New York Academy of Sciences, 1186,* 190–222.

59. Leary, M. R., & Baumeister, R. F. (2000). The nature and function of self-esteem: Sociometer theory. *Advances in Experimental Social Psychology, 32,* 1–62.

60. Peterson-Smith, K. (2015). Black lives matter: A new movement takes shape. *International Socialist Review,* 96.

61. Lerner, M. J. (1980). The belief in a just world. In *The belief in a just world* (pp. 9–30). New York: Springer US; Hafer, C. L., & Bègue, L. (2005). Experimental

research on just-world theory: Problems, developments, and future challenges. *Psychological Bulletin, 131,* 128.

62. Deci, E. L., & Ryan, R. M. (2000). The "what" and "why" of goal pursuits: Human needs and the self-determination of behavior. *Psychological Inquiry, 11,* 227–268; Fiske, S. T. (2009). *Social beings: Core motives in social psychology.* New York: John Wiley & Sons.

63. Webber, D., & Kruglanski, A. W. (2017). The social psychological makings of a terrorist. *Current Opinion in Psychology, 19,* 131–134; Kruglanski, A. W., Chen, X., Dechesne, M., Fishman, S., & Orehek, E. (2009). Fully committed: Suicide bombers' motivation and the quest for personal significance. *Political Psychology, 30,* 331–357.

64. Heider, F. (2013). *The psychology of interpersonal relations.* New York: Psychology Press; Kelley, H. H. (1967). Attribution theory in social psychology. In D. Levine (Ed.), *Nebraska symposium on motivation* (Vol. 15, pp. 192–241). Lincoln: University of Nebraska Press; Kelley, H. H. (1973). The process of causal attribution. *American Psychologist, 28,* 107–128; Interestingly, it has been argued that even scientists do not always think like scientists and instead fall prey to some of the biases described in this chapter. See Greenwald, A. G., Pratkanis, A. R., Leippe, M. R., & Baumgardner, M. H. (1986). Under what conditions does theory obstruct research progress? *Psychological Review, 93,* 216–229.

65. Gilbert, D. T., & Malone, P. S. (1995). The correspondence bias. *Psychological Bulletin, 117,* 21.

66. Ross, L., Amabile, T. M., & Steinmetz, J. L. (1977). Social roles, social control, and biases in social-perception processes. *Journal of Personality and Social Psychology, 35,* 485–494.

67. Buchanan, G. M., & Seligman, M. (2013). *Explanatory style.* New York: Routledge.

68. Rosenthal, R., & Jacobson, L. (1968). *Pygmalion in the classroom.* New York: Holt, Rinehart & Winston; Rosenthal, R. (2002). The Pygmalion effect and its mediating mechanisms. In J. Aronson (Ed.), *Improving academic achievement: Impact of psychological factors on education.* San Diego: Academic Press.

69. Jussim, L., & Harber, K. D. (2005). Teacher expectations and self-fulfilling prophecies: Knowns and unknowns, resolved and unresolved controversies. *Personality and Social Psychology Review, 9,* 131–155.

70. Simonson, I., & Tversky, A. (1992). Choice in context: Tradeoff contrast and extremeness aversion. *Journal of Marketing, 29,* 281; Gilbert, D. T. (2006). *Stumbling on happiness.* New York: Knopf.

71. Marsh, H. W., Kong, C.-K., & Hau, K.-T. (2000). Longitudinal multilevel models of the big-fish-little-pond effect on academic self-concept: Counterbalancing contrast and reflected glory effects in Hong Kong schools. *Journal of Personality and Social Psychology, 78,* 337–349.

72. Thornton, B., & Maurice, J. (1997). Physique contrast effect: Adverse impact of idealized body images for women. *Sex Roles, 37,* 433–439.

73. Shensa, A., Escobar-Viera, C. G., Sidani, J. E., Bowman, N. D., Marshal, M. P., & Primack, B. A. (2017). Problematic social media use and depressive symptoms among US young adults: A nationally-representative study. *Social Science & Medicine, 182,* 150–157.

74. Lyubomirsky, S. (2013). *The myths of happiness: What should make you happy, but doesn't, what shouldn't make you happy, but does.* New York: Penguin.

75. Dweck, C. S. (2006). *Mindset: The new psychology of success.* New York: Random House Incorporated.

76. Higgins, E. T., Rholes, W. S., & Jones, C. R. (1977). Category accessibility and impression formation. *Journal of Experimental Social Psychology, 13,* 141–154.

77. Graham, S., & Lowery, B. S. (2004). Priming unconscious racial stereotypes about adolescent offenders. *Law and Human Behavior, 28,* 483.

78. McCombs, M. E., & Shaw, D. L. (1972). The agenda-setting function of mass media. *Public Opinion Quarterly, 36,* 176–187; McCombs, M. (1994). News influence on our pictures of the world. In J. Bryant, & D. Zillmann (Eds.), *Media effects: Advances in theory and research* (pp. 1–16). Hillsdale, NJ: Erlbaum.

79. Cohen, B. (1963). *The press and foreign policy.* Princeton: Princeton University Press.

80. Asch, S. (1946). Forming impressions of personality. *Journal of Abnormal and Social Psychology, 41,* 258–290.

81. Jones, E. E., Rock, L., Shaver, K. G., Goethals, G. R., & Ward, L. M. (1968). Pattern of performance and ability attribution: An unexpected primacy effect. *Journal of Personality and Social Psychology, 10,* 317–340.

82. Aronson, J. M., & Jones, E. E. (1992). Inferring abilities after influencing performances. *Journal of Experimental Social Psychology, 28,* 277–299.

83. Tversky, A., & Kahneman, D. (1974). Judgment under uncertainty: Heuristics and biases. *Science, 185,* 1124–1131; Kahneman, D., & Tversky, A. (1973). On the psychology of prediction. *Psychological Review, 80,* 237–251.

84. Food and Agriculture Organization of the United Nations (1981). Which cereal for breakfast? *Consumer Reports,* 68–75.

85. Tversky, A., & Kahneman, D. (1973). Availability: A heuristic for judging frequency and probability. *Cognitive Psychology, 5,* 207–232; Signorielli, N., Gerbner, G., & Morgan, M. (1995). Violence on television: The Cultural Indicators Project. *Journal of Broadcasting and Electronic Media, 39,* 278–283.

86. Oppenheimer, D. M., & Frank, M. C. (2008). A rose in any other font would not smell as sweet: Effects of perceptual fluency on categorization. *Cognition, 106,* 1178–1194.

87. McGlone, M. S., & Tofighbakhsh, J. (2000). Birds of a feather flock conjointly (?): Rhyme as reason in aphorisms. *Psychological Science, 11.5*, 424–428.

88. Schwarz, N., & Clore, G. L. (1983). Mood, misattribution, and judgments of well-being: Informative and directive functions of affective states. *Journal of Personality and Social Psychology, 45*, 513.

89. Sinaceur, M., Heath, C., & Cole, S. (2005). Emotional and deliberative reactions to a public crisis: Mad cow disease in France. *Psychological Science, 16*, 247–254.

90. Pratkanis, A. R. (1989). The cognitive representation of attitudes. In A. R. Pratkanis, S. J. Breckler, & A. G. Greenwald (Eds.), *Attitude structure and function* (pp. 71–98). Hillsdale, NJ: Erlbaum.

91. Wilson, T. D., & Gilbert, D. T. (2003). Affective forecasting. *Advances in Experimental Social Psychology, 35*, 345–411; Gilbert, D. T. (2006). *Stumbling on happiness*. New York: Knopf.

92. Dunn, E. W., Wilson, T. D., & Gilbert, D. T. (2003). Location, location, location: The misprediction of satisfaction in housing lotteries. *Personality and Social Psychology Bulletin, 29*, 1421–1432.

93. Liberman, N., & Trope, Y. (1998). The role of feasibility and desirability considerations in near and distant future decisions: A test of temporal construal theory. *Journal of Personality and Social Psychology, 75*, 5.

94. Loftus, E. F., & Loftus, G. R. (1980). On the permanence of stored information in the human brain. *American Psychologist, 35*, 409–420; Loftus, E. F., & Palmer, J. C. (1974).

95. Loftus, E. F., & Palmer, J. C. (1974). Reconstruction of automobile destruction: An example of the interaction between language and memory. *Journal of Verbal Learning and Verbal Behavior, 13*, 585–589.

96. Loftus, E. F. (1977). Shifting human color memory. *Memory and Cognition, 5*, 696–699.

97. Markus, H. (1977). Self-schemata and processing information about the self. *Journal of Personality and Social Psychology, 35*, 63–78; Conway, M., & Ross, M. (1984). Getting what you want by revising what you had. *Journal of Personality and Social Psychology, 47*, 738.

98. Loftus, E. F. (1993). The reality of repressed memories. *American Psychologist, 48*, 518–537; Loftus, E. F., & Ketcham, K. (1994). *The myth of repressed memory: False memories and allegations of sexual abuse*. New York: St. Martin's Press.

99. Loftus, E. F., & Greenspan, R. L. (2017). If I'm certain, is it true? Accuracy and confidence in eyewitness memory. *Psychological Science in the Public Interest, 18*, 1–2.

100. Loftus, E. F., & Greenspan, R. L. (2017). If I'm certain, is it true? Accuracy and confidence in eyewitness memory. *Psychological Science in the Public Interest, 18*, 1–2.

Chapter 3   Self-Justification

1. Prasad, J. (1950). A comparative study of rumors and reports in earthquakes. *British Journal of Psychology, 41*, 129–144.

2. Sinha, D. (1952). Behavior in a catastrophic situation: A psychological study of reports and rumours. *British Journal of Psychology, 43*, 200–209.

3. Festinger, L. (1957). *A theory of cognitive dissonance.* Stanford, CA: Stanford University Press.

4. Fotuhi, O., Fong, G. T., Zanna, M P., Borland, R., Yong, H., & Cummings, K. M. (2013). Patterns of cognitive dissonance-reducing beliefs among smokers: A longitudinal analysis from the International Tobacco Control (ITC) Four Country Survey. *Tobacco Control: An International Journal, 22*, 52–58.

5. Kassarjian, H., & Cohen, J. (1965). Cognitive dissonance and consumer behavior. *California Management Review, 8*, 55–64.

6. Tagliacozzo, R. (1979). Smokers' self-categorization and the reduction of cognitive dissonance. *Addictive Behaviors, 4*, 393–399.

7. Gibbons, F. X., Eggleston, T. J., & Benthin, A. C. (1997). Cognitive reactions to smoking relapse: The reciprocal relation between dissonance and self-esteem. *Journal of Personality and Social Psychology, 72*, 184–195.

8. Goleman, D. (1982, January). Make-or-break resolutions. *Psychology Today,* 19.

9. Levin, M. (1997). Jury views CEO's "gummy bear" deposition. *Los Angeles Times,* July 18, D3.

10. Tavris, C., & Aronson, E. (2007/2015). *Mistakes were made (but not by me),* Revised edition. New York: Harcourt.

11. Bruce, L. (1966). *How to talk dirty and influence people.* Chicago: Playboy Press, and New York: Pocket Books.

12. Trump, D. (2016). Said at a campaign rally in Iowa, 23 January.

13. Jones, E., & Kohler, R. (1959). The effects of plausibility on the learning of controversial statements. *Journal of Abnormal and Social Psychology, 57*, 315–320.

14. Lord, C., Ross, L., & Lepper, M. (1979). Biased assimilation and attitude polarization: The effects of prior theories on subsequently considered evidence. *Journal of Personality and Social Psychology, 37*, 2098–2109; Edwards, K., & Smith, E. (1996). A disconfirmation bias in the evaluation of arguments. *Journal of Personality and Social Psychology, 71*, 5–24.

15. Haidt, J. (2012). *The righteous mind: Why good people are divided by politics and religion.* New York: Vintage; Cohen, G. L., Aronson, J., & Steele, C. M. (2000). When beliefs yield to evidence: Reducing biased evaluation by affirming the self. *Personality and Social Psychology Bulletin, 26*, 1151–1164.

16. Ehrlich, D., Guttman, I., Schonbach, P., & Mills, J. (1957). Post-decision exposure to relevant information. *Journal of Abnormal and Social Psychology, 57,*

98–102; Gilovich, T., Medvec, V. H., & Chen S. (1995). Commission, omission, and dissonance reduction: Coping with regret in the "Monty Hall" problem. *Personality and Social Psychology Bulletin, 21*, 182–190.

17. Brehm, J. (1956). Postdecision changes in the desirability of alternatives. *Journal of Abnormal and Social Psychology, 52*, 384–389.

18. Johnson, D. J., & Rusbult, C. E. (1989). Resisting temptation: Devaluation of alternative partners as a means of maintaining commitment in close relationships. *Journal of Personality and Social Psychology, 57*, 967–980.

19. Simpson, J. A., Gangestad, S. W., & Lerma, M. (1990). Perception of physical attractiveness: Mechanisms involved in the maintenance of romantic relationships. *Journal of Personality and Social Psychology, 59*, 1192–1201.

20. Gilbert, D. T. (2006). *Stumbling on happiness.* New York: Knopf.

21. Arad, A. (2013). Past decisions do affect future choices: An experimental demonstration. *Organizational Behavior and Human Decision Processes, 121*, 267–277.

22. Egan, L. C., Santos, L. R., & Bloom, P. (2007). The origins of cognitive dissonance: Evidence from children and monkeys. *Psychological Science, 18*, 978–983.

23. Harmon-Jones, E., Harmon-Jones, C., & Amodio, D. M. (2012). A neuroscientific perspective on dissonance, guided by the action-based model. In B. Gawronski & F. Strack (Eds.), *Cognitive consistency: A fundamental principle in social cognition* (pp. 47–65). New York: Guilford Press.

24. Westen, D., Blagov P. S., Harenski, K., Kilts, C., & Hamann, S. (2006). Neural bases of motivated reasoning: An FMRI study of emotional constraints on partisan political judgment in the 2004 U.S. Presidential election. *Journal of Cognitive Neuroscience, 18*, 1947–1958.

25. Kokkoris, M. D., & Kühnen, U. (2013). Choice and dissonance in a European cultural context: The case of Western and Eastern Europeans. *International Journal of Psychology, 48*, 1260–1266.

26. Sakai, H. (1999). A multiplicative power-function model of cognitive dissonance: Toward an integrated theory of cognition, emotion, and behavior after Leon Festinger. In E. Harmon-Jones & J. S. Mills (Eds.), *Cognitive dissonance: Progress on a pivotal theory in social psychology.* Washington, D.C.: American Psychological Association.

27. Imada, T., & Kitayama, S. (2010). Social eyes and choice justification: Culture and dissonance revisited. *Social Cognition, 28*, 589–608.

28. Knox, R., & Inkster, J. (1968). Postdecision dissonance at post time. *Journal of Personality and Social Psychology, 8*, 319–323.

29. Gilbert, D. T., & Ebert, J. E. (2002). Decisions and revisions: The affective forecasting of changeable outcomes. *Journal of Personality and Social Psychology, 82*, 503.

30. Cialdini, R., Cacioppo, J., Bassett, R., & Miller, J. (1978). Low-ball procedure for producing compliance: Commitment then cost. *Journal of Personality and Social Psychology, 36*, 463–476.

31. Mills, J. (1958). Changes in moral attitudes following temptation. *Journal of Personality, 26*, 517–531.

32. Freedman, J. L., & Fraser, S. C. (1966). Compliance without pressure: The foot-in-the-door technique. *Journal of Personality and Social Psychology, 4*, 195.

33. Pliner, P., Hart, H., Kohl, J., & Saari, D. (1974). Compliance without pressure: Some further data on the foot-in-the-door technique. *Journal of Experimental Social Psychology, 10*, 17–22.

34. Festinger, L., & Carlsmith, J. M. (1959). Cognitive consequences of forced compliance. *Journal of Abnormal and Social Psychology, 58*, 203–210.

35. Cohen, A. R. (1962). An experiment on small rewards for discrepant compliance and attitude change. In J. W. Brehm & A. R. Cohen, *Explorations in cognitive dissonance* (pp. 73–78). New York: Wiley.

36. Zimbardo, P. (1969). *The cognitive control of motivation*. Glencoe, IL: Scott, Foresman.

37. Brehm, J. (1962). Motivational effects of cognitive dissonance. In *Nebraska Symposium on Motivation, 1962* (pp. 51–77). Lincoln: University of Nebraska Press.

38. Zimbardo, P., Weisenberg, M., Firestone, I., & Levy, B. (1965). Communicator effectiveness in producing public conformity and private attitude change. *Journal of Personality, 33*, 233–255.

39. Aronson, E., & Carlsmith, J. M. (1963). Effect of the severity of threat on the devaluation of forbidden behavior. *Journal of Abnormal and Social Psychology, 66*, 584–588.

40. Freedman, J. (1965). Long-term behavioral effects of cognitive dissonance. *Journal of Experimental Social Psychology, 1*, 145–155.

41. Bryan, C. J., Adams, G. S., & Monin, B. (2013). When cheating would make you a cheater: Implicating the self prevents unethical behavior. *Journal of Experimental Psychology: General, 142*, 1001–1005.

42. Pitt, R. N. (2010). "Killing the messenger": Religious black gay men's neutralization of anti-gay religious messages. *Journal for the Scientific Study of Religion, 49*, 56–72.

43. Aronson, E. (1968). Dissonance theory: Progress and problems. In R. P. Abelson, E. Aronson, W. J. McGuire, T. M. Newcomb, M. J. Rosenberg, & P. H. Tannenbaum (Eds.), *Theories of cognitive consistency: A sourcebook* (pp. 5–27). Chicago: Rand McNally; Aronson, E. (1969). The theory of cognitive dissonance: A current perspective. In L. Berkowitz (Ed.), *Advances in experimental social psychology* (Vol. 4, pp. 1–34). New York: Academic Press.

44. Murray, A. A., Wood, J. M., & Lilienfeld, S. O. (2012). Psychopathic personality traits and cognitive dissonance: Individual differences in attitude change. *Journal of Research in Personality, 46*, 525–536.

45. Aronson, E., & Mettee, D., (1968). Dishonest behavior as a function of different levels of self-esteem. *Journal of Personality and Social Psychology, 9*, 121–127.

46. Cohen, G. L., Garcia, J., Apfel, N., & Master, A. (2006). Reducing the racial achievement gap: A social-psychological intervention. *Science, 313*, 1307–1310.

47. Kernis, M. H. (2001). Following the trail from narcissism to fragile self-esteem. *Psychological Inquiry, 12*, 223–225.

48. Baumeister, R. F., Bushman, B. J., & Campbell, W. K. (2000). Self-esteem, narcissism, and aggression: Does violence result from low self-esteem or from threatened egotism? *Current Directions in Psychological Science, 9*, 26–29.

49. Salmivalli, C., Kaukiainen, A., Kaistaniemi, L., & Lagerspetz, K. M. Self-evaluated self-esteem, peer-evaluated self-esteem, and defensive egotism as predictors of adolescents' participation in bullying situations. *Personality and Social Psychology Bulletin, 25*, 1268–1278.

50. Aronson, E., & Mills, J. (1959). The effect of severity of initiation on liking for a group. *Journal of Abnormal and Social Psychology, 59*, 177–181.

51. Gerard, H., & Mathewson, G. (1966). The effects of severity on initiation on liking for a group: A replication. *Journal of Experimental Social Psychology, 2*, 278–287.

52. Aronson, E. (1969). The theory of cognitive dissonance: A current perspective. In L. Berkowitz (Ed.), *Advances in experimental social psychology* (Vol. 4, pp. 1–34). New York: Academic Press.

53. Sapolsky, R. (1993). *Why zebras don't get ulcers.* New York: Freeman.

54. Conway, M., & Ross, M. (1984). Getting what you want by revising what you had. *Journal of Personality and Social Psychology, 47*, 738–748.

55. Michener, J. (1971). *Kent State: What happened and why.* New York: Random House.

56. Davis, K., & Jones, E. E. (1960). Changes in interpersonal perception as a means of reducing cognitive dissonance. *Journal of Abnormal and Social Psychology, 61*, 402–410; Gibbons, F. X., & McCoy, S. B. (1991). Self-esteem, similarity, and reactions to active versus passive downward comparison. *Journal of Personality and Social Psychology, 60*, 414–424.

57. Glass, D. (1964). Changes in liking as a means of reducing cognitive discrepancies between self-esteem and aggression. *Journal of Personality, 32*, 531–549; Sorrentino, R., & Boutilier, R. (1974). Evaluation of a victim as a function of fate similarity/dissimilarity. *Journal of Experimental Social Psychology, 10*, 84–93; Sorrentino, R., & Hardy, J. (1974). Religiousness and derogation of an innocent victim. *Journal of Personality, 42*, 372–382.

58. Berscheid, E., Boyce, D., & Walster (Hatfield), E. (1968). Retaliation as a means of restoring equity. *Journal of Personality and Social Psychology, 10,* 370–376.

59. Sturman, E.D. (2012). Dehumanizing just makes you feel better: The role of cognitive dissonance in dehumanization. *Journal of Social, Evolutionary, and Cultural Psychology, 6,* 527–531.

60. Jost, J. T., Kay, A. C., & Thorisdottir, H. (Eds.). (2009). *Social and psychological bases of ideology and system justification.* New York: Oxford University Press.

61. Harber, K. D., Podolski, P., & Williams, C. H. (2015). Emotional disclosure and victim blaming. *Emotion, 15,* 603–614.

62. Shaw, G. B. (1952). In D. Russel (Ed.), *Selected prose.* New York: Dodd, Mead.

63. Brehm, J. (1959). Increasing cognitive dissonance by a fait-accompli. *Journal of Abnormal and Social Psychology, 58,* 379.

64. Darley, J., & Berscheid, E. (1967). Increased liking as a result of the anticipation of personal contact. *Human Relations, 20,* 29–40.

65. Lehman, D., & Taylor, S. E. (1987). Date with an earthquake: Coping with a probable, unpredictable disaster. *Personality and Social Psychology Bulletin, 13,* 546–555.

66. Aronson, E. (1997). The giving away of psychology—and condoms. *APS Observer, 10,* 17–35.

67. Stone, J., Aronson, E., Crain, A. L., Winslow, M. P., & Fried, C. B. (1994). Inducing hypocrisy as a means of encouraging young adults to use condoms. *Personality and Social Psychology Bulletin, 20,* 116–128.

68. Aronson, E. (1998). Dissonance, hypocrisy, and the self-concept. In E. Harmon-Jones & J. S. Mills (Eds.), *Cognitive dissonance theory: Revival with revisions and controversies.* Washington, D.C.: American Psychological Association Books; Dickerson, C. A., Thibodeau, R., Aronson, E., & Miller, D. (1992). Using cognitive dissonance to encourage water conservation. *Journal of Applied Social Psychology, 22,* 841–854; Aronson, J., Fried, C. B., & Good, C. (2002). Reducing the effects of stereotype threat on African American college students by shaping theories of intelligence. *Journal of Experimental Social Psychology, 38,* 113–125.

69. Wiesel, E. (1969). *Night.* New York: Avon.

70. White, J. E. (1988). Bush's most valuable player. *Time,* November 14, 20–21.

71. McClellan, S. (2008). *What happened: Inside the Bush White House and Washington's culture of deception.* New York: Public Affairs.

72. Bush, G. (2010). *Decision points.* New York: Crown.

73. Rosenthal, A. (1988). Foes accuse Bush campaign of inflaming racial tension. *New York Times,* October 24, A1, B5.

74. Goodwin, D. K. (2005). *Team of rivals: The political genius of Abraham Lincoln.* New York: Simon & Schuster.

75. Risen, J. (2006). *State of war: The secret history of the C.I.A. and the Bush administration.* New York: Free Press.

76. Johnson, L. B. (1971). *The vantage point: Perspectives of the presidency 1963–69.* New York: Holt, Rinehart and Winston.

Chapter 4   Conformity

1. © 1933, 1961 by James Thurber. From "The day the dam broke" in *My life and hard times* (New York: Harper, 1933), pp. 41, 47. (Originally printed in the *New Yorker.*)

2. Schachter, S. (1951). Deviation, rejection, and communication. *Journal of Abnormal and Social Psychology, 46,* 190–207.

3. Kruglanski, A. W., & Webster, D. W. (1991). Group members' reaction to opinion deviates and conformists at varying degrees of proximity to decision deadline and of environmental noise. *Journal of Personality and Social Psychology, 61,* 212–225.

4. Speer, A. (1970). *Inside the Third Reich: Memoirs.* (R. Winston & C. Winston, Trans.). New York: Macmillan.

5. (1975). John Dean interview. *Playboy,* January, 78.

6. Janis, I. L. (1971). Groupthink. *Psychology Today,* November, 43–46; Janis, I. L. (1984). Counteracting the adverse effects of concurrence-seeking in policy-planning groups. In H. Brandstatter, J. H. Davis, & G. Stocker-Kreichgauer (Eds.), *Group decision making.* New York: Academic Press; Kameda, T., & Sugimori, S. (1993). Psychological entrapment in group decision making: An assigned decision rule and a groupthink phenomenon. *Journal of Personality and Social Psychology, 65,* 282–292.

7. Heyes, C. (2016). Imitation: Not in our genes. *Current Biology, 26,* R412–R414.

8. Meltzoff, A. N., & Moore, M. K. (1983). Newborn infants imitate adult facial gestures. *Child Development, 54,* 702–709.

9. Meltzoff, A. N., & Kuhl, P. K. (2016). Exploring the infant social brain: What's going on in there? *Zero to Three Journal, 36,* 1–9.

10. Chartrand, T. L., & Bargh, J. A. (1999). The chameleon effect: The perception–behavior link and social interaction. *Journal of Personality and Social Psychology, 76,* 893.

11. Lakin, J. L., Jefferis, V. E., Cheng, C. M., & Chartrand, T. L. (2003). The chameleon effect as social glue: Evidence for the evolutionary significance of nonconscious mimicry. *Journal of Nonverbal Behavior, 27,* 145–162.

12. Chartrand, T. L., & Bargh, J. A. (1999). The chameleon effect: The perception–behavior link and social interaction. *Journal of Personality and Social Psychology, 76,* 893.

13. Rist, D. (2013). *The chameleon effect*. Lulu.com; Berger, J. (2016). *Invisible influence: The hidden forces that shape behavior*. New York: Simon & Schuster.

14. https://www.theguardian.com/world/2007/may/02/hillaryclinton. uselections2008. Accessed August 14, 2017; Mills, C. (2015). http://www. washingtonexaminer.com/clintons-southern-strategy-hillary-fakes-accent-for-crowd/article/2574357. Accessed August 14, 2017; Clinton denied the charges of pandering, claiming that she unconsciously slips into the drawl and saying "Y'all," whenever in the South.

15. Stel, M., Blascovich, J., McCall, C., et al. (2010). Mimicking disliked others: Effects of a priori liking on the mimicry-liking link. *European Journal of Social Psychology, 40*, 867–880; Van Baaren, R., Janssen, L., Chartrand, T. L., & Dijksterhuis, A. (2009). Where is the love? The social aspects of mimicry. *Philosophical Transactions of the Royal Society of London, B: Biological Sciences, 364*, 2381–2389.

16. Haun, D. B., Rekers, Y., & Tomasello, M. (2014). Children conform to the behavior of peers; other great apes stick with what they know. *Psychological Science, 25*, 2160–2167.

17. Fein, S., Goethals, G. R., & Kugler, M. B. (2007). Social influence on political judgments: The case of presidential debates. *Political Psychology, 28*, 165–192.

18. Nisbett, R. E., & Wilson, T. D. (1977). Telling more than we can know: Verbal reports on mental processes. *Psychological Review, 84*, 231.

19. Sherif, M. (1937). An experimental approach to the study of attitudes. *Sociometry*, 1, 90–98; MacNeil, M. K., & Sherif, M. (1976). Norm change over subject generations as a function of arbitrariness of prescribed norms. *Journal of Personality and Social Psychology, 34*, 762.

20. Asch, S. (1951). Effects of group pressure upon the modification and distortion of judgment. In M. H. Guetzkow (Ed.), *Groups, leadership and men* (pp. 117–190). Pittsburgh: Carnegie; Asch, S. (1956). Studies of independence and conformity: A minority of one against a unanimous majority. *Psychological Monographs, 70* (9, Whole No. 416).

21. Gitow, A., & Rothenberg, F. (Producers). (1997). *Dateline NBC: Follow the leader*. Distributed by NBC News. (August 10).

22. Bond, R., & Smith, P. (1996). Culture and conformity: A meta-analysis of studies using Asch's (1952, 1956) line judgment task. *Psychological Bulletin, 119*, 111–137.

23. Berns, G. S., Chappelow, J., Zink, C. F., Pagnoni, G., Martin-Skurski, M. E., & Richards, J. (2005). Neurobiological correlates of social conformity and independence during mental rotation. *Biological Psychiatry, 58*, 245–253.

24. Wu, H., Luo, Y., & Feng, C. (2016). Neural signatures of social conformity: A coordinate-based activation likelihood estimation meta-analysis of functional brain imaging studies. *Neuroscience & Biobehavioral Reviews, 71*, 101–111.

25. Eisenberger, N. I., & Lieberman, M. D. (2004). Why rejection hurts: A common neural alarm system for physical and social pain. *Trends in Cognitive Sciences, 8*, 294–300; Baumeister, R., & Tice, D. (2017). The social animal encounters social rejection: Cognitive, behavioral, emotional, and interpersonal effects of being excluded. In J. Aronson & E. Aronson (Eds.), *Readings about the social animal,* 12th edition. New York: Worth/Freeman; Twenge, J. M., Baumeister, R. F., Tice, D. M., & Stucke, T. S. (2001). If you can't join them, beat them: Effects of social exclusion on aggressive behavior. *Journal of Personality and Social Psychology, 81*, 1058–1069.

26. Festinger, L. (1954). A theory of social comparison processes. *Human Relations, 7*, 117–140.

27. Wolosin, R., Sherman, S., & Cann, A. (1975). Predictions of own and others' conformity. *Journal of Personality, 43*, 357–378.

28. Mullen, B., Cooper, C., & Driskell, J. E. (1990). Jaywalking as a function of model behavior. *Personality and Social Psychology Bulletin, 16*, 320–330.

29. Gladwell, M. (2000). *The tipping point.* New York: Little, Brown.

30. Surowiecki, J. (2005). *The wisdom of crowds: Why the many are smarter than the few and how collective wisdom shapes business, economies, societies, and nations.* New York: Random House; Hertwig, R. (2012). Tapping into the wisdom of the crowd—with confidence. *Science, 336*, 303–304.

31. Boyanowsky, E., Allen, V., Bragg, B., & Lepinski, J. (1981). Generalization of independence created by social support. *Psychological Record, 31*, 475–488.

32. Allen, V., & Levine, J. (1971). Social support and conformity: The role of independent assessment of reality. *Journal of Experimental Social Psychology, 7*, 48–58.

33. Deutsch, M., & Gerard, H. (1955). A study of normative and informational social influence upon individual judgment. *Journal of Abnormal and Social Psychology, 51*, 629–636.

34. Pennington, J., & Schlenker, B. R. (1999). Accountability for consequential decisions: Justifying ethical judgments to audiences. *Personality and Social Psychology Bulletin, 25*, 1067–1981.

35. Quinn, A., & Schlenker, B. R. (2002). Can accountability produce independence? Goals as determinants of the impact of accountability on conformity. *Personality and Social Psychology Bulletin, 28*, 472–483.

36. Arndt, J., Schimel, J., Greenberg, J., & Pyszczynski, T. (2002). The intrinsic self and defensiveness: Evidence that activating the intrinsic self reduces self-handicapping and conformity. *Personality and Social Psychology Bulletin, 28*, 671–683.

37. Mausner, B. (1954). The effects of prior reinforcement of the interaction of observed pairs. *Journal of Abnormal and Social Psychology, 49*, 65–68; Mausner, B. (1954). The effect on one's partner's success in a relevant task on the

interaction of observed pairs. *Journal of Abnormal and Social Psychology, 49,* 557–560; Goldberg, S., & Lubin, A. (1958). Influence as a function of perceived judgment error. *Human Relations, 11,* 275–281; Wiesenthal, D., Endler, N., Coward, T., & Edwards, J. (1976). Reversibility of relative competence as a determinant of conformity across different perceptual tasks. *Representative Research in Social Psychology, 7,* 35–43.

38. Dittes, J., & Kelley, H. (1956). Effects of different conditions of acceptance upon conformity to group norms. *Journal of Abnormal and Social Psychology, 53,* 100–107.

39. Harris, J. R. (2011). *The nurture assumption: Why children turn out the way they do.* New York: Simon and Schuster.

40. Steinberg, L. (2007). Risk taking in adolescence. *Current Directions in Psychological Science, 16,* 55–59.

41. Steinberg, L. (2008). A social neuroscience perspective on adolescent risk-taking. *Developmental Review, 28,* 78–106; Botdorf, M., Rosenbaum, G. M., Patrianakos, J., Steinberg, L., & Chein, J. M. (2017). Adolescent risk-taking is predicted by individual differences in cognitive control over emotional, but not non-emotional, response conflict. *Cognition and Emotion, 31,* 972–979.

42. Kennedy, D. M. (2013). "Don't shoot." Guest lecture on youth violence. New York University.

43. Baird, A. A. (2008). Adolescent moral reasoning: The integration of emotion and cognition. *Moral Psychology, 3,* 323–342.

44. Gaither, S. E., Apfelbaum, E. P., Birnbaum, H. J., Babbitt, L. G., & Sommers, S. R. (2017). Mere membership in racially diverse groups reduces conformity. *Social Psychological and Personality Science.* DOI: 10.1177/1948550617708013.

45. Kindermann, T. A. (2007). Effects of naturally existing peer groups on changes in academic engagement in a cohort of sixth graders. *Child Development, 78,* 1186–1203; Kindermann, T. A., McCollam, T. L., & Gibson, E. (1996). Peer group influences on children's developing school motivation. In K. Wentzel & J. Juvonen (Eds.), *Social motivation: Understanding children's school adjustment* (pp. 279–312). Newbury Park, CA: Sage.

46. Newcomb, T. M. (1943). *Personality and social change: Attitude formation in a student community.* New York: Holt, Rinehart, & Winston.

47. Crandall, C. S. (1988). Social contagion of binge eating. *Journal of Personality and Social Psychology, 55,* 588–598; O'Connor, S. M., Burt, S. A., VanHuysse, J. L., & Klump, K. L. (2016). What drives the association between weight-conscious peer groups and disordered eating? Disentangling genetic and environmental selection from pure socialization effects. *Journal of Abnormal Psychology, 125,* 356–368.

48. Aronson, E., & O'Leary, M. (1982–1983). The relative effectiveness of models and prompts on energy conservation: A field experiment in a shower room. *Journal of Environmental Systems, 12,* 219–224.

49. Cialdini, R. B., Reno, R. R., & Kallgren, C. A. (1990). A focus theory of normative conduct: Recycling the concept of norms to reduce littering in public places. *Journal of Personality and Social Psychology, 58,* 1015–1029.

50. Reno, R., Cialdini, R., & Kallgren, C. A. (1993). The trans-situational influence of social norms. *Journal of Personality and Social Psychology, 64,* 104–112.

51. Keizer, K., Lindenberg, S., & Steg, L. (2008). The spreading of disorder. *Science, 322,* 1681–1685; Hinkle, J. C., & Yang, S. M. (2014). A new look into broken windows: What shapes individuals' perceptions of social disorder? *Journal of Criminal Justice, 42,* 26–35; Keuschnigg, M., & Wolbring, T. (2015). Disorder, social capital, and norm violation: Three field experiments on the broken windows thesis. *Rationality and Society, 27,* 96–126; Keizer, K., Lindenberg, S., & Steg, L. (2013). The importance of demonstratively restoring order. *PLoS One, 8,* e65137.

52. Wicherts, J. M., & Bakker, M. (2014). Broken windows, mediocre methods, and substandard statistics. *Group Processes & Intergroup Relations, 17,* 388–403; Wilson, J. Q., & Kelling, G. L. (1982). Broken windows. *Atlantic Monthly,* March, 29–38.

53. Goldstein, N. J., Cialdini, R. B., & Griskevicius, V. (2008). A room with a viewpoint: Using social norms to motivate environmental conservation in hotels. *Journal of Consumer Research, 35,* 472–482.

54. Cialdini, R. B. (2003). Crafting normative messages to protect the environment. *Current Directions in Psychological Science, 12(4),* 105–109.

55. Manning, R., Levine, M., & Collins, A. (2007). The Kitty Genovese murder and the social psychology of helping: The parable of the 38 witnesses. *American Psychologist, 62,* 555–562.

56. Pelonero, C. (2014). *Kitty Genovese: A true account of a public murder and its private consequences.* New York: Skyhorse Publishing.

57. Korte, C., & Kerr, N. (1975). Response to altruistic opportunities in urban and nonurban settings. *Journal of Social Psychology, 95,* 183–184; Rushton, J. P. (1978). Urban density and altruism: Helping strangers in a Canadian city, suburb, and small town. *Psychological Reports, 43,* 987–990.

58. Levine, R. V., Norenzayan, A., & Philbrick, K. (2001). Cross-cultural differences in helping strangers. *Journal of Cross-Cultural Psychology, 32,* 543–560.

59. Darley, J., & Latané, B. (1968). Bystander intervention in emergencies: Diffusion of responsibility. *Journal of Personality and Social Psychology, 8,* 377–383; Latané, B., & Darley, J. (1968). Group inhibition of bystander intervention in emergencies. *Journal of Personality and Social Psychology, 10,* 215–221; Latané, B., & Rodin, J. (1969). A lady in distress: Inhibiting effects of friends and strangers on bystander intervention. *Journal of Experimental Social Psychology, 5,* 189–202.

60. Latané, B., & Rodin, J. (1969). A lady in distress: Inhibiting effects of friends and strangers on bystander intervention. *Journal of Experimental Social Psychology, 5,* 189–202.

61. Darley, J., & Latané, B. (1968). Bystander intervention in emergencies: Diffusion of responsibility. *Journal of Personality and Social Psychology, 8,* 377–383.

62. Darley, J., & Batson, D. (1973). "From Jerusalem to Jericho": A study of situational and dispositional variables in helping behavior. *Journal of Personality and Social Psychology, 27,* 100–108.

63. Piliavin, I., Rodin, J., & Piliavin, J. (1969). Good samaritanism: An underground phenomenon? *Journal of Personality and Social Psychology, 13,* 289–299.

64. Fischer, P., Krueger, J. I., Greitemeyer, T., et al. (2011). The bystander-effect: A meta-analytic review on bystander intervention in dangerous and non-dangerous emergencies. *Psychological Bulletin, 137,* 517–537.

65. Gross, J. J. (1998). The emerging field of emotion regulation: An integrative review. *Review of General Psychology, 2,* 271–299; Gross, J. J., & John, O. P. (2003). Individual differences in two emotion regulation processes: Implications for affect, relationships, and wellbeing. *Journal of Personality and Social Psychology, 85,* 348–362.

66. Hochschild, A. R. (2003). *The managed heart: Commercialization of human feeling* (2nd edition). Berkeley, CA: University of California Press.

67. Jessor, R., Costa, F. M., Krueger, P. M., & Turbin, M. S. (2017). Problem drinking in college. In *Problem behavior theory and adolescent health* (pp. 123–138). Springer International Publishing; 2014 National Survey on Drug Use and Health (NSDUH). Table 6.88B—Alcohol Use in the Past Month among Persons Aged 18 to 22, by College Enrollment Status and Demographic Characteristics: Percentages, 2013 and 2014. https://www.samhsa.gov/data/sites/default/files/NSDUH-DetTabs2013/NSDUH-DetTabs2013.htm#tab6.88b.

68. Miller, D. T., & Prentice, D. A. (2016). Changing norms to change behavior. *Annual Review of Psychology, 67,* 339–361.

69. Schroeder, C. M., & Prentice, D. A. (1998). Exposing pluralistic ignorance to reduce alcohol use among college students. *Journal of Applied Social Psychology, 28,* 2150–2180.

70. Kennedy, D. M., Kleiman, M. A., & Braga, A. A. (2017). Beyond deterrence. *Handbook of Crime Prevention and Community Safety,* 157.

71. Interrupting violence with the message "Don't Shoot": Interview with David M. Kennedy." *Fresh Air.* November 11, 2011. Retrieved April 22, 2014: Kennedy, David M. (2011). *Don't shoot: One man, a street fellowship, and the end of violence in inner-city America.* New York: Bloomsbury.

72. Kelman, H. (1961). Processes of opinion change. *Public Opinion Quarterly, 25,* 57–78.

73. Cohen, G. L., & Prinstein, M. J. (2006). Peer contagion of aggression and health-risk behavior among adolescent males: An experimental investigation of effects on public conduct and private attitudes. *Child Development, 77,* 967–983.

74. Milgram, S. (1963). Behavioral study of obedience. *Journal of Abnormal and Social Psychology, 67,* 371–378.

75. Milgram, S. (1974). *Obedience to authority.* New York: Harper & Row; Elms, A. C., & Milgram, S. (1966). Personality characteristics associated with obedience and defiance toward authoritative command. *Journal of Experimental Research in Personality, 1,* 282–289.

76. Kilham, W., & Mann, L. (1974). Level of destructive obedience as a function of transmitter and executant roles in the Milgram obedience paradigm. *Journal of Personality and Social Psychology, 29,* 696–702; Shanab, M., & Yahya, K. (1977). A behavioral study of obedience in children. *Journal of Personality and Social Psychology, 35,* 530–536.

77. Meeus, W. H. J., & Raaijmakers, Q. A. W. (1995). Obedience in modern society: The Utrecht studies. *Journal of Social Issues, 51(3),* 155–175; A. G. Miller, B. E. Collins, & D. E. Brief. (1995). Perspectives on obedience to authority: The legacy of the Milgram experiments. *Journal of Social Issues, 51(3),* 1–19.

78. Burger, J. (2007). Milgram replication. ABC *20/20.* January 3; Burger, J. M. (2014). Situational features in Milgram's experiment that kept his participants shocking. *Journal of Social Issues, 70,* 489–500.

79. Democracy Now (2005). Abu Ghraib: Getting away with torture? Human rights watch calls for accountability into U.S. abuse of detainees. Retrieved January 2, 2010, from http://www.democracynow.org/2005/4/25/getting_away_with_torture_human_rights; Zimbardo, P. (2007). *The Lucifer effect.* New York: Random House.

80. Milgram, S. (1965). Some conditions of obedience and disobedience to authority. *Human Relations, 18,* 57–76; Milgram, S. (1974). *Obedience to authority: An experimental view.* New York: Harper & Row.

81. Meeus, W. H. J., & Raaijmakers, Q. A. W. (1995). Obedience in modern society: The Utrecht studies. *Journal of Social Issues, 51,* 155–176.

82. Vasquez-Heilig, J., & Darling-Hammond, L. (2008). Accountability Texas-style: The progress and learning of urban minority students in a high-stakes testing context. *Educational Evaluation and Policy Analysis, 30,* 75–110.

83. Martin, R., & Hewstone, M. (2017). Minority influence. *Social Psychology: Revisiting the Classic Studies,* 93.

84. O'Connor, S. D. (2007). *The majesty of the law: Reflections of a Supreme Court justice.* New York: Random House.

Chapter 5   Mass Communication, Propaganda, and Persuasion

1. For example, see http://www.hopkinsmedicine.org/health/healthy_aging/healthy_body/is-there-really-any-benefit-to-multivitamins. Accessed August 13, 2017.

2. Smith, A. (2015). US smartphone use in 2015. *Pew Research Center, 1*; Tsetsi, E., & Rains, S. A. (2017). Smartphone internet access and use: Extending the digital divide and usage gap. *Mobile Media & Communication*, DOI: 10.1177/2050157917708329.

3. Hamm, M. P., Newton, A. S., Chisholm, A., Shulhan, J., Milne, A., Sundar, P., & Hartling, L. (2015). Prevalence and effect of cyberbullying on children and young people: A scoping review of social media studies. *JAMA Pediatrics, 169*, 770–777; Groves, C. L., & Anderson, C. A. (2017). Negative effects of video game play 49. *Handbook of Digital Games and Entertainment Technologies*, 1297; Benotsch, E. G., Snipes, D. J., Martin, A. M., & Bull, S. S. (2013). Sexting, substance use, and sexual risk behavior in young adults. *Journal of Adolescent Health, 52*, 307–313.

4. Oulasvirta, A., Rattenbury, T., Ma, L., & Raita, E. (2012). Habits make smartphone use pervasive. *Personal and Ubiquitous Computing, 16*, 105–114.

5. Alter, A. (2017). *Irresistible: The rise of addictive technology and the business of keeping us hooked*. New York: Penguin.

6. Seo, D. G., Park, Y., Kim, M. K., & Park, J. (2016). Mobile phone dependency and its impacts on adolescents' social and academic behaviors. *Computers in Human Behavior, 63*, 282–292.

7. Centers for Disease Control and Prevention (2016). *Youth Risk Behavior Surveillance–United States, 2015. Morbidity and Mortality Weekly Report, 65*. Atlanta, GA: Centers for Disease Control and Prevention.

8. Thornton, B., Faires, A., Robbins, M., & Rollins, E. (2014). The mere presence of a cell phone may be distracting implications for attention and task performance. *Social Psychology, 45*, 479–488.

9. Przybylski, A. K., & Weinstein, N. (2013). Can you connect with me now? How the presence of mobile communication technology influences face-to-face conversation quality. *Journal of Social and Personal Relationships, 30*, 237–246.

10. Misra, S., Cheng, L., Genevie, J., & Yuan, M. (2016). The iPhone effect: The quality of in-person social interactions in the presence of mobile devices. *Environment and Behavior, 48*, 275–298.

11. https://techcrunch.com/2017/03/03/u-s-consumers-now-spend-5-hours-per-day-on-mobile-devices/. Accessed August 14, 2017; https://hackernoon.com/how-much-time-do-people-spend-on-their-mobile-phones-in-2017-e5f90a0b10a6. Accessed August 14, 2017.

12. Uhls, Y. T., Michikyan, M., Morris, J., Garcia, D., Small, G. W., Zgourou, E., & Greenfield, P. M. (2014). Five days at outdoor education camp without screens improves preteen skills with nonverbal emotion cues. *Computers in Human Behavior, 39*, 387–392.

13. Green, C. S., & Bavelier, D. (2012). Learning, attentional control, and action video games. *Current Biology, 22*, R197–R206.

14. Twenge, J. M. (2013). Does online social media lead to social connection or social disconnection? *Journal of College and Character, 14*, 11–20; Halpern, D., Valenzuela, S., & Katz, J. E. (2016). "Selfie-ists" or "Narci-selfiers"?: A cross-lagged panel analysis of selfie taking and narcissism. *Personality and Individual Differences, 97*, 98–101.

15. Jackson, M. (2008). *Distracted: The erosion of attention and the coming dark age.* New York: Prometheus Books; Carr, N. (2011). *The shallows: What the Internet is doing to our brains.* New York: W. W. Norton.

16. For an excellent list of scientific references on the benefits of walking in nature on mental energy, creativity, stress reduction, memory, and other cognitive areas, see http://www.businessinsider.com/scientific-benefits-of-nature-outdoors-2016-4/#1-improved-short-term-memory-1. Accessed August 14, 2017.

17. Verduyn, P., Lee, D. S., Park, J., Shablack, H., Orvell, A., Bayer, J., & Kross, E. (2015). Passive Facebook usage undermines affective well-being: Experimental and longitudinal evidence. *Journal of Experimental Psychology: General, 144*, 480.

18. Johnson, R. N. (1996). Bad news revisited: The portrayal of violence, conflict, and suffering on television news. *Peace and Conflict: Journal of Peace Psychology, 2*, 201–216.

19. Pollock, J. (2017). *Crime and criminal justice in America.* New York: Taylor & Francis.

20. Piccalo, G. (2001). *Los Angeles Times.* September 26.

21. Nowicki, Dan. The Arizona Republic retrieved from: https://www.usatoday.com/story/news/nation/2013/03/17/iraq-war-10-years-later/1993431/. Accessed August 14, 2017.

22. Gilbert, G. M. (1947). *Nuremberg diary* (pp. 278–279). New York: Farrar, Straus and Company.

23. (1982). *St. Petersburg Times.* October 21; (1982). *The Tennessean.* October 31.

24. (1982). *Newsbank, 19,* October, 1.

25. Phillips, D. P., & Carstensen, L. L. (1986). Clustering of teenage suicides after television news stories about suicide. *New England Journal of Medicine, 315*, 685–689; Phillips, D. P., Lesyna, K., & Paight, D. J. (1992). Suicide and the media. In R. W. Maris, A. L. Berman, J. T. Maltsberger, & R. I. Yufit (Eds.), *Assessment and prediction of suicide* (pp. 499–519). New York: Guilford Press.

26. Ma-Kellams, C., Baek, J. H., & Or, F. (2016). Suicide contagion in response to widely publicized celebrity deaths: The roles of depressed affect, death-thought accessibility, and attitudes. *Psychology of Popular Media Culture,* DOI: 10.1037/ppm0000115.

27. Jobes, D. A., Berman, A. L., O'Carroll, P. W., Eastgard, S., & Knickmeyer, S. (1996). The Kurt Cobain suicide crisis: Perspectives from research, public health, and the news media. *Suicide and Life Threatening Behavior, 26*, 260–269.

28. Jenkin, G., Madhvani, N., Signal, L., & Bowers, S. (2014). A systematic review of persuasive marketing techniques to promote food to children on television. *Obesity Reviews, 15*, 281–293.

29. Lyle, J., & Hoffman, H. (1971). Explorations in patterns of television viewing by preschool-age children. In J. P. Murray, E. A. Robinson, & G. A. Comstock (Eds.), *Television and social behavior* (Vol. 4, pp. 257–344). Rockville, MD: National Institutes of Health; Unnikrishnan, N., & Bajpai, S. (1996). *The impact of television advertising on children.* New Delhi: Sage.

30. Kunkel, D., & Roberts, D. (1991). Young minds and marketplace values: Issues in children's television advertising. *Journal of Social Issues, 47*, 57–72.

31. Borzekowski, D. L., & Robinson, T. N. (2001). The 30-second effect: An experiment revealing the impact of television commercials on food preferences of preschoolers. *Journal of the American Dietetic Association, 101*, 42–46.

32. Kunkel, D., & Roberts, D. (1991). Young minds and marketplace values: Issues in children's television advertising. *Journal of Social Issues, 47*, 57–72.

33. Levine, R. (2003). *The power of persuasion: How we're bought and sold.* New York: John Wiley & Sons.

34. Zajonc, R. (1968). The attitudinal effects of mere exposure. *Journal of Personality and Social Psychology, Monograph Supplement, 9*, 1–27.

35. Bornstein, R. F. (1989) Exposure and affect: Overview and meta-analysis of research, 1968–1987. *Psychological Bulletin, 106*, 265–289.

36. Nuttin, J. (1985). Narcissism beyond Gestalt and awareness: The name letter effect. *European Journal of Social Psychology, 15*, 353–361; Keller, B., & Gierl, H. (2017). Can advertisers benefit from the name-letter-and birthday-number effect? In *Advances in Advertising Research VIII* (pp. 31–44). New York: Springer Fachmedien Wiesbaden.

37. Brady, N., Campbell, M., & Flaherty, M. (2004). My left brain and me: A dissociation in the perception of self and others. *Neuropsychologia, 42*, 1156–1161.

38. McGuire, W. J. (1986). The myth of massive media impact: Savagings and salvagings. *Public Communication and Behavior, 1*, 173–257.

39. Grush, J., McKeough, K., & Ahlering, R. (1978). Extrapolating laboratory exposure research to actual political elections. *Journal of Personality and Social Psychology, 36*, 257–270; Grush, J. E. (1980). Impact of candidate expenditures, regionality, and prior outcomes on the 1976 presidential primaries. *Journal of Personality and Social Psychology, 38*, 337–347.

40. Pfau, M., Diedrich, T., Larson, K. M., & Van Winkle, K. M. (1995). Influence of communication modalities on voters' perceptions of candidates during presidential primary campaigns. *Journal of Communication, 45*, 122–133; Soley, L. C., Craig, R. L., & Cherif, S. (1988). Promotional expenditures in congressional elections: Turnout, political action committees and asymmetry

effects. *Journal of Advertising, 17,* 36–44; Kaid, L. L. (2004). Political advertising. *Handbook of Political Communication Research,* 155–202.

41. White, J. E. (1988). Bush's most valuable player. *Time,* November 14, 20–21.

42. Rosenthal, A. (1988). Foes accuse Bush campaign of inflaming racial tension. *New York Times,* October 24, A1, B5; Pandora's box (1988). *The New Republic,* October, 4, 45.

43. Tolchin, M. (1988). Study says 53,000 get prison furloughs in '87, and few did harm. *New York Times,* October 12, A23.

44. Pratkanis, A. R., & Aronson, E. (1992). *The age of propaganda: The everyday use and abuse of persuasion.* New York: W. H. Freeman.

45. Pratkanis, A. R. (1993). Propaganda and persuasion in the 1992 U.S. presidential election: What are the implications for a democracy? *Current World Leaders, 36,* 341–361.

46. Pariser, E. (2011). *The filter bubble: How the new personalized web is changing what we read and how we think.* New York: Penguin.

47. Newseum (2017). State of the first amendment. Freedom Forum.

48. CNN. (2016). That Trump quote calling Republicans "the dumbest group of voters"? Fake! http://www.cnn.com/2016/11/10/politics/trump-quote-facebook-trnd/index.html. Accessed August 14, 2017; *New York Magazine.* (2017). "The Fake Donald Trump Quote That Just Won't Die." http://nymag.com/selectall/2016/11/the-fake-donald-trump-quote-that-just-wont-die.html. Accessed August 14, 2017.

49. Petty, R. E., & Cacciopo, J. T. (1986). The elaboration likelihood model of persuasion. In L. Berkowitz (Ed.) *Advances in experimental social psychology* (pp. 123–205). Hillsdale, NJ: Erlbaum; Petty, R. E., Heesacker, M., & Hughes, J. N. (1997). The elaboration likelihood model: Implications for the practice of school psychology. *Journal of School Psychology, 35,* 107–136; Chaiken, S., Wood, W., & Eagly, A. H. (1996). Principles of persuasion. In E. T. Higgins, & A. W. Kruglanski (Eds.), *Social psychology: Handbook of basic principles* (pp. 702–742). New York: Guilford Press.

50. McGlone, M. S., & Tofighbakhsh, J. (2000). Birds of a feather flock conjointly (?): Rhyme as reason in aphorisms. *Psychological Science, 11,* 424–428; McGlone, M. S., & Tofighbakhsh, J. (1999). The Keats heuristic: Rhyme as reason in aphorism interpretation. *Poetics, 26,* 235–244.

51. Luntz, F. (2007). *Words that work.* New York: Hyperion.

52. See, for example, LiveScience (2012). https://www.livescience.com/36367-pink-slime-bad-health-beef.html. Accessed August 14, 2017.

53. Eagly, A. H., & Chaiken, S. (1993). *The psychology of attitudes.* Fort Worth, TX: Harcourt, Brace, & Jovanovich.

54. Aristotle. (1954). Rhetoric. In W. Roberts (Trans.), *Aristotle, rhetoric and poetics* (p. 25). New York: Modern Library.

55. Hovland, C., & Weiss, W. (1951). The influence of source credibility on communication effectiveness. *Public Opinion Quarterly, 15,* 635–650.

56. Aronson, E., & Golden, B. (1962). The effect of relevant and irrelevant aspects of communicator credibility on opinion change. *Journal of Personality, 30,* 135–146.

57. Walster (Hatfield), E., & Festinger, L. (1962). The effectiveness of "overheard" persuasive communications. *Journal of Abnormal and Social Psychology, 65,* 395–402.

58. Mills, J., & Aronson, E. (1965). Opinion change as a function of communicator's attractiveness and desire to influence. *Journal of Personality and Social Psychology, 1,* 173–177.

59. Eagly, A., & Chaiken, S. (1975). An attribution analysis of the effect of communicator characteristics on opinion change: The case of communicator attractiveness. *Journal of Personality and Social Psychology, 32,* 136–144; Eagly, A. H., Ashmore, R. D., Makhijani, M. G., & Longo, L. C. (1991). What is beautiful is good, but….: A meta-analytic review of research on the physical attractiveness stereotype. *Psychological Bulletin, 110,* 109–128.

60. (1987). *Santa Cruz Sentinel,* January 13, p. A8.

61. Walster (Hatfield), E., & Festinger, L. (1962). The effectiveness of "overheard" persuasive communications. *Journal of Abnormal and Social Psychology, 65,* 395–402.

62. Eckel, C. C., & Wilson, R. K. (2004). Is trust a risky decision? *Journal of Economic Behavior & Organization, 55,* 447–465.

63. Mills, J., & Aronson, E. (1965). Opinion change as a function of communicator's attractiveness and desire to influence. *Journal of Personality and Social Psychology, 1,* 173–177; Eagly, A., & Chaiken, S. (1975). An attribution analysis of the effect of communicator characteristics on opinion change: The case of communicator attractiveness. *Journal of Personality and Social Psychology, 32,* 136–144; Eagly, A. H., Ashmore, R. D., Makhijani, M. G., & Longo, L. C. (1991). What is beautiful is good, but. …: A meta-analytic review of research on the physical attractiveness stereotype. *Psychological Bulletin, 110,* 109–128.

64. Hartmann, G. (1936). A field experience on the comparative effectiveness of "emotional" and "rational" political leaflets in determining election results. *Journal of Abnormal and Social Psychology, 31,* 336–352.

65. Leventhal, H. (1970). Findings and theory in the study of fear communications. In L. Berkowitz (Ed.), *Advances in experimental social psychology* (Vol. 5, pp. 119–186). New York: Academic Press; Leventhal, H., Meyer, D., & Nerenz, D. (1980). The common sense representation of illness danger. In S. Rachman (Ed.), *Contributions to medical psychology* (Vol. 2), New York: Pergamon Press; Cameron, L. D., & Leventhal, H. (1995). Vulnerability beliefs, symptom experiences, and the processing of health threat information: A self-regulatory perspective. *Journal of Applied Social Psychology, 25,* 1859–1883.

66. Chapman University. (2016). https://blogs.chapman.edu/wilkinson/2016/10/11/americas-top-fears-2016/. Accessed August 14, 2017.

67. Gilbert, D. (2006). If only gay sex caused global warming. *Los Angeles Times*, July 2.

68. McGlone, M. S., Bell, R. A., Zaitchik, S. T., & McGlynn III, J. (2013). Don't let the flu catch you: Agency assignment in printed educational materials about the H1N1 influenza virus. *Journal of Health Communication, 18*, 740–756; McGlone, M. S., Stephens, K. K., Rodriguez, S. A., & Fernandez, M. E. (2017). Persuasive texts for prompting action: Agency assignment in HPV vaccination reminders. *Vaccine, 5,* 4295–4297.

69. Haidt, J. (2003). The moral emotions. *Handbook of Affective Sciences, 11*, 852–870.

70. Brady, W. J., Wills, J. A., Jost, J. T., Tucker, J. A., & Van Bavel, J. J. (2017). Emotion shapes the diffusion of moralized content in social networks. *Proceedings of the National Academy of Sciences, 114*, 7313–7318.

71. Lakoff, G. (2016). *Moral politics: How liberals and conservatives think* (3rd edition). Chicago: University of Chicago Press.

72. Hibbert, S., Smith, A., Davies, A., & Ireland, F. (2007). Guilt appeals: Persuasion knowledge and charitable giving. *Psychology & Marketing, 24*, 723–742; Carlsmith, J. M., & Gross, A. E. (1969). Some effects of guilt on compliance. *Journal of Personality and Social Psychology, 11*, 232.

73. Schnall, S., Roper, J., & Fessler, D. M. (2010). Elevation leads to altruistic behavior. *Psychological Science, 21*, 315–320; Algoe, S. B., & Haidt, J. (2009). Witnessing excellence in action: The "other-praising" emotions of elevation, gratitude, and admiration. *Journal of Positive Psychology, 4*, 105–127; Franklin Waddell, T., Bailey, E., & Davis, S. E. (2017). Does elevation reduce viewers' enjoyment of media violence? Testing the intervention potential of inspiring media. *Journal of Media Psychology, 1,* 1–7.

74. Grant, A. (2014). *Give and take: Why helping others drives our success.* New York: Penguin.

75. Nisbett, R., Borgida, E., Crandall, R., & Reed, H. (1976). Popular induction: Information is not always informative. In J. S. Carroll & J. W. Payne (Eds.), *Cognition and social behavior* (pp. 227–236). Hillsdale, NJ: Erlbaum; Nisbett, R., & Ross, L. (1980). *Human inference: Strategies and shortcomings of social judgment.* Englewood Cliffs, NJ: Prentice-Hall; Hamill, R., DeCamp Wilson, T., & Nisbett, R. (1980). Insensitivity to sample bias: Generalizing from atypical cases. *Journal of Personality and Social Psychology, 39*, 578–589.

76. Aronson, E., Gonzales, M. H., & Costanzo, M. (1988). Increasing the effectiveness of energy auditors: A field experiment. *Journal of Applied Social Psychology, 18*, 1049–1066.

77. McClure, T., & Spence, R. (2006). *Don't mess with Texas: The story behind the legend.* Austin, TX: Idea City Press.

78. Bryan, C. J., Walton, G. M., Rogers, T., & Dweck, C. S. (2011). Motivating voter turnout by invoking the self. *Proceedings of the National Academy of Sciences, 108*, 12653–12656.

79. Bryan, C. J. (2018). You are what you do: Implicating the self to influence behavior. In J. Aronson & E. Aronson (Eds.), *Readings about the social animal* (12th edition). New York: Worth.

80. Hovland, C., Lumsdain, A., & Sheffield, F. (1949). *Experiments on mass communications.* Princeton, NJ: Princeton University Press.

81. Zimbardo, P. (1960). Involvement and communication discrepancy as determinants of opinion conformity. *Journal of Abnormal and Social Psychology, 60,* 86–94.

82. Whittaker, J. O. (1963). Opinion change as a function of communication-attitude discrepancy. *Psychological Reports, 13,* 763–772.

83. Hovland, C., Harvey, O. J., & Sherif, M. (1957). Assimilation and contrast effects in reaction to communication and attitude change. *Journal of Abnormal and Social Psychology, 55,* 244–252.

84. Zellner, M. (1970). Self-esteem, reception, and influenceability. *Journal of Personality and Social Psychology, 15,* 87–93; Wood, W., & Stagner, B. (1994). Why are some people easier to influence than others? In S. Shavitt & T. Brock (Eds.), *Persuasion: Psychological insights and perspectives* (pp. 149–174). Boston: Allyn & Bacon.

85. Jost, J. T., Glaser, J., Kruglanski, A. W., & Sulloway, F. (2003). Political conservatism as motivated social cognition. *Psychological Bulletin, 129,* 339–375.

86. Graham, J., Haidt, J., & Nosek, B. A. (2009). Liberals and conservatives rely on different sets of moral foundations. *Journal of Personality and Social Psychology, 96,* 1029–1046; Jost, J. T., Nosek, B. A., & Gosling, S. D. (2008). Ideology: Its resurgence in social, personality, and political psychology. *Perspectives on Psychological Science, 3,* 126–136.

87. Haidt, J. (2012). *The righteous mind: Why good people are divided by politics and religion.* New York: Vintage/Random House.

88. Cialdini, R. (2016). *Pre-suasion.* New York: Simon & Schuster.

89. Janis, I. J., Kaye, D., & Kirschner, P. (1965). Facilitating effects of "eating-while-reading" on responsiveness to persuasive communication. *Journal of Personality and Social Psychology, 1,* 181–186.

90. Petty, R. E., Schumann, D. W., Richman, S. A., & Strathman, A. (1993). Positive mood and persuasion: Different roles for affect under high- and low-elaboration conditions. *Journal of Personality and Social Psychology, 64,* 5–20.

91. Cohen, G. T., Aronson, J., & Steele, C. (2000). When beliefs yield to evidence: Reducing biased evaluation by affirming the self. *Personality and Social Psychology Bulletin, 26,* 1151–1164.

92. Hass, R. G., & Grady, K. (1975). Temporal delay, type of forewarning, and resistance to influence. *Journal of Experimental Social Psychology, 11,* 459–469.

93. Freedman, J., & Sears, D. (1965). Warning, distraction, and resistance to influence. *Journal of Personality and Social Psychology, 1,* 262–266; Petty, R. E., & Cacioppo, J. T. (1979). Effects of forewarning of persuasive intent and involvement on cognitive responses and persuasion. *Personality and Social Psychology Bulletin, 5,* 173–176; Chen, H. C., Reardon, R., Rea, C., & Moore, D. J. (1992). Forewarning of content and involvement: Consequences for persuasion and resistance to persuasion. *Journal of Experimental Social Psychology, 28,* 523–541.

94. Brehm, J. (1966). *A theory of psychological reactance.* New York: Academic Press.

95. Pennebaker, J. W., & Sanders, D. Y. (1976). American graffiti: Effects of authority and reactance arousal. *Personality and Social Psychology Bulletin, 2,* 264–267.

96. Erceg-Hurn, D. M., & Steed, L. G. (2011). Does exposure to cigarette health warnings elicit psychological reactance in smokers? *Journal of Applied Social Psychology, 41,* 219–237; Miller, C. H., Lane, L. T., Deatrick, L. M., Young, A. M., & Potts, K. A. (2007). Psychological reactance and promotional health messages. *Human Communication Research, 33,* 219–240.

97. Heilman, M. (1976). Oppositional behavior as a function of influence attempt intensity and retaliation threat. *Journal of Personality and Social Psychology, 33,* 574–578.

98. McGuire, W. J. (1964). Inducing resistance to persuasion. In L. Berkowitz (Ed.), *Advances in experimental social psychology* (Vol. 1, pp. 192–229). New York: Academic Press; McGuire, W., & Papageorgis, D. (1961). The relative efficacy of various types of prior belief-defense in producing immunity against persuasion. *Journal of Abnormal and Social Psychology, 62,* 327–337.

99. Banas, J. A., & Miller, G. (2013). Inducing resistance to conspiracy theory propaganda: Testing inoculation and metainoculation strategies. *Human Communication Research, 39,* 184–207.

100. Barrett, L. F. (2017, July 16). When is speech violent? *New York Times,* Sunday Review, 9.

Chapter 6   Human Aggression

1. (1986). *Newsweek,* April 28, 22.

2. Mass Shooting Archive (2017). http://www.gunviolencearchive.org/reports/mass-shooting. Accessed August 16, 2017.

3. Freud, S. (1948). *Beyond the pleasure principle.* London: Hogarth Press and Institute of Psycho-Analysis.

4. Kuo, Z. Y. (1961). Genesis of the cat's response to the rat. In E. Aronson (Ed.), *Instinct* (p. 24). Princeton, NJ: Van Nostrand.

5. Eibl-Eibesfeldt, I. (1963). Aggressive behavior and ritualized fighting in animals. In J. H. Masserman (Ed.), *Science and psychoanalysis, Vol. VI. Violence and war.* New York: Grune & Stratton.

6. Watts, D., Muller, M., Amsler, S., Mbabazi, G., & Mitani, J. C. (2006). Lethal intergroup aggression by chimpanzees in the Kibale National Park, Uganda. *American Journal of Primatology, 68,* 161–180; Watts, D., & Mitani, J. C. (2001). Boundary patrols and intergroup encounters in wild chimpanzees. *Behaviour, 138,* 299–327.

7. De Waal, F. B. M. (1996). *Good natured: The origins of right and wrong in humans and other animals.* Cambridge, MA: Harvard University Press; Parish, A. R., & de Waal, F. B. M. (2000). The other "closest living relative": How bonobos (Pan paniscus) challenge traditional assumptions about females, dominance, intra- and intersexual interactions, and hominid evolution. *Annals of the New York Academy of Sciences, 907,* 97–113.

8. Hare, B. (2017). Survival of the friendliest: Homo sapiens evolved via selection for prosociality. *Annual review of psychology, 68,* 155–186; Muller, M. N., & Mitani, J. C. (2005). Conflict and cooperation in wild chimpanzees. *Advances in the Study of Behavior, 35,* 275–331.

9. Bergeron, N., & Schneider, B. H. (2005). Explaining cross-national differences in peer-directed aggression: A quantitative synthesis. *Aggressive Behavior, 31,* 116–137.

10. Baron, R. A., & Richardson, D. R. (1994). *Human aggression* (2nd edition). New York: Plenum.

11. Hunt, G. T. (1940). *The wars of the Iroquois.* Madison: The University of Wisconsin Press.

12. Pinker, S. (2011). *The better angels of our nature.* New York: Penguin; Pinker, S. (2016). Has the decline of violence reversed since *The Better Angels of Our Nature* was written? https://stevenpinker.com/files/pinker/files/has_the_decline_of_violence_reversed_since_the_better_angels_of_our_nature_was_written.pdf. Accessed August 16, 2017.

13. Nisbett, R. E. (1993). Violence and U.S. regional culture. *American Psychologist, 48,* 441–449.

14. Cohen, D., Nisbett, R., Bowdle, B. F., & Schwarz, N. (1996) Insult, aggression, and the Southern culture of honor: An "experimental ethnography." *Journal of Personality and Social Psychology, 70,* 945–960.

15. Cohen, D., & Nisbett, R. E. (1994). Self-protection and the culture of honor: Explaining Southern violence. *Personality and Social Psychology Bulletin, 20,* 551–567.

16. Cohen, D., & Nisbett, R. E. (1997). Field experiments examining the culture of honor: The role of institutions in perpetuating norms about violence. *Personality and Social Psychology Bulletin, 23,* 1188–1199.

17. Brown, R. P., Osterman, L. L., & Barnes, C. D. (2009). School violence and the culture of honor. *Psychological Science, 20,* 1400–1405.

18. Vandello, J. A., & Cohen, D. (1999). Patterns of individualism and collectivism across the United States. *Journal of Personality and Social Psychology, 77,*

279–292; Vandello, J. A., Cohen, D., & Ransom, S. (2008). U.S. Southern and Northern differences in perceptions of norms about aggression: Mechanisms for the perpetuation of a culture of honor. *Journal of Cross-Cultural Psychology*, *39*, 162–177.

19. Bosson, J. K., & Vandello, J. A. (2011). Precarious manhood and its links to action and aggression. *Current Directions in Psychological Science*, *20*, 82–86.

20. Gilmore, D. D. (1990). *Manhood in the making: Cultural concepts of masculinity*. New Haven, CT: Yale University Press; Kimmel, M. (2012). *The gendered society* (5th edition). New York: Oxford University Press.

21. Archer, J. (2004). Sex differences in aggression in real-world settings: A meta-analytic review. *Review of General Psychology*, *8*, 291.

22. Archer, D., & McDaniel, P. (1995). Violence and gender: Differences and similarities across societies. In R. B. Ruback & N. A. Weiner (Eds.), *Interpersonal violent behaviors: Social and cultural aspects* (pp. 63–88). New York: Springer.

23. Dabbs, J. M., Carr, T. S., Frady, R. L., & Riad, J. K. (1995). Testosterone, crime, and misbehavior among 692 male prison inmates. *Personality and Individual Differences, 7*, 269–275.

24. Dabbs, J. M., Jr., Hargrove, M. F., & Heusel, C. (1996). Testosterone differences among college fraternities: Well-behaved vs. rambunctious. *Personality and Individual Differences, 20*, 157–161.

25. Archer, J., & Carré, J. M. (2016). Testosterone and aggression. *Aggression and Violence: A Social Psychological Perspective*, 90.

26. Sapolsky, R. A.(2017). *Behave: The biology of humans at our best and worst*. London: Bodley Head. Quotes on pages 100 and 101.

27. Breiding, M. J., Chen J., & Black, M. C. (2014). *Intimate partner violence in the United States—2010*. Atlanta: National Center for Injury Prevention and Control, Centers for Disease Control and Prevention.

28. Testa, M., Hoffman, J. H., & Leonard, K. E. (2011). Female intimate partner violence perpetration: Stability and predictors of mutual and nonmutual aggression across the first year of college. *Aggressive Behavior, 37*, 362–373.

29. Straus, M. (2011). Gender symmetry and mutuality in perpetration of clinical-level partner violence: Empirical evidence and implications for prevention and treatment. *Aggression and Violent Behavior, 16*, 279–288.

30. Langhinrichsen-Rohling, J., Misra, T. A., Selwyn, C., & Rohling, M. L. (2012). Rates of bi-directional versus unidirectional intimate partner violence across samples, sexual orientations, and race/ethnicities: A comprehensive review. *Partner Abuse*, 3, 199–230.

31. Archer, J. (2004). Sex differences in aggression in real-world settings: A meta-analytic review. *Review of General Psychology, 8*, 291–322; Levy, B. (2008). *Women and violence*. Berkeley, CA: Seal Press.

32. Bettencourt, B. A., & Miller, N. (1996). Gender differences in aggression as a function of provocation: A meta-analysis. *Psychological Bulletin, 119*, 422–447.

33. Eisenstat, S. A., & Bancroft, L. (1999). Domestic violence. *New England Journal of Medicine, 341,* 886–892.

34. Archer, D., & McDaniel, P. (1995). Violence and gender: Differences and similarities across societies. In R. B. Ruback & N. A. Weiner (Eds.), *Interpersonal violent behaviors: Social and cultural aspects* (pp. 63–88). New York: Springer.

35. Harris, M. G. (2004). Cholas, Mexican-American girls, and gangs. *Sex Roles, 30,* 289–301.

36. O'Rourke, L. (2008). Behind the woman behind the bomb. *New York Times,* August 2.

37. Crick, N. R., Casas, J. F., & Mosher, M. (1997). Relational and overt aggression in preschool. *Developmental Psychology, 33,* 579–587.

38. Murray-Close, D., Nelson, D. A., Ostrov, J. M., Casas, J. F., & Crick, N. R. (2016). Relational aggression: A developmental psychopathology perspective. *Developmental Psychopathology.*

39. Ostrov, J. M., Woods, K. E., Jansen Yeh, E. A., Casas, J. F., & Crick, N. R. (2004). An observational study of delivered and received aggression, gender, and social-psychological adjustment in preschool. *Early Childhood Research Quarterly, 19,* 355–371.

40. Rivers I., Chesney T., & Coyne I. (2011). Cyberbullying. In: C. P. Monks & I. Coyne (Eds.), *Bullying in different contexts* (pp. 211–230). Cambridge: Cambridge University Press.

41. Palfrey, J., boyd, d.[sic], & Sacco, D. (2010). Enhancing child safety and online technologies. The Berkman Center for Internet & Society at Harvard University. Durham, NC: Carolina Academic Press. http://www.cap-press.com/pdf/1997.pdf. Accessed August 16, 2017.

42. Freud, S. (1959). Why war? (Letter to Albert Einstein, 1932). In E. Jones (Ed.), *Collected papers* (Vol. 5., p. 282). New York: Basic Books.

43. Menninger, W. (1948). Recreation and mental health. *Recreation, 42,* 340–346.

44. Bushman, B. (2002). Does venting anger feed or extinguish the flame? Catharsis, rumination, distraction, anger and aggressive responding. *Personality and Social Psychology Bulletin, 28,* 724–731.

45. Patterson, A. H. (1974). Hostility catharsis: A naturalistic quasi-experiment. *Proceedings of the Division of Personality and Society Psychology, 1,* 195–197.

46. Geen, R. (1981). Spectator moods at an aggressive sports event. *Journal of Social Psychology, 3,* 217–227.

47. Glass, D. (1964). Changes in liking as a means of reducing cognitive discrepancies between self-esteem and aggression. *Journal of Personality, 32,* 531–549.

48. Bushman, B. J., Baumeister, R. F., & Phillips, C. M. (2001). Do people aggress to improve their mood? Catharsis beliefs, affect regulation opportunity, and

aggressive responding. *Journal of Personality and Social Psychology, 81,* 17; Bushman, B. J., & Whitaker, J. L. (2010). Like a magnet: Catharsis beliefs attract angry people to violent video games. *Psychological Science, 21,* 790–792; Bushman, B. J., Baumeister, R. F., & Stack, A. D. (1999). Catharsis, aggression, and persuasive influence: Self-fulfilling or self-defeating prophecies? *Journal of Personality and Social Psychology, 76,* 367–376.

49. Kahn, M. (1966). The physiology of catharsis. *Journal of Personality and Social Psychology, 3,* 278–298.

50. Davis, K. E., & Jones, E. E. (1960). Changes in interpersonal perception as a means of reducing cognitive dissonance. *Journal of Abnormal and Social Psychology, 61,* 402–410.

51. Doob, A. N., & Wood, L. (1972). Catharsis and aggression: The effects of annoyance and retaliation on aggressive behavior. *Journal of Personality and Social Psychology, 22,* 156–162; Bushman, B.J., Bonacci, A. M., Pedersen, W. C., et al. (2005). Chewing on it can chew you up: Effects of rumination on triggered displaced aggression. *Journal of Personality and Social Psychology, 88,* 969–983.

52. Shergill S. S., Bays P. M., Frith, C. D., & Wolpert, D. M. (2003). Two eyes for an eye: The neuroscience of force escalation. *Science, 301,* 187.

53. Heinz, A., Kluge, U., Schouler-Ocak, M., & Beck, A. (2016). Alcohol and aggression. *European Psychiatry, 33,* S21.

54. Caetano, R., Schafer, J., & Cunradi, C. B. (2017). Alcohol-related intimate partner violence among white, black, and Hispanic couples in the United States. *Domestic Violence: The Five Big Questions.*

55. Taylor, S. P., & Leonard, K. E. (1983). Alcohol and human physical aggression. In R. Geen & E. Donnerstein (Eds.), *Aggression: Theoretical and empirical reviews.* New York: Academic Press; Pedersen, W. C., Vasquez, E. A., Bartholow, B. D., Grosvenor, M., & Truong, A. (2014). Are you insulting me? Exposure to alcohol primes increases aggression following ambiguous provocation. *Personality and Social Psychology Bulletin, 40,* 1037–1049.

56. Gable, P. A., Mechin, N. C., & Neal, L. B. (2016). Booze cues and attentional narrowing: Neural correlates of virtual alcohol myopia. *Psychology of Addictive Behaviors, 30,* 377–382.

57. Davis, D., & Loftus, E. (2003). What's good for the goose cooks the gander: Inconsistencies between the law and psychology of voluntary intoxication and sexual assault. *Handbook of Forensic Psychology* (pp. 997–1032). New York: Academic Press.

58. Marlatt, G. A., & Rohsenow, D. J. (1980). Cognitive processes in alcohol use: Expectancy and the balanced placebo design. In N. K. Mello (Ed.), *Advances in substance abuse* (Vol. 1). Greenwich, CT: JAI Press; Bègue, L., Subra, B., Arvers, P., Muller, D., Bricout, V., & Zorman, N. (2009). A message in a bottle: Extrapharmacological effects of alcohol on aggression. *Journal of Experimental Social Psychology, 45,* 137–142.

59. Hutchinson, R. R. (1983). The pain–aggression relationship and its expression in naturalistic settings. *Aggressive Behavior, 9*, 229–242.

60. Berkowitz, L. (1988). Frustrations, appraisals, and aversively stimulated aggression. *Aggressive Behavior, 14*, 3–11.

61. Stoff, D., & Cairns, R. (1996). *Aggression and violence: Genetic, neurobiological, and biosocial perspectives.* Mahwah, NJ: Erlbaum.

62. Bushman, B. J., DeWall, C. N., Pond, R. S., & Hanus, M. D. (2014). Low glucose relates to greater aggression in married couples. *Proceedings of the National Academy of Sciences, 111*, 6254–6257.

63. Carlsmith, J. M., & Anderson, C. A. (1979). Ambient temperature and the occurrence of collective violence: A new analysis. *Journal of Personality and Social Psychology, 37*, 337–344.

64. Anderson, C. A., Bushman, B. J., & Groom, R. W. (1997). Hot years and serious and deadly assault: Empirical tests of the heat hypothesis. *Journal of Personality and Social Psychology, 73*, 1213–1223.

65. Griffitt, W., & Veitch, R. (1971). Hot and crowded: Influences of population density and temperature on interpersonal affective behavior. *Journal of Personality and Social Psychology, 17*, 92–98; Anderson, C., Anderson, B., & Deuser, W. (1996). Examining an affective aggression framework: Weapon and temperature effects on aggressive thoughts, affect, and attitudes. *Personality and Social Psychology Bulletin, 22*, 366–376.

66. Reifman, A. S., Larrick, R., & Fein, S. (1991). Temper and temperature on the diamond: The heat-aggression relationship in major league baseball. *Personality and Social Psychology Bulletin, 17*, 580–585.

67. Kenrick, D. T., & MacFarlane, S. W. (1986). Ambient temperature and horn honking: A field study of the heat/aggression relationship. *Environment and Behavior, 18*, 179–191.

68. Hsiang, S. M., Burke, M., & Miguel, E. (2013). Quantifying the influence of climate on human conflict. *Science, 341*. DOI: 10.1126/science.1235367

69. Gladwell, M. (2015). Thresholds of violence: How school shootings catch on. *The New Yorker: Annals of Public Safety.*

70. Aronson, E. (2000). *Nobody left to hate: Teaching compassion after Columbine.* New York: Worth/Freeman.

71. Leary, M. R., Kowalski, R. M., Smith, L., & Phillips, S. (2003). Teasing, rejection, and violence: Case studies of the school shootings. *Aggressive Behavior, 29*, 202–214.

72. Twenge, J. M., Baumeister, R. F., Tice, D. M., & Stucke, T. S. If you can't join them, beat them: Effects of social exclusion on aggressive behavior. *Journal of Personality and Social Psychology, 81*, 1058–1069; Baumeister, R., & Tice, D. (2017). The social animal encounters social rejection: Cognitive, behavioral,

emotional, and interpersonal effects of being excluded. In J. Aronson & Aronson, E. (Eds.), *Readings about the social animal* (12th edition). New York: Worth/Freeman.

73. (1999). Quoted in *Time,* December 20.

74. Barker, R., Dembo, T., & Lewin, K. (1941). Frustration and aggression: An experiment with young children. *University of Iowa Studies in Child Welfare, 18,* 1–314.

75. Harris, M. (1974). Mediators between frustration and aggression in a field experiment. *Journal of Experimental and Social Psychology, 10,* 561–571.

76. Kulik, J., & Brown, R. (1979). Frustration, attribution of blame, and aggression. *Journal of Experimental and Social Psychology, 15,* 183–194.

77. Brosnan, S. F., and de Waal, F. B. M. (2014, Oct. 17). Evolution of responses to (un)fairness. *Science, 346,* 1251776–1–7.

78. DeCelles, K. A., & Norton, M. I. (2016). Physical and situational inequality on airplanes predicts air rage. *Proceedings of the National Academy of Sciences, 113,* 5588–5591.

79. Payne, K. (2017). *The broken ladder: How inequality affects the way we think, live, and die.* New York: Penguin.

80. de Tocqueville, A. (1981). *Democracy in America.* Westminster, MD: Random House.

81. Mallick, S., & McCandless, B. (1966). A study of catharsis of aggression. *Journal of Personality and Social Psychology, 4,* 591–596.

82. Johnson, T. E., & Rule, B. G. (1986). Mitigating circumstances information, censure, and aggression. *Journal of Personality and Social Psychology, 50,* 537–542.

83. Gill, M. J., & Cerce, S. C. (2017). He never willed to have the will he has: Historicist narratives, "civilized" blame, and the need to distinguish two notions of free will. *Journal of Personality and Social Psychology, 112,* 361–382.

84. Berkowitz, L. (1965). Some aspects of observed aggression. *Journal of Personality and Social Psychology, 2,* 359–369.

85. Berkowitz, L., & LePage, A. (1967). Weapons as aggression-eliciting stimuli. *Journal of Personality and Social Psychology, 7,* 202–207.

86. Benjamin, A. J., & Bushman, B. J. (2017). The weapons effect. *Current Opinion in Psychology, 19,* 93–97.

87. Bushman, B. J., Kerwin, T., Whitlock, T., & Weisenberger, J. M. (2017). The weapons effect on wheels: Motorists drive more aggressively when there is a gun in the vehicle. *Journal of Experimental Social Psychology, 73,* 82–85.

88. Berkowitz, L. (2016). Research on automatically elicited aggression. In. R. J. Sternberg, S. T. Fiske, & D. J. Foss (Eds.), *Scientists making a difference: One*

hundred eminent behavioral and brain scientists talk about their most important contributions (p. 332). New York: Cambridge University Press; Zimring, F. E. (2017). Firearms and violence in American law. In *Bridging the gap: A report on scholarship and criminal justice reform* (Erik Luna, Ed.). UC Berkeley Public Law Research Paper No. 2939902.

89. Zimbardo, P. (1969). The human choice: Individuation, reason, and order versus deindividuation, impulse, and chaos. In W. Arnold & D. Levine (Eds.), *Nebraska Symposium on Motivation, 17*, 237–307.

90. Silvia, P. J., & Duval, T. S. (2001). Objective self-awareness theory: Recent progress and enduring problems. *Personality and Social Psychology Review, 5*, 230–241.

91. Mullen, B. (1986). Atrocity as a function of lynch mob composition: A self-attention perspective. *Personality and Social Psychology Bulletin, 12*, 187–197.

92. Postmes, T., & Spears, R. (1998). Deindividuation and antinormative behavior: A meta-analysis. *Psychological Bulletin, 123*, 238–259.

93. Bandura, A., Ross, D., & Ross, S. (1961). Transmission of aggression through imitation of aggressive models. *Journal of Abnormal and Social Psychology, 63*, 575–582.

94. Bushman, B. J., Jamieson, P. E., Weitz, I., & Romer, D. (2013). Gun violence trends in movies. *Pediatrics, 132*, 1014–1018.

95. Huesmann, L. R., Dubow, E. F., & Yang, G. (2013). Why it is hard to believe that media violence causes aggression. In K. E. Dill (Ed.), *The Oxford handbook of media psychology* (pp. 159–171). Oxford: Oxford University Press; Anderson, C. A., Berkowitz, L., Donnerstein, E., Huesmann, L. R., Johnson, J. D., Linz, D., Malamuth, N. M., & Wartella, E. (2003). The influence of media violence on youth. *Psychological Science in the Public Interest, 4*, 81–110.

96. Ferguson, Christopher J. (2007). The good, the bad and the ugly: A meta-analytic review of positive and negative effects of violent video games. *Psychiatric Quarterly, 78*, 309–316; Ferguson, C. (2009). Media violence effects: Confirmed truth or just another X-file? *Journal of Forensic Psychology Practice, 9*, 103–126; Sherry, J. L. (2001). The effects of violent video games on aggression: A meta-analysis. *Human Communication Research, 27*, 409–431.

97. Liebert, R. M., & Baron, R. A. (1972). Some immediate effects of televised violence on children's behavior. *Developmental Psychology, 6*, 469–475; Anderson, C. A., Berkowitz, L., Donnerstein, E., Huesmann, L. R., Johnson, J. D., Linz, D., Malamuth, N. M., & Wartella, E. (2003). The influence of media violence on youth. *Psychological Science in the Public Interest, 4*, 81–110.

98. Anderson, C. A., Shibuya, A., Ihori, N., Swing, E. L., Bushman, B. J., Sakamoto, A., Rothstein, H. R., & Saleem, M. (2010). Violent video game effects on aggression, empathy, and prosocial behavior in eastern and western countries: A meta-analytic review. *Psychological Bulletin, 136*, 151–173.

99. Greitemeyer, T., & Mügge, D. O. (2014). Video games do affect social outcomes: A meta-analytic review of the effects of violent and prosocial video game play. *Personality and Social Psychology Bulletin, 40*, 578–589.

100. Gentile, D. A., Coyne, S., & Walsh, D. A. (2011). Media violence, physical aggression, and relational aggression in school age children: A short-term longitudinal study. *Aggressive Behavior, 37,* 193–206.

101. Crescioni, A. W., & Baumeister, R. F. (2009). Alone and aggressive: Social exclusion impairs self-control and empathy and increases hostile cognition and aggression. In M. Harris (Ed.), *Bullying, rejection, and peer victimization: A social cognitive neuroscience perspective* (pp. 251–258). New York: Springer; Ferguson, C. J., & Kilburn, J. (2010). Much ado about nothing: The misestimation and overinterpretation of violent video game effects in eastern and western nations: Comment on Anderson et al. *Psychological Bulletin, 136,* 174–178.

102. Ferguson, C. J. (2013). Violent video games and the Supreme Court: Lessons for the scientific community in the wake of *Brown v. Entertainment Merchants Association. American Psychologist, 68,* 57–74; Ferguson, C. J. (2014). A way forward for video game violence research. *American Psychologist, 69,* 307–309.

103. Josephson, W. D. (1987). Television violence and children's aggression: Testing the priming, social script, and disinhibition prediction. *Journal of Personality and Social Psychology, 53,* 882–890.

104. Anderson, C. A., & Dill, K. E. (2000). Video games and aggressive thoughts, feelings, and behavior in the laboratory and in life. *Journal of Personality and Social Psychology, 78,* 772–790.

105. Cline, V. B., Croft, R. G., & Courrier, S. (1973). Desensitization of children to television violence. *Journal of Personality and Social Psychology, 27,* 360–365.

106. Bushman, B. J., & Anderson, C. A. (2009). Comfortably numb: Desensitizing effects of violent media on helping others. *Psychological Science, 20,* 273–277.

107. Greitemeyer, T. (2014). Playing violent video games increases intergroup bias. *Personality and Social Psychology Bulletin, 40,* 70–78.

108. Gentile, D. A., & Gentile, J. R. (2008). Violent video games as exemplary teachers: A conceptual analysis. *Journal of Youth and Adolescence, 9,* 127–141.

109. Jamieson, P. E., & Romer, D. (2014). Violence in popular U.S. prime time TV dramas and the cultivation of fear: A time series analysis. *Media and Communication, 2,* 31–41.

110. Anderson, C. A., Berkowitz, L., Donnerstein, E., Huesmann, L. R., Johnson, J. D., Linz, D., Malamuth, N. M., & Wartella, E. (2003). The influence of media violence on youth. *Psychological Science in the Public Interest, 4.*

111. King, M., & Woollett, E. (1997). Sexually assaulted males: 115 men consulting a counseling service. *Archives of Sexual Behavior, 26,* 579–588; Stemple, L., & Meyer, I. H. (2014). The sexual victimization of men in America: New data challenge old assumptions. *American Journal of Public Health, 104,* e19–e26.

112. Malamuth, N. M., Hald, G., & Koss, M. (2012). Pornography, individual differences in risk and men's acceptance of violence against women in a representative sample. *Sex Roles, 66,* 427–439.

113. Laumann, E. O, & Gagnon, J. H. (1995). A sociological perspective on sexual action. In R. G. Parker & J. H. Gagnon (Eds.), *Conceiving sexuality: Approaches to sex research in a postmodern world*. New York: Routledge.

114. Hust, S. J. T., Marett, E. G., Ren, C., Adams, P. M., Willoughby, J. F., Lei, M., Ran, W., & Norman, C. (2014). Establishing and adhering to sexual consent: The association between reading magazines and college students' sexual consent negotiation. *Journal of Sex Research, 51*, 280–290; La France, B. H., Henningsen, D. D., Oates, A., & Shaw, C. M. (2009). Social-sexual interactions? Meta-analyses of sex differences in perceptions of flirtatiousness, seductiveness, and promiscuousness. *Communication Monographs, 76*, 263–285.

115. Davis, D., & Loftus, E. F. (2003). What's good for the goose cooks the gander: Inconsistencies between the law and psychology of voluntary intoxication and sexual assault. In W. T. O'Donohue & E. Levensky (Eds.), *Handbook of forensic psychology* (pp. 997–1032). New York, Elsevier Academic Press.

116. Villalobos, J. G., Davis, D., & Leo, R. A. (2015). His story, her story: Sexual miscommunication, motivated remembering, and intoxication as pathways to honest false testimony regarding sexual consent. In R. Burnett (Ed.), *Vilified: Wrongful allegations of person abuse*. Oxford: Oxford University Press.

117. Clark, K. (1971). The pathos of power: A psychological perspective. *American Psychologist, 26*, 1047–1057.

118. King, R. S., Mauer, M., & Young, M. C. (2005). *Incarceration and crime: A complex relationship*. Washington, DC: The Sentencing Project.

119. Eichmann, C. (1966). *The impact of the Gideon decision on crime and sentencing in Florida*. Tallahassee, FL: Division of Corrections Publications.

120. DPIC. (2017). https://deathpenaltyinfo.org/deterrence-states-without-death-penalty-have-had-consistently-lower-murder-rates. Accessed August 16, 2017; King, R. S., Mauer, M., & Young, M. C. (2005). *Incarceration and crime: A complex relationship*. Washington, DC: The Sentencing Project.

121. Durrant, J., & Ensom, R. (2012). Physical punishment of children: Lessons from 20 years of research. *Canadian Medical Association Journal, 184*, 1373–1377.

122. Aronson, E., & Carlsmith, J. M. (1963). The effect of severity of threat on the devaluation of forbidden behavior. *Journal of Abnormal and Social Psychology, 66*, 584–588; Freedman, J. (1965). Long-term behavioral effects of cognitive dissonance. *Journal of Experimental and Social Psychology, 1*, 145–155.

123. Olweus, D. (1991). Bully/victim problems among school children: Basic facts and effects of a school-based intervention program. In D. Pepler & K. Rubin (Eds.), *The development and treatment of childhood aggression* (pp. 411–448). Hillsdale, NJ: Erlbaum; Olweus, D., & Limber, S. P. (2010). Bullying in school: Evaluation and dissemination of the Olweus Bullying Prevention Program. *American Journal of Orthopsychiatry, 80*, 124–134; Ttofi, M. M., & Farrington, D. P. (2011). Effectiveness of school-based programs to reduce bullying: A systematic and meta-analytic review. *Journal of Experimental Criminology, 7*, 27–56.

124. Bandura, A., Ross, D., & Ross, S. (1963). Imitation of film-mediated aggressive models. *Journal of Abnormal and Social Psychology, 66,* 3–11.

125. Brown, P., & Elliot, R. (1965). Control of aggression in a nursery school class. *Journal of Experimental Child Psychology, 2,* 103–107.

126. Davitz, J. (1952). The effects of previous training on post-frustration behavior. *Journal of Abnormal and Social Psychology, 47,* 309–315.

127. Baron, R. A., & Kepner, C. R. (1970). Model's behavior and attraction toward the model as determinants of adult aggressive behavior. *Journal of Personality and Social Psychology, 14,* 335–344.

128. Baron, R. A. (1976). The reduction of human aggression: A field study of the influence of incompatible reactions. *Journal of Applied Social Psychology, 6,* 260–274.

129. Feshbach, N., & Feshbach, S. (1969). The relationship between empathy and aggression in two age groups. *Developmental Psychology, 1,* 102–107.

130. Feshbach, N. (1989). Empathy training and prosocial behavior. In J. Groebel & R. A. Hinde (Eds.), *Aggression and war: Their biological and social bases* (pp. 101–111). New York: Cambridge University Press; Feshbach, N. D., & Feshbach, S. (2009). Empathy and education. In J. Decety & W. Ickes (Eds.), *The social neuroscience of empathy* (pp. 85–97). Cambridge, MA: MIT Press.

131. Hammock, G. S., & Richardson, D. R. (1992). Aggression as one response to conflict. *Journal of Applied Social Psychology, 22,* 298–311.

132. Obuchi, K., Ohno, T., & Mukai, H. (1993) Empathy and aggression: Effects of self-disclosure and fearful appeal. *Journal of Social Psychology, 133,* 243–253.

133. Aknin, L. B., Barrington-Leigh, C. P., Dunn, E. W., Helliwell, J. F., Burns, J., Biswas-Diener, R., Kemeza, I., Nyende, P., Ashton-James, C. E., & Norton, M. I. (2013). Prosocial spending and well-being: Cross-cultural evidence for a psychological universal. *Journal of Personality and Social Psychology, 104,* 635–652; Dunn, E. W., Aknin, L. B., & Norton, M. I. (2008). Spending money on others promotes happiness. *Science, 319,* 1687–1688.

134. Jazaieri, H., Lee, I. A., McGonigal, K., Jinpa, T., Doty, J. R., Gross, J. J., & Goldin, P. R. (2016). A wandering mind is a less caring mind: Daily experience sampling during compassion meditation training. *Journal of Positive Psychology, 11,* 37–50; Mrazek, M. D., Phillips, D. T., Franklin, M. S., Broadway, J. M., & Schooler, J. W. (2013). Young and restless: Validation of the Mind-Wandering Questionnaire (MWQ) reveals disruptive impact of mind-wandering for youth. *Frontiers in Psychology, 4,* 560; Killingsworth, M. A., & Gilbert, D. T. (2010). A wandering mind is an unhappy mind. *Science, 330,* 932–932.

135. Milani, A., Nikmanesh, Z., & Farnam, A. (2013). Effectiveness of mindfulness-based cognitive therapy (MBCT) in reducing aggression of individuals at the juvenile correction and rehabilitation center. *International Journal of High Risk Behaviors & Addiction, 2,* 126–131; Long, E. C., & Christian, M. S. (2015). Mindfulness buffers retaliatory responses to injustice: A regulatory approach.

Journal of Applied Psychology, 100, 1409–1422; Fix, R. L., & Fix, S. T. (2013). The effects of mindfulness-based treatments for aggression: A critical review. *Aggression and Violent Behavior, 18*, 219–227.

136. Nidich, S. I., Rainforth, M. V., Haaga, D. A., Hagelin, J., Salerno, J. W., Travis, F., Tanner, M., Gaylord-King, C., Grosswald, S., & Schneider, R. H. (2009). A randomized controlled trial on effects of the Transcendental Meditation program on blood pressure, psychological distress, and coping in young adults. *American Journal of Hypertension, 22*, 1326–1331.

137. Sedlmeier, P., Eberth, J., Schwarz, M., Zimmermann, D., Haarig, F., Jaeger, S., & Kunze, S. (2012). The psychological effects of meditation: A meta-analysis. *Psychological Bulletin, 138*, 1139.

138. Lorenz, K. (1966). *On aggression* (M. Wilson, Trans.). New York: Harcourt, Brace & World.

139. Montagu, A. (1950). *On being human.* New York: Hawthorne Books.

140. Kropotkin, P. (1902). *Mutual aid.* New York: Doubleday.

141. Hölldobler, B., & Wilson, E. O. (2009). *The superorganism: The beauty, elegance, and strangeness of insect societies.* W.W. Norton & Company.

142. Mason, L. E. (2017). The significance of Dewey's democracy and education for 21st-century education. *Education and Culture, 33*, 41–57.

143. Eiseley, L. (1946). *The immense journey.* New York: Random House.

Chapter 7   Prejudice

1. Williams, J. (2011). *Thurgood Marshall: American revolutionary.* New York: Three Rivers Press.

2. American National Election Studies (2016). National survey results. http://www.electionstudies.org. Accessed August 24, 2017.

3. Liptak, A. (2013). Supreme Court invalidates key part of voting rights act. *New York Times*, June 25. http://www.nytimes.com/2013/06/26/us/supreme-court-ruling.html?mcubz=0. Accessed August 24, 2017.

4. Parrillo, V. N., & Donoghue, C. (2013). The national social distance study: Ten years later. In *Sociological Forum, 28*, 597–614.

5. Stephens-Davidowitz, S. (2014). The data of hate. *New York Times*, July 12.

6. Gerges, F. A. (2014). ISIS and the third wave of Jihadism. *Current History, 113*, 339; Cheterian, V. (2015). ISIS and the killing fields of the Middle East. *Survival, 57*, 105–118.

7. Obama on the N-Word: WTF Podcast with Marc Maron #613. June 22, 2015.

8. Trump, D. (2015). Republican debate: Analysis and highlights. *New York Times*, August 6. https://www.nytimes.com/live/republican-debate-election.../trump-on-political-correctness/?. Accessed August 24, 2017.

9. Wang, A. (2017). Airbnb host who stranded guest because of race ordered to take class in Asian American studies. *Washington Post*, July 14. https://www.washingtonpost.com/news/business/wp/2017/07/14/airbnb-host-who-stranded-guest-because-of-race-ordered-to-take-class-in-asian-american-studies/?utm_term=.50278a1198b8. Accessed August 24, 2017.

10. Stolberg, S. G., & Dickerson, C. (2017). Hangman's noose, symbol of racial animus, keeps cropping up. *New York Times*, July 5. https://www.nytimes.com/2017/07/05/us/nooses-hate-crimes-philadelphia-mint.html?emc=eta1. Accessed August 24, 2017.

11. Wang, A. B. (2017). "Final act of bravery": Men who were fatally stabbed trying to stop anti-Muslim rants identified. *Washington Post*, May 27. https://www.washingtonpost.com/news/post-nation/wp/2017/05/27/man-fatally-stabs-2-on-portland-ore-train-after-they-interrupted-his-anti-muslim-rants-police-say/?utm_term=.01835f7c26c9. Accessed August 24, 2017.

12. Cikara, M., & Van Bavel, J. J. (2014). The neuroscience of intergroup relations: An integrative review. *Perspectives on Psychological Science*, *9*, 245–274.

13. Anzures, G., Quinn, P. C., Pascalis, O., Slater, A. M., Tanaka, J. W., & Lee, K. (2013). Developmental origins of the other-race effect. *Current Directions in Psychological Science*, *22*, 173–178.

14. Lippmann, W. (1922) *Public opinion*. New York: MacMillan Co.

15. Bodenhausen, G. V. (1990). Stereotypes as judgmental heuristics: Evidence of circadian variations in discrimination. *Psychological Science*, *1*, 319–322.

16. Jussim, L. (2017). Accuracy, bias, self-fulfilling prophecies, and scientific self-correction. *Behavioral and Brain Sciences*, *40*, e18; Jussim, L., Crawford, J. T., & Rubinstein, R. S. (2015). Stereotype (in) accuracy in perceptions of groups and individuals. *Current Directions in Psychological Science*, *24*, 490–497.

17. Jussim, L., Crawford, J.T., Anglin, S. M., Chambers, J. R., Stevens, S. T., & Cohen, F. (2016). Stereotype accuracy: One of the largest and most replicable effects in all of social psychology. In T. Nelson (Ed.), *Handbook of prejudice, stereotyping, and discrimination*, 2nd edition (pp. 31–63). New York: Psychology Press.

18. Nisbett, R. E., Aronson, J., Blair, C., Dickens, W., Flynn, J., Halpern, D. F., & Turkheimer, E. (2012). Intelligence: New findings and theoretical developments. *American Psychologist*, *67*, 130–159.

19. Feagin, J. R. (2017). *Myth of the model minority: Asian Americans facing racism*. New York: Routledge.

20. Fiske, S. T., & Neuberg, S. L. (1990). A continuum of impression formation, from category-based to individuating processes: Influences of information and motivation on attention and interpretation. *Advances in Experimental Social Psychology*, *23*, 1–74.

21. Stone, J., Perry, W., & Darley, J. M. (1997). "White men can't jump": Evidence for the perceptual confirmation of racial stereotypes following a basketball game. *Basic and Applied Social Psychology*, *19*, 291–306.

22. Duncan, B. (1976). Differential social perception and attribution of intergroup violence: Testing the lower limits of stereotyping of blacks. *Journal of Personality and Social Psychology, 34,* 590–598.

23. Kite, M. E., Deaux, K., & Haines, E. L. (2008). Gender stereotypes. In F. L. Denmark & M. A. Paludi (Eds.), *Psychology of women: A handbook of issues and theories,* 2nd edition (pp. 205–236). Westport, CT: Praeger Publishers.

24. Haines, E. L., Deaux, K., & Lofaro, N. (2016). The times they are a-changing … or are they not? A comparison of gender stereotypes, 1983–2014. *Psychology of Women Quarterly, 40,* 353–363.

25. Fine, C. (2010). *Delusions of gender: How our minds, society, and neurosexism create difference.* New York: W.W. Norton.

26. Mehl, M. R., Vazire, S., Ramírez-Esparza, N., Slatcher, R. B., & Pennebaker, J. W. (2007). Are women really more talkative than men? *Science, 317,* 82.

27. Glick, P., & Fiske, S. T. (2001). An ambivalent alliance: Hostile and benevolent sexism as complementary justifications for gender inequality. *American Psychologist, 56,* 109; Becker, J. C., & Wright, S. C. (2011). Yet another dark side of chivalry: Benevolent sexism undermines and hostile sexism motivates collective action for social change. *Journal of Personality and Social Psychology, 101,* 62–77.

28. Christopher, A. N., & Wojda, M. R. (2008). Social dominance orientation, right-wing authoritarianism, sexism, and prejudice toward women in the workforce. *Psychology of Women Quarterly, 32,* 65–73.

29. Jung, K., Shavitt, S., Viswanathan, M., & Hilbe, J. M. (2014). Female hurricanes are deadlier than male hurricanes. *Proceedings of the National Academy of Sciences, 111,* 8782–8787.

30. Allport, G. W. (1954/1979). *The nature of prejudice.* New York: Basic Books.

31. Holmes, O. W. (1831). The autocrat of the breakfast table. *New-England Magazine, 1,* 431.

32. Cohen, F., Jussim, L., Harber, K. D., & Bhasin, G. (2009). Modern anti-Semitism and anti-Israeli attitudes. *Journal of Personality and Social Psychology, 97,* 290–306.

33. Crandall, C. S., Bahns, A. J., Warner, R., & Schaller, M. (2011). Stereotypes as justifications of prejudice. *Personality and Social Psychology Bulletin, 37,* 1488–1498.

34. Harris, L. T., & Fiske, S. T. (2006). Dehumanizing the lowest of the low: Neuroimaging responses to extreme out-groups. *Psychological Science, 17,* 847–853.

35. Stanley, D., Phelps, E., & Banaji, M. (2008). The neural basis of implicit attitudes. *Current Directions in Psychological Science, 17,* 164–170.

36. Phelps, E. A., O'Connor, K. J., Cunningham, W. A., Funayama, E. S., Gatenby, J. C., Gore, J. C., & Banaji, M. R. (2000). Performance on indirect measures of race evaluation predicts amygdala activation. *Journal of Cognitive Neuroscience, 12,* 729–738.

37. Wheeler, M.E., & Fiske, S. T. (2005). Controlling racial prejudice: Social–cognitive goals affect amygdala and stereotype activation. *Psychological Science, 16*, 56–63.

38. Flegal, K. M., Kruszon-Moran, D., Carroll, M. D., Fryar, C. D., & Ogden, C. L. (2016). Trends in obesity among adults in the United States, 2005 to 2014. *Journal of the American Medical Association, 315*, 2284–2291.

39. Miller Jr., D. P., Spangler, J. G., Vitolins, M. Z., Davis, M. S. W., Ip, E. H., Marion, G. S., & Crandall, S. J. (2013). Are medical students aware of their anti-obesity bias? *Academic Medicine, 88*, 978–982; Lydecker, J. A., O'Brien, E., & Grilo, C. (2017). Parents' implicit and explicit attitudes towards childhood obesity. *Journal of Adolescent Health, 60*, S11–S12; Randall, J. G., Zimmer, C. U., O'Brien, K. R., Trump-Steele, R. C., Villado, A. J., & Hebl, M. R. (2017). Weight discrimination in helping behavior. *Revue Européenne de Psychologie Appliquée/European Review of Applied Psychology, 67*, 125–137.

40. Centers for Disease Control (2016). Lesbian, gay, bisexual, and transgender health. https://www.cdc.gov/lgbthealth/youth.htm. Accessed August 24, 2017.

41. U.S. Department of Education, Office of Civil Rights. (2016). 2013–2014 civil rights data collection: Key data highlights on equity and opportunity gaps in our nation's public schools. http://www2.ed.gov/about/offices/list/ocr/docs/crdc-2013-14.html. Accessed August 24, 2017.

42. Skiba, R. J., Michael R., Nardo A., & Peterson R. (2002). The color of discipline: Sources of racial and gender disproportionality in school punishment. *The Urban Review, 34*, 317–342; Skiba, R. J., Arredondo, M. I., Gray, C., & Rausch, M. K. (2016). What do we know about discipline disparities? New and emerging research. In R. J. Skiba & K. Mediratta (Eds.), *Inequality in school discipline* (pp. 21–38). New York: Palgrave Macmillan US; Rausch, M. K., & Skiba, R. J. (2017). The need for systemic interventions. In E. C. Lopez, S. G. Nahari, & S. L. Proctor (Eds.), *Handbook of multicultural school psychology: An interdisciplinary perspective*, 2nd edition. NY: Routledge; Okonofua, J. A., Walton, G. M., & Eberhardt, J. A. (2016). A vicious cycle: A social-psychological account of extreme racial disparities in school discipline. *Perspectives on Psychological Science, 11*, 381–398.

43. Gilliam, W. S., Maupin, A. N., Reyes, C. R., Accavitti, M., & Shic, F. (2016). Do early educators' implicit biases regarding sex and race relate to behavior expectations and recommendations of preschool expulsions and suspensions? Research Study Brief. Yale University, Yale Child Study Center. New Haven, CT.

44. Bjerk, D. (2017). Mandatory minimums and the sentencing of federal drug crimes. *Journal of Legal Studies, 46*, 93–128.

45. Mitchell, O., & Caudy, M. S. (2015). Examining racial disparities in drug arrests. *Justice Quarterly, 32*, 288–313.

46. Alexander, M. (2012). *The new Jim Crow: Mass incarceration in the age of colorblindness*. New York: New Press.

47. Fryer Jr., R. G. (2016). *An empirical analysis of racial differences in police use of force* (No. w22399). National Bureau of Economic Research; Buehler, J. W. (2017). Racial/ethnic disparities in the use of lethal force by US Police, 2010–2014. *Journal Information, 107*(2).

48. Lavergne, M., & Mullainathan, S. (2004). Are Emily and Greg more employable than Lakisha and Jamal? A field experiment on labor market discrimination. *American Economic Review, 94*, 991–1013.

49. Pager, D. (2003). The mark of a criminal record. *American Journal of Sociology, 108,* 937–975; Sugie, N. F. (2017). Criminal record questions, statistical discrimination, and equity in a "Ban the Box" era. *Criminology & Public Policy, 16*, 167–175.

50. David, A., & Melanie, W. (2013). Wayward sons: The emerging gender gap in labor markets and education. http://www.thirdway.org/report/wayward-sons-the-emerging-gender-gap-in-labor-markets-and-education. Accessed August 24, 2016.

51. Joshi, A., Son J., & Roh, H. (2015). When can women close the gap? A meta-analytic test of sex differences in performance and rewards. *Academy of Management Journal, 58,* 1516–1545.

52. Webber, K. L., & Canché, M. G. (2015). Not equal for all: Gender and race differences in salary for doctoral degree recipients. *Research on Higher Education, 56,* 645–672.

53. Goldin, C., & Rouse, C. (2000). Orchestrating impartiality: The impact of "blind" auditions on female musicians. *American Economic Review, 90,* 715–741.

54. Greenwald, A. G., McGhee, D. E., & Schwartz, J. L. K. (1998). Measuring individual differences in implicit cognition: The Implicit Association Test. *Journal of Personality and Social Psychology, 74,* 1464–1480.

55. Nosek, B. A., Greenwald, A. G., & Banaji, M. R. (2007). The Implicit Association Test at 7: A methodological and conceptual review. In J. A. Bargh (Ed.), *Social psychology and the unconscious.* New York: Psychology Press; Miller Jr., D. P., Spangler, J. G., Vitolins, M. Z., Davis, S. W., Ip, E. H., et al. (2013). Are medical students aware of their anti-obesity bias? *Academic Medicine, 88,* 978–982.

56. Banaji, M. R., & Greenwald, A. G. (2013). *Blindspot: Hidden biases of good people.* New York: Delacorte.

57. Kinoshita, S., & Peek-O'Leary, M. (2005). Does the compatibility effect in the race Implicit Association Test reflect familiarity or affect? *Psychonomic Bulletin & Review, 12,* 442–452; Rothermund, K., & Wentura, D. (2004). Underlying processes in the Implicit Association Test: Dissociating salience from associations. *Journal of Experimental Psychology: General, 133,* 139–165.

58. Arkes, H., & Tetlock, P. (2004). Attributions of implicit prejudice, or "Would Jesse Jackson 'fail' the Implicit Association Test?" *Psychological Inquiry, 15,*

257–278; Olson, M. A., & Fazio, R. H. (2004). Reducing the influence of extrapersonal associations on the implicit association test: Personalizing the IAT. *Journal of Personality and Social Psychology, 86*, 653–667.

59. Stanley, D. A., Sokol-Hessner, P., Banaji, M. R., & Phelps, E. A. (2011). Implicit race attitudes predict trustworthiness judgments and economic trust decisions. *PNAS, 108*, 7710–7715.

60. Cooper, L. A., Roter, D. L., Carson, K. A., Beach, M. C., Sabin, J. A., Greenwald, A. G., & Inui, T. S. (2012). The associations of clinicians' implicit attitudes about race with medical visit communication and patient ratings of interpersonal care. *American Journal of Public Health, 102*, 979–987.

61. De Houwer, J., Teige-Mocigemba, S., Spruyt, A., & Moors, A. (2009). Implicit measures: A normative analysis and review. *Psychological Bulletin, 135*, 347–368.

62. Hahn, A., Judd, C. M., Hirsh, H. K., & Blair, I. V. (2014). Awareness of implicit attitudes. *Journal of Experimental Psychology: General, 143*, 1369–1392.

63. Dovidio, J. F., Gaertner, S. L., & Pearson, A. R. (2016). Racism among the well-intentioned: Bias without awareness. In A. G. Miller (Ed.), *The social psychology of good and evil*, 2nd edition. New York: Guilford Press.

64. Rogers, R. W., & Prentice-Dunn, S. (1981). Deindividuation and anger-mediated interracial aggression: Unmasking regressive racism. *Journal of Personality and Social Psychology, 41*, 63–73.

65. Fein, S., & Spencer, S. J. (1997). Prejudice as self-image maintenance: Affirming the self through derogating others. *Journal of Personality and Social Psychology, 73*, 31–44; Maass, A., Cadinu, M., Guarnieri, G., & Grasselli, A. (2003). Sexual harassment under social identity threat: The computer harassment paradigm. *Journal of Personality and Social Psychology, 85*, 853–870; Meindl, J. R., & Lerner, M. J. (1985). Exacerbation of extreme responses to an out-group. *Journal of Personality and Social Psychology, 47*, 71–84.

66. Crandall, C., & Eshelman, A. (2003). A justification-suppression model of the expression and experience of prejudice. *Psychological Bulletin, 129(3)*, 414–446.

67. Frey, D. L., & Gaertner, S. I. (1986). Helping and the avoidance of inappropriate interracial behavior: A strategy that perpetuates a nonprejudiced self-image. *Journal of Personality and Social Psychology, 50*, 1035–1090.

68. King, E. B., Shapiro, J. R., Hebl, M. R., Singletary, S. L., & Turner, S. (2006). The stigma of obesity in customer service: A mechanism for remediation and bottom-line consequences of interpersonal discrimination. *Journal of Applied Psychology, 91*, 579–593.

69. Quotes from Edwards and Crocker in Jacobs, P., & Landau, S. (1971). *To serve the devil* (Vol. 2, pp. 71 and 81). New York: Vintage Books.

70. Greeley, A., & Sheatsley, P. (1971). The acceptance of desegregation continues to advance. *Scientific American, 225*, 13–19; Vanneman, R. D., & Pettigrew, T. F.

(1972). Race and relative deprivation in the urban United States. *Race, 13,* 461–486.

71. Sherif, M., Harvey, O. J., White, B. J., et al. (1961). *Intergroup conflict and cooperation: The Robbers Cave experiment.* Norman: University of Oklahoma Institute of Intergroup Relations.

72. Miller, N., & Bugelski, R. (1948). Minor studies in aggression: The influence of frustrations imposed by the in-group on attitudes expressed by the out-group. *Journal of Psychology, 25,* 437–442.

73. Staub, E. (1996). Cultural-societal roots of violence: The examples of genocidal violence, and of contemporary youth violence in the United States. *American Psychologist, 51,* 117–132.

74. Lowenthal, L., & Guterman, N. (1949). *Prophets of deceit: A study of the techniques of the American agitator.* New York: Harper and Brothers. Cited in G. Allport, *The nature of prejudice.* Reading, MA: Addison-Wesley.

75. Choma, B. L., & Hanoch, Y. (2017). Cognitive ability and authoritarianism: Understanding support for Trump and Clinton. *Personality and Individual Differences, 106,* 287–291.

76. Minard, R. D. (1952). Race relations in the Pocahontas coal field. *Journal of Social Issues, 8,* 29–44.

77. Watson, J. (1950). Some social and psychological situations related to change in attitude. *Human Relations, 3,* 15–56.

78. Kirkland, S. L., Greenberg, J., & Pyszczynski, T. (1987). Further evidence of the deleterious effects of overheard derogatory ethnic labels: Derogation beyond the target. *Personality and Social Psychology Bulletin, 13,* 216–227.

79. Eccles, J. S., Jacobs, J. E., & Harold, R. D. (1990). Gender role stereotypes, expectancy effects, and parents' socialization of gender differences. *Journal of Social Issues, 46,* 183–201.

80. Harber, K. D. (1998). Feedback to minorities: Evidence of a positive bias. *Journal of Personality and Social Psychology, 74,* 622–628; Harber, K. D. (2018). The positive feedback bias. In J. Aronson and E. Aronson (Eds.), *Readings about the social animal,* 12th edition. New York: Worth/Freeman.

81. Turner, M. E., & Pratkanis, A. R. (1994). Affirmative action as help: A review of recipient reactions to preferential selection and affirmative action. *Basic and Applied Social Psychology, 15,* 43–69.

82. Steele, C. M., & Aronson, J. (1995). Stereotype threat and the intellectual test performance of African Americans. *Journal of Personality and Social Psychology, 69,* 797–811.

83. Steele, C. M., Spencer, S. J., & Aronson, J. (2002). Contending with group image: The psychology of stereotype and social identity threat. *Advances in Experimental Social Psychology, 34,* 379–440.

84. Spencer, S. J., Steele, C. M., & Quinn, D. M. (1999). Stereotype threat and women's math performance. *Journal of Experimental Social Psychology, 35*, 4–28; Schmader, T., Johns, M., & Forbes, C. (2008). An integrated process model of stereotype threat effects on performance. *Psychological Review, 115*, 336–356; Nguyen, H. H., & Ryan, A. M. (2008). Does stereotype threat affect test performance of minorities and women? A meta-analysis of experimental evidence. *Journal of Applied Psychology, 93*, 1314–1334; Gonzales, P. M., Blanton, H., & Williams, K. J. (2002). The effects of stereotype threat and double-minority status on the test performance of Latino women. *Personality and Social Psychology Bulletin, 28*, 659–670; Chu, H., & Brown, C. S. (2017). Stereotype threat among Latino school age children. *International Journal of Social Science and Humanity, 7*, 278–281; Hess, T. M., Auman, C., Colcombe, S. J., & Rahhal, T. A. (2003). The impact of stereotype threat on age differences in memory performance. *The Journals of Gerontology Series B: Psychological Sciences and Social Sciences, 58*, 3–11; Spencer, S. J., Logel, C., & Davies, P. G. (2016). Stereotype threat. *Annual Review of Psychology, 67*, 415–437; Taylor, V. J., & Walton, G. M. (2011). Stereotype threat undermines academic learning. *Personality and Social Psychology Bulletin, 37*, 1055–1067.

85. Aronson, J., Lustina, M. J., Good, C., Keough, K., Steele, C. M., & Brown, J. (1999). When white men can't do math: Necessary and sufficient factors in stereotype threat. *Journal of Experimental Social Psychology, 35*, 29–46.

86. McGlone, M. S., & Aronson, J. (2006). Stereotype threat, identity salience, and spatial reasoning. *Journal of Applied Developmental Psychology, 27*, 486–493.

87. Herrmann, S. D., Adelman, R. M., Bodford, J. E., Graudejus, O., Okun, M. A., & Kwan, V. S. (2016). The effects of a female role model on academic performance and persistence of women in STEM courses. *Basic and Applied Social Psychology, 38*, 258–268; Stout, J. G., Dasgupta, N., Hunsinger, M., & McManus, M. A. (2011). STEMing the tide: Using ingroup experts to inoculate women's self-concept in science, technology, engineering, and mathematics (STEM). *Journal of Personality and Social Psychology, 100*, 255–270; Martens, A., Johns, M., Greenberg, J., & Schimel, J. (2006). Combating stereotype threat: The effect of self-affirmation on women's intellectual performance. *Journal of Experimental Social Psychology, 42*, 236–243.

88. Good, C., Aronson, J., & Inzlicht, M. (2003). Improving adolescents' standardized test performance: An intervention to reduce the effects of stereotype threat. *Journal of Applied Developmental Psychology, 24*, 645–662.

89. Walton, G. M., Cohen, G. L., Cwir, D., & Spencer, S. J. (2012). Mere belonging: the power of social connections. *Journal of Personality and Social Psychology, 102*, 513–532; Walton, G. M., & Cohen, G. L. (2011). A brief social-belonging intervention improves academic and health outcomes of minority students. *Science, 331*, 1447–1451.

90. Martens, A., Johns, M., Greenberg, J., & Schimel, J. (2006). Combating stereotype threat: The effect of self-affirmation on women's intellectual performance. *Journal of Experimental Social Psychology, 42*, 236–243.

91. Cohen, G. L., Garcia, J., Purdie-Vaughns, V., Apfel, N., & Brzustoski, P. (2009). Recursive processes in self-affirmation: Intervening to close the minority achievement gap. *Science, 324*, 400–403; Hanselman, P., Bruch, S. K., Gamoran, A., & Borman, G. D. (2014). Threat in context: School moderation of the impact of social identity threat on racial/ethnic achievement gaps. *Sociology of Education, 87*, 106–124.

92. Lerner, M. J. (1980). *The belief in a just world: A fundamental delusion.* New York: Plenum.

93. Furnham, A., & Gunter, B. (1984). Just world beliefs and attitudes towards the poor. *British Journal of Social Psychology, 23*, 265–269.

94. Paluck, E. L., & Green, D. P. (2009). Prejudice reduction: What works? A review and assessment of research and practice. *Annual Review of Psychology, 60*, 339–367.

95. Deutsch, M., & Collins, M. E. (1951). *Interracial housing: A psychological evaluation of a social experiment.* Minneapolis: University of Minnesota Press; Wilner, D., Wallcley, R., & Cook, S. (1955). *Human relations in interracial housing.* Minneapolis: University of Minnesota Press.

96. Herek, G. M., & Capitanio, J. P. (1996). "Some of my best friends": Intergroup contact, concealable stigma, and heterosexuals' attitudes toward gay men and lesbians. *Personality and Social Psychology Bulletin, 22*, 412–424; Pettigrew, Thomas T., & Tropp, Linda R. (2006). A meta-analytic test of intergroup contact theory. *Journal of Personality and Social Psychology, 90*, 751–783; Wilner, Daniel, Walkley, Rosabelle, & Cook, Stuart (1955). *Human relations in interracial housing.* Minneapolis: University of Minnesota Press.

97. Van Laar, C., Levin, S., & Sidanius, J. (2008). Ingroup and outgroup contact: A longitudinal study of the effects of cross-ethnic friendships, dates, roommate relationships and participation in segregated organizations. In U. Wagner, L. R. Tropp, G. Finchilescu, & C. Tredoux (Eds.), *Improving intergroup relations: Building on the legacy of Thomas F. Pettigrew.* Malden: Blackwell.

98. Sidanius, J., Van Laar, C., Levin, S., & Sinclair, S. (2004). Ethnic enclaves and the dynamics of social identity on the college campus: The good, the bad, and the ugly. *Journal of Personality and Social Psychology, 87*, 96–110.

99. Mendoza-Denton, R., & Page-Gould, E. (2008). Can crossgroup friendships influence minority students' well-being at historically white universities? *Psychological Science, 19*, 933–993.

100. Saguy, T., Tausch, N., Dovidio, J. F., Pratto, F. & Singh, P. (2010). Tension and harmony in intergroup relations. In M. Mikulincer & P. Shaver (Eds.), *Understanding and reducing aggression, violence, and their consequences.* Washington, DC: American Psychological Association.

101. Stephan, W. G. (1978). School desegregation: An evaluation of predictions made in *Brown v. The Board of Education. Psychological Bulletin, 85*, 217–238; Stephan, W. G. (1985). Intergroup relations. In G. Lindzey & E. Aronson

(Eds.), *Handbook of social psychology*, 3rd edition (pp. 599–658). New York: McGraw-Hill.

102. Sherif, M. (1958). Superordinate goals in the reduction of intergroup conflicts. *American Journal of Sociology, 63,* 349–356.

103. Deutsch, M. (1949). A theory of cooperation and competition. *Human Relations, 2,* 129–152; Deutsch, M. (1949). An experimental study of the effects of cooperation and competition upon group process. *Human Relations, 2,* 199–232

104. Keenan, P., & Carnevale, P. (1989). Positive effects of within-group competition on between-group negotiation. *Journal of Applied Social Psychology, 19,* 977–992.

105. Aronson, E., Stephan, C., Sikes, J., Blaney, N., & Snapp, M. (1978). *The jigsaw classroom.* Beverly Hills, CA: Sage; Aronson, E., & Osherow, N. (1980). Cooperation, prosocial behavior, and academic performance: Experiments in the desegregated classroom. In L. Bickman (Ed.), *Applied social psychology annual* (Vol. 1, pp. 163–196). Beverly Hills, CA: Sage; Aronson, E. (1992). Stateways can change folkways. In R. Baird & S. Rosenbaum (Eds.), *Bigotry, prejudice and hatred: Definitions, causes and solutions* (pp. 111–124). Buffalo, NY: Prometheus Books; Aronson, E., & Gonzalez, A. (1988). Desegregation, jigsaw and the Mexican-American experience. In P. Katz and D. Taylor (Eds.), *Eliminating racism.* New York: Plenum; Aronson, E., & Thibodeau, R. (1992). The jigsaw classroom: A cooperative strategy for reducing prejudice. In J. Lynch, C. Modgil, and S. Modgil (Eds.), *Cultural diversity in the schools.* London: Falmer Press; Aronson, E., & Patnoe, S. (2011). *Cooperation in the classroom: The jigsaw method,* 2nd edition. London, England: Pinter & Martin; Jigsaw Classroom. https://www.jigsaw.org. Accessed August 24, 2017.

106. Aronson, E., & Osherow, N. (1980). Cooperation, prosocial behavior, and academic performance: Experiments in the desegregated classroom. In L. Bickman (Ed.), *Applied social psychology annual* (Vol. 1, pp. 163–196). Beverly Hills, CA: Sage; Aronson, E. (2002). Building empathy, compassion, and achievement in the jigsaw classroom. In J. Aronson (Ed.), *Improving academic achievement: Impact of psychological factors on education* (pp. 209–225). San Diego, CA: Academic Press.

107. Juergen-Lohmann, J., Borsch, F., & Giesen, H. (2001). Cooperative learning at the university: An evaluation of jigsaw in classes of educational psychology/ Kooperatives Lernen an der Hochschule. Evaluation des Gruppenpuzzles in Seminaren der Paedagogischen Psychologie. *Zeitschrift fuer Paedagogische Psychologie, 15,* 74–84; Perkins, D., & Saris, R. (2001). A "jigsaw classroom" technique for undergraduate statistics courses. *Teaching of Psychology, 28,* 111–113; Walker, I., & Crogan, M. (1998). Academic performance, prejudice, and the jigsaw classroom: New pieces to the puzzle. *Journal of Community & Applied Social Psychology, 8,* 381–393.

108. Desforges D. M., Lord, C. G., Ramsey, S. L., Mason, J. A., Van Leeuwen, M. D., West, S. C., & Lepper, M. R. (1991). Effects of structured cooperative

contact on changing negative attitudes towards stigmatized social groups. *Journal of Personality and Social Psychology, 60,* 531–544.

109. Gaertner, S. L., Mann, J., Dovidio, J. F., Marrell, A., & Pomare, M. (1990). How does cooperation reduce intergroup bias? *Journal of Personality and Social Psychology, 59,* 692–704; Gaertner, S. L., & Dovidio, J. F. (2000). *Reducing intergroup bias: The common ingroup identity model.* Philadelphia, PA: Psychology Press.

110. Leippe, M. R., & Eisenstadt, D. (1994). Generalization of dissonance reduction: Decreasing prejudice through induced compliance. *Journal of Personality and Social Psychology, 67,* 395–413.

111. Gaertner, S. L., Mann, J. A., Dovidio, J. F., Murrell, A. J., & Pomare, M. (1990). How does cooperation reduce intergroup bias? *Journal of Personality and Social Psychology, 59,* 692–704.

112. Bridgeman, D. (1981). Enhanced role-taking through cooperative interdependence: A field study. *Child Development, 52,* 1231–1238.

113. Aronson, E. (2000). *Nobody left to hate: Teaching compassion after Columbine.* New York: Henry Holt.

114. Slavin, R. (1996). Research on cooperative learning and achievement: What we know, what we need to know. *Contemporary Educational Psychology, 21,* 43–69; Qin, Z., Johnson, D. W., & Johnson, R. T. (1995). Cooperative versus competitive efforts and problem solving. *Review of Educational Research, 65,* 29–143; Deutsch, M. (1949). A theory of cooperation and competition. *Human Relations, 2,* 129–152; Deutsch, M. (1949). An experimental study of the effects of cooperation and competition upon group process. *Human Relations, 2,* 199–232.

115. Van Bavel, J. J., & Cunningham, W. A. (2009). Self-categorization with a novel mixed-race group moderates automatic social and racial biases. *Personality and Social Psychology Bulletin, 35,* 321–335.

116. Todd, A., Bodenhausen, G. V., Richeson, J. A., & Galinsky, A. D. (2011). Perspective taking combats automatic expressions of racial bias. *Journal of Personality and Social Psychology, 100,* 1027–1042.

117. McConahay, J. B. (1981). Reducing racial prejudice in desegregated schools. In W. D. Hawley (Ed.), *Elective school desegregation.* Beverly Hills, CA: Sage.

118. Shipler, D. K. (1997). *A country of strangers: Blacks and whites in America.* New York: Knopf.

Chapter 8   Liking, Loving, and Connecting

1. Kasper, S. (1992). *Annie Oakley.* Norman, OK: University of Oklahoma Press.

2. Ekman, P. (1982). *Emotion in the human face,* 2nd edition. New York: Cambridge University Press.

3. Baumeister, R. F., & Leary, M. R. (1995). The need to belong: Desire for interpersonal attachments as a fundamental human motivation. *Psychological Bulletin, 117,* 497–529.

4. Waldinger, R., quoted in Curtin, M., (2017). This 75-year Harvard study found the 1 secret to leading a fulfilling life. *Inc.*, February 27. https://www.inc.com/melanie-curtin/want-a-life-of-fulfillment-a-75-year-harvard-study-says-to-prioritize-this-one-t.html.

5. Uchino, B. N., Cacioppo, J. T., & Kiecolt-Glaser, J. K. (1996). The relationship between social support and physiological processes: A review with emphasis on underlying mechanisms and implications for health. *Psychological Bulletin, 119*, 488–531.

6. Cacioppo, J. T., & Hawkley, L. C. (2003). Social isolation and health, with an emphasis on underlying mechanisms. *Perspectives in Biology and Medicine, 46*, S39–S52.

7. Cacioppo, J. T., Hawkley, L. C., & Thisted, R. A. (2010). Perceived social isolation makes me sad: 5-year cross-lagged analyses of loneliness and depressive symptomatology in the Chicago Health, Aging, and Social Relations Study. *Psychology and Aging, 25*, 453–463.

8. Klinenberg, E. (2013). *Going solo: The extraordinary rise and surprising appeal of living alone.* New York: Penguin.

9. DePaulo, B. M., & Morris, W. L. (2005). Singles in society and in science. *Psychological Inquiry, 16*, 57–83.

10. Quoted in Gregoire, C. (2013). The 75-year study that found the secrets to a fulfilling life. *Huffington Post*, August 23. http://www.huffingtonpost.com/2013/08/11/how-this-harvard-psycholo_n_3727229.html.

11. Carnegie, D. (1937/2010). *How to win friends and influence people.* New York: Simon and Schuster.

12. Remmers, H. H., & Radler, D. H. (1958). Teenage attitudes. *Scientific American, 198*, 25–29; Dawes, M., & Xie, H. (2014). The role of popularity goal in early adolescents' behaviors and popularity status. *Developmental Psychology, 50*, 489–497.

13. Lemann, T., & Solomon, R. (1952). Group characteristics as revealed in sociometric patterns and personality ratings. *Sociometry, 15*, 7–90.

14. Homans, G. (1961). *Social behavior: Its elementary forms.* New York: Harcourt, Brace and World.

15. Kelley, H. H., & Thibaut, J. W. (1978). *Interpersonal relations: A theory of interdependence.* John Wiley & Sons.

16. Festinger, L., Schachter, S., & Back, K. (1950). *Social pressures in informal groups: A study of human factors in housing.* New York: Harper.

17. Darley, J. M., & Berscheid, E. (1967). Increased liking as a result of the anticipation of personal contact. *Human Relations, 20*, 29–40.

18. Bossard, J. H. (1932). Residential propinquity as a factor in marriage selection. *American Journal of Sociology, 38*, 219–224.

19. Ansari, A., & Klinenberg, E. (2015). *Modern romance*. New York: Penguin.

20. Quoted in Ansari, A. (2015). *Modern romance,* New York: Penguin, p. 14.

21. Collisson, B., & Howell, J. L. (2014). The liking-similarity effect: Perceptions of similarity as a function of liking. *Journal of Social Psychology, 154,* 384–400; Aronson, E., & Worchel, S. (1966). Similarity versus liking as determinants of interpersonal attractiveness. *Psychometric Science, 5,* 157–158.

22. Tidwell, N. D., Eastwick, P. W., & Finkel, E. J. (2013), Perceived, not actual, similarity predicts initial attraction in a live romantic context: Evidence from the speed-dating paradigm. *Personal Relationships, 20,* 199–215.

23. Cialdini, R. B. (2004). The science of persuasion. *Scientific American Mind, 14,* 70–77.

24. Gehlbach, H., Brinkworth, M. E., King, A. M., Hsu, L. M., McIntyre, J., & Rogers, T. (2016). Creating birds of similar feathers: Leveraging similarity to improve teacher–student relationships and academic achievement. *Journal of Educational Psychology, 108,* 342–352.

25. Bales, R. (1958). Task roles and social roles in problem solving groups. In E. E. Maccoby, T. M. Newcomb, & E. L. Hartley (Eds.), *Readings in social psychology,* 3rd edition (pp. 437–447). New York: Holt.

26. Aronson, E., Willerman, B., & Floyd, J. (1966). The effect of a pratfall on increasing interpersonal attractiveness. *Psychonomic Science, 4,* 227–228.

27. Tesser, A., Millar, M., & Moore, J. (1988). Some affective consequences of social comparison and reflection processes: The pain and pleasure of being close. *Journal of Personality and Social Psychology, 54,* 49–61.

28. Cialdini, R. B., Borden, R. J., Thorne, A., Walker, M. R., Freeman, S., & Sloan, L. R. (1976). Basking in reflected glory: Three (football) field studies. *Journal of Personality and Social Psychology, 34,* 366–375.

29. Eastwick, P. W., Luchies, L. B., Finkel, E. J., & Hunt, L. L. (2014). The predictive validity of ideal partner preferences: A review and meta-analysis. *Psychological Bulletin, 140,* 623–665.

30. Todd, P. M., Penke, L., Fasolo, B., & Lenton, A. P. (2007). Different cognitive processes underlie human mate choices and mate preferences. *Proceedings of the National Academy of Sciences, 104,* 15011–15016.

31. Walster, E., Aronson, V., Abrahams, D., & Rottman, L. (1966). Importance of physical attractiveness in dating behavior. *Journal of Personality and Social Psychology, 5,* 508–516.

32. White, G. (1980). Physical attractiveness and courtship progress. *Journal of Personality and Social Psychology, 39,* 660–668.

33. Dion, K., Berscheid, E., & Walster (Hatfield), E. (1972). What is beautiful is good. *Journal of Personality and Social Psychology, 24,* 285–290.

34. Fink, B., Neave, N., Manning, J. T., & Grammer, K. (2006). Facial symmetry and judgements of attractiveness, health and personality. *Personality and Individual Differences, 41*, 491–499; Reber, R., Schwarz, N., & Winkielman, P. (2004). Processing fluency and aesthetic pleasure: Is beauty in the perceiver's processing experience? *Personality and Social Psychology Review, 8*, 364–382.

35. Tan, A. S. (1979). TV beauty ads and role expectations of adolescent female viewers. *Journalism Quarterly, 56*, 283–288.

36. Dion, K. (1972). Physical attractiveness and evaluations of children's transgressions. *Journal of Personality and Social Psychology, 24*, 207–213.

37. Frieze, I. H., Olson, J. E., & Russell, J. (1991). Attractiveness and income for men and women in management. *Journal of Applied Social Psychology, 21*, 1037–1039.

38. Sigall, H., & Aronson, E. (1969). Liking for an evaluator as a function of her physical attractiveness and nature of the evaluations. *Journal of Experimental and Social Psychology, 5*, 93–100.

39. Snyder, M., Tanke, E. D., & Berscheid, E. (1977). Social perception and interpersonal behavior: On the self-fulfilling nature of social stereotypes. *Journal of Personality and Social Psychology, 35*, 656–666.

40. Kniffin, K. M., & Wilson, D. S. (2004). The effect of nonphysical traits on the perception of physical attractiveness: Three naturalistic studies. *Evolution and Human Behavior, 25*, 88–101.

41. Gross, A. E., & Crofton, C. (1977). What is good is beautiful. *Personality and Social Psychology Bulletin, 3*, 262–265.

42. Freeman, J. (2011). Stereotypes and status symbols impact if a face is viewed as black or white. https://medicalxpress.com/news/2011-09-stereotypes-status-impact-viewed-black.html. Accessed September 3, 2017.

43. Curtis, R. C., & Miller, K. (1986). Believing another likes or dislikes you: Behaviors making the beliefs come true. *Journal of Personality and Social Psychology, 51*, 284–290.

44. Walster (Hatfield), E. (1965). The effect of self-esteem on romantic liking. *Journal of Experimental and Social Psychology, 1*, 184–197.

45. Kiesler, S. B., & Baral, R. L. (1970). The search for a romantic partner: The effects of self-esteem and physical attractiveness on romantic behavior. In K. J. Gergen & D. Marlowe (Eds.), *Personality and social behavior.* Reading, MA: Addison-Wesley.

46. Finkel, E. J., & Eastwick, P. W. (2009). Arbitrary social norms influence sex differences in romantic selectivity. *Psychological Science, 20*, 1290–1295.

47. Schwartz, B. (2004). *The paradox of choice: Why less is more.* New York: Ecco.

48. Iyengar, S. S., & Lepper, M. R. (2000). When choice is demotivating: Can one desire too much of a good thing? *Journal of Personality and Social Psychology, 79*, 995–1006.

49. Ansari, A. (2015). *Modern romance*. New York: Penguin.

50. Iyengar, S. S., Wells, R. E., & Schwartz, B. (2006). Doing better but feeling worse: Looking for the "best" job undermines satisfaction. *Psychological Science, 17*, 143–150.

51. Ansari, A. (2015). *Modern romance*. New York: Penguin.

52. Amabile, T. M. (1983). Brilliant but cruel: Perceptions of negative evaluators. *Journal of Experimental Social Psychology, 19*, 146–156.

53. Swann, Jr., W. B. (1990). To be adored or to be known? The interplay of self-enhancement and self-verification. In R.M. Sorrentino & E.T. Higgins (Eds.), *Foundations of social behavior* (Vol. 2), pp. 408–448. New York: Guilford.

54. Lawrence, J. S., Crocker, J., & Blanton, H. (2011). Stigmatized and dominant cultural groups differentially interpret positive feedback. *Journal of Cross-Cultural Psychology, 42*, 165–169.

55. Jones, E.E. (1964) *Ingratiation*. New York: Appleton-Century-Crofts.

56. Brehm J., & Cole, A. (1966). Effect of a favor which reduces freedom. *Journal of Personality and Social Psychology, 3*, 420–426.

57. Bigelow, J. (Ed.). (1916). *The autobiography of Benjamin Franklin*. New York: G. P. Putnam's Sons.

58. Jecker, J., & Landy, D. (1969). Liking a person as a function of doing him a favor. *Human Relations, 22,* 371–378.

59. Aronson, E., & Linder, D. (1965). Gain and loss of esteem as determinants of interpersonal attractiveness. *Journal of Experimental and Social Psychology, 1,* 156–171; Gerard, H., & Greenbaum, C. W. (1962). Attitudes toward an agent of uncertainty reduction. *Journal of Personality, 30,* 485–495; Mettee, D., Taylor, S. E., & Friedman, H. (1973). Affect conversion and the gain-loss like effect. *Sociometry, 36,* 505–519; Aronson, E., & Mettee, D. (1974). Affective reactions to appraisal from others. In *Foundations of interpersonal attraction.* New York: Academic Press; Clore, G. L., Wiggins, N. H., & Itkin, S. (1975). Gain and loss in attraction: Attributions from nonverbal behavior. *Journal of Personality and Social Psychology, 31,* 706–712; Turcotte, S. J., & Leventhal, L. (1984). Gain-loss versus reinforcement-affect ordering of student ratings of teaching: Effect of rating instructions. *Journal of Educational Psychology, 76,* 782–791.

60. Aronson, E., & Linder, D. (1965). Gain and loss of esteem as determinants of interpersonal attractiveness. *Journal of Experimental and Social Psychology, 1,* 156–171.

61. Spinoza, B. de. (1910). The ethics. In A. Boyle (Trans.), *Spinoza's ethics and "De Intellectus Emendatione"* (pp. 232–233). New York: Dutton.

62. Mettee, D. R., Taylor, S. E., & Friedman, H. (1973). Affect conversion and the gain-loss like effect. *Sociometry, 36,* 505–519.

63. Mettee, D. R., & Aronson, E. (1974). Affective reactions to appraisal from others. In T. L. Huston (Ed.), *Foundations of interpersonal attraction* (pp. 235–283). New York: Academic Press.

64. Strauss, N. (2012). *The game: Penetrating the secret society of pickup artists.* New York: It Books.

65. Clark, M. S., & Mills, J. (1979). Interpersonal attraction in exchange and communal relationships. *Journal of Personality and Social Psychology, 37,* 12–24.

66. Walster, E., Walster, G. W., & Traupmann, J. (1979). Equity and premarital sex. In M. Cook & G. Wilson (Eds.), *Love and attraction.* New York: Pergamon Press.

67. Pillemer, J., Hatfield, E., & Sprecher, S. (2008). The importance of fairness and equity for the marital satisfaction of older women. *Journal of Women and Aging, 20,* 215–229.

68. Clark, M. S., Mills, J. R., & Corcoran, D. M. (1989). Keeping track of needs and inputs of friends and strangers. *Personality and Social Psychology Bulletin, 15,* 533–542.

69. Hatfield, E., & Rapson, R. L. (2008). Passionate love and sexual desire: Multidisciplinary perspectives. In J. P. Forgas & J. Fitness (Eds.), *Social relationships: Cognitive, affective, and motivational processes.* New York: Psychology Press.

70. Baumeister, R. F., & Bratslavsky, E. (1999). Passion, intimacy, and time: Passionate love as a function of change in intimacy. *Personality and Social Psychology Review, 3,* 49–67.

71. Aron, A., Fisher, H., Mashek, D. J., Strong, G., Li, H., & Brown, L. L. (2005). Reward, motivation, and emotion systems associated with early-stage intense romantic love. *Journal of Neurophysiology, 94,* 327–337; Scheele, D., Willie, S., Kendrick, K. M., Stoffel-Wagner, B., Becker, B., Güntürkün, O., Maier, W., & Hurlemann, R. (2013). Oxytocin enhances brain reward system responses in men viewing the face of their female partner. *PNAS, 110,* 20308–20313.

72. Haidt, J. (2006). *The happiness hypothesis.* New York: Hachette.

73. Solomon, R. (1994). *About love.* Lanham, MD: Littlefield Adams.

74. Aron, A., Fisher, H. E., Strong, G., et al. (2008). Falling in love. In S. Sprecher, A. Wenzel, & J. Harvey (Eds.), *Handbook of relationship initiation.* New York: Psychology Press; Acevedo, B. P., & Aron, A. (2009). Does a long-term relationship kill romantic love? *Review of General Psychology, 13,* 59–65.

75. Epstein, R., Pandit, M., & Thakar, M. (2013). How love emerges in arranged marriages: Two cross-cultural studies. *Journal of Comparative Family Studies, 44,* 341–360.

76. Lee, S. W. S., & Schwarz, N. (2014). Framing love: When it hurts to think we were made for each other. *Journal of Experimental Social Psychology, 54,* 61–67.

77. Knee, C. R. (1998). Implicit theories of relationships: Assessment and prediction of romantic relationship initiation, coping, and longevity. *Journal of Personality and Social Psychology, 74*, 360–370; Knee, C. R., Nanayakkara, A., Vietor, N. A., Neighbors, C., & Patrick, H. (2001). Implicit theories of relationships: Who cares if romantic partners are less than ideal? *Personality and Social Psychology Bulletin, 27*, 808–819.

78. Shaver, P. R., & Hazan, C. (1993). Adult romantic attachment: Theory and evidence. In D. Perlman & W. H. Jones (Eds.), *Advances in personal relationships* (Vol. 4). London: Kingsley.

79. Mikulincer, M., & Shaver, P. R. (2007). *Attachment in adulthood: Structure, dynamics, and change*. New York: Guilford Press.

80. Dinero, R. E., Conger, R. D., Shaver, P. R., Widaman, K. F., & Larsen-Rife, D. (2008). Influence of family of origin and adult romantic partners on romantic attachment security. *Journal of Family Psychology, 22*, 622–632.

81. Feeney, B. C., & Cassidy, J. (2003). Reconstructive memory related to adolescent–parent conflict interactions. *Journal of Personality and Social Psychology, 85*, 945–955.

82. Fraley, R. C., Vicary, A. M., Brumbaugh, C. C., & Roisman, G. I. (2011). Patterns of stability in adult attachment: An empirical test of two models of continuity and change. *Journal of Personality and Social Psychology, 101*, 974–992; Gillath, O., Shaver, P. R., Baek, J.-M., & Chun, D. S. (2008). Genetic correlates of adult attachment style. *Personality and Social Psychology Bulletin, 34*, 1396–1405.

83. Sroufe, L. A. (2005). Attachment and development: A prospective, longitudinal study from birth to adulthood. *Attachment and Human Development, 7*, 349–367; Simpson, J. A., Collins, W. A., Salvatore, J. E., & Sung, S. (2014). The impact of early interpersonal experience on romantic relationship functioning in adulthood. In M. Mikulincer & P. R. Shaver (Eds.), *Mechanisms of social connections: From brain to group* (pp. 221–234). Washington, DC: American Psychological Association.

84. Reis, H. T., Clark, M. S., & Holmes, J. G. (2004). Perceived partner responsiveness as an organizing construct in the study of intimacy and closeness. In D. J. Mashek & A. Aron (Eds.), *Handbook of closeness and intimacy* (pp. 201–225). New York: Psychology Press; Downey, G., Freitas, A. L., Michaelis, B., & Khouri, H. (1998). The self-fulfilling prophecy in close relationships: Rejection sensitivity and rejection by romantic partners. *Journal of Personality and Social Psychology, 75*, 545–560.

85. Oriña, M. M., Collins, W. A., Simpson, J. A., Salvatore, J. E., Haydon, K. C., Kim, J. S. (2011). Developmental and dyadic perspectives on commitment in adult romantic relationships. *Psychological Science, 22*, 908–915; Simpson, J. A., Collins, W. A., & Salvatore, J. E. (2011). The impact of early interpersonal experience on adult romantic relationship functioning: Recent findings from the Minnesota Longitudinal Study of Risk and Adaptation. *Current Directions in Psychological Science, 20*, 355–359.

86. Finkel, E. J. (2017). *The all-or-nothing marriage*. New York: Dutton.

87. Arriaga, X. B., Kumashiro, M., Finkel, E. J., VanderDrift, L. E., & Luchies, L. B. (2014). Filling the void: Bolstering attachment security in committed relationships. *Social Psychological and Personality Science*, *5*, 398–406.

88. Duck, S. (1995). Stratagems, spoils and a serpent's tooth: On the delights and dilemmas of personal relationships. In W. R. Cupach & B. H. Spitzberg (Eds.), *The dark side of interpersonal communication*. Hillsdale, NJ: LEA.

89. Harvey, O. J. (1962). Personality factors in resolution of conceptual incongruities. *Sociometry*, *25*, 336–352.

90. Schopenhauer, A. (1851). *Parerga and Paralipomena* (Vol. 2, Chapter XXXI). Translation: E. F. J. Payne. Oxford: Oxford University Press.

91. Clark, M. S., & Lemay, E. P. (2010). Close relationships. In S. T. Fiske, D. T. Gilbert, and G. Lindzey (Eds.), *Handbook of social psychology*, 5th edition (pp. 898–940). New York: Wiley.

92. Murray, S. L., Holmes, J. G., & Collins, N. L. (2006). Optimizing assurance: The risk regulation system in relationships. *Psychological Bulletin*, *132*, 641–666.

93. Finkel, E. (2017). *The all or nothing marriage*. New York: Dutton.

94. Aron, A., Melinat, E., Aron, E. N., Vallone, R. D., & Bator, R. J. (1997). The experimental generation of interpersonal closeness: A procedure and some preliminary findings. *Personality and Social Psychology Bulletin*, *23*, 363–377.

95. Swann, Jr., W. B. (1990). To be adored or to be known? The interplay of self-enhancement and self-verification. In R. M. Sorrentino & E. T. Higgins (Eds.), *Foundations of social behavior*, Vol. 2 (pp. 408–448). New York: Guilford; Swann, Jr., W. B., De La Ronde, C., & Hixon, J. G. (1994). Authenticity and positivity strivings in marriage and courtship. *Journal of Personality and Social Psychology*, *66*, 857–869; Swann, Jr., W. B., & Pelham, B. (2002). Who wants out when the going gets good? Psychological investment and preference for self-verifying college roommates. *Self and Identity*, *1*, 219–233.

96. Gable, S. L., Gonzaga, G. C., & Strachman, A. (2006). Will you be there for me when things go right? Supportive responses to positive event disclosures. *Journal of Personality and Social Psychology*, *91*, 904–917.

97. Harvey, J. H., Weber, A. L., & Orbuch, T. L. (1990). *Interpersonal accounts: A social psychological perspective*. Oxford: Blackwell.

98. Gottman, J. (2012). *Why marriages succeed or fail*. New York: Simon & Schuster.

99. Gottman, J. S. (Ed.) (2004). *The Marriage Clinic Casebook*. New York: W. W. Norton.

100. Fincham, F. D., & Bradbury, T. N. (1993). Marital satisfaction, depression, and attributions: A longitudinal analysis. *Journal of Personality and Social Psychology*, *64*, 442–452; Karney, B., & Bradbury, T. N. (2000). Attributions in marriage: State or trait? A growth curve analysis. *Journal of Personality and Social Psychology*, *78*, 295–309.

101. Finkel (2017), Ibid.

Chapter 9   Social Psychology as a Science

1. Kunen, J. S. (1995, July 10). Teaching prisoners a lesson. *New Yorker*, pp. 34–39.

2. Feynman, R. (1993, December 21). The best mind since Einstein. http://www.pbs.org/wgbh/nova/education/programs/2019_bestmind.html. Accessed November 28, 2017.

3. P. Semonov (1997). Personal communication.

4. Nisbett & Wilson; also Gilovich, T., & Ross, L. (2015). *The wisest one in the room: How you can benefit from social psychology's most powerful insights.* New York: Free Press.

5. Aronson, E., Willerman, B., & Floyd, J. (1966). The effect of a pratfall on increasing interpersonal attractiveness. *Psychonomic Science, 4,* 227–228.

6. Aronson, E., & Mills, J. (1959). The effect of severity of initiation on liking for a group. *Journal of Abnormal and Social Psychology, 59,* 177–181.

7. Liebert, R., & Baron, R. (1972). Some immediate effects of televised violence on children's behavior. *Developmental Psychology, 6,* 469–475.

8. Aronson, E., & Carlsmith, J. M. (1969). Experimentation in social psychology. In G. Lindzey & E. Aronson (Eds.), *Handbook of social psychology,* 2nd edition (Vol. 2, pp. 1–79). Reading, MA: Addison-Wesley; Aronson, E., Brewer, M., & Carlsmith, J. M. (1985). Experimentation in social psychology. In G. Lindzey & E. Aronson (Eds.), *Handbook of social psychology,* 3rd edition (Vol. 1, pp. 441–486). New York: Random House.

9. Milgram, S. (1963). Behavioral study of obedience. *Journal of Abnormal and Social Psychology, 67,* 371–378.

10. Aronson, E., Sigall, H., & Van Hoose, T. (1970). The cooperative subject: Myth or reality? *Journal of Experimental and Social Psychology, 6,* 1–10.

11. Asch, S. (1951). Effects of group pressure upon the modification and distortion of judgment. In M. H. Guetzkow (Ed.), *Groups, leadership, and men* (pp. 177–190). Pittsburgh: Carnegie; Asch, S. (1951). Studies of independence and conformity: I. A minority of one against a unanimous majority. *Psychological Monographs: General and Applied, 70(9),* 1–70.

12. Oostenbroek, J., Suddendorf, T., Nielsen, M., Redshaw, J., Kennedy-Costantini, S., Davis, J., Clark, S., & Slaughter, V. (2016). Comprehensive longitudinal study challenges the existence of neonatal imitation in humans. *Current Biology, 26,* 1334–1338.

13. Cohen, G. L., Garcia, J., Purdie-Vaughns, V., Apfel, N., & Brzustoski, P. (2009). Recursive processes in self-affirmation: Intervening to close the minority achievement gap. *Science, 324,* 400–403.

14. Borman, G. D., Grigg, J., & Hanselman, P. (2016). An effort to close achievement gaps at scale through self-affirmation. *Educational Evaluation and*

Policy Analysis, 38, 21–24; Hanselman, P., Rozek, C. S., Grigg, J., & Borman, G. D. (2017). New evidence on self-affirmation effects and theorized sources of heterogeneity from large-scale replications. *Journal of Educational Psychology, 109,* 405.

15. Simmons, J. P., & Simonsohn, U. (2017). Power posing: *P*-curving the evidence. *Psychological Science, 28,* 687–693; Ranehill E., Dreber A., Johannesson M., Leiberg S., Sul S., & Weber R. A. (2015). Assessing the robustness of power posing: No effect on hormones and risk tolerance in a large sample of men and women. *Psychological Science, 26,* 653–656.

16. Van Bavel, J. J., Mende-Siedlecki, P., Brady, W.J., & Reinero, D. A. (2016, August 9). Contextual sensitivity helps explain the reproducibility gap between social and cognitive psychology. http://dx.doi.org/10.2139/ssrn.2820883. Accessed September 4, 2017.

17. Dawes, R., McTavish, J., & Shaklee, H. (1977). Behavior, communication, and assumptions about other people's behavior in a common dilemma situation. *Journal of Personality and Social Psychology, 35,* 1–11.

18. Aronson, E., & Mettee, D. (1968). Dishonest behavior as a function of differential levels of induced self-esteem. *Journal of Personality and Social Psychology, 9,* 121–127.

19. Bickman, L., & Zarantonello, M. (1978). The effects of deception and level of obedience on subjects' ratings of the Milgram study. *Personality and Social Psychology Bulletin, 4,* 81–85.

20. Milgram, S. (1964). Issues in the study of obedience: A reply to Baumrind. *American Psychologist, 19,* 848–852.

Name Index

Subject Index